International Air Carrier Liability

International Air Carrier Liability brings together essential treaties and airline-to-airline agreements on air carrier liability, safety and security, and supplements these with expert commentary and analysis. The examination considers the general regulatory framework of international civil aviation (including the Chicago Convention and related documents) and how the liability regime fits within that framework.

The book is divided into three parts: dealing in turn with liability, safety and security, and civil aviation regulation. Part I, for example, provides comment on and analysis of the international air-carrier liability regime, how the main liability conventions operate, and the application of these conventions to international carriage by air (passengers, baggage and cargo). Given its subject matter and the universal state party participation in these conventions, this book has truly global application.

David Hodgkinson and Rebecca Johnston aim to provide a reference aid for legal practitioners (at law firms, airlines, manufacturers, aviation-related corporations, government departments and agencies), as well as academics, students (undergraduate and postgraduate) and government officials regarding treaties, laws and documents concerned with these vital legal issues.

David Hodgkinson is a partner at HodgkinsonJohnston and an associate professor at the University of Western Australia. He is the author of books and numerous journal articles on aviation and climate change, and was Director of Legal at IATA, the organisation of the world's airlines.

Rebecca Johnston is a partner at aviation and aerospace law firm, HodgkinsonJohnston, and teaches at the University of Western Australia. She is admitted to practice law in Australia and New York. She advises international clients on a range of commercial and regulatory aviation law matters.

International Air Carrier Liability

Safety and Security

David Hodgkinson and
Rebecca Johnston

Routledge
Taylor & Francis Group

LONDON AND NEW YORK

First published 2017 by Routledge

2 Park Square, Milton Park, Abingdon, Oxfordshire OX14 4RN
52 Vanderbilt Avenue, New York, NY 10017

Routledge is an imprint of the Taylor & Francis Group, an informa business

First issued in paperback 2019

Copyright © 2017 David Hodgkinson and Rebecca Johnston

The right of David Hodgkinson and Rebecca Johnston to be identified as
authors of this work has been asserted by them in accordance with sections
77 and 78 of the Copyright, Designs and Patents Act 1988.

All rights reserved. No part of this book may be reprinted or reproduced or
utilised in any form or by any electronic, mechanical, or other means, now
known or hereafter invented, including photocopying and recording, or in
any information storage or retrieval system, without permission in writing
from the publishers.

Notice:
Product or corporate names may be trademarks or registered trademarks,
and are used only for identification and explanation without intent to
infringe.

British Library Cataloguing in Publication Data
A catalogue record for this book is available from the British Library

Library of Congress Cataloging in Publication Data
Names: Hodgkinson, David (David Ivor), author. | Johnston, Rebecca,
author.
Title: International air carrier liability: safety and security / David
Hodgkinson and Rebecca Johnston.
Description: Abingdon, Oxon [UK]; New York: Routledge, 2017. |
Includes bibliographical references and index.
Identifiers: LCCN 2016027649| ISBN 9781138200494 (hardback) |
ISBN 9781315514338 (ebook)
Subjects: LCSH: Liability for aircraft accidents. | Aeronautics--Law and
legislation. | Aeronautics, Commercial--Law and legislation. | Carriers--
Law and legislation. | Aeronautics--Safety measures. | Freight and
freightage.
Classification: LCC K4122 .H63 2017 | DDC 346.03/22--dc23
LC record available at https://lccn.loc.gov/2016027649

ISBN: 978-1-138-20049-4 (hbk)
ISBN: 978-0-367-88962-3 (pbk)

Typeset in Bembo
by Florence Production Ltd, Stoodleigh, Devon, UK

Every effort has been made to contact copyright holders for their permission
to reprint material in this book. The publishers would be grateful to hear from
any copyright holder who is not here acknowledged and will undertake to
rectify any errors or omissions in future editions of this book.

Contents

Foreword

Globalisation is a protean concept, and increasingly so these days, a decidedly polemical notion. As a purely descriptive rather than a normative proposition, however, globalisation is an inexorable fact of modern life – pervasive, persistent and irreversible. To be 'against' globalisation in this sense, would be, as Jacques Barzun said more than 50 years ago about the pointlessness of being 'against' science, tantamount to being 'against' the tides or sunsets.[1]

In this century and the last, few phenomena have been, at once, so indicative of, and contributory to, the processes of globalisation as air transport. To be sure, it was a distinctively militarised expression of technological creativity that provided the impetus for the extraordinary development of ever more sophisticated aircraft. But it was a decidedly civil and consciously civilising response to the devastation of two world wars that gave rise to the beneficial expansion of the air transport industry, harnessing those artefacts of power and destruction with a view to securing and extending the constructive social and economic benefits that technology had come to be recognised as remarkably capable of delivering.

Over this same period, and in the same crucible of war and its aftermath, what was once a fine and fragile filigree of international law, has grown into a more tightly woven fabric of honoured obligations, reasonable expectations and binding agreements, providing a framework for treaty-based multilateralism in which the interstices contract measurably with each passing decade. Today, to understand the contours and content of these arrangements is as essential to successful international air navigation as is the hardware and software that make contemporary flight as safe, affordable and accessible as it is. In the business and law of international aviation, as much as, if not more than, any other sphere of trans-national activity in an increasingly integrated world, multilateralism matters[2] – perhaps more so now than ever.[3]

Successfully navigating through the complex domain of international air transport law in the 21st century requires more than a conventional map. Even an intimate familiarity with the myriad multi-lateral treaties and inter-national agreements on the basis of which these dynamic affairs are played out is simply not enough. Conversancy and mastery require a deeper, more nuanced and contextualised understanding of wider, inter-related principles and the thoughtful analysis of competing, often conflicting, objectives and motives. That is precisely what this volume offers.

Adeptly elaborating on the legal foundations of air carrier liability, safety and security, with a further and equally lucid account of the regulatory framework within which – and, as an equally important foundational element itself, upon which – some of the most challenging realities of international air commerce arise, David Hodgkinson and Rebecca Johnston describe, explain, clarify and expand compellingly on the very issues that demand the informed attention of professional practitioners, students and academics alike. What is more, they do so in a way that is readily accessible, presenting sometimes unavoidably complex ideas in an articulate, uncomplicated manner, without compromising a vital fidelity to the principles underpinning the important concepts and issues to hand, for the sake of the kind of glib oversimplification that is sometimes advanced nowadays as 'reader friendliness'.

Without diminishing the singular and significantly beneficial contribution *International Air Carrier Liability: Safety and Security* makes to the scholarly literature, it is, I believe, to serious and circumspect practitioners – of international air law, the commercial and political endeavours governed by that law and those charged with responsibility for interpreting and applying such laws – that this volume will pay its greatest and most enduring dividends. This book is a tool for the adroit craftsperson, for whom fashioning a compelling proposition, a winning argument, effective policy or viable strategy, no less so than sound, tenable answers to real, immediate and practical questions, is the driving objective. What is provided here will make readers think and help them to do so.

The volume is thematically and logically organised into three parts. The first two are usefully arranged around the major conventions, protocols and agreements germane to air carrier liability, and safety and security issues, respectively. Reflecting the growing importance European legislation is coming to play, both within the European Union and for a growing number of other jurisdictions where European models are being adopted and adapted with increasing frequency, Part I concludes with a section devoted specifically to the relevant European regulations.

With the horror of 11 September 2001 now 15 years behind us, the impact of those shocking events continue to have a profound influence on the evolution of security-related considerations in the international aviation community. The historical antecedents to, and the most recent expressions of, contemporary approaches to aviation security are canvassed in Part II, along with the consideration of pertinent safety-related issues reflected in the 2010 Beijing Convention and Protocol, and the Montreal protocol 2014, which, although not yet in force, are most informatively considered Part II. Part III focuses on the regulation of international aviation under the umbrella of the Convention on International Civil Aviation (the Chicago Convention).

Each of the book's three parts is replete with extended extracts from the relevant documents themselves, and extensive references to pertinent discussions of those texts by other contributors to the contemporary literature. For all that, the authors' own distinctive remarks and rich commentary are what gives *International Air Carrier Liability: Safety and Security* its exceptional depth and dimension, and it is the probing and incisive gloss of their annotations that give this volume its exceptional and what I am sure will be its lasting lustre.

Dr Jonathan Aleck
Legal Affairs, Regulatory Policy & International Strategy
Civil Aviation Safety Authority

Notes

1   *Science: The Glorious Entertainment*. New York: Harper & Row, 1964, 6.
2   See J.G. Ruggie (ed.), *Multilateralism Matter: The Theory and Praxis of an Institutional Form*. New York: Columbia University Press, 1993.
3   *The Economist*, 11 October 2008, 30.

Preface

Of all the great steps in mankind's progress, from the wheel to the printing press, the sailing ship to the computer, few have had such an enormous impact as aviation. Aircraft have shrunk the world, ended the isolation of cultures, invigorated trade and human communication; they have also created a terrible new dimension to warfare. Within the first 30 years of the 20th century – a blink of an eye in the magnitude of human existence – man mastered movement through the one basic element hitherto denied him – the air.[1]

The history of the twentieth and the twenty-first centuries is, in essence, the history of flight. Flight has been instrumental in bringing people and nations together. More than a century after Wilbur Wright's first flight in 1903, passenger air travel has become globally commonplace. Aviation has transformed the world politically, socially, economically and militarily.

This transformation has necessitated the development of international rules governing carriage by air. It is these legal rules and that development which form the subject matter of this book.

———————————

We extend our sincere appreciation and thanks to a number of people and organisations for assistance in the production of this book. In particular, we would like to thank our commissioning editor, Guy Loft from Routledge.

We are indebted to Dr Jonathan Aleck, General Manager of the Legal Affairs, Regulatory Policy and International Strategy Branch of Australia's Civil Aviation Safety Authority (CASA) for agreeing to write the foreword to this book and for his unwavering enthusiasm and support for our various aviation endeavours however unconventional they may have appeared to be.

We acknowledge the support of our aviation and aerospace law firm, HodgkinsonJohnston. Establishing this legal practice has been, for each of us, perhaps the most rewarding experience of our professional legal careers. True it is that, without making this move, our book may well not have been written. We are also grateful for the support of our colleagues and students at the Law School of the University of Western Australia.

We owe a debt of thanks to the many academics and aviation law experts whose work we have drawn on in writing this book. In particular, we wish to recognise the contributions of leading aviation law authors, excerpts of whose work appear in this book.

Finally, David would like to thank his partner, Lucy Young. Rebecca would like to thank her parents, James and Sandra Johnston, her sister Laura Johnston, and her partner Hudson Wheeler.

Note

1   Almond, Peter. *Aviation: The Early Years*. London: Konemann, 1997, 10.

Abbreviations and acronyms

BCN	Biological, chemical or nuclear weapons
CITEJA	Comité International Technique d'Experts Juridiques Aériens (succeeded by ICAO's Legal Committee)
DOT	United States Department of Transport
DVT	Deep vein thrombosis
EU	European Union
GATS	Global Agreement on Trade in Services
IASTA	International Air Services Transit Agreement
IATA	International Air Transport Association
ICAO	International Civil Aviation Organization
MALIAT	Multilateral Agreement on Liberalization of International Air Transportation
MC99	Montreal Convention 1999
NPT	Nuclear Non-Proliferation Treaty
PANS	Procedures for Air Navigation Services
SARPS	Standards and Recommended Practices
SDR	Special Drawing Right
UN	United Nations
USD	United States Dollar

Introduction

This book brings together essential documents on air carrier liability, safety and security, as well as commentary and analysis. It is distinctive in that, in addition to setting out air carrier liability, safety and security treaties and other documentation, it also provides analysis with regard to the general regulatory framework of international civil aviation (including the Chicago Convention) without which one cannot fully understand those air carrier treaties.

The book's aim is to provide a ready reference for legal practitioners (at law firms, airlines, manufacturers, aviation-related corporations and government departments and agencies), academics, students (undergraduate and graduate), government officials and interested members of the public regarding treaties, domestic laws and documents concerned with air carrier and passenger liability and airline safety and security.

No similar book to *International Air Carrier Liability: Safety and Security* currently exists. The International Air Transport Association produced successive books, which dealt with air carrier liability, but their scope was much more limited than this title, and they provided almost no commentary or material of an academic nature. Further, they did not provide documents regarding safety and security matters. They are also now out of date.

There is a clear need on the part of legal practitioners, academics, government officials and others for aviation liability, safety and security documentation to be gathered together in one publication as a ready reference. There is a need for a foundation source for academic research and a reference for day-to-day use on the part of the aviation industry broadly defined.

We hope that this book is that source.

In Part I, the development of air carrier liability regimes from the 1929 Warsaw Convention to the 1999 Montreal Convention and their futures are examined. We also set out the main provisions of the relevant treaties and instruments. Part II provides analysis of international air safety and security treaties and their development. These treaties deal with matters involving passengers in the air and persons on the ground. In Part III, the final part, the evolution of civil aviation regulation is reviewed with a focus on the Chicago Convention. The book also includes a comprehensive bibliography of key aviation law sources.

This book is not an exhaustive treatment of international air law. Its documentary focus is air carrier liability, safety and security, and public law regulation of civil aviation. Select commentary has been provided in essential areas and in areas that have provoked either the most discussion or the most controversy. For example, matters relating to air carrier liability for passenger injury or death receive more discussion and analysis than cargo-related matters.

For consistency and ease of reference, primary sources have been reformatted. Some headings and footnotes from secondary sources have been omitted. Formatting and numbering have not been changed where meaning or interpretation would be affected.

The law stated in this book is as it appeared to us on 1 June 2016. Any errors or inaccuracies are entirely the responsibility of the authors.

PART I
LIABILITY

Commentary

Accidents have been common to air travel since flight began. As with any new mode of transport, aviation necessitated the development of rules concerning the responsibilities of carriers and the rights of passengers. The inclusion of rules with respect to carrier liability for passengers, as well as baggage and cargo, was inevitable.

International air carrier liability today is governed by a complex web of treaties and international agreements. These agreements are supplemented by a range of national and regional arrangements.

Against this background we examine the development of air carrier liability regimes from the 1929 Warsaw Convention to the 1999 Montreal Convention and the future of such regimes. We set out the key provisions of the relevant treaties and instruments, and we address the often-hard questions regarding their operation. In so doing it becomes clear that the establishment of an international framework for air carrier liability has been difficult. As a result, in addition to state-based agreements, liability regimes have, from time to time, been governed by agreements made between carriers.

DEVELOPMENT OF WARSAW TO MONTREAL

Air carrier liability for international carriage of passengers, baggage and cargo is governed by a series of international conventions (or treaties) and various instruments, which amend those conventions. The first such convention was the 1929 Warsaw Convention and the most recent is the Montreal Convention of 1999. Each successive convention offers – in general – more generous compensation for passenger injury or death and for loss, damage or delay in terms of baggage or cargo.

The following passages provide the rationale and some background to the formation of the first set of legal rules governing international air carrier liability.

Origins of the Warsaw Convention of 1929

Legal rules of carrier liability in international air transport owe their origin to the efforts of a number of international aeronautical organizations in the 1920s, during the infancy of commercial aviation, to create a uniform legal regime, and shield carriers from potentially devastating aviation disaster damage awards. The absence of uniform law governing international commercial aviation and the consequent plethora of conflicting national laws on the subject led thee organizations to pass resolutions calling upon governments to formulate a uniform system of private air law on the foundation of the Paris Convention of 1919.[1]

A Search for a Universal Cap on Liability

At two international conferences held between 1925 and 1929, States debated the merits of constructing a system of harmonized rules governing liability for international carriage by air. Although cross-border air travel was still in its infancy, States and their air carriers realized that uniform standards of liability could not exist in a legal environment where national courts applied inconsistent conflict of laws (choice of law) rules to select a governing law in a particular dispute. More important, from the airlines' perspective, was the need to create a universal cap on their liability for damages arising out of international air transportation. According to the airlines, their fledgling status, combined with uncertainty surrounding the causes of many airline accidents, made the uniquely vulnerable to lawsuits. Unlimited liability would deter investors and limit the scope of services that air carriers would be able to provide. Other options besides a universal liability cap were available to narrow the industry's exposure. Airlines concerned about risky cross-border transit could have negotiated liability limits or other protections into their contracts of carriage, perhaps foregoing some profit through reduced fares in exchange for the consent of passengers or shippers to a fixed level of damages in the event of an accident.[2]

It was at these 1925 and 1929 conferences that the original legal framework for air carrier liability principles were established. A draft text of the Warsaw Convention, formally titled the Convention for the Unification of Certain Rules Relating to International Carriage by Air, was considered at this second conference and signed by 23 countries on 12 October 1929. The influence of the Warsaw Convention can be seen throughout the 20th century; it provided the foundation and sets out the underpinnings of modern air carrier liability law.

The Convention came into effect on 13 February 1933, that date being ninety days after the deposit of the fifth instrument of ratification with the Polish Government.

Principles of the Warsaw Convention

By providing a set of uniform rules, the Convention eliminated many of the troublesome conflict of laws questions which would otherwise arise. It resolved jurisdictional questions, prescribed a limitation period, and by an elaborate set of provisions created a uniform system of documentation. By establishing a uniform law as to the carrier's liability, the Convention side-stepped most choice-of-law problems. It must be admitted, however, that there is not complete agreement among courts and commentators as to the precise effect of the Convention on choice-of-law questions.

In the liability area, the main feature of the Convention was a reversal of the burden of proof. A carrier's liability under common law rules is based on negligence, with the burden of proof on the plaintiff. Under the Convention it remained a fault-based liability, but fault would be assumed on proof of damage, and did not have to be established by the plaintiff. The carrier could escape liability by proving that he, and his servants and agents, had taken all necessary measures to avoid the damage, but the burden of establishing this defence was on him.

To balance this reversal of the burden of proof, the liability of the carrier, in terms of the amount of damages to be awarded, was limited. The Convention fixed maximum sums, 125,000 gold francs in the case of injury to a passenger; the plaintiff could only recover more that this figure if he discharged the burden of proving 'wilful misconduct' on the part of the carrier, his servants or agents.'

Kirby J of the High Court of Australia made this comment on the nature of the Convention:

> A study of the minutes of the Second International Conference on Private Aeronautical Law that preceded the adoption of the Warsaw Convention in its original form in 1929 bares out the conclusion that the text ultimately endorsed was not so much the product of considerations of principle, justice and equity as of international and domestic politics, business pressures, a consideration of the technical advances in aviation, as well as changing policy judgments and the differing approaches of municipal judges to such claims. These considerations have continued to effect the later revisions of the text [of the Convention].[3]

Central to the Warsaw Convention (and the ensuing Warsaw regime) is the provision of air carrier compensation for passenger injury or death. Notwithstanding that this provision is fundamental to that regime, key terms in relation to air carrier liability are not defined in the regime's instruments.

Article 17 of the 1929 Warsaw Convention, for example, provides that:

> [t]he carrier is liable for damage sustained in the event of the death or wounding of a passenger or any other bodily injury suffered by a passenger,

if the accident which caused the damage so sustained took place on board the aircraft or in the course of any of the operations of embarking or disembarking.

Among other words and terms, none of either 'bodily injury', 'accident', 'embarking' or 'disembarking' are defined in the Convention.

This definitional lacuna has understandably caused both uncertainty and ambiguity as to the meaning and scope of relevant words and terms. Courts in jurisdictions around the world have filled this void through thousands of decisions regarding the interpretation of such words and terms, the most important of which is arguably 'accident'.

The Term "Accident"

Definition

For the carrier to be liable, there must have been an 'accident' under Article 17 of the Warsaw Convention, and the Warsaw Convention as amended by the Hague Protocol. Said treaties do not define 'accident'. In Annex 13 of ICAO, accident is defined as

> "an occurrence associated with the operation of an aircraft which takes place between the time any person board the aircraft with the intention of flight until such time as all such persons have disembarked"

in which passengers are fatally or seriously injured, the aircraft sustains damage or structural failure, or the aircraft is missing or is completely inaccessible. Other occurrences associated with the operation of an aircraft which affect or could affect the safety of an aircraft are termed as 'incidents'.

Under case law made in private international air law, other definitions are drawn up. Depending upon their contents, definitions of the term 'accident' may limit or extend the liability of the carrier, making a definition crucial for liability purposes. The US Supreme Court in the case of *Saks v. Air France* [470 US 392 (1985) at 405] has given what has become a 'classical' definition of the term 'accident'. According to the court, an accident occurs:

> " . . . when a passenger's injury is caused by an unexpected or unusual event that is external to the passenger."[4]

Like any original instrument, with the passage of time and increasing experience with the international air carrier liability regime, it was clear that amendments needed to be made to the Warsaw Convention. This was particularly so with regard to passenger compensation limits (the limits of which were so low that they arguably gave air carriers greater assurance that they would not be required to bear the full costs of damages incurred by such passengers), damage to baggage and cargo, and passenger delay.

In the 1920s and 1930s, airline passengers were generally wealthy and could self-insure, although needless to say, this changed over time as air travel became more accessible to the general public. As the number of airline passengers increased, pressure attended carriers to raise compensation limits and to amend liability rules to provide further protection for passengers in the event of an accident.

Increased compensation and further legal protections for passengers were implemented over time through a patchwork quilt of amending and supplementing Warsaw instruments and stand-alone treaties. These treaties are set out below:

The Amendments to the Original Warsaw Convention

The amendments to the Warsaw Convention ratified by a number of countries were the following:

(1) The Hague Protocol of 1955 which, among other things, raised the carrier's per passenger limit of liability to USD16,600;
(2) The 1961 Guadalajara Supplementary Convention which extended the Convention rules to a carrier performing the international flight (as substituted carrier or operating carrier in a code-share flight), even if that carrier did not have a contract of carriage with the passenger;
(3) The Guatemala City Protocol which created an unbreakable per passenger limit of liability of 100,000 SDRs, but provided for a Supplementary Compensation Plan funded by passenger contributions to allow for the payment of damages in excess of the 100,000 SDR limit;
(4) Montreal Protocols No. 1, 2 and 3 which provided for limits in terms of SDRs and incorporated the provisions of the Guatemala City Protocol; and
(5) Montreal Protocol No. 4 which modernized the cargo provisions of the Warsaw Convention.[5]

The Hague Protocol of 1955 was the first significant addition to the Warsaw Convention; the Protocol increased passenger liability limits and entered into force on 1 August 1963 (ninety days after receipt of the thirtieth instrument of ratification). A supplementary treaty – the Guadalajara Convention of 1961 for the Unification of Certain Rules Relating to International Carriage by Air Performed by a Person Other than the Contracting Carrier – entered into force on 1 May 1964.

The 1971 Guatemala City Protocol was drafted as an amending agreement, which updates the Hague Protocol with an absolute cap on liability. The Guatemala City Protocol, an International Civil Aviation Organisation (**ICAO**) initiative, is effectively a protocol to a protocol. The Guatemala City Protocol proposes an unbroken, absolute liability cap of USD100,000. This Protocol never entered into force although provisions contained in the Protocol have influenced air carrier liability treaties subsequent to it.

Four additional protocols were agreed in 1975, the effect of which was to replace the unit of measurement of liability limits from Poincaré gold francs to Special Drawing Rights (**SDR**). The SDR is an international reserve asset determined by the International Monetary Fund; it is based on the market exchange rates of a basket of major currencies (the US dollar, the euro, pound sterling and the Japanese yen).

On one view, Montreal Protocol 4 is the most important of the four additional protocols, amending as it does (among other things) the cargo provisions of the Warsaw regime.

Montreal Protocol 3 alone has not entered into force.

Aftermath of the Montreal Protocols

The Montreal Protocols marked the last efforts by public international law treaty-making to modify the Warsaw System. But they did not obviate any need for further change. The Warsaw System was now plagued by inconsistent and uneven ratifications of various instruments. The United States, as noted, had rejected all of the agreements that followed Warsaw (and had even threatened to reject Warsaw itself). Moreover, other than in the technical sense of consolidating prior agreements, the Protocols largely avoided the fraught question of moving (or removing) Warsaw's liability caps. Despite enthusiastic U.S. support for the Montreal Protocols at the time of drafting, once again U.S. ratification was not forthcoming. And . . . other States revealed displeasure with the Warsaw System by adopting less airline-friendly variances of the prevailing international rules for international air carrier liability.

Continued U.S. Dissatisfaction with Warsaw

. . . [T]he United States had little stake in further multilateral negotiations to modify the Warsaw System. Preservation of the concept of liability limits, however many times the caps were elevated, ran counter to its interests (or, rather, to the vocal interests of the U.S. plaintiffs' tort bar). Critics accused the United States of undermining the Warsaw System through unilateralism, but those attacks were overstated. From the beginning, after all, the Warsaw Convention presented no *textual* objection to waving its ground rules for liability and defenses. . . . Article 22 allowed air carriers, "by special contract," to "agree to a higher limit of liability" than that codified in the treaty. Added to that, Article 33 of the Convention provided that "[n]othing in [the] Convention shall prevent [a carrier] . . . from making regulations which do not conflict with the provisions of the Convention." Besides, few would have denied that the Warsaw System had failed to keep pace with the huge expansion of international air services during the second half of the twentieth century. The economic justifications for inoculating the airlines against high liability that were so convincing in 1929 had lost much of their directive force by the 1970s. Finally, U.S. domestic air transport had not perished as a result of decades-long exposure to the rigors of uncapped liability under common law. To U.S. critics of the Warsaw System, it was absurd that an accident befalling a passenger on a flight between Chicago and Toronto could be subject to severe liability caps while a similar event on the much longer Los Angeles/New York route would be controlled by the common law rules on common carrier liability.[6]

INTERCARRIER AND CARRIER AGREEMENTS

The Montreal Agreement of 1966

The United States gave notice of its denunciation of the Warsaw Convention in October 1965 as a result of the Warsaw regime's very low liability limits and failure on the part of governments to raise those limits. The United States' goal was to secure a new passenger liability agreement prior to the denunciation taking effect at the expiration of the six-month notice period. Following the notice, a conference was held under the auspices of ICAO in Montreal in February 1966. Although that Montreal Conference itself failed to reach an agreement, subsequent agreement was reached between *carriers* as opposed to states.

> The Montreal Conference ended without agreement due to an impasse between the United States proposal of $100,000 and the lower proposals of other nations. The failure of the conference to reach a consensus did not, however, end efforts to reach an agreement. The airlines themselves stepped in to fill the void. These efforts were successful in achieving a so-called "interim solution," and in May 1966, only two days before the United States' denunciation would have become effective, notice of the denunciation was retracted. This "interim solution" is officially termed "Agreement Relating to Liability Limitation of the Warsaw Convention and The Hague Protocol" and has become known as the "Montreal Agreement."
>
> The Montreal Agreement is a private agreement, signed by each airline operating to, from or through the territory of the United States, waiving the Warsaw Convention's liability limitations on personal injury (via a special contract under Article 22(1) up to $75,000 for each individual claimant, inclusive of attorney's fees and costs. It retains the requirement that the claimant prove wilful misconduct to recover more than $75,000), and waives the defences available under Article 20(1) (thereby subjecting themselves to strict liability without fault). Though not an inter-

governmental agreement, convention, or treaty, the United States has made it legally binding under its regulatory powers over certification of all domestic and foreign carriers serving the United States. Under U.S. domestic law, the agreement applies to all flights originating, terminating or stopping in the United States. Foreign carriers seeking a permit to serve the United States must first sign the agreement. U.S. carriers seeking a Certificate of Public Convenience and Necessity must also adhere to the Agreement.

It is important to emphasize that the Montreal Agreement is not a treaty, but an agreement among international air carriers that imposes a "quasi-legal and largely experimental system of liability that is . . . contractual in nature." The Agreement applies only to death or personal injury, and not to loss or damage of baggage or cargo. The waiver of the Article 20(1) defences, which amounts to strict liability without regard to fault, is a *quid pro quo* for the limitation on air carrier liability. For personal injury, the plaintiff need only prove damages up to the $75,000 limit. Although intended to be an "interim solution," it remained the dominant liability regime over thirty years after its 1966 creation, although only in a limited territorial scope of carriage to, from or through the United States.[7]

The Japanese Initiative 1992

It was not only the United States that expressed dissatisfaction with the Warsaw regime and the unreasonably low passenger liability limits. A quarter of a century later, the Japanese carriers – as opposed to states – took action with regard to low liability limits. Ten Japanese airlines voluntarily contracted out of the Warsaw Convention's liability limits by way of amendment to their conditions of carriage in a unilateral action known as the 'Japanese Initiative'. Such action, together with the International Air Transport Association (**IATA**) intercarrier agreements three years later, led to the Montreal Convention of 1999.

Continued concern about the liability ceiling for passenger injury prompted the airlines themselves to address the governmental inability to amend the Warsaw regime. In 1992, the Japanese air carriers asked their government to eliminate the liability ceiling on negligence litigation in international aviation. The vast difference in plaintiffs' recovery under the domestic automobile liability regime vis-à-vis recovery for international aviation disasters made a continuation of the ceiling implausible. Moreover, average recovery for the 1985 domestic crash of a Japan Air Lines 747, in which 520 people died, was $850,000, well above Warsaw limits.

In 1992, Japanese carriers filed tariffs providing they would not invoke the Article 20 "all necessary measures" defense up to 100,000 SDRs; in other words, strict liability would exist up to 100,000 SDRs, and a fault-based reversed burden of proof would exist on claims for compensatory damages above that threshold without any monetary limit. The so-called "Japanese initiative" received much attention in aviation litigation circles.[8]

The IATA Intercarrier Agreements 1995–1996

Absent significant and comprehensive action by states to increase passenger compensation limits, carriers – in addition to Japanese carriers – together took private action through a number of intercarrier agreements paving the way for a new passenger liability regime. These agreements did not amend any of the Warsaw or related instruments, such amendment requiring state-based action. At the heart of the intercarrier agreements is a waiver of the Warsaw/Hague liability limits for passenger injury or death by way of 'special contract' between the carrier and the passenger (such special contract possible under Article 22 of the Warsaw Convention).

The principal Intercarrier Agreements were:

(1) The 1966 Montreal Intercarrier Agreement under which an airline agreed to raise the limits of the Convention by special contract under Article 22 to USD 75,000 if the transportation involved a point in the United States. The carriers also agreed to waive the 'all necessary measures defense' of Article 20(1); and

(2) The 1995–1996 IATA Intercarrier Agreements under which the airline agreed to waive all limits of liability, but retained the right to invoke the 'all necessary measures' defense of Article 20 for that portion of a claim in excess of 100,000 SDRs. The carrier, except where it could prove contributory negligence, was, in effect, strictly liable for provable damages up to 100,000 SDRs for bodily injury or wrongful death as a result of an accident, and was presumptively liable to an unlimited amount.

These instruments (the Protocols, the Supplementary Convention and 1995–1996 IATA Intercarrier Agreements) and the Warsaw Convention itself can be fairly described as the *status quo*. The liability of the many international carriers, particularly US carriers, and the major non-US carriers, currently are governed by the Warsaw Convention and the 1995–1996 IATA Intercarrier Agreements. The new Montreal Convention incorporates provisions of each of these instruments in an attempt to create a single document, setting forth a uniform regime for carrier liability in international transportation.[9]

By way of background to the formation of the intercarrier agreements, the United States Department of Transport (**DOT**), in 1995, provided IATA with antitrust immunity so as to allow discussions relating to the international air carrier liability regime and its modernisation. The DOT was of the view that "the current regime should be updated to provide sufficient protection to the travelling public" and that liability limits under that current regime were inadequate to keep pace with contemporary compensation standards generally.

Among the objectives established by DOT to guide the intercarrier negotiations were:

> First, with regard to passenger claims arising from international journeys ticketed in the United States, passengers would be entitled to prompt and complete compensation on a strict liability basis with no per passenger limits and with measures of damages consistent with those available in cases arising in U.S. domestic air transportation; second, this coverage should be extended to U.S. citizens and permanent residents travelling internationally on tickets not issued in the United States.

Sixty-seven airlines attended IATA's first session thereunder, held in Washington, D.C., in June 1995. The airlines agreed that the Warsaw Convention must be preserved, but acknowledged that "the existing passenger liability limits for international carriage by air are grossly inadequate in many jurisdictions and should be revised as a matter of urgency." At its 1995 Annual General Meeting in Kuala Lumpur, IATA endorsed a new "Washington Intercarrier Agreement" providing for "Full compensatory recoverable damages." Described as "the most dramatic development in the 66 year history of the Warsaw Convention," the agreement was signed by twelve airlines in Kuala Lumpur, Malaysia on October 30, 1995. U.S. airlines followed suit a week later, effectively clearing the way for the new liability regime.

The agreement preserves the "all necessary measures" defense of Article 20 for claims exceeding 100,000 SDRs. Article 25 litigation on the issue of "wilful misconduct" becomes irrelevant. For personal injury, the plaintiff must prove the existence of an Article 17 accident and damages, while in rebuttal and defendant must prove that it took "all necessary measures" to avoid the injury.

[. . .]

[W]herefrom came the sudden goodwill of airlines to radically improve the protection of their passengers [?] In the case of the "Japanese initiative" it could well have been a matter of moral principle and a sense "common justice" to treat their international passengers equally with the claimants in domestic carriage; moreover, the Japanese carriers enjoyed a remarkable safety record and could manage the increased risk by effective insurance. Among the other airlines of the world it would not be credible to expect the same Oriental sense of "rectitude" and it is more likely that they understood the unrealistic liability regime and limits of liability under the "Warsaw" system and were rightly concerned that States – unable to agree on the modernization of the system - might start denouncing the Convention when the Guatemala City attempt at its modernization was evidently failing. A demise of the unified system of law, however unsatisfactory, would have left airlines to face unpredictable conflicts of laws and conflict of jurisdiction, unpredictable claims, and difficulty in obtaining adequate insurance.[10]

MONTREAL CONVENTION 1999

The Montreal Convention 1999 for the Unification of Certain Rules for International Carriage by Air (**MC99**) in its preamble recognised the need to "modernise and consolidate the Warsaw Convention and related instruments". As part of this modernisation and consolidation, MC99, following the 1961 Guadalajara Supplementary Convention, distinguishes between 'contracting' and 'actual' carriers.

The Convention aims to better protect the interests of passengers (and other consumers) and ensure equitable compensation. It redresses the previous imbalance between the interests of the carrier and those of the passenger. It is clear that for state parties to the Convention, MC99 – as a separate and distinct treaty, some 70 years after the Warsaw Convention – was the best mechanism through which to achieve, arguably, an equitable balance of interests between a carrier and its passengers.

MC99 is not an amendment of the 1929 Warsaw Convention and related international law instruments and intercarrier agreements which, together, comprised the Warsaw System in 1999. MC99 is an entirely new Convention intended to consolidate in one instrument the principal and internationally accepted liability rules of the Warsaw System.

While MC99 was drafted and adopted to replace the Warsaw System, the drafters and the States Party fully intended to preserve the seventy years of judicial decisions interpreting and applying the liability rules of the Warsaw System to be used in interpreting and applying the MC99 liability rules. To that end, there was no substantive change made to the wording of the liability rules of the Warsaw System which were adopted in MC99.

To ensure universality in the interpretation and application of the MC99 liability rules, the drafters and States Party to MC99 intended that the rules, where applicable to the transportation, be exclusive and preempt all national and local laws and regulations that otherwise might be applicable to the claims presented and, further, that the rules be interpreted and applied by the courts of the States Party in a uniform manner.

The key features of MC99 are: (1) strict liability of the carrier for Article 17 passenger death and bodily injury, with no limitation on recoverable damages, except as may be provided by applicable local law pursuant to Article 29; (2) strict liability for cargo damage with an unbreakable limitation of liability of 19 SDRs per kilogram of the cargo involved; (3) a per passenger limitation of liability for baggage damage, but the liability limitation is breakable if the damage is caused by intentional or reckless wrongdoing of the carrier; (4) a per passenger limitation of liability for delay, also breakable if the damage is caused by intentional or reckless wrongdoing of the carrier; (5) a new fifth jurisdiction for the bringing of Article 17 passenger death and bodily injury damage claims only, being the principal and permanent residence of the passenger at the time of the Article 17 accident, provided that the air carrier has a specified business presence in that jurisdiction.[11]

Central to the Montreal Convention is the passenger compensation regime and its carrier liability framework. That framework is considered to be a passenger-friendly one. The key provision is Article 21 "Compensation in Case of Death or Injury of Passengers".

Article 21 provides for two tiers of liability for the death of, or bodily injury to, a passenger. The first tier, with a compensation limit up to 100,000 SDRs, is based on strict (no-fault) liability and can only be reduced or excluded in cases of contributory negligence on the part of the passenger or claimant.

The second tier of compensation (from 100,000 SDRs) is potentially unlimited, such unlimited liability being fault-based. The carrier will be liable unless it can prove (the burden of proof being on the carrier) that:

a) the damage was not due to negligence or any other wrongful act or omission of the carrier; or
b) that the damage was solely due to the negligence or the wrongful act or omission of a third party for which the carrier is not responsible.

Terms of Liability

[. . .]

[Further], the carrier can exonerate itself if it proves that the damage was cause or contributed to by the negligence or otherwise wrongful actor omission of the person claiming compensation, or a person rightfully representing him or her. Hence, failing such proof by the carrier, it is liable for all proven damages sustained by the passenger as a result of the death or bodily injury caused by such an accident.

The passenger/claimant never has to prove fault of any kind to recover 100 percent of the proven damages sustained as a result of the bodily injury caused by the accident under Article 17 of the Montreal Convention. Hence, assuming that all the requirements of Article 17 are met, if the damage claims is for 100,000 SDRs there is no defence to the liability of the carrier. However, the carrier may be able to reduce wholly or partly the damage claim pursuant to the combined effect of Articles 20 and 29 of the Montreal Convention – by virtue of the application local laws. Theoretically, the passenger could recover no damages at all by the application of local law.

Thus, if the applicable local law limits the recoverable damages to for instance USD 50,000 that amount caps the recover in a case coming under the terms of the Montreal Convention involving passenger death or injury.

Hence, Article 21 of the Convention does not limit air carrier liability; rather, it established strict liability for all recoverable damages, as determined by application of Article 29 of the same convention, with the carrier having:

- [N]o defence to liability for the first 100,000 SDRs of proven damages;
- [T]he option to try to avoid liability for the proven damages in excess of 100,000 SDRs by proof of either element of Article 21(2) (liability not due to its negligence or that of a third party).[12]

The Warsaw liability regime and the Montreal Convention both contemplate the occurrence of an accident (again, 'accident' is not defined). As previously noted, under the Warsaw regime, carrier liability is limited in the event of an accident. Warsaw, then, provides a measure of protection for carriers where an accident has occurred. For the Montreal Convention, unlike the Warsaw regime, carriers face potentially unlimited liability in the event of an accident. Montreal, then, can be considered a passenger-friendly treaty (in this and in other ways), affording protection for *passengers* where an accident has occurred.

The Term 'Accident'

The wording of the compensable damages for passengers in the Convention is similar to but not identical with the wording of the Warsaw Convention: "damage sustained in the event of the death or wounding of a passenger or any other bodily injury suffered by a passenger" in the Warsaw Convention (Article 17) became somewhat more concise "damage sustained in case of death or bodily injury" in the Montreal Convention, 1999 (also Article 17). The damage must be caused by an *accident*. Also:

(1) there must be a causal link between the damage and the accident; and:
(2) the event giving rise to the damage must be qualified as an 'accident'.

Again, reference is made to myriad cases made under the Warsaw regime, and the criteria which were developed thereof or the determination of the term 'accident'.

Under the regime of the Montreal Convention, 1999, the presence of a discarded blanket bag on the floor of the aircraft which made a passenger slip does not constitute an 'accident', as it is not an unexpected or unusual event. According to the court, the crew had not violated standards of care. A passenger who fell on an inoperable escalator which she was ascending has not suffered an 'accident' under Article 17. Being hit by a bottle of liquid falling from an overhead bin constitutes an 'accident'. The carrier's failure to equip the aircraft with an Automate External Defibrillator does not constitute an 'accident' under the Montreal Convention.

From an Australian case, it can be concluded that a plaintiff will not necessarily be required to establish precisely what caused the bodily injury causing event that is claimed to be an accident under Article 17 of the

Montreal Convention. As a result, it may be sufficient for the plaintiff to state that the injury was caused by an event that was external to the passenger and that the event was unusual and unexpected, In the words of English and Australian courts: "... a distinct event, not being part of the usual, normal and expected operation of the aircraft, which happens independently of anything down or omitted by the passenger."

Does the airline's failure to recognise or respond to a heart attack suffered by a decedent passenger constitute an 'accident'? In a judgment from 2003, the court found that the airline's employee's conduct did not constitute an accident. In 2007, a court determined that there was a question of fact whether or not the airline' behaviour could be termed an "accident". An English Court of Appeal has ruled that a slip, trip or fall, unless caused by a distinct event independent of the passenger, does not qualify as an 'accident' within the meaning of Article 17 of the Montreal Convention, 1999.

As under the Warsaw Convention, DVT and related illnesses such as thrombosis embolism are not accidents in the meaning of Article 17 of the Montreal Convention. The failure to warn of the risk of DVT is not an accident either. Finally, the court confirmed that such claims are exclusively governed by the Montreal Convention, pre-empting the application of local law or other sources of law. So far, an Italian court has followed case law on DVT in the US, Australia, Canada and the UK.[13]

The Future of Montreal

The Montreal Convention brings an end to the patchwork quilt of international air carrier liability conventions and associated instruments, the first of which dates from 1929. But, as Havel and Sanchez note in their commentary below, in some respects the regime is an unfinished one. The scope and application of the Montreal Convention will continue to evolve through judicial interpretation of its provisions and further state ratification. Nevertheless, it would appear to be the end point – at least for the foreseeable future – in terms of the creation of further air carrier liability conventions.

An Unfinished Regime

As important as the Montreal Convention has been to overcoming problems encountered in the Warsaw System, it is not a terminal point in the evolution of this area of law. The treaty is only a decade old and has not yet won "universal" ratification. Although its circle of adhering States is expanding (103 States had ratified as of 2013), the total number is just over half that of the Chicago Convention. Thus, it is premature to declare the Montreal Convention an unqualified success or to extol it as the private law complement to the Chicago Convention. Many commentators have suggested that further work on the Convention needs to be done and that issues ranging from the amount of strict liability to more specific provisions on psychic injury will require future amendments to the treaty. Like Warsaw, Montreal fails to define several key terms including "carrier," "accident," "embarkation" and "disembarkation," and "delay." Nor does the treaty elucidate fully the role of insurance, establish uniform conflict of laws (choice of law) rules, or give detailed guidance on recoverable compensatory damages. There is concern, however, that meddling with the Montreal Convention through amendments before wider ratification is achieved will not only slow the accession of new States, but also duplicate Warsaw's history by developing another fractured, piecemeal system that squanders global uniformity and coherence. Some States, for example, might ratify the Montreal Convention but not an amending instrument. Montreal, it is argued, was designed to unclutter the confusion of Warsaw, not to compound it.[14]

At some point, the Montreal Convention will likely cover the global air carrier liability and passenger compensation field. Until that time, coverage will be somewhat patchy – with a number of states still signatories to various versions of the Warsaw regime.

Patchy Coverage

It is easy to think that when each of these Conventions are opened for signature, it is like wiping the slate clean and providing a fresh, new consistent and uniform Convention that will answer all the problems identified in the previous versions. The statement of ICAO Council President Dr Assad Kotaite provides the public perception of the success of the Montreal Convention and its unifying and homogenizing effect on private international air law:

> We have succeeded in modernizing a seventy-year old system of international instruments of private international law into one legal instrument that will provide, for years to come, an adequate level of compensation for those involved in international air accidents.

Alas, this is simply not true. The strength of any Convention is gauged by the number of ratifications it has received: A Convention only begins to apply once States have ratified it. In the case of the Montreal Convention, this means both the departure and the destination State. Until that time, it will simply not apply, rendering it useless, no matter how progressive it is; the more ratifications it receives, the more flights it will apply to, and therefore, the 'stronger' it will be. This is never more evident than the case of the Guatemala City Protocol that received so few ratifications that it never even became law. Now, twelve years since the conclusion of the Montreal Conference that gave birth to the Montreal Convention, the Montreal Convention has received numerous signatures and ratifications, in total 102 States have ratified the Convention, but this is still many less than the Warsaw Convention (152) and the Hague Protocol (137). ICAO currently has 190 members, which means that only 54% of Member States have ratified the Montreal Convention.

While those States that have ratified the Montreal Convention have made the vital step towards ensuring that their citizens are fairly compensated, there are many that have not and leave their citizens, like the families of the Lokomotiv Yaroslavl ice hockey team, facing the horror of a future without financial certainty and security. This is not the fault of the Montreal Convention, but this is the fault of those States that continue to refuse to ratify it.

[. . .]

So what in reality are we left with? Like a damaged quilt, we have failed to rid ourselves of the former Conventions and they glaringly shine through the gaps. The new Convention, a fresh quilt, has been thrown over the failing, unfair, and inappropriate Conventions of yesteryear, but alas the quilt remains riddled with holes. Until those States whose airlines are statistically at a higher risk of crashing finally ratify the Montreal Convention, we will not have succeeded in modernizing the Warsaw Regime.[15]

At the time of writing, more than a decade after the Montreal Convention entered into force, 119 of 191 ICAO Member States are parties to the Convention. This represents about 60 per cent of all states. On one view, this represents significant progress across the period since the Convention's conclusion. On another view, however, in terms of ratifications, it could be seen as something of a failure given the nature of international carriage by air and the need for universal ratification for the benefits of the Montreal Convention to be fully realised.

The Potential for the Failure of MC99 Due to Lack of Universal Acceptance

For MC99 to achieve its intended objective for universality in application, MC99 must be ratified by all ICAO Member States, of which there are 191.

Yet, although MC99 entered into force on 4 November 2003, there are as of this date [28 February 2014], slightly over ten years later, only 103 States Party to MC99.

Since 2010, there have been only six (6) ratifications of MC99; four (4) in 2011, one (1) in 2012 and one (1) in 2013.

Sixteen of the original signatories to MC99 on 28 May 1999 have not yet ratified MC99. The Representative of one of these non-ratifying State signatories at the Montreal Conference, Mauritius, was the Rapporteur at the Montreal Conference.

Twenty-eight States represented at the Montreal Conference did not sign MC99. Several of these States are significant air transportation States; for example, Guatemala, Indonesia, Iran, Philippines, Russian Federation, Sri Lanka, Thailand, Trinidad and Tobago, Tunisia, Venezuela.[16]

The potential for the Montreal Convention to fail in achieving its objectives has further been emphasised with respect to the interpretation of its liability provisions by domestic state courts, such interpretation arguably different to that of the original drafters and signatories to the Convention. A number of actions have been suggested, both with respect to ratification and interpretation of the Montreal Convention, to give full effect to that Convention.

Suggested Actions to Get MC99 Back on the Intended Flight Path for Global Acceptance and Correct Court Interpretation and Application of the MC99 Liability Rules

(1) The Council of ICAO should take appropriate steps to ensure that all Member States of ICAO ratify, accept, approve or accede to MC99 at the earliest time possible.

(2) The IATA member airlines of non-MC99 States should take appropriate steps to ensure that their respective governments ratify, accept, approve or accede to MC99 at the earliest possible time.

(3) The Governments of MC99 States Party should not hesitate to intervene in court cases pending in their respective jurisdictions to make their views known as to the intended meaning of the liability rules of MC99, whenever a court decision is rendered contrary to that intent. The USA already has done so.

(4) As perhaps a last resort, ICAO should re-convene the Montreal Conference of 1999 to make even clearer the intent of the States Party to MC99 as to the meaning of those Articles of MC99 which have been misconstrued, misinterpreted, misread and misapplied by courts when applying MC99 to actual cases and expressly confirm, once again and in no uncertain terms, that, where applicable to the transportation, MC99 is exclusive and preempts all local and national laws and regulations that otherwise may apply to the claim presented.[17]

EUROPEAN REGULATIONS

Air Carrier Liability in the Event of an Accident

The 1999 Montreal Convention provides a legal framework to govern international air carrier liability and passenger compensation. At a regional level, by way of example, the most significant uniform system for air carrier liability is that of the European Union (**EU**), which we examine below.

Council Regulation (EC) No 2027/97

Prior to the advent of the Montreal Convention, air carrier liability in the event of an accident in the European Union was governed by Council Regulation (EC) No 2027/97. Council Regulation (EC) No 2027/97 provides for EU carrier unlimited liability in the event of passenger injury or death and ensures consistent liability limits across all EU states, between EU states, and between EU states and third countries.

This Regulation did not, however, provide uniform liability limits for baggage or cargo, such limits subject to the Warsaw regime.

The Regulation has application to damage sustained in the event of passenger death or bodily injury if the relevant accident took place either on board an aircraft or during the process of embarkation or disembarkation. As set out in its preface, it "defines and harmonises the obligations of Community air carriers as regards the nature and limits of their liability in the event of accidents to passengers".

European action in the face of limited changes to the international air carrier liability regime (the Warsaw regime) have been described as follows:

> Given the fact that the 'Sleeping Beauty' called Warsaw Convention . . . has slumbered for decades as far as upward adjustment of liability limits is concerned, it comes as somewhat of a surprise that a horde of 'princes' are now virtually standing in line to wake 'her' with a kiss. As in the fairy tale by the Grimm brothers, it appears as though some of these saviors are likely to get caught in the brier bushes, although others will suffer the consequences: the airlines, the passengers, the certainty of the law, the original idea of a unification of rules relating to liability in international air transport, etc.[18]

European Parliament and Council Regulation No 889/2002

Regulation (EC) No 889/2002 amends Regulation No 2027/97 so as to take account of the provisions of the Montreal Convention with respect to domestic and international flights operated by EU carriers.

The Regulation ensures consistency between EU regulations and the relevant provisions of the Montreal Convention; it harmonises liability limits and carrier defences regardless of whether the accident occurs on a domestic EU, intra-EU or international journey.

> Parliament and Council Regulation 889/2002 amending Council Regulation (EC) 2027/97 on air carrier liability in the event of accidents was adopted on 13 May 2002. The essential purpose of the Regulation is to amend the existing Regulation on air carrier liability by implementing the provisions of the Montreal Convention 1999 in respect of the carriage of passengers and baggage by air (but not cargo), when it comes into effect.

In contrast to Regulation 2027/97, which unwisely sought to re-enact provisions of the Warsaw Convention, the new Regulation provides simply that the liability of a Community air carrier in respect of passengers and their baggage shall be governed by the relevant provisions of the Montreal Convention. Hence, it applies to all carriage by Community air carriers, including domestic carriage. It also contains four further provisions:

- An obligation on each Community air carrier to be insured up to a level adequate to ensure that all persons entitled to compensation in respect of passengers receive the full amount to which they are entitled;
- A provision requiring that any supplementary sum required by a Community carrier when a passenger makes a special declaration in respect of baggage should be based on a transparent tariff related to additional costs;
- An obligation on Community carriers to make advance payments required to meet immediate economic needs, similar to the current requirement, except that the minimum in the case of death has been increased from SDR15,000 to SDR 16,000;
- Certain notice and information requirements.

While in other respects unobjectionable, in two important respects the Regulation is unsatisfactory. In the first place, the fact that it obliges Community air carriers to apply the Montreal Convention regime even as regards carriage which under the Convention system would be governed rather by the Warsaw Convention will lead to EC Member States infringing their international law obligations to those parties of the Warsaw Convention who are not also party to the Montreal Convention, as confirmed in *R v. Secretary of State for the Environment, Transport and the Regions ex p IATA*. Secondly, significant problems are raised by the information and notice requirements . . .[19]

Denied Boarding, Cancellation and Long Delay of Flights

EC Regulation 261/2004 sets out common rules on compensation and assistance to passengers in the event of denied boarding, cancellation and long delay of flights. Compensation amounts depend both on the length of the flight as well as alternative flights available by the carrier. In addition to an immediate legal challenge in the United Kingdom High Court by carriers soon after the Regulation entered into force, the Regulation has been the subject of much litigation and academic comment.

European Parliament and Council Regulation No 261/2004

Given the low cost and high frequency of intra-European flights today, air travel is popular as never before. The benefits to Union citizens are considerable: new routes and operators are launched with astonishing regularity, and traditional 'legacy' carriers have revamped their business models to cater to increasingly broader groups of consumers. The resulting increase in traffic, however, brings with it a host of potential problems for operators and passengers: yield prediction becomes difficult as passengers book and throw away cheap tickets at random, intensive airframe utilization can put pressure on already tight maintenance schedules, and as runways and air traffic control systems reach capacity, the knock-on effects even of small delays can quickly spiral out of control.

It is perhaps unsurprising, then, that the European Union (EU's) Regulation 261/2004 on compensation and assistance to passengers in the event of denied boarding and of cancellation or long delay of flights has become one of the most high-profile areas of EU law in the perception of the travelling public. From a legal perspective, it has similarly resulted in heated academic discussion and analysis, building on a wide range of cases at domestic and European level. The Regulation has, on the one hand, been one of the most successful areas of EU action in the field of consumer protection, contributing significantly to the creation of an internal market in aviation services: following early action to ensure market liberalization, the Union is now working to ensure that service recipients' rights are protected when travelling across the Continent. On the other, the Regulation has come in for heavy criticism from the aviation industry: the obligations as laid down in its provisions, and later expanded upon by the Court of Justice of the European Union ('CJEU'), are said to impose significant financial burdens on air operators. They furthermore pose challenging questions as regards the relationship between EU law and international norms, notably in the form of the Montreal Convention for the Unification of Certain Rules for International Carriage by Air of 1999 ('Montreal Convention'), which purports to regulate exclusively liability arising from the contract of carriage by air.

Given these polar opposite viewpoints, fuelled further by the involvement of representative interest bodies on both air carrier and passenger sides, the application of Regulation 261/2004 in practice has led to considerable inconsistency and persistent compliance problems across different Member States. Even the very legality of the measures has repeatedly been at stake, as airlines challenge the validity and interpretation of the Regulation. A point has thus been reached where the only issue all parties seemingly manage to agree upon is an urgent need for reform – while of course disagreeing significantly as to what shape such measures should take: the industry hopes to reduce the scope of obligations imposed on it, whereas passengers are primarily interested in improving the Regulation's patchy enforcement record. On 13 March 2013 the European Commission finally heeded these calls, and put forward a set of proposals for a new Regulation to amend, and potentially extend, the existing regime of passenger rights protection.[20]

International Uniformity or Regional Harmonisation

Given the exclusivity provisions set out in the Montreal Convention for claims which fall within its ambit, and the potential overlap with relevant national or regional air carrier liability regimes, difficult questions as to scope and interpretation could arise. Such provisions of the Montreal Convention lead to the conclusion that priority is to be given to international uniformity above regional harmonisation. That said, it is clear that regional or domestic aviation liability rules can be used to supplement those of the Montreal Convention.

The EU has joined the Montreal Convention along with all the EU Member States, and thus, the Montreal Convention belongs to the mixed agreements category. The EU legislation includes several regulations, among them Regulation No 2027/97 and Regulation No 261/2004. The first one deals with air carrier liability in cases of accidents. Regulation (EC) No 261/2004 establishes common rules on compensation and assistance to passengers in the event boarding is denied and of cancellation or long delays of flights. In the Preamble, a high level of protection for passengers is indicated as the objective. As noted, it was the first instrument that established immediate measures to take care for passengers in case of denied boarding, delayed flights or cancellations compared to other international instruments or national law.

The main text of the Regulation stipulates that passengers of cancelled flights are entitled to receive assistance, re-routing and even compensation. Article 7 establishes a fixed amount of compensation with regard to the distance of the route. The provisions on delay are silent with respect to compensation; however, the passengers, depending on the length of their delay and the distance of the route, are to be offered assistance or re-routing or reimbursement. It should be noted that denial of boarding and cancellation preceding the carriage are not covered by the Montreal Convention as such. However, the Court's interpretation of 'cancellation' sometimes overlaps with damages due to delay and it is apparent that carrier's liability for delay is governed by the Montreal Convention.

It must be recalled that the Montreal Convention establishes the liability regime for personal injury and death to a passenger, damage to cargo and delay in relation to passengers and cargo. Article 29 establishes exclusivity of the cause of action under the Montreal Convention. It entails that where the carrier is clearly liable under the Convention, claims based on other causes of action are precluded. The purpose of this exclusivity is to maintain a balance between the rights of passengers to be compensated on the one hand and the air carriers on the other hand, that are protected from all possible claims that might arise during carriage by air, and also to ensure the uniform application of the Convention by Contracting States.

It is notable that most courts in common law jurisdictions have with a striking similarity, endorsed the exclusivity of a cause of action for passenger claims arising out of death, bodily injury, delay and damage to baggage in international air carriage and have dismissed claims for which the Convention did not provide a remedy including any non-material damage regarding the carriage of passengers and their baggage. The leading authority emanating from the British House of Lords is the position established in *Sidhu* by Lord Hope. According to him, the word 'all' concerning the scope of application stated in Article 1(1) has a particular significance for being all-embracing, meaning that solutions proposed in the Convention can be suitable for universal application in all cases. Otherwise, the whole system will be distorted, especially in cases where the Convention did not establish any liability for the carrier. Lord Hope also stated that the domestic courts by virtue of Article 24 are precluded from providing any remedy according to their own law, since the whole scheme of the Convention would be undermined. It is noteworthy that the decision in Sidhu has been applied and followed in numerous other cases decided by the English courts and also in other common law jurisdictions.

The courts of the USA have adopted a similar approach. It was held in *Tseng* that the Warsaw Convention precludes a passenger from maintaining an action for personal (psychological) injury damages under local law when her claim does not satisfy the conditions for liability under the Convention. In *Thibodeau v. Air Canada* the Supreme Court of Canada confirmed that even though the Montreal Convention does not deal with all aspects of international carriage by air, within the areas with which it deals, it is exclusive and thus bars resort to other bases for liability in those areas.[21]

Notes

1 Dempsey, Paul S. and Milde, Michael. *International Air Carrier Liability: The Montreal Convention of 1999*. Montreal: McGill University Centre for Research in Air & Space Law, 2005, 11.
2 Havel, Brian F. and Sanchez, Gabriel S. *The Principles and Practice of International Aviation Law*. New York: Cambridge University Press, 2014, 258–259.
3 Shawcross, C.N. and Beaumont, K.C. *Shawcross and Beaumont: Air Law*. London: Lexis Nexis Butterworths, 1997 (as updated, loose-leaf service), VII [127].
4 Diederiks-Verschoor, I.H. Ph. and Mendes de Leon, Pablo. *An Introduction to Air Law*. Alphen aan den Rijn: Kluwer Law International, 2012, 9th edition, 153–154.
5 Whalen, Thomas. "The New Warsaw Convention: The Montreal Convention", *Air and Space Law* 25(1) (2000): 13.
6 Havel and Sanchez, *Principles and Practice*, 268–269.
7 Dempsey and Milde, *International Air Carrier Liability*, 29–31.
8 Dempsey and Milde, *International Air Carrier Liability*, 32.
9 Whalen, Thomas. "The New Warsaw Convention", 13.
10 Dempsey and Milde, *International Air Carrier Liability*, 33–35.
11 Tompkins Jr. George N. "Are the Objectives of the 1999 Montreal Convention in Danger of Failure?", *Air and Space Law* 39(3) (2014): 204.
12 Diederiks-Verschoor and Mendes de Leon, *Air Law*, 223–225.
13 Diederiks-Verschoor and Mendes de Leon, *Air Law*, 226–227.
14 Havel and Sanchez, *Principles and Practice*, 313–314.

15 Neenan, Peter. "The Damaged Quilt: Inadequate Coverage of the Montreal Convention", *Air and Space Law* 37(1) (2012): 55–56, 64.
16 Tompkins. "Objectives of the 1999 Montreal Convention", 204–205.
17 Tompkins. "Objectives of the 1999 Montreal Convention", 213–214.
18 Giemulla, Elmar and Schmid, Ronald. "Council Regulation (EC) No. 2027/97 on Air Carrier Liability in the Event of Accidents and its Implications for Air Carriers", *Air and Space Law* 23(3) (1998): 98–99.
19 Balfour, John. "EC Aviation Scene (No 1: 2002)", *Air and Space Law* 27(4/5) (2002): 249–265.
20 Prassl, Jeremias. "Reforming Air Passenger Rights in the European Union", *Air and Space Law* 39(1) (2014): 59–60.
21 Bokareva, Olena. "Air Passengers' Rights in the EU: International Uniformity versus Regional Harmonization", *Air and Space Law* 41(1) (2016): 5–7.

Section 1

Main Conventions

1.1 Warsaw Convention 1929

CONVENTION FOR THE UNIFICATION OF CERTAIN RULES RELATING TO INTERNATIONAL CARRIAGE BY AIR

Chapter I – Scope – Definitions

Article 1

1. This Convention applies to all international carriage of persons, luggage or goods performed by aircraft for reward. It applies equally to gratuitous carriage by aircraft performed by an air transport undertaking.
2. For the purposes of this Convention the expression "international carriage" means any carriage in which, according to the contract made by the parties, the place of departure and the place of destination, whether or not there be a break in the carriage or a transhipment, are situated either within the territories of two High Contracting Parties, or within the territory of a single High Contracting Party, if there is an agreed stopping place within a territory subject to the sovereignty, suzerainty, mandate or authority of another Power, even though that Power is not a party to this Convention. A carriage without such an agreed stopping place between territories subject to the sovereignty, suzerainty, mandate or authority of the same High Contracting Party is not deemed to be international for the purposes of this Convention.
3. A carriage to be performed by several successive air carriers is deemed, for the purposes of this Convention, to be one undivided carriage, if it has been regarded by the parties as a single operation, whether it had been agreed upon under the form of a single contract or of a series of contracts, and it does not lose its international character merely because one contract or a series of contracts is to be performed entirely within a territory subject to the sovereignty, suzerainty, mandate or authority of the same High Contracting Party.

Article 2

1. This Convention applies to carriage performed by the State or by legally constituted public bodies provided it falls within the conditions laid down in Article 1.

2. This Convention does not apply to carriage performed under the terms of any international postal Convention.

Chapter II – Documents of Carriage

Section 1 – Passenger Ticket

Article 3

1. For the carriage of passengers the carrier must deliver a passenger ticket which shall contain the following particulars:

    (a) the place and date of issue;
    (b) the place of departure and of destination;
    (c) the agreed stopping places, provided that the carrier may reserve the right to alter the stopping places in case of necessity, and that if he exercises that right, the alteration shall not have the effect of depriving the carriage of its international character;
    (d) the name and address of the carrier or carriers;
    (e) a statement that the carriage is subject to the rules relating to liability established by this Convention.

2. The absence, irregularity or loss of the passenger ticket does not affect the existence or the validity of the contract of carriage, which shall none the less be subject to the rules of this Convention. Nevertheless, if the carrier accepts a passenger without a passenger ticket having been delivered he shall not be entitled to avail himself of those provisions of this Convention which exclude or limit his liability.

Section 2 – Luggage Ticket

Article 4

1. For the carriage of luggage, other than small personal objects of which the passenger takes charge himself, the carrier must deliver a luggage ticket.
2. The luggage ticket shall be made out in duplicate, one part for the passenger and the other part for the carrier.
3. The luggage ticket shall contain the following particulars:

    (a) the place and date of issue;
    (b) the place of departure and of destination;
    (c) the name and address of the carrier or carriers;
    (d) the number of the passenger ticket;
    (e) a statement that delivery of the luggage will be made to the bearer of the luggage ticket;
    (f) the number and weight of the packages;

(g) the amount of the value declared in accordance with Article 22(2);

(h) a statement that the carriage is subject to the rules relating to liability established by this Convention.

4. The absence, irregularity or loss of the luggage ticket does not affect the existence or the validity of the contract of carriage, which shall none the less be subject to the rules of this Convention. Nevertheless, if the carrier accepts luggage without a luggage ticket having been delivered, or if the luggage ticket does not contain the particulars set out at (d), (f) and (h) above, the carrier shall not be entitled to avail himself of those provisions of the Convention which exclude or limit his liability.

Section 3 – Air Consignment Note

Article 5

1. Every carrier of goods has the right to require the consignor to make out and hand over to him a document called an "air consignment note"; every consignor has the right to require the carrier to accept this document.
2. The absence, irregularity or loss of this document does not affect the existence or the validity of the contract of carriage which shall, subject to the provisions of Article 9, be none the less governed by the rules of this Convention.

Article 6

1. The air consignment note shall be made out by the consignor in three original parts and be handed over with the goods.
2. The first part shall be marked "for the carrier", and shall be signed by the consignor. The second part shall be marked "for the consignee"; it shall be signed by the consignor and by the carrier and shall accompany the goods. The third part shall be signed by the carrier and handed by him to the consignor after the goods have been accepted.
3. The carrier shall sign on acceptance of the goods.
4. The signature of the carrier may be stamped; that of the consignor may be printed or stamped.
5. If, at the request of the consignor, the carrier makes out the air consignment note, he shall be deemed, subject to proof to the contrary, to have done so on behalf of the consignor.

Article 7

The carrier of goods has the right to require the consignor to make out separate consignment notes when there is more than one package.

Article 8

The air consignment note shall contain the following particulars:
(a)   the place and date of its execution;
(b)   the place of departure and of destination;
(c)   the agreed stopping places, provided that the carrier may reserve the right to alter the stopping places in case of necessity, and that if he exercises that right the alteration shall not have the effect of depriving the carriage of its international character;
(d)   the name and address of the consignor;
(e)   the name and address of the first carrier;
(f)   the name and address of the consignee, if the case so requires;
(g)   the nature of the goods;
(h)   the number of the packages, the method of packing and the particular marks or numbers upon them;
(i)   the weight, the quantity and the volume or dimensions of the goods;
(j)   the apparent condition of the goods and of the packing;
(k)   the freight, if it has been agreed upon, the date and place of payment, and the person who is to pay it;
(l)   if the goods are sent for payment on delivery, the price of the goods, and, if the case so requires, the amount of the expenses incurred;
(m)   the amount of the value declared in accordance with Article 22 (2);
(n)   the number of parts of the air consignment note;
(o)   the documents handed to the carrier to accompany the air consignment note;
(p)   the time fixed for the completion of the carriage and a brief note of the route to be followed, if these matters have been agreed upon;
(q)   a statement that the carriage is subject to the rules relating to liability established by this Convention.

Article 9

If the carrier accepts goods without an air consignment note having been made out, or if the air consignment note does not contain all the particulars set out in Article 8(a) to (i) inclusive and (q), the carrier shall not be entitled to avail himself of the provisions of this Convention which exclude or limit his liability.

Article 10

1.   The consignor is responsible for the correctness of the particulars and statements relating to the goods which he inserts in the air consignment note.
2.   The consignor will be liable for all damage suffered by the carrier or any other person by reason of the irregularity, incorrectness or incompleteness of the said particulars and statements.

Article 11

1. The air consignment note is *prima facie* evidence of the conclusion of the contract, of the receipt of the goods and of the conditions of carriage.
2. The statements in the air consignment note relating to the weight, dimensions and packing of the goods, as well as those relating to the number of packages, are *prima facie* evidence of the facts stated; those relating to the quantity, volume and condition of the goods do not constitute evidence against the carrier except so far as they both have been, and are stated in the air consignment note to have been, checked by him in the presence of the consignor, or relate to the apparent condition of the goods.

Article 12

1. Subject to his liability to carry out all his obligations under the contract of carriage, the consignor has the right to dispose of the goods by withdrawing them at the aerodrome of departure or destination, or by stopping them in the course of the journey on any landing, or by calling for them to be delivered at the place of destination or in the course of the journey to a person other than the consignee named in the air consignment note, or by requiring them to be returned to the aerodrome of departure. He must not exercise this right of disposition in such a way as to prejudice the carrier or other consignors and he must repay any expenses occasioned by the exercise of this right.
2. If it is impossible to carry out the orders of the consignor the carrier must so inform him forthwith.
3. If the carrier obeys the orders of the consignor for the disposition of the goods without requiring the production of the part of the air consignment note delivered to the latter, he will be liable, without prejudice to his right of recovery from the consignor, for any damage which may be caused thereby to any person who is lawfully in possession of that part of the air consignment note.
4. The right conferred on the consignor ceases at the moment when that of the consignee begins in accordance with Article 13. Nevertheless, if the consignee declines to accept the consignment note or the goods, or if he cannot be communicated with, the consignor resumes his right of disposition.

Article 13

1. Except in the circumstances set out in the preceding Article, the consignee is entitled, on arrival of the goods at the place of destination, to require the carrier to hand over to him the air consignment note and to deliver the goods to him, on payment of the charges due and on complying with the conditions of carriage set out in the air consignment note.

2. Unless it is otherwise agreed, it is the duty of the carrier to give notice to the consignee as soon as the goods arrive.
3. If the carrier admits the loss of the goods, or if the goods have not arrived at the expiration of seven days after the date on which they ought to have arrived, the consignee is entitled to put into force against the carrier the rights which flow from the contract of carriage.

Article 14

The consignor and the consignee can respectively enforce all the rights given them by Articles 12 and 13, each in his own name, whether he is acting in his own interest or in the interest of another, provided that he carries out the obligations imposed by the contract.

Article 15

1. Articles 12, 13 and 14 do not affect either the relations of the consignor or the consignee with each other or the mutual relations of third parties whose rights are derived either from the consignor or from the consignee.
2. The provisions of Articles 12, 13 and 14 can only be varied by express provision in the air consignment note.

Article 16

1. The consignor must furnish such information and attach to the air consignment note such documents as are necessary to meet the formalities of customs, octroi or police before the goods can be delivered to the consignee. The consignor is liable to the carrier for any damage occasioned by the absence, insufficiency or irregularity of any such information or documents, unless the damage is due to the fault of the carrier or his agents.
2. The carrier is under no obligation to enquire into the correctness or sufficiency of such information or documents.

Chapter III – Liability of the Carrier

Article 17

The carrier is liable for damage sustained in the event of the death or wounding of a passenger or any other bodily injury suffered by a passenger, if the accident which caused the damage so sustained took place on board the aircraft or in the course of any of the operations of embarking or disembarking.

Article 18

1. The carrier is liable for damage sustained in the event of the destruction or loss of, or of damage to, any registered luggage or any goods, if the occurrence which caused the damage so sustained took place during the carriage by air.
2. The carriage by air within the meaning of the preceding paragraph comprises the period during which the luggage or goods are in charge of the carrier, whether in an aerodrome or on board an aircraft, or, in the case of a landing outside an aerodrome, in any place whatsoever.
3. The period of the carriage by air does not extend to any carriage by land, by sea or by river performed outside an aerodrome. If, however, such a carriage takes place in the performance of a contract for carriage by air, for the purpose of loading, delivery or transhipment, any damage is presumed, subject to proof to the contrary, to have been the result of an event which took place during the carriage by air.

Article 19

The carrier is liable for damage occasioned by delay in the carriage by air of passengers, luggage or goods.

Article 20

1. The carrier is not liable if he proves that he and his agents have taken all necessary measures to avoid the damage or that it was impossible for him or them to take such measures.
2. In the carriage of goods and luggage the carrier is not liable if he proves that the damage was occasioned by negligent pilotage or negligence in the handling of the aircraft or in navigation and that, in all other respects, he and his agents have taken all necessary measures to avoid the damage.

Article 21

If the carrier proves that the damage was caused by or contributed to by the negligence of the injured person the Court may, in accordance with the provisions of its own law, exonerate the carrier wholly or partly from his liability.

Article 22

1. In the carriage of passengers the liability of the carrier for each passenger is limited to the sum of 125,000 francs. Where, in accordance with the law of the Court seised of the case, damages may be awarded in the form of periodical payments, the equivalent capital value of the said payments

shall not exceed 125,000 francs. Nevertheless, by special contract, the carrier and the passenger may agree to a higher limit of liability.

2.   In the carriage of registered luggage and of goods, the liability of the carrier is limited to a sum of 250 francs per kilogram, unless the consignor has made, at the time when the package was handed over to the carrier, a special declaration of the value at delivery and has paid a supplementary sum if the case so requires. In that case the carrier will be liable to pay a sum not exceeding the declared sum, unless he proves that that sum is greater than the actual value to the consignor at delivery.

3.   As regards objects of which the passenger takes charge himself the liability of the carrier is limited to 5,000 francs per passenger.

4.   The sums mentioned above shall be deemed to refer to the French franc consisting of 65½ milligrams gold of millesimal fineness 900. These sums may be converted into any national currency in round figures.

Article 23

Any provision tending to relieve the carrier of liability or to fix a lower limit than that which is laid down in this Convention shall be null and void, but the nullity of any such provision does not involve the nullity of the whole contract, which shall remain subject to the provisions of this Convention.

Article 24

1.   In the cases covered by Articles 18 and 19 any action for damages, however founded, can only be brought subject to the conditions and limits set out in this Convention.

2.   In the cases covered by Article 17 the provisions of the preceding paragraph also apply, without prejudice to the questions as to who are the persons who have the right to bring suit and what are their respective rights.

Article 25

1.   The carrier shall not be entitled to avail himself of the provisions of this Convention which exclude or limit his liability, if the damage is caused by his wilful misconduct or by such default on his part as, in accordance with the law of the Court seised of the case, is considered to be equivalent to wilful misconduct.

2.   Similarly the carrier shall not be entitled to avail himself of the said provisions, if the damage is caused as aforesaid by any agent of the carrier acting within the scope of his employment.

Article 26

1. Receipt by the person entitled to delivery of luggage or goods without complaint is *prima facie* evidence that the same have been delivered in good condition and in accordance with the document of carriage.
2. In the case of damage, the person entitled to delivery must complain to the carrier forthwith after the discovery of the damage, and, at the latest, within three days from the date of receipt in the case of luggage and seven days from the date of receipt in the case of goods. In the case of delay the complaint must be made at the latest within fourteen days from the date on which the luggage or goods have been placed at his disposal.
3. Every complaint must be made in writing upon the document of carriage or by separate notice in writing despatched within the times aforesaid.
4. Failing complaint within the times aforesaid, no action shall lie against the carrier, save in the case of fraud on his part.

Article 27

In the case of the death of the person liable, an action for damages lies in accordance with the terms of this Convention against those legally representing his estate.

Article 28

1. An action for damages must be brought, at the option of the plaintiff, in the territory of one of the High Contracting Parties, either before the Court having jurisdiction where the carrier is ordinarily resident, or has his principal place of business, or has an establishment by which the contract has been made or before the Court having jurisdiction at the place of destination.
2. Questions of procedure shall be governed by the law of the Court seised of the case.

Article 29

1. The right to damages shall be extinguished if an action is not brought within two years, reckoned from the date of arrival at the destination, or from the date on which the aircraft ought to have arrived, or from the date on which the carriage stopped.
2. The method of calculating the period of limitation shall be determined by the law of the Court seised of the case.

Article 30

1. In the case of carriage to be performed by various successive carriers and falling within the definition set out in the third paragraph of Article 1, each carrier who accepts passengers, luggage or goods is subjected to the rules set out in this Convention, and is deemed to be one of the contracting parties to the contract of carriage in so far as the contract deals with that part of the carriage which is performed under his supervision.
2. In the case of carriage of this nature, the passenger or his representative can take action only against the carrier who performed the carriage during which the accident or the delay occurred, save in the case where, by express agreement, the first carrier has assumed liability for the whole journey.
3. As regards luggage or goods, the passenger or consignor will have a right of action against the first carrier, and the passenger or consignee who is entitled to delivery will have a right of action against the last carrier, and further, each may take action against the carrier who performed the carriage during which the destruction, loss, damage or delay took place. These carriers will be jointly and severally liable to the passenger or to the consignor or consignee.

Chapter IV – Provisions Relating to Combined Carriage

Article 31

1. In the case of combined carriage performed partly by air and partly by any other mode of carriage, the provisions of this Convention apply only to the carriage by air, provided that the carriage by air falls within the terms of Article 1.
2. Nothing in this Convention shall prevent the parties in the case of combined carriage from inserting in the document of air carriage conditions relating to other modes of carriage, provided that the provisions of this Convention are observed as regards the carriage by air.

Chapter V – General and Final Provisions

Article 32

Any clause contained in the contract and all special agreements entered into before the damage occurred by which the parties purport to infringe the rules laid down by this Convention, whether by deciding the law to be applied, or by altering the rules as to jurisdiction, shall be null and void. Nevertheless for the carriage of goods arbitration clauses are allowed, subject to this Convention, if the arbitration is to take place within one of the jurisdictions referred to in the first paragraph of Article 28.

Article 33

Nothing contained in this Convention shall prevent the carrier either from refusing to enter into any contract of carriage, or from making regulations which do not conflict with the provisions of this Convention.

Article 34

This Convention does not apply to international carriage by air performed by way of experimental trial by air navigation undertakings with the view to the establishment of a regular line of air navigation, nor does it apply to carriage performed in extraordinary circumstances outside the normal scope of an air carrier's business.

Article 35

The expression "days" when used in this Convention means current days not working days.

Article 36

The Convention is drawn up in French in a single copy which shall remain deposited in the archives of the Ministry for Foreign Affairs of Poland and of which one duly certified copy shall be sent by the Polish Government to the Government of each of the High Contracting Parties.

Article 37

1. This Convention shall be ratified. The instruments of ratification shall be deposited in the archives of the Ministry for Foreign Affairs of Poland, which will notify the deposit to the Government of each of the High Contracting Parties.
2. As soon as this Convention shall have been ratified by five of the High Contracting Parties it shall come into force as between them on the ninetieth day after the deposit of the fifth ratification. Thereafter it shall come into force between the High Contracting Parties who shall have ratified and the High Contracting Party who deposits his instrument of ratification on the ninetieth day after the deposit.
3. It shall be the duty of the Government of the Republic of Poland to notify to the Government of each of the High Contracting Parties the date on which this Convention comes into force as well as the date of the deposit of each ratification.

Article 38

1. This Convention shall, after it has come into force, remain open for accession by any State.
2. The accession shall be effected by a notification addressed to the Government of the Republic of Poland, which will inform the Government of each of the High Contracting Parties thereof.
3. The accession shall take effect as from the nineteenth day after the notification made to the Government of the Republic of Poland.

Article 39

1. Any one of the High Contracting Parties may denounce this Convention by a notification addressed to the Government of the Republic of Poland, which will at once inform the Government of each of the High Contracting Parties.
2. Denunciation shall take effect six months after the notification of denunciation, and shall operate only as regards the Party who shall have proceeded to denunciation.

Article 40

1. Any High Contracting Party may, at the time of signature or of deposit of ratification or of accession declare that the acceptance which he gives to this Convention does not apply to all or any of his colonies, protectorates, territories under mandate, or any other territory subject to his sovereignty or his authority, or any territory under his suzerainty.
2. Accordingly any High Contracting Party may subsequently accede separately in the name of all or any of his colonies, protectorates, territories under mandate or any other territory subject to his sovereignty or to his authority or any territory under his suzerainty which has been thus excluded by his original declaration.
3. Any High Contracting Party may denounce this Convention, in accordance with its provisions, separately or for all or any of his colonies, protectorates, territories under mandate or any other territory subject to his sovereignty or to his authority, or any other territory under his suzerainty.

Article 41

Any High Contracting Party shall be entitled not earlier than two years after the coming into force of this Convention to call for the assembling of a new international Conference in order to consider any improvements which may be made in this Convention. To this end he will communicate with the Government of the French Republic which will take the necessary measures to make preparations for such Conference.

This Convention done at Warsaw on the 12th October, 1929, shall remain open for signature until the 31st January, 1930.

Additional Protocol (with reference to Article 2)

The High Contracting Parties reserve to themselves the right to declare at the time of ratification or of accession that the first paragraph of Article 2 of this Convention shall not apply to international carriage by air performed directly by the State, its colonies protectorates or mandated territories or by any other territory under its sovereignty, suzerainty or authority.

1.2 Warsaw Convention 1929 as amended at The Hague 1955

WARSAW CONVENTION, 1929, AS AMENDED AT THE HAGUE, 1955

Chapter I – Scope – Definitions

Article 1

1. This Convention applies to all international carriage of persons, baggage or cargo performed by aircraft for reward. It applies equally to gratuitous carriage by aircraft performed by an air transport undertaking.
2. For the purposes of this Convention, the expression *international carriage* means any carriage in which, according to the agreement between the parties, the place of departure and the place of destination, whether or not there be a break in the carriage or a transhipment, are situated either within the territories of two High Contracting Parties or within the territory of a single High Contracting Party if there is an agreed stopping place within the territory of another State, even if that State is not a High Contracting Party. Carriage between two points within the territory of a single High Contracting Party without an agreed stopping place within the territory of another State is not international carriage for the purposes of this Convention.
3. Carriage to be performed by several successive air carriers is deemed, for the purposes of this Convention, to be one undivided carriage if it has been regarded by the parties as a single operation, whether it had been agreed upon under the form of a single contract or of a series of contracts, and it does not lose its international character merely because one contract or a series of contracts is to be performed entirely within the territory of the same State.

Article 2

1. The Convention applies to carriage performed by the State or by legally constituted public bodies provided it falls within the conditions laid down in Article 1.
2. This Convention shall not apply to carriage of mail and postal packages.

Chapter II – Documents of Carriage

Section I – Passenger Ticket

Article 3

1. In respect of the carriage of passengers a ticket shall be delivered containing:

   (a) an indication of the places of departure and destination;
   (b) if the places of departure and destination are within the territory of a single High Contracting Party, one or more agreed stopping places being within the territory of another State, an indication of at least one such stopping place;
   (c) a notice to the effect that, if the passenger's journey involves an ultimate destination or stop in a country other than the country of departure, the Warsaw Convention may be applicable and that the Convention governs and in most cases limits the liability of carriers for death or personal injury and in respect of loss of or damage to baggage.

2. The passenger ticket shall constitute *prima facie* evidence of the conclusion and conditions of the contract of carriage. The absence, irregularity or loss of the passenger ticket does not affect the existence or the validity of the contract of carriage which shall, none the less, be subject to the rules of this Convention. Nevertheless, if, with the consent of the carrier, the passenger embarks without a passenger ticket having been delivered, or if the ticket does not include the notice required by paragraph 1(c) of this Article, the carrier shall not be entitled to avail himself of the provisions of Article 22.

Section II – Baggage Check

Article 4

1. In respect of the carriage of registered baggage, a baggage check shall be delivered, which, unless combined with or incorporated in a passenger ticket which complies with the provisions of Article 3, paragraph 1, shall contain:

   (a) an indication of the places of departure and destination;
   (b) if the places of departure and destination are within the Territory of a single High Contracting Party, one or more agreed stopping places being within the territory of another State, an indication of at least one such stopping place;
   (c) a notice to the effect that, if the carriage involves an ultimate destination or stop in a country other than the country of departure, the Warsaw Convention may be applicable and that the Convention governs and in most cases limits the liability of carriers in respect of loss of or damage to baggage.

2. The baggage check shall constitute *prima facie* evidence of the registration of the baggage and of the conditions of the contract of carriage. The absence, irregularity or loss of the baggage check does not affect the existence or the validity of the contract of carriage which shall, none the less, be subject to the rules of this Convention. Nevertheless, if the carrier takes charge of the baggage without a baggage check having been delivered or if the baggage check (unless combined with or incorporated in the passenger ticket which complies with the provisions of Article 3, paragraph 1(c)) does not include the notice required by paragraph 1(c) of this Article, he shall not be entitled to avail himself of the provisions of Article 22, paragraph 2.

Section III – Air Waybill

Article 5

1. Every carrier of cargo has the right to require the consignor to make out and hand over to him a document called an "air waybill"; every consignor has the right to require the carrier to accept this document.
2. The absence, irregularity, or loss of this document does not affect the existence or the validity of the contract of carriage which shall, subject to the provisions of Article 9, be none the less governed by the rules of this Convention.

Article 6

1. The air waybill shall be made out by the consignor in three original parts and be handed over with the cargo.
2. The first part shall be marked "for the carrier", and shall be signed by the consignor. The second part shall be marked "for the consignee"; it shall be signed by the consignor and by the carrier and shall accompany the cargo. The third part shall be signed by the carrier and handed by him to the consignor after the cargo has been accepted.
3. The carrier shall sign prior to the loading of the cargo on board the aircraft.
4. The signature of the carrier may be stamped; that of the consignor may be printed or stamped.
5. If, at the request of the consignor, the carrier makes out the air waybill, he shall be deemed, subject to proof to the contrary, to have done so on behalf of the consignor.

Article 7

The carrier of cargo has the right to require the consignor to make out separate air waybills when there is more than one package.

Article 8

The air waybill shall contain:

(a) an indication of the places of departure and destination;

(b) if the places of departure and destination are within the territory of a single High Contracting Party, one or more agreed stopping places being within the territory of another State, an indication of at least one such stopping place;

(c) a notice to the consignor to the effect that, if the carriage involves an ultimate destination or stop in a country other than the country of departure, the Warsaw Convention may be applicable and that the Convention governs and in most cases limits the liability of carriers in respect of loss of or damage to cargo.

Article 9

If, with the consent of the carrier, cargo is loaded on board the aircraft without an air waybill having been made out, or if the air waybill does not include the notice required by Article 8, paragraph (c), the carrier shall not be entitled to avail himself of the provisions of Article 22, paragraph 2.

Article 10

1. The consignor is responsible for the correctness of the particulars and statements relating to the cargo which he inserts in the air waybill.

2. The consignor shall indemnify the carrier against all damage suffered by him, or by any other person to whom the carrier is liable, by reason of the irregularity, incorrectness or incompleteness of the particulars and statements furnished by the consignor.

Article 11

1. The air waybill shall be *prima facie* evidence of the conclusion of the contract, of the receipt of the cargo and of the conditions of carriage.

2. The statements in the air waybill relating to the weight, dimensions and packing of the cargo, as well as those relating to the number of packages, shall be *prima facie* evidence of the facts stated; those relating to the quantity, volume and condition of the cargo shall not constitute evidence against the carrier except so far as they both have been, and are stated in the air waybill to have been, checked by him in the presence of the consignor, or relate to the apparent condition of the cargo.

Article 12

1. Subject to his liability to carry out all his obligations under the contract of carriage, the consignor shall have the right to dispose of the cargo by withdrawing them at the airport of departure or destination, or by stopping them in the course of the journey on any landing, or by calling for them to be delivered at the place of destination, or in the course of the journey to a person other than the consignee named in the air waybill, or by requiring them to be returned to the airport of departure. He must not exercise this right of disposition in such a way as to prejudice the carrier or other consignors, and he must repay any expenses occasioned by the exercise of this right.
2. If it is impossible to carry out the orders of the consignor the carrier must so inform him forthwith.
3. If the carrier obeys the orders of the consignor for the disposition of the cargo without requiring the production of the part of the air waybill delivered to the latter, he will be liable, without prejudice to his right of recovery from the consignor, for any damage which may be caused thereby to any person who is lawfully in possession of that part of the air waybill.
4. The right conferred on the consignor ceases at the moment when that of the consignee begins in accordance with Article 13, below. Nevertheless, if the consignee declines to accept the air waybill or the cargo, or if he cannot be communicated with, the consignor shall resume his right of disposition.

Article 13

1. Except in the circumstances set out in the preceding Article, the consignee shall be entitled, on arrival of the cargo at the place of destination, to require the carrier to hand over to him the air waybill and to deliver the cargo to him, on payment of the charges due and on complying with the conditions of carriage set out in the air waybill.
2. Unless it is otherwise agreed, it shall be the duty of the carrier to give notice to the consignee as soon as the cargo arrives.
3. If the carrier admits the loss of the cargo, or if the cargo has not arrived at the expiration of seven days after the date on which it ought to have arrived, the consignee shall be entitled to put into force against the carrier the rights which flow from the contract of carriage.

Article 14

The consignor and the consignee can respectively enforce all the rights given them by Articles 12 and 13, each in his own name, whether he is acting in his own interest or in the interest of another, provided that he carries out the obligations imposed by the contract.

Article 15

1. Articles 12, 13 and 14 shall not affect either the relations of the consignor and the consignee with each other or the relations of third parties whose rights are derived either from the consignor or from the consignee.
2. The provisions of Articles 12, 13 and 14 can only be varied by express provision in the air waybill.
3. Nothing in this Convention prevents the issue of a negotiable air waybill.

Article 16

1. The consignor must furnish such information and attach to the air waybill such documents as are necessary to meet the formalities of customs, octroi, or police before the cargo can be delivered to the consignee. The consignor is liable to the carrier for any damage occasioned by the absence, insufficiency or irregularity of any such information or documents, unless the damage is due to the fault of the carrier or his agents.
2. The carrier is under no obligation to inquire into the correctness or sufficiency of such information or documents.

Chapter III – Liability of the Carrier

Article 17

The carrier shall be liable for damage sustained in the event of the death or wounding of a passenger or any other bodily injury suffered by a passenger, if the accident which caused the damage so sustained took place on board the aircraft or in the course of any of the operations of embarking or disembarking.

Article 18

1. The carrier shall be liable for damages sustained in the event of the destruction or loss of, or of damage to, any checked baggage or any cargo, if the occurrence which caused the damage so sustained took place during the carriage by air.
2. The carriage by air within the meaning of the preceding paragraph shall comprise the period during which the baggage or cargo are in [the] charge of the carrier, whether in an airport or on board an aircraft, or, in the case of a landing outside an airport, in any place whatsoever.
3. The period of the carriage by air does not extend to any carriage by land, by sea or by river performed outside an airport. If, however, such carriage takes place in the performance of a contract for carriage by air, for the purpose of loading, delivery or transshipment, any damage is presumed, subject to proof to the contrary, to have been the result of an event which took place during the carriage by air.

Article 19

The carrier shall be liable for damage occasioned by delay in the carriage by air of passengers, baggage or cargo.

Article 20

The carrier shall not be liable if he proves that he and his agents have taken all necessary measures to avoid the damage or that it was impossible for him or them to take such measures.

Article 21

If the carrier proves that the damage was caused by or contributed to by the negligence of the injured person the court may, in accordance with the provisions of its own law, exonerate the carrier wholly or partly from his liability.

Article 22

1.   In the carriage of persons the liability of the carrier for each passenger is limited to the sum of two hundred and fifty thousand francs. Where, in accordance with the law of the court seised of the case, damages may be awarded in the form of periodical payments, the equivalent capital value of the said payments shall not exceed two hundred and fifty thousand francs. Nevertheless, by special contract, the carrier and the passenger may agree to a higher limit of liability.

2.   (a)   In the carriage of registered baggage and of cargo, the liability of the carrier is limited to a sum of two hundred and fifty francs per kilogramme, unless the passenger or consignor has made, at the time when the package was handed over to the carrier, a special declaration of interest in delivery at destination and has paid a supplementary sum if the case so requires. In that case the carrier will be liable to pay a sum not exceeding the declared sum, unless he proves that the sum is greater than the passenger's or consignor's actual interest in delivery at destination.

     (b)   In the case of loss, damage or delay of part of registered baggage or cargo, or of any object contained therein, the weight to be taken into consideration in determining the amount to which the carrier's liability is limited shall be only the total weight of the package or packages concerned. Nevertheless, when the loss, damage or delay of a part of the registered baggage or cargo, or of an object contained therein, affects the value of other packages covered by the same baggage check or the same air waybill, the total weight of such package or packages shall also be taken into consideration in determining the limit of liability.

3. As regards objects of which the passenger takes charge himself the liability of the carrier is limited to five thousand francs per passenger.

4. The limits prescribed in this article shall not prevent the court from awarding, in accordance with its own law, in addition, the whole or part of the court costs and of the other expenses of the litigation incurred by the plaintiff. The foregoing provision shall not apply if the amount of the damages awarded, excluding court costs and other expenses of the litigation, does not exceed the sum which the carrier has offered in writing to the plaintiff within a period of six months from the date of the occurrence causing the damage, or before the commencement of the action, if that is later.

5. The sums mentioned in francs in this Article shall be deemed to refer to a currency unit consisting of sixty-five and a half milligrammes of gold of millesimal fineness nine hundred. These sums may be converted into national currencies in round figures. Conversion of the sums into national currencies other than gold shall, in case of judicial proceedings, be made according to the gold value of such currencies at the date of the judgment.

Article 23

1. Any provision tending to relieve the carrier of liability or to fix a lower limit than that which is laid down in this Convention shall be null and void, but the nullity of any such provision does not involve the nullity of the whole contract, which shall remain subject to the provisions of this Convention.

2. Paragraph 1 of this Article shall not apply to provisions governing loss or damage resulting from the inherent defect, quality or vice of the cargo carried.

Article 24

1. In the cases covered by Articles 18 and 19 any action for damages, however founded, can only be brought subject to the conditions and limits set out in this Convention.

2. In the cases covered by Article 17 the provisions of the preceding paragraph shall also apply, without prejudice to the questions as to who are the persons who have the right to bring suit and what are their respective rights.

Article 25

The limits of liability specified in Article 22 shall not apply if it is proved that the damage resulted from an act or omission of the carrier, his servants or agents, done with intent to cause damage or recklessly and with knowledge that damage would probably result; provided that, in the case of such act or omission of a servant or agent, it is also proved that he was acting within the scope of his employment.

Article 25A

1. If an action is brought against a servant or agent of the carrier arising out of damage to which this Convention relates, such servant or agent, if he proves that he acted within the scope of his employment, shall be entitled to avail himself of the limits of liability which that carrier himself is entitled to invoke under Article 22.
2. The aggregate of the amounts recoverable from the carrier, his servants and agents, in that case, shall not exceed the said limits.
3. The provisions of paragraphs 1 and 2 of this Article shall not apply if it is proved that the damage resulted from an act or omission of the servant or agent done with intent to cause damage or recklessly and with knowledge that damage would probably result.

Article 26

1. Receipt by the person entitled to delivery of baggage or cargo without complaint shall be *prima facie* evidence that the same has been delivered in good condition and in accordance with the document of carriage.
2. In the case of damage, the person entitled to delivery must complain to the carrier forthwith after the discovery of the damage, and, at the latest, within seven days from the date of receipt in the case of baggage and fourteen days from the date of receipt in the case of cargo. In the case of delay the complaint must be made at the latest within twenty-one days from the date on which the baggage or cargo have been placed at his disposal.
3. Every complaint must be made in writing upon the document of carriage or by separate notice in writing despatched within the times aforesaid.
4. Failing complaint within the times aforesaid, no action shall lie against the carrier, save in the case of fraud on his part.

Article 27

In the case of the death of the person liable, an action for damages lies in accordance with the terms of this Convention against those legally representing his estate.

Article 28

1. An action for damages must be brought, at the option of the plaintiff, in the territory of one of the High Contracting Parties, either before the court having jurisdiction where the carrier is ordinarily resident or has his principal place of business, or has an establishment by which the contract has been made, or before the court having jurisdiction at the place of destination.

2. Questions of procedure shall be governed by the law of the court seised of the case.

Article 29

1. The right to damages shall be extinguished if an action is not brought within 2 (two) years, reckoned from the date of arrival at the destination, or from the date on which the aircraft ought to have arrived, or from the date on which the carriage stopped.
2. The method of calculating the period of limitation shall be determined by the law of the court seised of the case is submitted.

Article 30

1. In the case of carriage to be performed by various successive carriers and falling within the definition set out in the third paragraph of Article 1, each carrier who accepts passengers, baggage or cargo is subject to the rules set out in this Convention, and shall be deemed to be one of the contracting parties to the contract of carriage insofar as the contract deals with that part of the carriage which is performed under his supervision.
2. In the case of carriage of this nature, the passenger or his representative can take action only against the carrier who performed the carriage during which the accident or the delay occurred, save in the case where, by express agreement, the first carrier has assumed liability for the whole journey.
3. As regards baggage or cargo, the passenger or consignor will have a right of action against the first carrier, and the passenger or consignee who is entitled to delivery will have a right of action against the last carrier, and further, each may take action against the carrier who performed the carriage during which the destruction, loss, damage or delay took place. These carriers will be jointly and severally liable to the passenger or to the consignor or consignee.

Chapter IV – Provisions Relating to Combined Carriage

Article 31

1. In the case of combined carriage performed partly by air and partly by any other mode of carriage, the provisions of this Convention shall apply only to the carriage by air, provided that the carriage by air falls within the terms of Article 1.
2. Nothing in this Convention shall prevent the parties in the case of combined carriage from inserting in the document of air carriage conditions relating to other modes of carriage, provided that the provisions of this Convention are observed as regards the carriage by air.

Chapter V – General and Final Provisions

Article 32

Any clause contained in the contract and all special agreements entered into before the damage occurred by which the parties purport to infringe the rules laid down by this Convention, whether by deciding the law to be applied, or by altering the rules as to jurisdiction, shall be null and void. Nevertheless for the carriage of cargo arbitration clauses are allowed, subject to this Convention, if the arbitration is to take place within one of the jurisdictions referred to in the first paragraph of Article 28.

Article 33

Nothing contained in this Convention shall prevent the carrier either from refusing to enter into any contract of carriage or from making regulations which do not conflict with the provisions of this Convention.

Article 34

The provisions of Articles 3 to 9 inclusive relating to documents of carriage shall not apply in the case of carriage performed in extraordinary circumstances outside the normal scope of an air carrier's business.

Article 35

The expression "days" when used in this Convention means current days, not working days.

[. . .]

Article 40A

1. In Article 37, paragraph 2 and Article 40, paragraph 1, the expression High Contracting Party shall mean State. In all other cases, the expression High Contracting Party shall mean a State whose ratification of or adherence to the Convention has become effective and whose denunciation thereof has not become effective.
2. For the purposes of the Convention the word territory means not only the metropolitan territory of a State but also all other territories for the foreign relations of which that State is responsible.

[. . .]

Additional Protocol (with reference to Article 2)

The High Contracting Parties reserve to themselves the right to declare at the time of ratification or of accession that the first paragraph of Article 2 of this Convention shall not apply to international carriage by air performed directly by the State, its colonies, protectorates or mandated territories or by any other territory under its sovereignty, suzerainty or authority.

REMAINING PROVISIONS OF THE HAGUE PROTOCOL[1]

Chapter II – Scope of Application of the Convention as Amended

Article XVIII

The Convention as amended by this Protocol shall apply to international carriage as defined in Article 1 of the Convention, provided that the places of departure and destination referred to in that Article are situated either in the territories of two parties to this Protocol or within the territory of a single party to this Protocol with an agreed stopping place within the territory of another State.

Chapter III – Final Clauses

Article XIX

As between the Parties to this Protocol, the Convention and the Protocol shall be read and interpreted together as one single instrument and shall be known as the *Warsaw Convention as amended at The Hague, 1955.*

Article XX

Until the date on which this Protocol comes into force in accordance with the provisions of Article XXII, paragraph 1, it shall remain open for signature on behalf of any State which up to that date has ratified or adhered to the Convention or which has participated in the Conference at which this Protocol was adopted.

Article XXI

1. This Protocol shall be subject to ratification by the signatory States.
2. Ratification of this Protocol by any State which is not a Party to the Convention shall have the effect of adherence to the Convention as amended by this Protocol.
3. The instruments of ratification shall be deposited with the Government of the People's Republic of Poland.

Article XXII

1. As soon as thirty signatory States have deposited their instruments of ratification of this Protocol, it shall come into force between them on the ninetieth day after the deposit of the thirtieth instrument of ratification. It shall come into force for each State ratifying thereafter on the ninetieth day after the deposit of its instrument of ratification.
2. As soon as this Protocol comes into force it shall be registered with the United Nations by the Government of the People's Republic of Poland.

Article XXIII

1. This Protocol shall, after it has come into force, be open for adherence by any non-signatory State.
2. Adherence to this Protocol by any State which is not a Party to the Convention shall have the effect of adherence to the Convention as amended by this Protocol.
3. Adherence shall be effected by the deposit of an instrument of adherence with the Government of the People's Republic of Poland and shall take effect on the ninetieth day after the deposit.

Article XXIV

1. Any Party to this Protocol may denounce the Protocol by notification addressed to the Government of the People's Republic of Poland.
2. Denunciation shall take effect six months after the date of receipt by the Government of the People's Republic of Poland of the notification of denunciation.
3. As between the Parties to this Protocol, denunciation by any of them of the Convention in accordance with Article 39 thereof shall not be construed in any way as a denunciation of the Convention as amended by this Protocol.

Article XXV

1. This Protocol shall apply to all territories for the foreign relations of which a State Party to this Protocol is responsible, with the exception of territories in respect of which a declaration has been made in accordance with paragraph 2 of this Article.
2. Any State may, at the time of deposit of its instrument of ratification or adherence, declare that its acceptance of this Protocol does not apply to any one or more of the territories for the foreign relations of which such State is responsible.
3. Any State may subsequently, by notification to the Government of the People's Republic of Poland, extend the application of this Protocol to

any or all of the territories regarding which it has made a declaration in accordance with paragraph 2 of this Article. The notification shall take effect on the ninetieth day after its receipt by that Government.

4. Any State Party to this Protocol may denounce it, in accordance with the provisions of Article XXIV, paragraph 1, separately for any or all of the territories for the foreign relations of which such State is responsible.

Article XXVI

No reservation may be made to this Protocol except that a State may at any time declare by a notification addressed to the Government of the People's Republic of Poland that the Convention as amended by this Protocol shall not apply to the carriage of persons, cargo and baggage for its military authorities on aircraft, registered in that State, the whole capacity of which has been reserved by or on behalf of such authorities.

Article XXVII

The Government of the People's Republic of Poland shall give immediate notice to the Governments of all States signatories to the Convention or this Protocol, all States Parties to the Convention or this Protocol, and all States Members of the International Civil Aviation Organization or of the United Nations and to the International Civil Aviation Organization:

(a) of any signature of this Protocol and the date thereof;
(b) of the deposit of any instrument of ratification or adherence in respect of this Protocol and the date thereof;
(c) of the date on which this Protocol comes into force in accordance with Article XXII, paragraph 1;
(d) of the receipt of any notification of denunciation and the date thereof;
(e) of the receipt of any declaration or notification made under Article XXV and the date thereof; and
(f) of the receipt of any notification made under Article XXVI and the date thereof.

IN WITNESS WHEREOF the undersigned Plenipotentiaries, having been duly authorized, have signed this Protocol.

DONE at The Hague on the twenty-eighth day of the month of September of the year One Thousand Nine Hundred and Fifty-five, in three authentic texts in the English, French and Spanish languages. In the case of any inconsistency, the text in the French language, in which language the Convention was drawn up, shall prevail.

This Protocol shall be deposited with the Government of the People's Republic of Poland with which, in accordance with Article XX, it shall remain open for signature, and that Government shall send certified copies thereof to the Governments of all States signatories to the Convention or this Protocol, all States Parties to the Convention or this Protocol, and all States Members of the International Civil Aviation Organization or of the United Nations, and to the International Civil Aviation Organization.

1.3 Guadalajara Supplementary Convention 1961

**CONVENTION SUPPLEMENTARY TO THE WARSAW
CONVENTION FOR THE UNIFICATION OF CERTAIN
RULES RELATING TO INTERNATIONAL CARRIAGE
BY AIR PERFORMED BY A PERSON OTHER THAN
THE CONTRACTING CARRIER**

THE STATES SIGNATORY TO THE PRESENT CONVENTION

NOTING that the Warsaw Convention does not contain particular rules relating to international carriage by air performed by a person who is not a party to the agreement for carriage.

CONSIDERING that it is therefore desirable to formulate rules to apply in such circumstances.

HAVE AGREED as follows:

Article I

In this Convention:

(a) "Warsaw Convention" means the Convention for the Unification of Certain Rules Relating to International Carriage by Air signed at Warsaw on 12 October 1929, or the Warsaw Convention as amended at The Hague, 1955, according to whether the carriage under the agreement referred to in paragraph (b) is governed by the one or by the other;

(b) "contracting carrier" means a person who as a principal makes an agreement for carriage governed by the Warsaw Convention with a passenger or consignor or with a person acting on behalf of the passenger or consignor;

(c) "actual carrier" means a person other than the contracting carrier, who, by virtue of authority from the contracting carrier, performs the whole or part of the carriage contemplated in paragraph (b) but who is not with respect to such part a successive carrier within the meaning of the Warsaw Convention. Such authority is presumed in the absence of proof to the contrary.

Article II

If an actual carrier performs the whole or part of carriage which, according to the agreement referred to in Article I, paragraph (b), is governed by the Warsaw Convention, both the contracting carrier and the actual carrier shall, except as otherwise provided in this Convention, be subject to the rules of the Warsaw Convention, the former for the whole of the carriage contemplated in the agreement, the latter solely for the carriage which he performs.

Article III

1. The acts and omissions of the actual carrier and of his servants and agents acting within the scope of their employment shall, in relation to the carriage performed by the actual carrier, be deemed to be also those of the contracting carrier.
2. The acts and omissions of the contracting carrier and of his servants and agents acting within the scope of their employment shall, in relation to the carriage performed by the actual carrier, be deemed to be also those of the actual carrier. Nevertheless, no such act or omission shall subject the actual carrier to liability exceeding the limits specified in Article 22 of the Warsaw Convention. Any special agreement under which the contracting carrier assumes obligations not imposed by the Warsaw Convention or any waiver of rights conferred by that Convention or any special declaration of interest in delivery at destination contemplated in Article 22 of the said Convention, shall not affect the actual carrier unless agreed to by him.

Article IV

Any complaint to be made or order to be given under the Warsaw Convention to the carrier shall have the same effect whether addressed to the contracting carrier or to the actual carrier. Nevertheless, orders referred to in Article 12 of the Warsaw Convention shall only be effective if addressed to the contracting carrier.

Article V

In relation to the carriage performed by the actual carrier, any servant or agent of that carrier or of the contracting carrier shall, if he proves that he acted within the scope of his employment, be entitled to avail himself of the limits of liability which are applicable under this Convention to the carrier whose servant or agent he is unless it is proved that he acted in a manner which, under the Warsaw Convention, prevents the limits of liability from being invoked.

Article VI

In relation to the carriage performed by the actual carrier, the aggregate of the amounts recoverable from that carrier and the contracting carrier, and from their servants and agents acting within the scope of their employment, shall not exceed the highest amount which could be awarded against either the contracting carrier or the actual carrier under this Convention, but none of the persons mentioned shall be liable for a sum in excess of the limit applicable to him.

Article VII

In relation to the carriage performed by the actual carrier, an action for damages may be brought, at the option of the plaintiff, against that carrier or the contracting carrier, or against both together or separately. If the action is brought against only one of those carriers, that carrier shall have the right to require the other carrier to be joined in the proceedings, the procedure and effects being governed by the law of the court seised of the case.

Article VIII

Any action for damages contemplated in Article VII of this Convention must be brought, at the option of the plaintiff, either before a court in which an action may be brought against the contracting carrier, as provided in Article 28 of the Warsaw Convention, or before the court having jurisdiction at the place where the actual carrier is ordinarily resident or has his principal place of business.

Article IX

1. Any contractual provision tending to relieve the contracting carrier or the actual carrier of liability under this Convention or to fix a lower limit than that which is applicable according to this Convention shall be null and void, but the nullity of any such provision does not involve the nullity of the whole agreement, which shall remain subject to the provisions of this Convention.
2. In respect of the carriage performed by the actual carrier, the preceding paragraph shall not apply to contractual provisions governing loss or damage resulting from the inherent defect, quality or vice of the cargo carried.
3. Any clause contained in an agreement for carriage and all special agreements entered into before the damage occurred by which the parties purport to infringe the rules laid down by this Convention, whether by deciding the law to be applied, or by altering the rules as to jurisdiction, shall be null and void. Nevertheless, for the carriage of cargo arbitration clauses are

allowed, subject to this Convention, if the arbitration is to take place in one of the jurisdictions referred to in Article VIII.

Article X

Except as provided in Article VII, nothing in this Convention shall affect the rights and obligations of the two carriers between themselves.

Article XI

Until the date on which the Convention comes into force in accordance with the provisions of Article XIII, it shall remain open for signature on behalf of any State which at that date is a Member of the United Nations or of any of the Specialised Agencies.

Article XII

1. This Convention shall be subject to ratification by the signatory States.
2. The instruments of ratification shall be deposited with the Government of the United States of Mexico.

Article XIII

1. As soon as five of the signatory States have deposited their instruments of ratification of this Convention, it shall come into force between them on the ninetieth day after the date of the deposit of the fifth instrument of ratification. It shall come into force for each State ratifying thereafter on the ninetieth day after the deposit of its instrument of ratification.
2. As soon as this Convention comes into force, it shall be registered with the United Nations and the International Civil Aviation Organization by the Government of the United States of Mexico.

Article XIV

1. This Convention shall, after it has come into force, be open for accession by any State Member of the United Nations or of any of the Specialized Agencies.
2. The accession of a State shall be effected by the deposit of an instrument of accession with the Government of the United States of Mexico and shall take effect as from the ninetieth day after the date of such deposit.

Article XV

1. Any Contracting State may denounce this Convention by notification addressed to the Government of the United States of Mexico.

2. Denunciation shall take effect six months after the date of receipt by the Government of the United States of Mexico of the notification of denunciation.

Article XVI

1. Any Contracting State may at the time of its ratification of or accession to this Convention or at any time thereafter declare by notification to the Government of the United States of Mexico that the Convention shall extend to any of the territories for whose international relations it is responsible.
2. The Convention shall, ninety days after the date of the receipt of such notification by the Government of the United States of Mexico, extend to the territories named therein.
3. Any Contracting State may denounce this Convention, in accordance with the provisions of Article XV, separately for any or all of the territories for the international relations of which such State is responsible.

Article XVII

No reservation may be made to this Convention.

Article XVIII

The Government of the United States of Mexico shall give notice to the International Civil Aviation Organization and to all States Members of the United Nations or of any of the Specialized Agencies:

(a) of any signature of this Convention and the date thereof;
(b) of the deposit of any instrument of ratification or accession and the date thereof;
(c) of the date on which this Convention comes into force in accordance with Article XIII, paragraph 1;
(d) of the receipt of any notification of denunciation and the date thereof;
(e) of the receipt of any declaration or notification made under Article XVI and the date thereof.

IN WITNESS WHEREOF the undersigned Plenipotentiaries, having been duly authorized, have signed this Convention.

DONE at Guadalajara on the eighteenth day of September One Thousand Nine Hundred and Sixty-one in three authentic texts drawn up in the English, French and Spanish languages. In case of any inconsistency, the text in the French language, in which language the Warsaw Convention of 12 October 1929 was drawn up, shall prevail. The Government of the United States of Mexico will establish an official translation of the text of the Convention in the Russian language.

This Convention shall be deposited with the Government of the United States of Mexico with which, in accordance with Article XI, it shall remain open for signature, and that Government shall send certified copies thereof to the International Civil Aviation Organization and to all States Members of the United Nations or of any Specialized Agency.

1.4 Warsaw Convention 1929 as Amended at The Hague 1955 and by Protocol No. 4 of Montreal 1975

WARSAW CONVENTION AS AMENDED AT THE HAGUE AND BY MONTREAL PROTOCOL NO. 4

Chapter I – Scope – Definitions

Article 1

1. This Convention applies to all international carriage of persons, baggage or cargo performed by aircraft for reward. It applies equally to gratuitous carriage by aircraft performed by an air transport undertaking.
2. For the purposes of this Convention, the expression *international carriage* means any carriage in which, according to the agreement between the parties, the place of departure and the place of destination, whether or not there be a break in the carriage or a transhipment, are situated either within the territories of two High Contracting Parties or within the territory of a single High Contracting Party if there is an agreed stopping place within the territory of another State, even if that State is not a High Contracting Party. Carriage between two points within the territory of a single High Contracting Party without an agreed stopping place within the territory of another State is not international carriage for the purpose of this Convention.
3. Carriage to be performed by several successive air carriers is deemed, for the purposes of this Convention, to be one undivided carriage if it has been regarded by the parties as a single operation, whether it had been agreed upon under the form of a single contract or of a series of contracts, and it does not lose its international character merely because one contract or a series of contracts is to be performed entirely within the territory of the same State.

Article 2

1. The Convention applies to carriage performed by the State or by legally constituted public bodies provided it falls within the conditions laid down in Article 1.

2.   In the carriage of postal items the carrier shall be liable only to the relevant postal administration in accordance with the rules applicable to the relationship between the carriers and the postal administrations.

3.   Except as provided in paragraph 2 of this Article, the provisions of this Convention shall not apply to the carriage of postal items.

Chapter II – Documents of Carriage

Section I – Passenger Ticket

Article 3

1.   In respect of the carriage of passengers a ticket shall be delivered containing:

   (a)   an indication of the places of departure and destination;

   (b)   if the places of departure and destination are within the territory of a single High Contracting Party, one or more agreed stopping places being within the territory of another State, an indication of at least one such stopping place;

   (c)   a notice to the effect that, if the passenger's journey involves an ultimate destination or stop in a country other than the country of departure, the Warsaw Convention may be applicable and that the Convention governs and in most cases limits the liability of carriers for death or personal injury and in respect of loss of or damage to baggage.

2.   The passenger ticket shall constitute *prima facie* evidence of the conclusion and conditions of the contract of carriage. The absence, irregularity or loss of the passenger ticket does not affect the existence or the validity of the contract of carriage which shall, none the less, be subject to the rules of this Convention. Nevertheless, if, with the consent of the carrier, the passenger embarks without a passenger ticket having been delivered, or if the ticket does not include the notice required by paragraph 1 (c) of this Article, the carrier shall not be entitled to avail himself of the provisions of Article 22.

Section II – Baggage Check

Article 4

1.   In respect of the carriage of registered baggage, a baggage check shall be delivered, which, unless combined with or incorporated in a passenger ticket which complies with the provisions of Article 3, paragraph 1, shall contain:

   (a)   an indication of the places of departure and destination;

   (b)   if the places of departure and destination are within the territory of a single High Contracting Party, one or more agreed stopping places being within the territory of another State, an indication of at least one such stopping place;

(c) a notice to the effect that, if the carriage involves an ultimate destination or stop in a country other than the country of departure, the Warsaw Convention may be applicable and that the Convention governs and in most cases limits the liability of carriers in respect of loss of or damage to baggage.

2. The baggage check shall constitute *prima facie* evidence of the registration of the baggage and of the conditions of the contract of carriage. The absence, irregularity or loss of the baggage check does not affect the existence or the validity of the contract of carriage which shall, none the less, be subject to the rules of this Convention. Nevertheless, if the carrier takes charge of the baggage without a baggage check having been delivered or if the baggage check (unless combined with or incorporated in the passenger ticket which complies with the provisions of Article 3, paragraph 1 (c)) does not include the notice required by paragraph 1 (c) of this Article, he shall not be entitled to avail himself of the provisions of Article 22, paragraph 2.

Section III – Documentation Relating to Cargo

Article 5

1. In respect of the carriage of cargo an air waybill shall be delivered.
2. Any other means which would preserve a record of the carriage to be performed may, with the consent of the consignor, be substituted for the delivery of an air waybill. If such other means are used, the carrier shall, if so requested by the consignor, deliver to the consignor a receipt for the cargo permitting identification of the consignment and access to the information contained in the record preserved by such other means.
3. The impossibility of using, at points of transit and destination, the other means which would preserve the record of the carriage referred to in paragraph 2 of this Article does not entitle the carrier to refuse to accept the cargo for carriage.

Article 6

1. The air waybill shall be made out by the consignor in three original parts.
2. The first part shall be marked "for the carrier"; it shall be signed by the consignor. The second part shall be marked "for the consignee"; it shall be signed by the consignor and by the carrier. The third part shall be signed by the carrier and handed by him to the consignor after the cargo has been accepted.
3. The signature of the carrier and that of the consignor may be printed or stamped.

4. If, at the request of the consignor, the carrier makes out the air waybill, he shall be deemed, subject to proof to the contrary, to have done so on behalf of the consignor.

Article 7

When there is more than one package:

(a) the carrier of cargo has the right to require the consignor to make out separate air waybills;
(b) the consignor has the right to require the carrier to deliver separate receipts when the other means referred to in paragraph 2 of Article 5 are used.

Article 8

The air waybill and the receipt for the cargo shall contain:

(a) an indication of the places of departure and destination;
(b) if the places of departure and destination are within the territory of a single High Contracting Party, one or more agreed stopping places being within the territory of another State, an indication of at least one such stopping place;
(c) an indication of the weight of the consignment.

Article 9

Non-compliance with the provisions of Articles 5 to 8 shall not affect the existence or the validity of the contract of carriage, which shall, none the less, be subject to the rules of this Convention including those relating to limitation of liability.

Article 10

1. The consignor is responsible for the correctness of the particulars and statements relating to the cargo inserted by him or on his behalf in the air waybill or furnished by him or on his behalf to the carrier for insertion in the receipt for the cargo or for insertion in the record preserved by the other means referred to in paragraph 2 of Article 5.
2. The consignor shall indemnify the carrier against all damage suffered by him, or by any other person to whom the carrier is liable, by reason of the irregularity, incorrectness or incompleteness of the particulars and statements furnished by the consignor or on his behalf.
3. Subject to the provisions of paragraphs 1 and 2 of this Article, the carrier shall indemnify the consignor against all damage suffered by him, or by

any other person to whom the consignor is liable, by reason of the irregularity, incorrectness or incompleteness of the particulars and statements inserted by the carrier or on his behalf in the receipt for the cargo or in the record preserved by the other means referred to in paragraph 2 of Article 5.

Article 11

1. The air waybill or the receipt for the cargo is *prima facie* evidence of the conclusion of the contract, of the acceptance of the cargo and of the conditions of carriage mentioned therein.
2. Any statements in the air waybill or the receipt for the cargo relating to the weight, dimensions and packing of the cargo, as well as those relating to the number of packages, are *prima facie* evidence of the facts stated; those relating to the quantity, volume and condition of the cargo do not constitute evidence against the carrier except so far as they both have been, and are stated in the air waybill to have been, checked by him in the presence of the consignor, or relate to the apparent condition of the cargo.

Article 12

1. Subject to his liability to carry out all his obligations under the contract of carriage, the consignor has the right to dispose of the cargo by withdrawing it at the airport of departure or destination, or by stopping it in the course of the journey on any landing, or by calling for it to be delivered at the place of destination or in the course of the journey to a person other than the consignee originally designated, or by requiring it to be returned to the airport of departure. He must not exercise this right of disposition in such a way as to prejudice the carrier or other consignors and he must repay any expenses occasioned by the exercise of this right.
2. If it is impossible to carry out the orders of the consignor the carrier must so inform him forthwith.
3. If the carrier obeys the orders of the consignor for the disposition of the cargo without requiring the production of the part of the air waybill or the receipt for the cargo delivered to the latter, he will be liable, without prejudice to his right of recovery from the consignor, for any damage which may be caused thereby to any person who is lawfully in possession of that part of the air waybill or the receipt for the cargo.
4. The right conferred on the consignor ceases at the moment when that of the consignee begins in accordance with Article 13. Nevertheless, if the consignee declines to accept the cargo, or if he cannot be communicated with, the consignor resumes his right of disposition.

Article 13

1. Except when the consignor has exercised his right under Article 12, the consignee is entitled, on arrival of the cargo at the place of destination, to require the carrier to deliver the cargo to him, on payment of the charges due and on complying with the conditions of carriage.
2. Unless it is otherwise agreed, it is the duty of the carrier to give notice to the consignee as soon as the cargo arrives.
3. If the carrier admits the loss of the cargo, or if the cargo has not arrived at the expiration of seven days after the date on which it ought to have arrived, the consignee is entitled to enforce against the carrier the rights which flow from the contract of carriage.

Article 14

The consignor and the consignee can respectively enforce all the rights given them by Articles 12 and 13, each in his own name, whether he is acting in his own interest or in the interest of another, provided that he carries out the obligations imposed by the contract of carriage.

Article 15

1. Articles 12, 13 and 14 do not affect either the relations of the consignor and the consignee with each other or the mutual relations of third parties whose rights are derived either from the consignor or from the consignee.
2. The provisions of Articles 12, 13 and 14 can only be varied by express provision in the air waybill or the receipt for the cargo.

Article 16

1. The consignor must furnish such information and such documents as are necessary to meet the formalities of customs, octroi or police before the cargo can be delivered to the consignee. The consignor is liable to the carrier for any damage occasioned by the absence, insufficiency or irregularity of any such information or documents, unless the damage is due to the fault of the carrier, his servants or agents.
2. The carrier is under no obligation to inquire into the correctness or sufficiency of such information or documents.

Chapter III – Liability of the Carrier

Article 17

The carrier is liable for damage sustained in the event of the death or wounding of a passenger or any other bodily injury suffered by a passenger, if the accident which caused the damage so sustained took place on board the aircraft or in the course of any of the operations of embarking or disembarking.

Article 18

1. The carrier is liable for damage sustained in the event of the destruction or loss of, or damage to, any registered baggage, if the occurrence which caused the damage so sustained took place during the carriage by air.
2. The carrier is liable for damage sustained in the event of the destruction or loss of, or damage to, cargo upon condition only that the occurrence which caused the damage so sustained took place during the carriage by air.
3. However, the carrier is not liable if he proves that the destruction, loss of, or damage to, the cargo resulted solely from one or more of the following:
   (a) inherent defect, quality or vice of that cargo;
   (b) defective packing of that cargo performed by a person other than the carrier or his servants or agents;
   (c) an act of war or an armed conflict;
   (d) an act of public authority carried out in connexion with the entry, exit or transit of the cargo.
4. The carriage by air within the meaning of the preceding paragraphs of this Article comprises the period during which the baggage or cargo is in the charge of the carrier, whether in an airport or on board an aircraft, or, in the case of a landing outside an airport, in any place whatsoever.
5. The period of the carriage by air does not extend to any carriage by land, by sea or by river performed outside an airport. If, however, such carriage takes place in the performance of a contract for carriage by air, for the purpose of loading, delivery or transhipment, any damage is presumed, subject to proof to the contrary, to have been the result of an event which took place during the carriage by air.

Article 19

The carrier is liable for damage occasioned by delay in the carriage by air of passengers, baggage or cargo.

Article 20

In the carriage of passengers and baggage, and in the case of damage occasioned by delay in the carriage of cargo, the carrier shall not be liable if he proves that he and his servants and agents have taken all necessary measures to avoid the damage or that it was impossible for them to take such measures.

Article 21

1. In the carriage of passengers and baggage, if the carrier proves that the damage was caused by or contributed to by the negligence of the person suffering the damage the Court may, in accordance with the provisions of its own law, exonerate the carrier wholly or partly from his liability.
2. In the carriage of cargo, if the carrier proves that the damage was caused by or contributed to by the negligence or other wrongful act or omission of the person claiming compensation, or the person from whom he derives his rights, the carrier shall be wholly or partly exonerated from his liability to the claimant to the extent that such negligence or wrongful act or omission caused or contributed to the damage.

Article 22

1. In the carriage of persons the liability of the carrier for each passenger is limited to the sum of two hundred and fifty thousand francs. Where, in accordance with the law of the Court seised of the case, damages may be awarded in the form of periodical payments, the equivalent capital value of the said payments shall not exceed two hundred and fifty thousand francs. Nevertheless, by special contract, the carrier and the passenger may agree to a higher limit of liability.

2. (a) In the carriage of registered baggage, the liability of the carrier is limited to a sum of two hundred and fifty francs per kilogramme, unless the passenger or consignor has made, at the time when the package was handed over to the carrier, a special declaration of interest in delivery at destination and has paid a supplementary sum if the case so requires. In that case the carrier will be liable to pay a sum not exceeding the declared sum, unless he proves that the sum is greater than the passenger's or consignor's actual interest in delivery at destination.
    (b) In the carriage of cargo, the liability of the carrier is limited to a sum of 17 Special Drawing Rights per kilogramme, unless the consignor has made, at the time when the package was handed over to the carrier, a special declaration of interest in delivery at destination and has paid a supplementary sum if the case so requires. In that case the carrier will be liable to pay a sum not exceeding the declared sum, unless he proves that the sum is greater than the consignor's actual interest in delivery at destination.
    (c) In the case of loss, damage or delay of part of registered baggage or cargo, or of any object contained therein, the weight to be taken into consideration in determining the amount to which the carrier's liability is limited shall be only the total weight of the package or packages concerned. Nevertheless, when the loss, damage or delay of a part of the registered baggage or cargo, or of an object contained therein, affects the value of other packages covered by the same baggage check

or the same air waybill, the total weight of such package or packages shall also be taken into consideration in determining the limit of liability.

3. As regards objects of which the passenger takes charge himself the liability of the carrier is limited to five thousand francs per passenger.

4. The limits prescribed in this article shall not prevent the court from awarding, in accordance with its own law, in addition, the whole or part of the court costs and of the other expenses of the litigation incurred by the plaintiff. The foregoing provision shall not apply if the amount of the damages awarded, excluding court costs and other expenses of the litigation, does not exceed the sum which the carrier has offered in writing to the plaintiff within a period of six months from the date of the occurrence causing the damage, or before the commencement of the action, if that is later.

5. The sums mentioned in francs in this Article shall be deemed to refer to a currency unit consisting of sixty-five and a half milligrammes of gold of millesimal fineness nine hundred. These sums may be converted into national currencies in round figures. Conversion of the sums into national currencies other than gold shall, in case of judicial proceedings, be made according to the gold value of such currencies at the date of the judgment.

6. The sums mentioned in terms of the Special Drawing Right in this Article shall be deemed to refer to the Special Drawing Right as defined by the International Monetary Fund. Conversion of the sums into national currencies shall, in case of judicial proceedings, be made according to the value of such currencies in terms of the Special Drawing Right at the date of the judgment. The value of a national currency, in terms of the Special Drawing Right, of a High Contracting Party which is a Member of the International Monetary Fund, shall be calculated in accordance with the method of valuation applied by the International Monetary Fund, in effect at the date of the judgment, for its operations and transactions. The value of a national currency, in terms of the Special Drawing Right, of a High Contracting Party which is not a Member of the International Monetary Fund, shall be calculated in a manner determined by that High Contracting Party.

   Nevertheless, those States which are not Members of the International Monetary Fund and whose law does not permit the application of the provisions of paragraph 2 (b) of Article 22 may, at the time of ratification or accession or at any time thereafter, declare that the limit of liability of the carrier in judicial proceedings in their territories is fixed at a sum of two hundred and fifty monetary units per kilogramme. The monetary unit corresponds to sixty-five and a half milligrammes of gold of millesimal fineness nine hundred. This sum may be converted into the national currency concerned in round figures. The conversion of this sum into the national currency shall be made according to the law of the State concerned.

Article 23

1. Any provision tending to relieve the carrier of liability or to fix a lower limit than that which is laid down in this Convention shall be null and void, but the nullity of any such provision does not involve the nullity of the whole contract, which shall remain subject to the provisions of this Convention.
2. Paragraph 1 of this Article shall not apply to provisions governing loss or damage resulting from the inherent defect, quality or vice of the cargo carried.

Article 24

1. In the carriage of passengers and baggage, any action for damages, however founded, can only be brought subject to the conditions and limits set out in this Convention, without prejudice to the question as to who are the persons who have the right to bring suit and what are their respective rights.
2. In the carriage of cargo, any action for damages, however founded, whether under this Convention or in contract or in tort or otherwise, can only be brought subject to the conditions and limits of liability set out in this Convention without prejudice to the question as to who are the persons who have the right to bring suit and what are their respective rights. Such limits of liability constitute maximum limits and may not be exceeded whatever the circumstances which gave rise to the liability.

Article 25

In the carriage of passengers and baggage, the limits of liability specified in Article 22 shall not apply if it is proved that the damage resulted from an act or omission of the carrier, his servants or agents, done with intent to cause damage or recklessly and with knowledge that damage would probably result; provided that, in the case of such act or omission of a servant or agent, it is also proved that he was acting within the scope of his employment.

Article 25A

1. If an action is brought against a servant or agent of the carrier arising out of damage to which this Convention relates, such servant or agent, if he proves that he acted within the scope of his employment, shall be entitled to avail himself of the limits of liability which that carrier himself is entitled to invoke under Article 22.
2. The aggregate of the amounts recoverable from the carrier, his servants and agents, in that case, shall not exceed the said limits.
3. In the carriage of passengers and baggage, the provisions of paragraphs 1 and 2 of this Article shall not apply if it is proved that the damage resulted

from an act or omission of the servant or agent done with intent to cause damage or recklessly and with knowledge that damage would probably result.

Article 26

1. Receipt by the person entitled to delivery of baggage or cargo without complaint is *prima facie* evidence that the same has been delivered in good condition and in accordance with the document of carriage.
2. In the case of damage, the person entitled to delivery must complain to the carrier forthwith after the discovery of the damage, and, at the latest, within seven days from the date of receipt in the case of baggage and fourteen days from the date of receipt in the case of cargo. In the case of delay the complaint must be made at the latest within twenty-one days from the date on which the baggage or cargo have been placed at his disposal.
3. Every complaint must be made in writing upon the document of carriage or by separate notice in writing despatched within the times aforesaid.
4. Failing complaint within the times aforesaid, no action shall lie against the carrier, save in the case of fraud on his part.

Article 27

In the case of the death of the person liable, an action for damages lies in accordance with the terms of this Convention against those legally representing his estate.

Article 28

1. An action for damages must be brought, at the option of the plaintiff, in the territory of one of the High Contracting Parties, either before the court having jurisdiction where the carrier is ordinarily resident or has his principal place of business, or has an establishment by which the contract has been made, or before the court having jurisdiction at the place of destination.
2. Questions of procedure shall be governed by the law of the court seised of the case.

Article 29

1. The right to damages shall be extinguished if an action is not brought within 2 (two) years, reckoned from the date of arrival at the destination, or from the date on which the aircraft ought to have arrived, or from the date on which the carriage stopped.
2. The method of calculating the period of limitation shall be determined by the law of the court seised of the case.

Article 30

1. In the case of carriage to be performed by various successive carriers and falling within the definition set out in the third paragraph of Article 1, each carrier who accepts passengers, baggage or cargo is subject to the rules set out in this Convention, and is deemed to be one of the contracting parties to the contract of carriage insofar as the contract deals with that part of the carriage which is performed under his supervision.
2. In the case of transportation of this nature, the passenger or his representative can take action only against the carrier who performed the carriage during which the accident or the delay occurred, save in the case where, by express agreement, the first carrier has assumed liability for the whole journey.
3. As regards baggage or cargo, the passenger or consignor will have a right of action against the first carrier, and the passenger or consignee who is entitled to delivery will have a right of action against the last carrier, and further, each may take action against the carrier who performed the carriage during which the destruction, loss, damage, or delay took place. These carriers will be jointly and severally liable to the passenger or to the consignor or consignee.

Article 30A

Nothing in this Convention shall prejudice the question whether a person liable for damage in accordance with its provisions has a right of recourse against any other person.

Chapter IV – Provisions Relating to Combined Carriage

Article 31

1. In the case of combined carriage performed partly by air and partly by any other mode of carriage, the provisions of this Convention shall apply only to the carriage by air, provided that the carriage by air falls within the terms of Article 1.
2. Nothing in this Convention shall prevent the parties in the case of combined carriage from inserting in the document of air carriage conditions relating to other modes of carriage, provided that the provisions of this Convention are observed as regards the carriage by air.

Chapter V – General and Final Provisions

Article 32

Any clause contained in the contract and all special agreements entered into before the damage occurred by which the parties purport to infringe the rules laid down by this Convention, whether by deciding the law to be applied, or by altering the rules as to jurisdiction, shall be null and void. Nevertheless for the carriage of cargo arbitration clauses are allowed, subject to this Convention, if the arbitration is to take place within one of the jurisdictions referred to in the first paragraph of Article 28.

Article 33

Except as provided in paragraph 3 of Article 5, nothing in this Convention shall prevent the carrier either from refusing to enter into any contract of carriage or from making regulations which do not conflict with the provisions of this Convention.

Article 34

The provisions of Articles 3 to 8 inclusive relating to documents of carriage shall not apply in the case of carriage performed in extraordinary circumstances outside the normal scope of an air carrier's business.

Article 35

The expression "days" when used in this Convention means current days, not working days.

[. . .]

Article 40A

1. In Article 37, paragraph 2 and Article 40, paragraph 1, the expression High Contracting Party shall mean State. In all other cases, the expression High Contracting Party shall mean a State whose ratification of or adherence to the Convention has become effective and whose denunciation thereof has not become effective.
2. For the purposes of the Convention the word territory means not only the metropolitan territory of a State but also all other territories for the foreign relations of which that State is responsible.

[. . .]

Additional Protocol (with reference to Article 2)

The High Contracting Parties reserve to themselves the right to declare at the time of ratification or of accession that the first paragraph of Article 2 of this Convention shall not apply to international carriage by air performed directly by the State, its colonies, protectorates or mandated territories or by any other territory under its sovereignty, suzerainty or authority.

REMAINING PROVISIONS OF THE WARSAW CONVENTION[2]

Article 36

The Convention is drawn up in French in a single copy which shall remain deposited in the archives of the Ministry for Foreign Affairs of Poland and of which one duly certified copy shall be sent by the Polish Government to the Government of each of the High Contracting Parties.

Article 37

1. This Convention shall be ratified. The instruments of ratification shall be deposited in the archives of the Ministry for Foreign Affairs of Poland, which will notify the deposit to the Government of each of the High Contracting Parties.
2. As soon as this Convention shall have been ratified by five of the High Contracting Parties it shall come into force as between them on the nineteenth day after the deposit of the fifth ratification. Thereafter it shall come into force between the High Contracting Parties who shall have ratified and the High Contracting Party who deposits his instrument of ratification on the nineteenth day after the deposit.
3. It shall be the duty of the Government of the Republic of Poland to notify to the Government of each of the High Contracting Parties the date on which this Convention comes into force as well as the date of the deposit of each ratification.

Article 38

1. This Convention shall, after it has come into force, remain open for accession by any State.
2. The accession shall be effected by a notification addressed to the Government of the Republic of Poland, which will inform the Government of each of the High Contracting Parties thereof.
3. The accession shall take effect as from the nineteenth day after the notification made to the Government of the Republic of Poland.

Article 39

1. Any one of the High Contracting Parties may denounce this Convention by a notification addressed to the Government of the Republic of Poland, which will at once inform the Government of each of the High Contracting Parties.
2. Denunciation shall take effect six months after the notification of denunciation, and shall operate only as regards the Party who shall have proceeded to denunciation.

Article 40

1. Any High Contracting Party may, at the time of signature or of deposit of ratification or of accession declare that the acceptance which he gives to this Convention does not apply to all or any of his colonies, protectorates, territories under mandate, or any other territory subject to his sovereignty or his authority, or any territory under his suzerainty.
2. Accordingly any High Contracting Party may subsequently accede separately in the name of all or any of his colonies, protectorates, territories under mandate or any other territory subject to his sovereignty or to his authority or any territory under his suzerainty which has been thus excluded by his original declaration.
3. Any High Contracting Party may denounce this Convention, in accordance with its provisions, separately or for all or any of his colonies, protectorates, territories under mandate or any other territory subject to his sovereignty or to his authority, or any other territory under his suzerainty.

Article 41

Any High Contracting Party shall be entitled not earlier than two years after the coming into force of this Convention to call for the assembling of a new international Conference in order to consider any improvements which may be made in this Convention. To this end he will communicate with the Government of the French Republic which will take the necessary measures to make preparations for such Conference.

This Convention done at Warsaw on the 12th October, 1929, shall remain open for signature until the 31st January, 1930.

REMAINING PROVISIONS OF THE HAGUE PROTOCOL[3]

Chapter II – Scope of Application of the Convention as Amended

Article XVIII

The Convention as amended by this Protocol shall apply to international carriage as defined in Article 1 of the Convention, provided that the places of departure and destination referred to in that Article are situated either in the territories of two parties to this Protocol or within the territory of a single party to this Protocol with an agreed stopping place within the territory of another State.

Chapter III – Final Clauses

Article XIX

As between the Parties to this Protocol, the Convention and the Protocol shall be read and interpreted together as one single instrument and shall be known as the *Warsaw Convention as amended at The Hague, 1955.*

Article XX

Until the date on which this Protocol comes into force in accordance with the provisions of Article XXII, paragraph 1, it shall remain open for signature on behalf of any State which up to that date has ratified or adhered to the Convention or which has participated in the Conference at which this Protocol was adopted.

Article XXI

1. This Protocol shall be subject to ratification by the signatory States.
2. Ratification of this Protocol by any State which is not a Party to the Convention shall have the effect of adherence to the Convention as amended by this Protocol.
3. The instruments of ratification shall be deposited with the Government of the People's Republic of Poland.

Article XXII

1. As soon as thirty signatory States have deposited their instruments of ratification of this Protocol, it shall come into force between them on the ninetieth day after the deposit of the thirtieth instrument of ratification. It shall come into force for each State ratifying thereafter on the ninetieth day after the deposit of its instrument of ratification.
2. As soon as this Protocol comes into force it shall be registered with the United Nations by the Government of the People's Republic of Poland.

Article XXIII

1. This Protocol shall, after it has come into force, be open for adherence by any non-signatory State.
2. Adherence to this Protocol by any State which is not a Party to the Convention shall have the effect of adherence to the Convention as amended by this Protocol.
3. Adherence shall be effected by the deposit of an instrument of adherence with the Government of the People's Republic of Poland and shall take effect on the ninetieth day after the deposit.

Article XXIV

1. Any Party to this Protocol may denounce the Protocol by notification addressed to the Government of the People's Republic of Poland.
2. Denunciation shall take effect six months after the date of receipt by the Government of the People's Republic of Poland of the notification of denunication.
3. As between the Parties to this Protocol, denunciation by any of them of the Convention in accordance with Article 39 thereof shall not be construed in any way as a denunciation of the Convention as amended by this Protocol.

Article XXV

1. This Protocol shall apply to all territories for the foreign relations of which a State Party to this Protocol is responsible, with the exception of territories in respect of which a declaration has been made in accordance with paragraph 2 of this Article.
2. Any State may, at the time of deposit of its instrument of ratification or adherence, declare that its acceptance of this Protocol does not apply to any one or more of the territories for the foreign relations of which such State is responsible.
3. Any State may subsequently, by notification to the Government of the People's Republic of Poland, extend the application of this Protocol to any or all of the territories regarding which it has made a declaration in accordance with paragraph 2 of this Article. The notification shall take effect on the ninetieth day after its receipt by that Government.
4. Any State Party to this Protocol may denounce it, in accordance with the provisions of Article XXIV, paragraph 1, separately for any or all of the territories for the foreign relations of which such State is responsible.

Article XXVI

No reservation may be made to this Protocol except that a State may at any time declare by a notification addressed to the Government of the People's Republic of Poland that the Convention as amended by this Protocol shall not apply to the carriage of persons, cargo and baggage for its military authorities on aircraft, registered in that State, the whole capacity of which has been reserved by or on behalf of such authorities.

Article XXVII

The Government of the People's Republic of Poland shall give immediate notice to the Governments of all States signatories to the Convention or this Protocol, all States Parties to the Convention or this Protocol, and all States

Members of the International Civil Aviation Organization or of the United Nations and to the International Civil Aviation Organization:

(a) of any signature of this Protocol and the date thereof;
(b) of the deposit of any instrument of ratification or adherence in respect of this Protocol and the date thereof;
(c) of the date on which this Protocol comes into force in accordance with Article XXII, paragraph 1;
(d) of the receipt of any notification of denunciation and the date thereof;
(e) of the receipt of any declaration or notification made under Article XXV and the date thereof; and
(f) of the receipt of any notification made under Article XXVI and the date thereof.

IN WITNESS WHEREOF the undersigned Plenipotentiaries, having been duly authorized, have signed this Protocol.

DONE at The Hague on the twenty-eighth day of the month of September of the year One Thousand Nine Hundred and Fifty-five, in three authentic texts in the English, French and Spanish languages. In the case of any inconsistency, the text in the French language, in which language the Convention was drawn up, shall prevail.

This Protocol shall be deposited with the Government of the People's Republic of Poland with which, in accordance with Article XX, it shall remain open for signature, and that Government shall send certified copies thereof to the Governments of all States signatories to the Convention or this Protocol, all States Parties to the Convention or this Protocol, and all States Members of the International Civil Aviation Organization or of the United Nations, and to the International Civil Aviation Organization.

REMAINING PROVISIONS OF THE MONTREAL NO. 4 PROTOCOL[4]

Chapter II – Scope of Application of the Convention as Amended

Article XIV

The Warsaw Convention as amended at The Hague in 1955 and by this Protocol shall apply to international carriage as defined in Article 1 of the Convention, provided that the places of departure and destination referred to in that Article are situated either in the territories of two parties to this Protocol or within the territory of a single party to this Protocol with an agreed stopping place in the territory of another State.

Chapter III – Final Clauses

Article XV

As between the Parties to this Protocol, the Warsaw Convention as amended at The Hague in 1955 and this Protocol shall be read and interpreted together as one single instrument and shall be known as the *Warsaw Convention as amended at The Hague, 1955, and by Protocol No. 4 of Montreal, 1975.*

Article XVI

Until the date on which this Protocol comes into force in accordance with the provisions of Article XVIII, it shall remain open for signature by any State.

Article XVII

1. This Protocol shall be subject to ratification by the signatory States.
2. Ratification of this Protocol by any State which is not a Party to the Warsaw Convention or by any State which is not a Party to the Warsaw Convention as amended at The Hague, 1955, shall have the effect of accession to the *Warsaw Convention as amended at The Hague, 1955, and by Protocol No. 4 of Montreal, 1975.*
3. The instruments of ratification shall be deposited with the Government of the Polish People's Republic.

Article XVIII

1. As soon as thirty signatory States have deposited their instruments of ratification of this Protocol, it shall come into force between them on the ninetieth day after the deposit of the thirtieth instrument of ratification. It shall come into force for each State ratifying thereafter on the ninetieth day after the deposit of its instrument of ratification.
2. As soon as this Protocol comes into force it shall be registered with the United Nations by the Government of the Polish People's Republic.

Article XIX

1. This Protocol, after it has come into force, shall be open for accession by any non-signatory State.
2. Accession to this Protocol by any State which is not a Party to the Warsaw Convention or by any State which is not a Party to the Warsaw Convention as amended at The Hague, 1955, shall have the effect of accession to the *Warsaw Convention as amended at The Hague, 1955, and by Protocol No. 4 of Montreal, 1975.*

3. Accession shall be effected by the deposit of an instrument of accession with the Government of the Polish People's Republic and shall take effect on the ninetieth day after the deposit.

Article XX

1. Any Party to this Protocol may denounce the Protocol by notification addressed to the Government of the Polish People's Republic.
2. Denunciation shall take effect six months after the date of receipt by the Government of the Polish People's Republic of the notification of denunciation.
3. As between the Parties to this Protocol, denunciation by any of them of the Warsaw Convention in accordance with Article 39 thereof or of The Hague Protocol in accordance with Article XXIV thereof shall not be construed in any way as denunciation of the *Warsaw Convention as amended at The Hague, 1955, and by Protocol No. 4 of Montreal, 1975.*

Article XXI

1. Only the following reservations may be made to this Protocol:

    (a) a State may at any time declare by a notification addressed to the Government of the Polish People's Republic that the *Warsaw Convention as amended at The Hague, 1955, and by Protocol No. 4 of Montreal, 1975,* shall not apply to the carriage of persons, baggage and cargo for its military authorities on aircraft, registered in that State, the whole capacity of which has been reserved by or on behalf of such authorities; and

    (b) any State may declare at the time of ratification of or accession to the Additional Protocol No. 3 of Montreal, 1975, or at any time thereafter, that it is not bound by the provisions of the *Warsaw Convention as amended at The Hague, 1955, and by Protocol No. 4 of Montreal, 1975,* in so far as they relate to the carriage of passengers and baggage. Such declaration shall have effect ninety days after the date of receipt of the declaration by the Government of the Polish People's Republic.

2. Any State having made a reservation in accordance with the preceding paragraph may at any time withdraw such reservation by notification to the Government of the Polish People's Republic.

Article XXII

The Government of the Polish People's Republic shall promptly inform all States Parties to the Warsaw Convention or to that Convention as amended, all signatory or acceding States to the present Protocol, as well as the International Civil Aviation Organization, of the date of each signature, the date of deposit of each instrument of ratification or accession, the date of coming into force of this Protocol, and other relevant information.

Article XXIII

As between the Parties to this Protocol which are also Parties to the Convention, Supplementary to the Warsaw Convention, for the Unification of Certain Rules Relating to International Carriage by Air Performed by a Person Other than the Contracting Carrier, signed at Guadalajara on 18 September 1961 (hereinafter referred to as the "Guadalajara Convention") any reference to the "Warsaw Convention" contained in the Guadalajara Convention shall include reference to the *Warsaw Convention as amended at The Hague, 1955, and by Protocol No. 4 of Montreal, 1975*, in cases where the carriage under the agreement referred to in Article 1, paragraph (b) of the Guadalajara Convention is governed by this Protocol.

Article XXIV

If two or more States are Parties both to this Protocol and to the Guatemala City Protocol, 1971, or to the Additional Protocol No. 3 of Montreal, 1975, the following rules shall apply between them:

(a) the provisions resulting from the system established by this Protocol, concerning cargo and postal items, shall prevail over the provisions resulting from the system established by the Guatemala City Protocol, 1971, or by the Additional Protocol No. 3 of Montreal, 1975;
(b) the provisions resulting from the system established by the Guatemala City Protocol, 1971, or by the Additional Protocol No. 3 of Montreal, 1975, concerning passengers and baggage, shall prevail over the provisions resulting from the system established by this Protocol.

Article XXV

This Protocol shall remain open for signature until 1 January 1976 at the Headquarters of the International Civil Aviation Organization and thereafter until it comes into force in accordance with Article XVIII at the Ministry for Foreign Affairs of the Polish People's Republic. The International Civil Aviation Organization shall promptly inform the Government of the Polish People's Republic of any signature and the date thereof during the time that the Protocol shall be open for signature at the Headquarters of the International Civil Aviation Organization.

IN WITNESS WHEREOF the undersigned Plenipotentiaries, having been duly authorized, have signed this Protocol.

DONE AT MONTREAL on the twenty-fifth day of September of the year One Thousand Nine Hundred and Seventy-five in four authentic texts in the English, French, Russian and Spanish languages. In the case of any inconsistency, the text in the French language, in which language the Warsaw Convention of 12 October 1929 was drawn up, shall prevail.

1.5 Montreal Convention 1999

CONVENTION FOR THE UNIFICATION OF CERTAIN RULES FOR INTERNATIONAL CARRIAGE BY AIR

THE STATES PARTIES TO THIS CONVENTION

RECOGNIZING the significant contribution of the Convention for the Unification of Certain Rules Relating to International Carriage by Air signed in Warsaw on 12th October 1929, hereinafter referred to as the "Warsaw Convention", and other related instruments to the harmonization of private international air law;

RECOGNIZING the need to modernize and consolidate the Warsaw Convention and related instruments;

RECOGNIZING the importance of ensuring protection of the interests of consumers in international carriage by air and the need for equitable compensation based on the principle of restitution;

REAFFIRMING the desirability of an orderly development of international air transport operations and the smooth flow of passengers, baggage and cargo in accordance with the principles and objectives of the Convention on International Civil Aviation, done at Chicago on 7 December 1944;

CONVINCED that collective State action for further harmonization and codification of certain rules governing international carriage by air through a new Convention is the most adequate means of achieving an equitable balance of interests;

HAVE AGREED AS FOLLOWS:

Chapter I – General Provisions

Article 1 – Scope of Application

1. This Convention applies to all international carriage of persons, baggage or cargo performed by aircraft for reward. It applies equally to gratuitous carriage by aircraft performed by an air transport undertaking.
2. For the purposes of this Convention, the expression *international carriage* means any carriage in which, according to the agreement between the parties, the place of departure and the place of destination, whether or not there be a break in the carriage or a transhipment, are situated either within the territories of two States Parties, or within the territory of a single State Party if there is an agreed stopping place within the territory of another State, even if that State is not a State Party. Carriage between two points within the territory of a single State Party without an agreed stopping place within the territory of another State is not international carriage for the purposes of this Convention.
3. Carriage to be performed by several successive carriers is deemed, for the purposes of this Convention, to be one undivided carriage if it has been regarded by the parties as a single operation, whether it had been agreed upon under the form of a single contract or of a series of contracts, and it does not lose its international character merely because one contract or a series of contracts is to be performed entirely within the territory of the same State.
4. This Convention applies also to carriage as set out in Chapter V, subject to the terms contained therein.

Article 2 – Carriage Performed by State and Carriage of Postal Items

1. This Convention applies to carriage performed by the State or by legally constituted public bodies provided it falls within the conditions laid down in Article 1.
2. In the carriage of postal items, the carrier shall be liable only to the relevant postal administration in accordance with the rules applicable to the relationship between the carriers and the postal administrations.
3. Except as provided in paragraph 2 of this Article, the provisions of this Convention shall not apply to the carriage of postal items.

Chapter II – Documentation and Duties of the Parties Relating to the Carriage of Passengers, Baggage and Cargo

Article 3 – Passengers and Baggage

1. In respect of carriage of passengers, an individual or collective document of carriage shall be delivered containing:

(a)   an indication of the places of departure and destination;

(b)   if the places of departure and destination are within the territory of a single State Party, one or more agreed stopping places being within the territory of another State, an indication of at least one such stopping place.

2.   Any other means which preserves the information indicated in paragraph 1 may be substituted for the delivery of the document referred to in that paragraph. If any such other means is used, the carrier shall offer to deliver to the passenger a written statement of the information so preserved.

3.   The carrier shall deliver to the passenger a baggage identification tag for each piece of checked baggage.

4.   The passenger shall be given written notice to the effect that where this Convention is applicable it governs and may limit the liability of carriers in respect of death or injury and for destruction or loss of, or damage to, baggage, and for delay.

5.   Non-compliance with the provisions of the foregoing paragraphs shall not affect the existence or the validity of the contract of carriage, which shall, nonetheless, be subject to the rules of this Convention including those relating to limitation of liability.

Article 4 – Cargo

1.   In respect of the carriage of cargo, an air waybill shall be delivered.

2.   Any other means which preserves a record of the carriage to be performed may be substituted for the delivery of an air waybill. If such other means are used, the carrier shall, if so requested by the consignor, deliver to the consignor a cargo receipt permitting identification of the consignment and access to the information contained in the record preserved by such other means.

Article 5 – Contents of Air Waybill or Cargo Receipt

The air waybill or the cargo receipt shall include:

(a)   an indication of the places of departure and destination;

(b)   if the places of departure and destination are within the territory of a single State Party, one or more agreed stopping places being within the territory of another State, an indication of at least one such stopping place; and

(c)   an indication of the weight of the consignment.

Article 6 – Document Relating to the Nature of the Cargo

The consignor may be required, if necessary to meet the formalities of customs, police and similar public authorities, to deliver a document indicating the nature of the cargo. This provision creates for the carrier no duty, obligation or liability resulting therefrom.

Article 7 – Description of Air Waybill

1. The air waybill shall be made out by the consignor in three original parts.
2. The first part shall be marked "for the carrier"; it shall be signed by the consignor. The second part shall be marked "for the consignee"; it shall be signed by the consignor and by the carrier. The third part shall be signed by the carrier who shall hand it to the consignor after the cargo has been accepted.
3. The signature of the carrier and that of the consignor may be printed or stamped.
4. If, at the request of the consignor, the carrier makes out the air waybill, the carrier shall be deemed, subject to proof to the contrary, to have done so on behalf of the consignor.

Article 8 – Documentation for Multiple Packages

When there is more than one package:

(a) the carrier of cargo has the right to require the consignor to make out separate air waybills;
(b) the consignor has the right to require the carrier to deliver separate cargo receipts when the other means referred to in paragraph 2 of Article 4 are used.

Article 9 – Non-compliance with Documentary Requirements

Non-compliance with the provisions of Articles 4 to 8 shall not affect the existence or the validity of the contract of carriage, which shall, nonetheless, be subject to the rules of this Convention including those relating to limitation of liability.

Article 10 – Responsibility for Particulars of Documentation

1. The consignor is responsible for the correctness of the particulars and statements relating to the cargo inserted by it or on its behalf in the air waybill or furnished by it or on its behalf to the carrier for insertion in the cargo receipt or for insertion in the record preserved by the other means referred to in paragraph 2 of Article 4. The foregoing shall also apply where the person acting on behalf of the consignor is also the agent of the carrier.
2. The consignor shall indemnify the carrier against all damage suffered by it, or by any other person to whom the carrier is liable, by reason of the

irregularity, incorrectness or incompleteness of the particulars and statements furnished by the consignor or on its behalf.

3.   Subject to the provisions of paragraphs 1 and 2 of this Article, the carrier
     shall indemnify the consignor against all damage suffered by it, or by any
     other person to whom the consignor is liable, by reason of the irregularity,
     incorrectness or incompleteness of the particulars and statements inserted
     by the carrier or on its behalf in the cargo receipt or in the record preserved
     by the other means referred to in paragraph 2 of Article 4.

Article 11 – Evidentiary Value of Documentation

1.   The air waybill or the cargo receipt is *prima facie* evidence of the conclusion
     of the contract, of the acceptance of the cargo and of the conditions of
     carriage mentioned therein.
2.   Any statements in the air waybill or the cargo receipt relating to the weight,
     dimensions and packing of the cargo, as well as those relating to the number
     of packages, are *prima facie* evidence of the facts stated; those relating to
     the quantity, volume and condition of the cargo do not constitute evidence
     against the carrier except so far as they both have been, and are stated in
     the air waybill or the cargo receipt to have been, checked by it in the
     presence of the consignor, or relate to the apparent condition of the cargo.

Article 12 – Right of Disposition of Cargo

1.   Subject to its liability to carry out all its obligations under the contract of
     carriage, the consignor has the right to dispose of the cargo by withdrawing
     it at the airport of departure or destination, or by stopping it in the course
     of the journey on any landing, or by calling for it to be delivered at the
     place of destination or in the course of the journey to a person other than
     the consignee originally designated, or by requiring it to be returned to
     the airport of departure. The consignor must not exercise this right of
     disposition in such a way as to prejudice the carrier or other consignors
     and must reimburse any expenses occasioned by the exercise of this right.
2.   If it is impossible to carry out the instructions of the consignor, the carrier
     must so inform the consignor forthwith.
3.   If the carrier carries out the instructions of the consignor for the disposition
     of the cargo without requiring the production of the part of the air waybill
     or the cargo receipt delivered to the latter, the carrier will be liable, without
     prejudice to its right of recovery from the consignor, for any damage which
     may be caused thereby to any person who is lawfully in possession of that
     part of the air waybill or the cargo receipt.
4.   The right conferred on the consignor ceases at the moment when that of
     the consignee begins in accordance with Article 13. Nevertheless, if the
     consignee declines to accept the cargo, or cannot be communicated with,
     the consignor resumes its right of disposition.

Article 13 – Delivery of the Cargo

1. Except when the consignor has exercised its right under Article 12, the consignee is entitled, on arrival of the cargo at the place of destination, to require the carrier to deliver the cargo to it, on payment of the charges due and on complying with the conditions of carriage.
2. Unless it is otherwise agreed, it is the duty of the carrier to give notice to the consignee as soon as the cargo arrives.
3. If the carrier admits the loss of the cargo, or if the cargo has not arrived at the expiration of seven days after the date on which it ought to have arrived, the consignee is entitled to enforce against the carrier the rights which flow from the contract of carriage.

Article 14 – Enforcement of the Rights of Consignor and Consignee

The consignor and the consignee can respectively enforce all the rights given to them by Articles 12 and 13, each in its own name, whether it is acting in its own interest or in the interest of another, provided that it carries out the obligations imposed by the contract of carriage.

Articles 15 – Relations of Consignor and Consignee or Mutual Relations of Third Parties

1. Articles 12, 13 and 14 do not affect either the relations of the consignor and the consignee with each other or the mutual relations of third parties whose rights are derived either from the consignor or from the consignee.
2. The provisions of Articles 12, 13 and 14 can only be varied by express provision in the air waybill or the cargo receipt.

Article 16 – Formalities of Customs, Police or Other Public Authorities

1. The consignor must furnish such information and such documents as are necessary to meet the formalities of customs, police and any other public authorities before the cargo can be delivered to the consignee. The consignor is liable to the carrier for any damage occasioned by the absence, insufficiency or irregularity of any such information or documents, unless the damage is due to the fault of the carrier, its servants or agents.
2. The carrier is under no obligation to enquire into the correctness or sufficiency of such information or documents.

Chapter III – Liability of the Carrier and Extent of Compensation for Damage

Article 17 – Death and Injury of Passengers – Damage to Baggage

1. The carrier is liable for damage sustained in case of death or bodily injury of a passenger upon condition only that the accident which caused the death or injury took place on board the aircraft or in the course of any of the operations of embarking or disembarking.
2. The carrier is liable for damage sustained in case of destruction or loss of, or of damage to, checked baggage upon condition only that the event which caused the destruction, loss or damage took place on board the aircraft or during any period within which the checked baggage was in the charge of the carrier. However, the carrier is not liable if and to the extent that the damage resulted from the inherent defect, quality or vice of the baggage. In the case of unchecked baggage, including personal items, the carrier is liable if the damage resulted from its fault or that of its servants or agents.
3. If the carrier admits the loss of the checked baggage, or if the checked baggage has not arrived at the expiration of twenty-one days after the date on which it ought to have arrived, the passenger is entitled to enforce against the carrier the rights which flow from the contract of carriage.
4. Unless otherwise specified, in this Convention the term "baggage" means both checked baggage and unchecked baggage.

Article 18 – Damage to Cargo

1. The carrier is liable for damage sustained in the event of the destruction or loss of, or damage to, cargo upon condition only that the event which caused the damage so sustained took place during the carriage by air.
2. However, the carrier is not liable if and to the extent it proves that the destruction, or loss of, or damage to, the cargo resulted from one or more of the following:

    (a) inherent defect, quality or vice of that cargo;
    (b) defective packing of that cargo performed by a person other than the carrier or its servants or agents;
    (c) an act of war or an armed conflict;
    (d) an act of public authority carried out in connection with the entry, exit or transit of the cargo.

3. The carriage by air within the meaning of paragraph 1 of this Article comprises the period during which the cargo is in the charge of the carrier.
4. The period of the carriage by air does not extend to any carriage by land, by sea or by inland waterway performed outside an airport. If, however,

such carriage takes place in the performance of a contract for carriage by air, for the purpose of loading, delivery or transhipment, any damage is presumed, subject to proof to the contrary, to have been the result of an event which took place during the carriage by air. If a carrier, without the consent of the consignor, substitutes carriage by another mode of transport for the whole or part of a carriage intended by the agreement between the parties to be carriage by air, such carriage by another mode of transport is deemed to be within the period of carriage by air.

Article 19 – Delay

The carrier is liable for damage occasioned by delay in the carriage by air of passengers, baggage or cargo. Nevertheless, the carrier shall not be liable for damage occasioned by delay if it proves that it and its servants and agents took all measures that could reasonably be required to avoid the damage or that it was impossible for it or them to take such measures.

Article 20 – Exoneration

If the carrier proves that the damage was caused or contributed to by the negligence or other wrongful act or omission of the person claiming compensation, or the person from whom he or she derives his or her rights, the carrier shall be wholly or partly exonerated from its liability to the claimant to the extent that such negligence or wrongful act or omission caused or contributed to the damage. When by reason of death or injury of a passenger compensation is claimed by a person other than the passenger, the carrier shall likewise be wholly or partly exonerated from its liability to the extent that it proves that the damage was caused or contributed to by the negligence or other wrongful act or omission of that passenger. This Article applies to all the liability provisions in this Convention, including paragraph 1 of Article 21.

Article 21 – Compensation in Case of Death or Injury of Passengers

1. For damages arising under paragraph 1 of Article 17 not exceeding 100,000 Special Drawing Rights for each passenger, the carrier shall not be able to exclude or limit its liability.
2. The carrier shall not be liable for damages arising under paragraph 1 of Article 17 to the extent that they exceed for each passenger 100,000 Special Drawing Rights if the carrier proves that:

    (a) such damage was not due to the negligence or other wrongful act or omission of the carrier or its servants or agents; or
    (b) such damage was solely due to the negligence or other wrongful act or omission of a third party.

Article 22 – Limits of Liability in Relation to Delay, Baggage and Cargo

1. In the case of damage caused by delay as specified in Article 19 in the carriage of persons, the liability of the carrier for each passenger is limited to 4,150 Special Drawing Rights.

2. In the carriage of baggage, the liability of the carrier in the case of destruction, loss, damage or delay is limited to 1,000 Special Drawing Rights for each passenger unless the passenger has made, at the time when the checked baggage was handed over to the carrier, a special declaration of interest in delivery at destination and has paid a supplementary sum if the case so requires. In that case the carrier will be liable to pay a sum not exceeding the declared sum, unless it proves that the sum is greater than the passenger's actual interest in delivery at destination.

3. In the carriage of cargo, the liability of the carrier in the case of destruction, loss, damage or delay is limited to a sum of 17 Special Drawing Rights per kilogramme, unless the consignor has made, at the time when the package was handed over to the carrier, a special declaration of interest in delivery at destination and has paid a supplementary sum if the case so requires. In that case the carrier will be liable to pay a sum not exceeding the declared sum, unless it proves that the sum is greater than the consignor's actual interest in delivery at destination.

4. In the case of destruction, loss, damage or delay of part of the cargo, or of any object contained therein, the weight to be taken into consideration in determining the amount to which the carrier's liability is limited shall be only the total weight of the package or packages concerned. Nevertheless, when the destruction, loss, damage or delay of a part of the cargo, or of an object contained therein, affects the value of other packages covered by the same air waybill, or the same receipt or, if they were not issued, by the same record preserved by the other means referred to in paragraph 2 of Article 4, the total weight of such package or packages shall also be taken into consideration in determining the limit of liability.

5. The foregoing provisions of paragraphs 1 and 2 of this Article shall not apply if it is proved that the damage resulted from an act or omission of the carrier, its servants or agents, done with intent to cause damage or recklessly and with knowledge that damage would probably result; provided that, in the case of such act or omission of a servant or agent, it is also proved that such servant or agent was acting within the scope of its employment.

6. The limits prescribed in Article 21 and in this Article shall not prevent the court from awarding, in accordance with its own law, in addition, the whole or part of the court costs and of the other expenses of the litigation incurred by the plaintiff, including interest. The foregoing provision shall not apply if the amount of the damages awarded, excluding court costs and other expenses of the litigation, does not exceed the sum which the carrier has offered in writing to the plaintiff within a period of six months

from the date of the occurrence causing the damage, or before the commencement of the action, if that is later.

Article 23 – Conversion of Monetary Units

1. The sums mentioned in terms of Special Drawing Right in this Convention shall be deemed to refer to the Special Drawing Right as defined by the International Monetary Fund. Conversion of the sums into national currencies shall, in case of judicial proceedings, be made according to the value of such currencies in terms of the Special Drawing Right at the date of the judgement. The value of a national currency, in terms of the Special Drawing Right, of a State Party which is a Member of the International Monetary Fund, shall be calculated in accordance with the method of valuation applied by the International Monetary Fund, in effect at the date of the judgement, for its operations and transactions. The value of a national currency, in terms of the Special Drawing Right, of a State Party which is not a Member of the International Monetary Fund, shall be calculated in a manner determined by that State.

2. Nevertheless, those States which are not Members of the International Monetary Fund and whose law does not permit the application of the provisions of paragraph 1 of this Article may, at the time of ratification or accession or at any time thereafter, declare that the limit of liability of the carrier prescribed in Article 21 is fixed at a sum of 1,500,000 monetary units per passenger in judicial proceedings in their territories; 62,500 monetary units per passenger with respect to paragraph 1 of Article 22; 15,000 monetary units per passenger with respect to paragraph 2 of Article 22; and 250 monetary units per kilogramme with respect to paragraph 3 of Article 22. This monetary unit corresponds to sixty-five and a half milligrammes of gold of millesimal fineness nine hundred. These sums may be converted into the national currency concerned in round figures. The conversion of these sums into national currency shall be made according to the law of the State concerned.

3. The calculation mentioned in the last sentence of paragraph 1 of this Article and the conversion method mentioned in paragraph 2 of this Article shall be made in such manner as to express in the national currency of the State Party as far as possible the same real value for the amounts in Articles 21 and 22 as would result from the application of the first three sentences of paragraph 1 of this Article. States Parties shall communicate to the depositary the manner of calculation pursuant to paragraph 1 of this Article, or the result of the conversion in paragraph 2 of this Article as the case may be, when depositing an instrument of ratification, acceptance, approval of or accession to this Convention and whenever there is a change in either.

Article 24 – Review of Limits

1. Without prejudice to the provisions of Article 25 of this Convention and subject to paragraph 2 below, the limits of liability prescribed in Articles 21, 22 and 23 shall be reviewed by the Depositary at five-year intervals, the first such review to take place at the end of the fifth year following the date of entry into force of this Convention, or if the Convention does not enter into force within five years of the date it is first open for signature, within the first year of its entry into force, by reference to an inflation factor which corresponds to the accumulated rate of inflation since the previous revision or in the first instance since the date of entry into force of the Convention. The measure of the rate of inflation to be used in determining the inflation factor shall be the weighted average of the annual rates of increase or decrease in the Consumer Price Indices of the States whose currencies comprise the Special Drawing Right mentioned in paragraph 1 of Article 23.

2. If the review referred to in the preceding paragraph concludes that the inflation factor has exceeded 10 per cent, the Depositary shall notify States Parties of a revision of the limits of liability. Any such revision shall become effective six months after its notification to the States Parties. If within three months after its notification to the States Parties a majority of the States Parties register their disapproval, the revision shall not become effective and the Depositary shall refer the matter to a meeting of the States Parties. The Depositary shall immediately notify all States Parties of the coming into force of any revision.

3. Notwithstanding paragraph 1 of this Article, the procedure referred to in paragraph 2 of this Article shall be applied at any time provided that one-third of the States Parties express a desire to that effect and upon condition that the inflation factor referred to in paragraph 1 has exceeded 30 per cent since the previous revision or since the date of entry into force of this Convention if there has been no previous revision. Subsequent reviews using the procedure described in paragraph 1 of this Article will take place at five-year intervals starting at the end of the fifth year following the date of the reviews under the present paragraph.

Article 25 – Stipulation on Limits

A carrier may stipulate that the contract of carriage shall be subject to higher limits of liability than those provided for in this Convention or to no limits of liability whatsoever.

Article 26 – Invalidity of Contractual Provisions

Any provision tending to relieve the carrier of liability or to fix a lower limit than that which is laid down in this Convention shall be null and void, but the nullity of any such provision does not involve the nullity of the whole contract, which shall remain subject to the provisions of this Convention.

Article 27 – Freedom to Contract

Nothing contained in this Convention shall prevent the carrier from refusing to enter into any contract of carriage, from waiving any defences available under the Convention, or from laying down conditions which do not conflict with the provisions of this Convention.

Article 28 – Advance Payments

In the case of aircraft accidents resulting in death or injury of passengers, the carrier shall, if required by its national law, make advance payments without delay to a natural person or persons who are entitled to claim compensation in order to meet the immediate economic needs of such persons. Such advance payments shall not constitute a recognition of liability and may be offset against any amounts subsequently paid as damages by the carrier.

Article 29 – Basis of Claims

In the carriage of passengers, baggage and cargo, any action for damages, however founded, whether under this Convention or in contract or in tort or otherwise, can only be brought subject to the conditions and such limits of liability as are set out in this Convention without prejudice to the question as to who are the persons who have the right to bring suit and what are their respective rights. In any such action, punitive, exemplary or any other non-compensatory damages shall not be recoverable.

Article 30 – Servants, Agents – Aggregation of Claims

1. If an action is brought against a servant or agent of the carrier arising out of damage to which the Convention relates, such servant or agent, if they prove that they acted within the scope of their employment, shall be entitled to avail themselves of the conditions and limits of liability which the carrier itself is entitled to invoke under this Convention.
2. The aggregate of the amounts recoverable from the carrier, its servants and agents, in that case, shall not exceed the said limits.
3. Save in respect of the carriage of cargo, the provisions of paragraphs 1 and 2 of this Article shall not apply if it is proved that the damage resulted from an act or omission of the servant or agent done with intent to cause damage or recklessly and with knowledge that damage would probably result.

Article 31 – Timely Notice of Complaints

1. Receipt by the person entitled to delivery of checked baggage or cargo without complaint is *prima facie* evidence that the same has been delivered in good condition and in accordance with the document of carriage or with the record preserved by the other means referred to in paragraph 2 of Article 3 and paragraph 2 of Article 4.
2. In the case of damage, the person entitled to delivery must complain to the carrier forthwith after the discovery of the damage, and, at the latest, within seven days from the date of receipt in the case of checked baggage and fourteen days from the date of receipt in the case of cargo. In the case of delay, the complaint must be made at the latest within twenty-one days from the date on which the baggage or cargo have been placed at his or her disposal.
3. Every complaint must be made in writing and given or dispatched within the times aforesaid.
4. If no complaint is made within the times aforesaid, no action shall lie against the carrier, save in the case of fraud on its part.

Article 32 – Death of Person Liable

In the case of the death of the person liable, an action for damages lies in accordance with the terms of this Convention against those legally representing his or her estate.

Article 33 – Jurisdiction

1. An action for damages must be brought, at the option of the plaintiff, in the territory of one of the States Parties, either before the court of the domicile of the carrier or of its principal place of business, or where it has a place of business through which the contract has been made or before the court at the place of destination.
2. In respect of damage resulting from the death or injury of a passenger, an action may be brought before one of the courts mentioned in paragraph 1 of this Article, or in the territory of a State Party in which at the time of the accident the passenger has his or her principal and permanent residence and to or from which the carrier operates services for the carriage of passengers by air, either on its own aircraft, or on another carrier's aircraft pursuant to a commercial agreement, and in which that carrier conducts its business of carriage of passengers by air from premises leased or owned by the carrier itself or by another carrier with which it has a commercial agreement.
3. For the purposes of paragraph 2,
    (a) "commercial agreement" means an agreement, other than an agency agreement, made between carriers and relating to the provision of their joint services for carriage of passengers by air;

(b) "principal and permanent residence" means the one fixed and permanent abode of the passenger at the time of the accident. The nationality of the passenger shall not be the determining factor in this regard.

4. Questions of procedure shall be governed by the law of the court seised of the case.

Article 34 – Arbitration

1. Subject to the provisions of this Article, the parties to the contract of carriage for cargo may stipulate that any dispute relating to the liability of the carrier under this Convention shall be settled by arbitration. Such agreement shall be in writing.
2. The arbitration proceedings shall, at the option of the claimant, take place within one of the jurisdictions referred to in Article 33.
3. The arbitrator or arbitration tribunal shall apply the provisions of this Convention.
4. The provisions of paragraphs 2 and 3 of this Article shall be deemed to be part of every arbitration clause or agreement, and any term of such clause or agreement which is inconsistent therewith shall be null and void.

Article 35 – Limitation of Actions

1. The right to damages shall be extinguished if an action is not brought within a period of two years, reckoned from the date of arrival at the destination, or from the date on which the aircraft ought to have arrived, or from the date on which the carriage stopped.
2. The method of calculating that period shall be determined by the law of the court seised of the case.

Article 36 – Successive Carriage

1. In the case of carriage to be performed by various successive carriers and falling within the definition set out in paragraph 3 of Article 1, each carrier which accepts passengers, baggage or cargo is subject to the rules set out in this Convention and is deemed to be one of the parties to the contract of carriage in so far as the contract deals with that part of the carriage which is performed under its supervision.
2. In the case of carriage of this nature, the passenger or any person entitled to compensation in respect of him or her can take action only against the carrier which performed the carriage during which the accident or the delay occurred, save in the case where, by express agreement, the first carrier has assumed liability for the whole journey.
3. As regards baggage or cargo, the passenger or consignor will have a right of action against the first carrier, and the passenger or consignee who is

entitled to delivery will have a right of action against the last carrier, and further, each may take action against the carrier which performed the carriage during which the destruction, loss, damage or delay took place. These carriers will be jointly and severally liable to the passenger or to the consignor or consignee.

Article 37 – Right of Recourse against Third Parties

Nothing in this Convention shall prejudice the question whether a person liable for damage in accordance with its provisions has a right of recourse against any other person.

Chapter IV – Combined Carriage

Article 38 – Combined Carriage

1. In the case of combined carriage performed partly by air and partly by any other mode of carriage, the provisions of this Convention shall, subject to paragraph 4 of Article 18, apply only to the carriage by air, provided that the carriage by air falls within the terms of Article 1.
2. Nothing in this Convention shall prevent the parties in the case of combined carriage from inserting in the document of air carriage conditions relating to other modes of carriage, provided that the provisions of this Convention are observed as regards the carriage by air.

Chapter V – Carriage by Air Performed by a Person other than the Contracting Carrier

Article 39 – Contracting Carrier – Actual Carrier

The provisions of this Chapter apply when a person (hereinafter referred to as "the contracting carrier") as a principal makes a contract governed by this Convention with a passenger or consignor or with a person acting on behalf of the passenger or consignor, and another person (hereinafter referred to as "the actual carrier") performs, by virtue of authority from the contracting carrier, the whole or part of the carriage, but is not with respect to such part a successive carrier within the meaning of this Convention. Such authority shall be presumed in the absence of proof to the contrary.

Article 40 – Respective Liability of Contracting and Actual Carriers

If an actual carrier performs the whole or part of carriage which, according to the contract referred to in Article 39, is governed by this Convention, both the contracting carrier and the actual carrier shall, except as otherwise provided in this Chapter, be subject to the rules of this Convention, the former for the whole of the carriage contemplated in the contract, the latter solely for the carriage which it performs.

Article 41 – Mutual Liability

1. The acts and omissions of the actual carrier and of its servants and agents acting within the scope of their employment shall, in relation to the carriage performed by the actual carrier, be deemed to be also those of the contracting carrier.
2. The acts and omissions of the contracting carrier and of its servants and agents acting within the scope of their employment shall, in relation to the carriage performed by the actual carrier, be deemed to be also those of the actual carrier. Nevertheless, no such act or omission shall subject the actual carrier to liability exceeding the amounts referred to in Articles 21, 22, 23 and 24. Any special agreement under which the contracting carrier assumes obligations not imposed by this Convention or any waiver of rights or defences conferred by this Convention or any special declaration of interest in delivery at destination contemplated in Article 22 shall not affect the actual carrier unless agreed to by it.

Article 42 – Addressee of Complaints and Instructions

Any complaint to be made or instruction to be given under this Convention to the carrier shall have the same effect whether addressed to the contracting carrier or to the actual carrier. Nevertheless, instructions referred to in Article 12 shall only be effective if addressed to the contracting carrier.

Article 43 – Servants and Agents

In relation to the carriage performed by the actual carrier, any servant or agent of that carrier or of the contracting carrier shall, if they prove that they acted within the scope of their employment, be entitled to avail themselves of the conditions and limits of liability which are applicable under this Convention to the carrier whose servant or agent they are, unless it is proved that they acted in a manner that prevents the limits of liability from being invoked in accordance with this Convention.

Article 44 – Aggregation of Damages

In relation to the carriage performed by the actual carrier, the aggregate of the amounts recoverable from that carrier and the contracting carrier, and from their servants and agents acting within the scope of their employment, shall not exceed the highest amount which could be awarded against either the contracting carrier or the actual carrier under this Convention, but none of the persons mentioned shall be liable for a sum in excess of the limit applicable to that person.

Article 45 – Addressee of Claims

In relation to the carriage performed by the actual carrier, an action for damages may be brought, at the option of the plaintiff, against that carrier or the contracting carrier, or against both together or separately. If the action is brought against only one of those carriers, that carrier shall have the right to require the other carrier to be joined in the proceedings, the procedure and effects being governed by the law of the court seised of the case.

Article 46 – Additional Jurisdiction

Any action for damages contemplated in Article 45 must be brought, at the option of the plaintiff, in the territory of one of the States Parties, either before a court in which an action may be brought against the contracting carrier, as provided in Article 33, or before the court having jurisdiction at the place where the actual carrier has its domicile or its principal place of business.

Article 47 – Invalidity of Contractual Provisions

Any contractual provision tending to relieve the contracting carrier or the actual carrier of liability under this Chapter or to fix a lower limit than that which is applicable according to this Chapter shall be null and void, but the nullity of any such provision does not involve the nullity of the whole contract, which shall remain subject to the provisions of this Chapter.

Article 48 – Mutual Relations of Contracting and Actual Carriers

Except as provided in Article 45, nothing in this Chapter shall affect the rights and obligations of the carriers between themselves, including any right of recourse or indemnification.

Chapter VI – Other Provisions

Article 49 – Mandatory Application

Any clause contained in the contract of carriage and all special agreements entered into before the damage occurred by which the parties purport to infringe the rules laid down by this Convention, whether by deciding the law to be applied, or by altering the rules as to jurisdiction, shall be null and void.

Article 50 – Insurance

States Parties shall require their carriers to maintain adequate insurance covering their liability under this Convention. A carrier may be required by the State Party into which it operates to furnish evidence that it maintains adequate insurance covering its liability under this Convention.

Article 51 – Carriage Performed in Extraordinary Circumstances

The provisions of Articles 3 to 5, 7 and 8 relating to the documentation of carriage shall not apply in the case of carriage performed in extraordinary circumstances outside the normal scope of a carrier's business.

Article 52 – Definition of Days

The expression "days" when used in this Convention means calendar days, not working days.

Chapter VII – Final Clauses

Article 53 – Signature, Ratification and Entry into Force

1. This Convention shall be open for signature in Montreal on 28 May 1999 by States participating in the International Conference on Air Law held at Montreal from 10 to 28 May 1999. After 28 May 1999, the Convention shall be open to all States for signature at the Headquarters of the International Civil Aviation Organization in Montreal until it enters into force in accordance with paragraph 6 of this Article.
2. This Convention shall similarly be open for signature by Regional Economic Integration Organisations. For the purpose of this Convention, a "Regional Economic Integration Organisation" means any organisation which is constituted by sovereign States of a given region which has competence in respect of certain matters governed by this Convention and has been duly authorized to sign and to ratify, accept, approve or accede to this Convention. A reference to a "State Party" or "States Parties" in this Convention, otherwise than in paragraph 2 of Article 1, paragraph 1(b) of Article 3, paragraph (b) of Article 5, Articles 23, 33, 46 and paragraph (b) of Article 57, applies equally to a Regional Economic Integration Organisation. For the purpose of Article 24, the references to "a majority of the States Parties" and "one-third of the States Parties" shall not apply to a Regional Economic Integration Organisation.
3. This Convention shall be subject to ratification by States and by Regional Economic Integration Organisations which have signed it.
4. Any State or Regional Economic Integration Organisation which does not sign this Convention may accept, approve or accede to it at any time.
5. Instruments of ratification, acceptance, approval or accession shall be deposited with the International Civil Aviation Organization, which is hereby designated the Depositary.
6. This Convention shall enter into force on the sixtieth day following the date of deposit of the thirtieth instrument of ratification, acceptance, approval or accession with the Depositary between the States which have deposited such instrument. An instrument deposited by a Regional

Economic Integration Organisation shall not be counted for the purpose of this paragraph.

7. For other States and for other Regional Economic Integration Organisations, this Convention shall take effect sixty days following the date of deposit of the instrument of ratification, acceptance, approval or accession.

8. The Depositary shall promptly notify all signatories and States Parties of:

    (a) each signature of this Convention and date thereof;
    (b) each deposit of an instrument of ratification, acceptance, approval or accession and date thereof;
    (c) the date of entry into force of this Convention;
    (d) the date of the coming into force of any revision of the limits of liability established under this Convention;
    (e) any denunciation under Article 54.

Article 54 – Denunciation

1. Any State Party may denounce this Convention by written notification to the Depositary.

2. Denunciation shall take effect one hundred and eighty days following the date on which notification is received by the Depositary.

Article 55 – Relationship with other Warsaw Convention Instruments

This Convention shall prevail over any rules which apply to international carriage by air:

1. between States Parties to this Convention by virtue of those States commonly being Party to

    (a) the *Convention for the Unification of Certain Rules Relating to International Carriage by Air* Signed at Warsaw on 12 October 1929 (hereinafter called the Warsaw Convention);
    (b) the *Protocol to Amend the Convention for the Unification of Certain Rules Relating to International Carriage by Air Signed, at Warsaw on 12 October 1929*, Done at The Hague on 28 September 1955 (hereinafter called The Hague Protocol);
    (c) the *Convention, Supplementary to the Warsaw Convention, for the Unification of Certain Rules Relating to International Carriage by Air Performed by a Person Other than the Contracting Carrier*, Signed at Guadalajara on 18 September 1961 (hereinafter called the Guadalajara Convention);
    (d) the *Protocol to Amend the Convention for the Unification of Certain Rules Relating to International Carriage by Air Signed at Warsaw on 12 October 1929 as Amended by the Protocol Done at The Hague on 28 September*

> 1955 Signed at Guatemala City on 8 March 1971 (hereinafter called the Guatemala City Protocol);
>
> (e) Additional Protocol Nos. 1 to 3 and Montreal Protocol No. 4 to amend the Warsaw Convention as amended by The Hague Protocol or the Warsaw Convention as amended by both The Hague Protocol and the Guatemala City Protocol Signed at Montreal on 25 September 1975 (hereinafter called the Montreal Protocols); or

2. within the territory of any single State Party to this Convention by virtue of that State being Party to one or more of the instruments referred to in sub-paragraphs (a) to (e) above.

Article 56 – States with more than one System of Law

1. If a State has two or more territorial units in which different systems of law are applicable in relation to matters dealt with in this Convention, it may at the time of signature, ratification, acceptance, approval or accession declare that this Convention shall extend to all its territorial units or only to one or more of them and may modify this declaration by submitting another declaration at any time.
2. Any such declaration shall be notified to the Depositary and shall state expressly the territorial units to which the Convention applies.
3. In relation to a State Party which has made such a declaration:

   (a) references in Article 23 to "national currency" shall be construed as referring to the currency of the relevant territorial unit of that State; and
   (b) the reference in Article 28 to "national law" shall be construed as referring to the law of the relevant territorial unit of that State.

Article 57 – Reservations

No reservation may be made to this Convention except that a State Party may at any time declare by a notification addressed to the Depositary that this Convention shall not apply to:

(a) international carriage by air performed and operated directly by that State Party for non-commercial purposes in respect to its functions and duties as a sovereign State; and/or
(b) the carriage of persons, cargo and baggage for its military authorities on aircraft registered in or leased by that State Party, the whole capacity of which has been reserved by or on behalf of such authorities.

IN WITNESS WHEREOF the undersigned Plenipotentiaries, having been duly authorized, have signed this Convention.

DONE at Montreal on the 28th day of May of the year one thousand nine hundred and ninety-nine in the English, Arabic, Chinese, French, Russian and Spanish languages, all texts being equally authentic. This Convention shall remain deposited in the archives of the International Civil Aviation Organization, and certified copies thereof shall be transmitted by the Depositary to all States Parties to this Convention, as well as to all States Parties to the Warsaw Convention, The Hague Protocol, the Guadalajara Convention, the Guatemala City Protocol, and the Montreal Protocols.

Notes

1   Not included in the consolidated version of the Warsaw Convention as amended at The Hague.
2   Not included in the consolidated version of the Warsaw Convention as amended at The Hague and by Montreal Protocol No. 4.
3   Not included in the consolidated version of the Warsaw Convention as amended at The Hague and by Montreal Protocol No. 4.
4   Not included in the consolidated version of the Warsaw Convention as amended at The Hague and by Montreal Protocol No. 4.

Section 2

Additional Protocols

2.1 The Hague Protocol 1955

**PROTOCOL TO AMEND THE CONVENTION FOR
THE UNIFICATION OF CERTAIN RULES RELATING
TO INTERNATIONAL CARRIAGE BY AIR, SIGNED AT
WARSAW ON 12 OCTOBER 1929, DONE AT THE
HAGUE ON 28 SEPTEMBER 1955**

THE GOVERNMENTS UNDERSIGNED

CONSIDERING that it is desirable to amend the Convention for the Unification of Certain Rules Relating to International Carriage by Air signed at Warsaw on 12 October 1929,

HAVE AGREED as follows:

Chapter I – Amendments to the Convention

Article I

In Article 1 of the Convention –

(a) paragraph 2 shall be deleted and replaced by the following:

"2. For the purposes of this Convention, the expression international carriage means any carriage in which, according to the agreement between the parties, the place of departure and the place of destination, whether or not there be a break in the carriage or a transhipment, are situated either within the territories of two High Contracting Parties or within the territory of a single High Contracting Party if there is an agreed stopping place within the territory of another State, even if that State is not a High Contracting Party. Carriage between two points within the territory of a single High Contracting Party without an agreed stopping place within the territory of another State is not international carriage for the purposes of this Convention."

(b) paragraph 3 shall be deleted and replaced by the following:

> "3. Carriage to be performed by several successive air carriers is deemed, for the purposes of this Convention, to be one undivided carriage if it has been regarded by the parties as a single operation, whether it had been agreed upon under the form of a single contract or of a series of contracts, and it does not lose its international character merely because one contract or a series of contracts is to be performed entirely within the territory of the same State."

Article II

In Article 2 of the Convention paragraph 2 shall be deleted and replaced by the following:

> "2. This Convention shall not apply to carriage of mail and postal packages."

Article III

In Article 3 of the Convention –

(a) paragraph 1 shall be deleted and replaced by the following:

> "1. In respect of the carriage of passengers a ticket shall be delivered containing:
>
> (a) an indication of the places of departure and destination;
> (b) if the places of departure and destination are within the territory of a single High Contracting Party, one or more agreed stopping places being within the territory of another State, an indication of at least one such stopping place;
> (c) a notice to the effect that, if the passenger's journey involves an ultimate destination or stop in a country other than the country of departure, the Warsaw Convention may be applicable and that the Convention governs and in most cases limits the liability of carriers for death or personal injury and in respect of loss of or damage to baggage."

(b) paragraph 2 shall be deleted and replaced by the following:

> "2. The passenger ticket shall constitute *prima facie* evidence of the conclusion and conditions of the contract of carriage. The absence, irregularity or loss of the passenger ticket does not affect the existence or the validity of the contract of carriage which shall, none the less, be subject to the rules of this Convention. Nevertheless, if, with the consent of the carrier, the passenger embarks without a passenger ticket having been delivered, or if the ticket does not include the notice required by paragraph

1 (c) of this Article, the carrier shall not be entitled to avail himself of the provisions of Article 22."

Article IV

In Article 4 of the Convention –

(a) paragraphs 1, 2 and 3 shall be deleted and replaced by the following:

"1. In respect of the carriage of registered baggage, a baggage check shall be delivered, which, unless combined with or incorporated in a passenger ticket which complies with the provisions of Article 3, paragraph 1, shall contain:

(a) an indication of the places of departure and destination;
(b) if the places of departure and destination are within the territory of a single High Contracting Party, one or more agreed stopping places being within the territory of another State, an indication of at least one such stopping place;
(c) a notice to the effect that, if the carriage involves an ultimate destination or stop in a country other than the country of departure, the Warsaw Convention may be applicable and that the Convention governs and in most cases limits the liability of carriers in respect of loss of or damage to baggage."

(b) paragraph 4 shall be deleted and replaced by the following:

"2. The baggage check shall constitute *prima facie* evidence of the registration of the baggage and of the conditions of the contract of carriage. The absence, irregularity or loss of the baggage check does not affect the existence or the validity of the contract of carriage which shall, none the less, be subject to the rules of this Convention. Nevertheless, if the carrier takes charge of the baggage without a baggage check having been delivered or if the baggage check (unless combined with or incorporated in the passenger ticket which complies with the provisions of Article 3, paragraph 1(c)) does not include the notice required by paragraph 1(c) of this Article, he shall not be entitled to avail himself of the provisions of Article 22, paragraph 2."

Article V

In Article 6 of the Convention – paragraph 3 shall be deleted and replaced by the following:

"3. The carrier shall sign prior to the loading of the cargo on board the aircraft."

Article VI

Article 8 of the Convention shall be deleted and replaced by the following:

"The air waybill shall contain:

(a) an indication of the places of departure and destination;
(b) if the places of departure and destination are within the territory of a single High Contracting Party, one or more agreed stopping places being within the territory of another State, an indication of at least one such stopping place;
(c) a notice to the consignor to the effect that, if the carriage involves an ultimate destination or stop in a country other than the country of departure, the Warsaw Convention may be applicable and that the Convention governs and in most cases limits the liability of carriers in respect of loss of or damage to cargo."

Article VII

Article 9 of the Convention shall be deleted and replaced by the following:

"If, with the consent of the carrier, cargo is loaded on board the aircraft without an air waybill having been made out, or if the air waybill does not include the notice required by Article 8, paragraph (c), the carrier shall not be entitled to avail himself of the provisions of Article 22, paragraph 2."

Article VIII

In Article 10 of the Convention – paragraph 2 shall be deleted and replaced by the following:

"2. The consignor shall indemnify the carrier against all damage suffered by him, or by any other person to whom the carrier is liable, by reason of the irregularity, incorrectness or incompleteness of the particulars and statements furnished by the consignor."

Article IX

To Article 15 of the Convention – the following paragraph shall be added:

"3. Nothing in this Convention prevents the issue of a negotiable air waybill."

Article X

Paragraph 2 of Article 20 of the Convention shall be deleted.

Article XI

Article 22 of the Convention shall be deleted and replaced by the following:

"Article 22

1. In the carriage of persons the liability of the carrier for each passenger is limited to the sum of two hundred and fifty thousand francs where, in accordance with the law of the court seised of the case, damages may be awarded in the form of periodical payments, the equivalent capital value of the said payments shall not exceed two hundred and fifty thousand francs. Nevertheless, by special contract, the carrier and the passenger may agree to a higher limit of liability.

2. (a) In the carriage of registered baggage and of cargo, the liability of the carrier is limited to a sum of two hundred and fifty francs per kilogramme, unless the passenger or consignor has made, at the time when the package was handed over to the carrier, a special declaration of interest in delivery at destination and has paid a supplementary sum if the case so requires. In that case the carrier will be liable to pay a sum not exceeding the declared sum, unless he proves that that sum is greater than the passenger's or consignor's actual interest in delivery at destination.

   (b) In the case of loss, damage or delay of part of registered baggage or cargo, or of any object contained therein, the weight to be taken into consideration in determining the amount to which the carrier's liability is limited shall be only the total weight of the package or packages concerned. Nevertheless, when the loss, damage or delay of a part of the registered baggage or cargo, or of an object contained therein, affects the value of other packages covered by the same baggage check or the same air waybill, the total weight of such package or packages shall also be taken into consideration in determining the limit of liability.

3. As regards objects of which the passenger takes charge himself the liability of the carrier is limited to five thousand francs per passenger.

4. The limits prescribed in this article shall not prevent the court from awarding, in accordance with its own law, in addition, the whole or part of the court costs and of the other expenses of the litigation incurred by the plaintiff. The foregoing provision shall not apply if the amount of the damages awarded, excluding court costs and other expenses of the litigation, does not exceed the sum which the carrier has offered in writing

to the plaintiff within a period of six months from the date of the occurrence causing the damage, or before commencement of the action, if that is later.

5.   The sums mentioned in francs in this Article shall be deemed to refer to a currency unit consisting of sixty-five and a half milligrammes of gold of millesimal fineness nine hundred. These sums may be converted into national currencies in round figures. Conversion of the sums into national currencies other than gold shall, in case of judicial proceedings, be made according to the gold value of such currencies at the date of the judgment."

Article **XII**

In Article 23 of the Convention, the existing provision shall be renumbered as paragraph 1 and another paragraph shall be added as follows:

"2. Paragraph 1 of this Article shall not apply to provisions governing loss or damage resulting from the inherent defect, quality or vice of the cargo carried."

Article **XIII**

In Article 25 of the Convention – paragraphs 1 and 2 shall be deleted and replaced by the following:

"The limits of liability specified in Article 22 shall not apply if it is proved that the damage resulted from an act or omission of the carrier, his servants or agents, done with intent to cause damage or recklessly and with knowledge that damage would probably result; provided that, in the case of such act or omission of a servant or agent, it is also proved that he was acting within the scope of his employment."

Article **XIV**

After Article 25 of the Convention, the following article shall be inserted:

"**Article 25A**

1.   If an action is brought against a servant or agent of the carrier arising out of damage to which this Convention relates, such servant or agent, if he proves that he acted within the scope of his employment, shall be entitled to avail himself of the limits of liability which that carrier himself is entitled to invoke under Article 22.

2.   The aggregate of the amounts recoverable from the carrier, his servants and agents, in that case, shall not exceed the said limits.

3.   The provisions of paragraphs 1 and 2 of this article shall not apply if it is proved that the damage resulted from an act or omission of the servant or

agent done with intent to cause damage or recklessly and with knowledge that damage would probably result."

Article XV

In Article 26 of the Convention – paragraph 2 shall be deleted and replaced by the following:

"2. In the case of damage, the person entitled to delivery must complain to the carrier forthwith after the discovery of the damage, and, at the latest, within seven days from the date of receipt in the case of baggage and fourteen days from the date of receipt in the case of cargo. In the case of delay the complaint must be made at the latest within twenty-one days from the date on which the baggage or cargo have been placed at his disposal."

Article XVI

Article 34 of the Convention shall be deleted and replaced by the following:

"The provisions of Articles 3 to 9 inclusive relating to documents of carriage shall not apply in the case of carriage performed in extraordinary circumstances outside the normal scope of an air carrier's business."

Article XVII

After Article 40 of the Convention, the following Article shall be inserted:

"Article 40A

1. In Article 37, paragraph 2 and Article 40, paragraph 1, the expression High Contracting Party shall mean State. In all other cases, the expression High Contracting Party shall mean a State whose ratification of or adherence to the Convention has become effective and whose denunciation thereof has not become effective.
2. For the purposes of the Convention the word territory means not only the metropolitan territory of a State but also all other territories for the foreign relations of which that State is responsible."

Chapter II – Scope of Application of the Convention as Amended

Article XVIII

The Convention as amended by this Protocol shall apply to international carriage as defined in Article 1 of the Convention, provided that the places of departure and destination referred to in that Article are situated either in the territories of two parties to this Protocol or within the territory of a single party to this Protocol with an agreed stopping place within the territory of another State.

Chapter III – Final Clauses

Article XIX

As between the Parties to this Protocol, the Convention and the Protocol shall be read and interpreted together as one single instrument and shall be known as the Warsaw Convention as amended at The Hague, 1955.

Article XX

Until the date on which this Protocol comes into force in accordance with the provisions of Article XXII, paragraph 1, it shall remain open for signature on behalf of any State which up to that date has ratified or adhered to the Convention or which has participated in the Conference at which this Protocol was adopted.

Article XXI

1. This Protocol shall be subject to ratification by the signatory States.
2. Ratification of this Protocol by any State which is not a Party to the Convention shall have the effect of adherence to the Convention as amended by this Protocol.
3. The instruments of ratification shall be deposited with the Government of the People's Republic of Poland.

Article XXII

1. As soon as thirty signatory States have deposited their instruments of ratification of this Protocol, it shall come into force between them on the ninetieth day after the deposit of the thirtieth instrument of ratification. It shall come into force for each State ratifying thereafter on the ninetieth day after the deposit of its instrument of ratification.
2. As soon as this Protocol comes into force it shall be registered with the United Nations by the Government of the People's Republic of Poland.

Article XXIII

1. This Protocol shall, after it has come into force, be open for adherence by any non-signatory State.

2. Adherence to this Protocol by any State which is not a Party to the Convention shall have the effect of adherence to the Convention as amended by this Protocol.

3. Adherence shall be effected by the deposit of an instrument of adherence with the Government of the People's Republic of Poland and shall take effect on the ninetieth day after the deposit.

Article XXIV

1. Any Party to this Protocol may denounce the Protocol by notification addressed to the Government of the People's Republic of Poland.

2. Denunciation shall take effect six months after the date of receipt by the Government of the People's Republic of Poland of the notification of denunication.

3. As between the Parties to this Protocol, denunciation by any of them of the Convention in accordance with Article 39 thereof shall not be construed in any way as a denunciation of the Convention as amended by this Protocol.

Article XXV

1. This Protocol shall apply to all territories for the foreign relations of which a State Party to this Protocol is responsible, with the exception of territories in respect of which a declaration has been made in accordance with paragraph 2 of this Article.

2. Any State may, at the time of deposit of its instrument of ratification or adherence, declare that its acceptance of this Protocol does not apply to any one or more of the territories for the foreign relations of which such State is responsible.

3. Any State may subsequently, by notification to the Government of the People's Republic of Poland, extend the application of this Protocol to any or all of the territories regarding which it has made a declaration in accordance with paragraph 2 of this Article. The notification shall take effect on the ninetieth day after its receipt by that Government.

4. Any State Party to this Protocol may denounce it, in accordance with the provisions of Article XXIV, paragraph 1, separately for any or all of the territories for the foreign relations of which such State is responsible.

Article XXVI

No reservation may be made to this Protocol except that a State may at any time declare by a notification addressed to the Government of the People's Republic of Poland that the Convention as amended by this Protocol shall not apply to the carriage of persons, cargo and baggage for its military authorities on aircraft, registered in that State, the whole capacity of which has been reserved by or on behalf of such authorities.

Article XXVII

The Government of the People's Republic of Poland shall give immediate notice to the Governments of all States signatories to the Convention or this Protocol, all States Parties to the Convention or this Protocol, and all States Members of the International Civil Aviation Organization or of the United Nations and to the International Civil Aviation Organization:

(a) of any signature of this Protocol and the date thereof;
(b) of the deposit of any instrument of ratification or adherence in respect of this Protocol and the date thereof;
(c) of the date on which this Protocol comes into force in accordance with Article XXII, paragraph 1;
(d) of the receipt of any notification of denunciation and the date thereof;
(e) of the receipt of any declaration or notification made under Article XXV and the date thereof; and
(f) of the receipt of any notification made under Article XXVI and the date thereof.

IN WITNESS WHEREOF the undersigned Plenipotentiaries, having been duly authorized, have signed this Protocol.

DONE at The Hague on the twenty-eighth day of the month of September of the year One Thousand Nine Hundred and Fifty-five, in three authentic texts in the English, French and Spanish languages. In the case of any inconsistency, the text in the French language, in which language the Convention was drawn up, shall prevail.

This Protocol shall be deposited with the Government of the People's Republic of Poland with which, in accordance with Article XX, it shall remain open for signature, and that Government shall send certified copies thereof to the Governments of all States signatories to the Convention or this Protocol, all States Parties to the Convention or this Protocol, and all States Members of the International Civil Aviation Organization or of the United Nations, and to the International Civil Aviation Organization.

2.2 Guatemala City Protocol 1971

PROTOCOL TO AMEND THE CONVENTION FOR THE UNIFICATION OF CERTAIN RULES RELATING TO INTERNATIONAL CARRIAGE BY AIR, SIGNED AT WARSAW ON 12 OCTOBER 1929, AS AMENDED BY THE PROTOCOL DONE AT THE HAGUE ON 28 SEPTEMBER 1955, SIGNED AT GUATEMALA CITY ON 8 MARCH 1971

THE GOVERNMENTS UNDERSIGNED

CONSIDERING that it is desirable to amend the Convention for the Unification of Certain Rules Relating to International Carriage by Air signed at Warsaw on 12 October 1929 as amended by the Protocol done at The Hague on 28 September 1955,

HAVE AGREED as follows:

Chapter I – Amendments to the Convention

Article I

The Convention which the provisions of the present Chapter modify is the Warsaw Convention as amended at The Hague in 1955.

Article II

Article 3 of the Convention shall be deleted and replaced by the following:

"Article 3

1. In respect of the carriage of passengers an individual or collective document of carriage shall be delivered containing:

    (a) an indication of the places of departure and destination;
    (b) if the places of departure and destination are within the territory of a single High Contracting Party, one or more agreed stopping places

being within the territory of another State, an indication of at least one such stopping place.

2.   Any other means which would preserve a record of the information indicated in (a) and (b) of the foregoing paragraph may be substituted for the delivery of the document referred to in that paragraph.

3.   Non-compliance with the provisions of the foregoing paragraphs shall not affect the existence or the validity of the contract of carriage, which shall, none the less, be subject to the rules of this Convention including those relating to limitation of liability."

Article III

Article 4 of the Convention shall be deleted and replaced by the following:

"Article 4

1.   In respect of the carriage of checked baggage, a baggage check shall be delivered, which, unless combined with or incorporated in a document of carriage which complies with the provisions of Article 3,

(a)   an indication of the places of departure and destination;
(b)   if the places of departure and destination are within the territory of a single High Contracting Party, one or more agreed stopping places being within the territory of another State, an indication of at least one such stopping place.

2.   Any other means which would preserve a record of the information indicated in (a) and (b) of the foregoing paragraph may be substituted for the delivery of the baggage check referred to in that paragraph.

3.   Non-compliance with the provisions of the foregoing paragraphs shall not affect the existence or the validity of the contract of carriage, which shall, none the less, be subject to the rules of this Convention including those relating to limitation of liability."

Article IV

Article 17 of the Convention shall be deleted and replaced by the following:

"Article 17

1.   The carrier is liable for damage sustained in case of death or personal injury of a passenger upon condition only that the event which caused the death or injury took place on board the aircraft or in the course of any of the operations of embarking or disembarking. However, the carrier is not liable if the death or injury resulted solely from the state of health of the passenger.

2. The carrier is liable for damage sustained in case of destruction or loss of, or of damage to, baggage upon condition only that the event which caused the destruction, loss or damage took place on board the aircraft or in the course of any of the operations of embarking or disembarking or during any period within which the baggage was in charge of the carrier. However, the carrier is not liable if the damage resulted solely from the inherent defect, quality or vice of the baggage.
3. Unless otherwise specified, in this Convention the term "baggage" means both checked baggage and objects carried by the passenger."

Article V

In Article 18 of the Convention – paragraphs 1 and 2 shall be deleted and replaced by the following:

"1. The carrier is liable for damage sustained in the event of the destruction or loss of, or of damage to, any cargo, if the occurrence which caused the damage so sustained took place during the carriage by air.
 2. The carriage by air within the meaning of the preceding paragraph comprises the period during which the cargo is in charge of the carrier, whether in an airport or on board an aircraft, or, in the case of a landing outside an airport, in any place whatsoever."

Article VI

Article 20 of the Convention shall be deleted and replaced by the following:

"Article 20

1. In the carriage of passengers and baggage the carrier shall not be liable for damage occasioned by delay if he proves that he and his servants and agents have taken all necessary measures to avoid the damage or that it was impossible for them to take such measures.
2. In the carriage of cargo the carrier shall not be liable for damages resulting from destruction, loss, damage or delay if he proves that he and his servants and agents have taken all necessary measures to avoid the damage or that it was impossible for them to take such measures."

Article VII

Article 21 of the Convention shall be deleted and replaced by the following:

"Article 21

If the carrier proves that the damage was caused or contributed to by the negligence or other wrongful act or omission of the person claiming compensation, the carrier shall be wholly or partly exonerated from his liability to such person to the extent that such negligence or wrongful act or omission caused or contributed to the damage. When by reason of the death or injury of a passenger compensation is claimed by a person other than the passenger, the carrier shall likewise be wholly or partly exonerated from his liability to the extent that he proves that the damage was caused or contributed to by the negligence or other wrongful act or omission of that passenger."

Article VIII

Article 22 of the Convention shall be deleted and replaced by the following:

"Article 22

1. (a) In the carriage of persons the liability of the carrier is limited to the sum of one million five hundred thousand francs for the aggregate of the claims, however founded, in respect of damage suffered as a result of the death or personal injury of each passenger. Where, in accordance with the law of the court seised of the case, damages may be awarded in the form of periodic payments, the equivalent capital value of the said payments shall not exceed one million five hundred thousand francs.

   (b) In the case of delay in the carriage of persons the liability of the carrier for each passenger is limited to sixty-two thousand five hundred francs.

   (c) In the carriage of baggage the liability of the carrier in the case of destruction, loss, damage or delay is limited to fifteen thousand francs for each passenger.

2. (a) In the carriage of cargo, the liability of the carrier is limited to a sum of two hundred and fifty francs per kilogramme, unless the consignor has made, at the time when the package was handed over to the carrier, a special declaration of interest in delivery at destination and has paid supplementary sum if the case so requires. In that case the carrier will be liable to pay a sum not exceeding the declared sum, unless he proves that that sum is greater than the consignor's actual interest in delivery at destination.

   (b) In the case of loss, damage or delay of part of the cargo, or of any object contained therein, the weight to be taken into consideration in determining the amount to which the carrier's liability is limited shall be only the total weight of the package or packages concerned. Nevertheless, when the loss, damage or delay of a part of the cargo or of an object contained therein, affects the value of other packages covered by the same air waybill, the total weight of such package or packages shall also be taken into consideration in determining the limit of liability.

3. (a) The courts of the High Contracting Parties which are not authorized under their law to award the costs of the action, including lawyers' fees, shall, in actions to which this Convention applies, have the power to award, in their discretion, to the claimant the whole or part of the costs of the action, including lawyers' fees which the court considers reasonable.

    (b) The costs of the action including lawyers' fees shall be awarded in accordance with subparagraph (a) only if the claimant gives a written notice to the carrier of the amount claimed including the particulars of the calculation of that amount and the carrier does not make, within a period of six months after his receipt of such notice, a written offer of settlement in an amount at least equal to the compensation awarded within the applicable limit. This period will be extended until the time of commencement of the action if that is later.

    (c) The costs of the action including lawyers' fees shall not be taken into account in applying the limits under this Article.

4. The sums mentioned in francs in this Article and Article 42 shall be deemed to refer to a currency unit consisting of sixty-five and a half milligrammes of gold of millesimal fineness nine hundred. These sums may be converted into national currencies in round figures. Conversion of the sums into national currencies other than gold shall, in case of judicial proceedings, be made according to the gold value of such currencies at the date of the judgment."

Article IX

Article 24 of the Convention shall be deleted and replaced by the following:

"Article 24

1. In the carriage of cargo, any action for damages, however founded, can only be brought subject to the conditions and limits set out in this Convention.

2. In the carriage of passengers and baggage any action for damages, however founded, whether under this Convention or in contract or in tort or otherwise, can only be brought subject to the conditions and limits of liability set out in this Convention without prejudice to the question as to who are the persons who have the right to bring suit and what are their respective rights. Such limits of liability constitute maximum limits and may not be exceeded whatever the circumstances which gave rise to the liability."

Article X

Article 25 of the Convention shall be deleted and replaced by the following:

"Article 25

The limit of liability specified in paragraph 2 of Article 22 shall not apply if it is proved that the damage resulted from an act or omission of the carrier, his servants or agents, done with intent to cause damage or recklessly and with knowledge that damage would probably result; provided that, in the case of such act or omission of a servant or agent, it is also proved that he was acting within the scope of his employment."

Article XI

In Article 25 A of the Convention – paragraphs 1 and 3 shall be deleted and replaced by the following:

"1. If an action is brought against a servant or agent of the carrier arising out of damage to which the Convention relates, such servant or agent, if he proves that he acted within the scope of his employment, shall be entitled to avail himself of the limits of liability which that carrier himself is entitled to invoke under this Convention.

3. The provisions of paragraphs 1 and 2 of this Article shall not apply to the carriage of cargo if it is proved that the damage resulted from an act or omission of the servant or agent done with intent to cause damage or recklessly and with knowledge that damage would probably result."

Article XII

In Article 28 of the Convention – the present paragraph 2 shall be renumbered as paragraph 3 and a new paragraph 2 shall be inserted as follows:

"2. In respect of damage resulting from the death, injury or delay of a passenger or the destruction, loss, damage or delay of baggage, the action may be brought before one of the Courts mentioned in paragraph 1 of this Article, or in the territory of one of the High Contracting Parties, before the Court within the jurisdiction of which the carrier has an establishment if the passenger has his domicile or permanent residence in the territory of the same High Contracting Party."

Article XIII

After Article 30 of the Convention, the following Article shall be inserted:

"**Article 30 A**

Nothing in this Convention shall prejudice the question whether a person liable for damage in accordance with its provisions has a right of recourse against any other person."

Article XIV

After Article 35 of the Convention, the following Article shall be inserted:

"**Article 35A**

No provision contained in this Convention shall prevent a State from establishing and operating within its territory a system to supplement the compensation payable to claimants under the Convention in respect of death, or personal injury, of passengers. Such a system shall fulfil the following conditions:

(a) it shall not in any circumstances impose upon the carrier, his servants or agents, any liability in addition to that provided under this Convention;

(b) it shall not impose upon the carrier any financial or administrative burden other than collecting in that State contributions from passengers if required so to do;

(c) it shall not give rise to any discrimination between carriers with regard to the passengers concerned and the benefits available to the said passengers under the system shall be extended to them regardless of the carrier whose services they have used;

(d) if a passenger has contributed to the system, any person suffering damage as a consequence of death or personal injury of such passenger shall be entitled to the benefits of the system."

Article XV

After Article 41 of the Convention, the following Article shall be inserted:

"**Article 42**

1. Without prejudice to the provisions of Article 41, Conferences of the Parties to the Protocol done at Guatemala City on the eighth March 1971 shall be convened during the fifth and tenth years respectively after the date of entry into force of the said Protocol for the purpose of reviewing the limit established in Article 22, paragraph 1 (a) of the Convention as amended by that Protocol.

2. At each of the Conferences mentioned in paragraph 1 of this Article the limit of liability in Article 22, paragraph 1 (a) in force at the respective dates of these Conferences shall not be increased by an amount exceeding one hundred and eighty-seven thousand five hundred francs.
3. Subject to paragraph 2 of this Article, unless before the thirty-first December of the fifth and tenth years after the date of entry into force of the Protocol referred to in paragraph 1 of this Article the aforesaid Conferences decide otherwise by a two-thirds majority vote of the Parties present and voting, the limit of liability in Article 22, paragraph 1 (a) in force at the respective dates of these Conferences shall on those dates be increased by one hundred and eighty-seven thousand five hundred francs.
4. The applicable limit shall be that which, in accordance with the preceding paragraphs, is in effect on the date of the event which caused the death or personal injury of the passenger."

Chapter II – Scope of Application of the Convention as Amended

Article XVI

The Warsaw Convention as amended at The Hague in 1955 and by this Protocol shall apply to international carriage as defined in Article 1 of the Convention, provided that the places of departure and destination referred to in that Article are situated either in the territories of two Parties to this Protocol or within the territory of a single Party to this Protocol with an agreed stopping place in the territory of another State.

Chapter III – Final Clauses

Article XVII

As between the Parties to this Protocol, the Warsaw Convention as amended at The Hague in 1955 and this Protocol shall be read and interpreted together as one single instrument and shall be known as the *Warsaw Convention as amended at The Hague, 1955,* and at *Guatemala City, 1971.*

Article XVIII

Until the date on which this Protocol enters into force in accordance with the provisions of Article XX, it shall remain open for signature by all States Members of the United Nations or of any of the Specialized Agencies or of the International Atomic Energy Agency or Parties to the Statute of the International Court of Justice, and by any other State invited by the General Assembly of the United Nations to become a Party to this Protocol.

Article XIX

1. This Protocol shall be subject to ratification by the signatory States.
2. Ratification of this Protocol by any State which is not a Party to the Warsaw Convention or by any State which is not a Party to the Warsaw Convention as amended at The Hague, 1955, shall have the effect of accession to the Warsaw Convention as amended at the Hague, 1955, and at Guatemala City, 1971.
3. The instruments of ratification shall be deposited with the International Civil Aviation Organization.

Article XX

1. This Protocol shall enter into force on the ninetieth day after the deposit of the thirtieth instrument of ratification on the condition, however, that the total international scheduled air traffic, expressed in passenger-kilometers, according to the statistics for the year 1970 published by the International Civil Aviation Organization, of the airlines of five States which have ratified this Protocol, represents at least 40% of the total international scheduled air traffic of the airlines of the member States of the International Civil Aviation Organization in that year. If, at the time of deposit of the thirtieth instrument of ratification, this condition has not been fulfilled, the Protocol shall not come into force until the ninetieth day after this condition shall have been satisfied. This Protocol shall come into force for each State ratifying after the deposit of the last instrument of ratification necessary for entry into force of this Protocol on the ninetieth day after the deposit of its instrument of ratification.
2. As soon as this Protocol comes into force it shall be registered with the United Nations by the International Civil Aviation Organization.

Article XXI

1. After the entry into force of this Protocol it shall be open for accession by any State referred to in Article XVIII.
2. Accession to this Protocol by any State which is not a Party to the Warsaw Convention or by any State which is not a Party to the Warsaw Convention as amended at The Hague, 1955, shall have the effect of accession to the Warsaw Convention as amended at The Hague, 1955, and at Guatemala City, 1971.
3. Accession shall be effected by the deposit of an instrument of accession with the International Civil Aviation Organization and shall take effect on the ninetieth day after the deposit.

Article XXII

1. Any Party to this Protocol may denounce the Protocol by notification addressed to the International Civil Aviation Organization.
2. Denunciation shall take effect six months after the date of receipt by the International Civil Aviation Organization of the notification of denunciation.
3. As between the Parties to this Protocol, denunciation by any of them of the Warsaw Convention in accordance with Article 39 thereof or of the Hague Protocol in accordance with Article XXIV thereof shall not be construed in any way as a denunciation of the Warsaw Convention as amended at The Hague, 1955, and at Guatemala City, 1971.

Article XXIII

1. Only the following reservations may be made to this Protocol:

    (a) a State whose courts are not authorized under its law to award the costs of the action including lawyers' fees may at any time by a notification addressed to the International Civil Aviation Organization declare that Article 22, paragraph 3 (a) shall not apply to its courts; and
    (b) a State may at any time declare by a notification addressed to the International Civil Aviation Organization that the Warsaw Convention as amended at The Hague 1955, and at Guatemala City, 1971 shall not apply to the carriage of persons, baggage and cargo for its military authorities on aircraft, registered in that State, the whole capacity of which has been reserved by or on behalf of such authorities.

2. Any State having made a reservation in accordance with the preceding paragraph may at any time withdraw such reservation by notification to the International Civil Aviation Organization.

Article XXIV

The International Civil Aviation Organization shall promptly inform all signatory or acceding States of the date of each signature, the date of deposit of each instrument of ratification or accession, the date of entry into force of this Protocol, and other relevant information.

Article XXV

As between the Parties to this Protocol which are also Parties to the Convention, Supplementary to the Warsaw Convention, for the Unification of Certain Rules Relating to International Carriage by Air Performed by a Person Other than the Contracting Carrier, signed at Guadalajara on 18 September 1961 (hereinafter referred to as the "Guadalajara Convention") any reference to the

"Warsaw Convention" contained in the Guadalajara Convention shall include reference to the Warsaw Convention as amended at The Hague, 1955, and at Guatemala City, 1971, in cases where the carriage under the agreement referred to in Article 1, paragraph (b) of the Guadalajara Convention is governed by this Protocol.

Article XXVI

This Protocol shall remain open, until 30 September 1971, for signature by any State referred to in Article XVIII, at the Ministry of External Relations of the Republic of Guatemala and thereafter, until it enters into force in accordance with Article XX, at the International Civil Aviation Organization. The Government of the Republic of Guatemala shall promptly inform the International Civil Aviation Organization of any signature and the date thereof during the time that the Protocol shall be open for signature in Guatemala.

IN WITNESS WHEREOF the undersigned Plenipotentiaries, having been duly authorized, have signed this Protocol.

DONE at Guatemala City on the eighth day of the month of March of the year One Thousand Nine Hundred and Seventy-one in three authentic texts in the English, French and Spanish languages. The International Civil Aviation Organization shall establish an authentic text of this Protocol in the Russian language. In the case of any inconsistency, the text in the French language, in which language the Warsaw Convention of 12 October 1929 was drawn up, shall prevail.

2.3 Montreal Additional Protocol No. 1, 1975

ADDITIONAL PROTOCOL NO. 1 TO AMEND CONVENTION FOR THE UNIFICATION OF CERTAIN RULES RELATING TO INTERNATIONAL CARRIAGE BY AIR SIGNED AT WARSAW ON 12 OCTOBER 1929, SIGNED AT MONTREAL, ON 25 SEPTEMBER 1975

THE GOVERNMENTS UNDERSIGNED

CONSIDERING that it is desirable to amend the Convention for the Unification of Certain Rules Relating to International Carriage by Air signed at Warsaw on 12 October 1929,

HAVE AGREED as follows:

Chapter I – Amendments to the Convention

Article I

The Convention which the provisions of the present Chapter modify is the Warsaw Convention, 1929.

Article II

Article 22 of the Convention shall be deleted and replaced by the following:

"Article 22

1. In the carriage of passengers the liability of the carrier for each passenger is limited to the sum of 8 300 Special Drawing Rights. Where, in accordance with the law of the court seised of the case, damages may be awarded in the form of periodic payments, the equivalent capital value of the said payments shall not exceed this limit. Nevertheless, by special contract, the carrier and the passenger may agree to a higher limit of liability.

2. In the carriage of registered baggage and of cargo, the liability of the carrier is limited to a sum of 17 Special Drawing Rights per kilogramme, unless the consignor has made, at the time when the package was handed over to the carrier, a special declaration of interest in delivery at destination and has paid a supplementary sum if the case so requires. In that case the carrier will be liable to pay a sum not exceeding the declared sum, unless he proves that that sum is greater than the consignor's actual interest in delivery at destination.

3. As regards objects of which the passenger takes charge himself the liability of the carrier is limited to 332 Special Drawing Rights per passenger.

4. The sums mentioned in terms of the Special Drawing Right in this Article shall be deemed to refer to the Special Drawing Right as defined by the International Monetary Fund. Conversion of the sums into national currencies shall, in case of judicial proceedings, be made according to the value of such currencies in terms of the Special Drawing Right at the date of the judgment. The value of a national currency, in terms of the Special Drawing Right, of a High Contracting Party which is a Member of the International Monetary Fund, shall be calculated in accordance with the method of valuation applied by the International Monetary Fund, in effect at the date of the judgment, for its operations and transactions. The value of a national currency, in terms of the Special Drawing Right, of a High Contracting Party which is not a Member of the International Monetary Fund, shall be calculated in a manner determined by that High Contracting Party.

   Nevertheless, those States which are not Members of the International Monetary Fund and whose law does not permit the application of the provisions of paragraphs 1, 2 and 3 of Article 22 may, at the time of ratification or accession or at any time thereafter, declare that the limit of liability of the carrier in judicial proceedings in their territories is fixed at a sum of 125 000 monetary units per passenger with respect to paragraph 1 of Article 22; 250 monetary units per kilogramme with respect to paragraph 2 of Article 22; and 5 000 monetary units per passenger with respect to paragraph 3 of Article 22. This monetary unit corresponds to sixty-five and a half milligrammes of gold of millesimal fineness nine hundred. These sums may be converted into the national currency concerned in round figures. The conversion of these sums into national currency shall be made according to the law of the State concerned."

Chapter II – Scope of Application of the Convention as Amended

Article III

The Warsaw Convention as amended by this Protocol shall apply to international carriage as defined in Article 1 of the Convention, provided that the place of departure and destination referred to in that Article are situated either in the territories of two Parties to this Protocol, or within the territory of a single Party to this Protocol with an agreed stopping place in the territory of another State.

Chapter III – Final Clauses

Article IV

As between the Parties to this Protocol, the Convention and the Protocol shall be read and interpreted together as one single instrument and shall be known as the *Warsaw Convention as amended by Additional Protocol No. 1 of Montreal, 1975.*

Article V

Until the date on which this Protocol comes into force in accordance with the provisions of Article VII, it shall remain open for signature by any State.

Article VI

1. This Protocol shall be subject to ratification by the signatory States.
2. Ratification of this Protocol by any State which is not a Party to the Warsaw Convention shall have the effect of accession to the Convention as amended by this Protocol.
3. The instruments of ratification shall be deposited with the Government of the Polish People's Republic.

Article VII

1. As soon as thirty signatory States have deposited their instruments of ratification of this Protocol, it shall come into force between them on the ninetieth day after the deposit of the thirtieth instrument of ratification. It shall come into force for each State ratifying thereafter on the ninetieth day after the deposit of its instrument of ratification.
2. As soon as this Protocol comes into force it shall be registered with the United Nations by the Government of the Polish People's Republic.

Article VIII

1. This Protocol, after it has come into force, shall be open for accession by any non-signatory State.
2. Accession to this Protocol by any State which is not a Party to the Convention shall have the effect of accession to the Convention as amended by this Protocol.

3. Accession shall be effected by the deposit of an instrument of accession with the Government of the Polish People's Republic and shall take effect on the ninetieth day after the deposit.

Article IX

1. Any Party to this Protocol may denounce the Protocol by notification addressed to the Government of the Polish People's Republic.
2. Denunciation shall take effect six months after the receipt by the Government of the Polish People's Republic of the notification of denunciation.
3. As between the Parties to this Protocol, denunciation by any of them of the Convention in accordance with Article 39 thereof shall not be construed in any way as a denunciation of the Convention as amended by this Protocol.

Article X

No reservation may be made to this Protocol.

Article XI

The Government of the Polish People's Republic shall promptly inform all States Parties to the Warsaw Convention or of that Convention as amended, all signatory or acceding States to the present Protocol, as well as the International Civil Aviation Organization, of the date of each signature, the date of deposit of each instrument of ratification or accession, the date of coming into force of this Protocol, and other relevant information.

Article XII

As between the Parties to this Protocol which are also Parties to the Convention, Supplementary to the Warsaw Convention, for the Unification of Certain Rules Relating to International Carriage by Air Performed by a Person Other than the Contracting Carrier, signed at Guadalajara on 18 September 1961 (hereinafter referred to as the "Guadalajara Convention") any reference to the "Warsaw Convention" contained in the Guadalajara Convention shall include reference to the *Warsaw Convention as amended by Additional Protocol No. 1 of Montreal, 1975*, in cases where the carriage under the agreement referred to in Article 1, paragraph (b) of the Guadalajara Convention is governed by this Protocol.

Article XIII

This Protocol shall remain open for signature until 1 January 1976 at the Headquarters of the International Civil Aviation Organization and thereafter until it comes into force in accordance with Article VII at the Ministry for Foreign Affairs of the Polish People's Republic. The International Civil Aviation Organization shall promptly inform the Government of the Polish People's Republic of any signature and the date thereof during the time that the Protocol shall be open for signature at the Headquarters of the International Civil Aviation Organization.

IN WITNESS WHEREOF the undersigned Plenipotentiaries, having been duly authorized, have signed this Protocol.

DONE at Montreal on the twenty-fifth day of the month of September of the year One Thousand Nine Hundred and Seventy-five in four authentic texts in the English, French, Russian and Spanish languages. In the case of any inconsistency, the text in the French language, in which language the Warsaw Convention of 12 October 1929 was drawn up, shall prevail.

2.4 Montreal Additional Protocol No. 2, 1975

ADDITIONAL PROTOCOL NO. 2 TO AMEND THE CONVENTION FOR THE UNIFICATION OF CERTAIN RULES RELATING TO INTERNATIONAL CARRIAGE BY AIR, SIGNED AT WARSAW ON 12 OCTOBER 1929, AS AMENDED BY THE PROTOCOL DONE AT THE HAGUE ON 28 SEPTEMBER 1955, SIGNED AT MONTREAL ON 25 SEPTEMBER 1975

THE GOVERNMENTS UNDERSIGNED

CONSIDERING that it is desirable to amend the Convention for the Unification of Certain Rules Relating to International Carriage by Air signed at Warsaw on 12 October 1929 as amended by the Protocol done at The Hague on 28 September 1955,

HAVE AGREED as follows:

Chapter I – Amendments to the Convention

Article I

The Convention which the provisions of the present Chapter modify is the Warsaw Convention as amended at The Hague in 1955.

Article II

Article 22 of the Convention shall be deleted and replaced by the following:

"Article 22

1. In the carriage of persons the liability of the carrier for each passenger is limited to the sum of 16 600 Special Drawing Rights. Where, in accordance with the law of the court seised of the case, damages may be awarded in the form of periodic payments, the equivalent capital value of the said

payments shall not exceed this limit. Nevertheless, by special contract, the carrier and the passenger may agree to a higher limit of liability.

2. (a) In the carriage of registered baggage and of cargo, the liability of the carrier is limited to a sum of 17 Special Drawing Rights per kilogramme, unless the passenger or consignor has made, at the time when the package was handed over to the carrier, a special declaration of interest in delivery at destination and has paid a supplementary sum if the case so requires. In that case the carrier will be liable to pay a sum not exceeding the declared sum, unless he proves that that sum is greater than the passenger's or consignor's actual interest in delivery at destination.

    (b) In the case of loss, damage or delay of part of registered baggage or cargo, or of any object contained therein, the weight to be taken into consideration in determining the amount to which the carrier's liability is limited shall be only the total weight of the package or packages concerned. Nevertheless, when the loss, damage or delay of a part of the registered baggage or cargo, or of an object contained therein, affects the value of other packages covered by the same baggage check or the same air waybill, the total weight of such package or packages shall also be taken into consideration in determining the limit of liability.

3. As regards objects of which the passenger takes charge himself the liability of the carrier is limited to 332 Special Drawing Rights per passenger.

4. The limits prescribed in this Article shall not prevent the court from awarding, in accordance with its own law, in addition, the whole or part of court costs and of the other expenses of the litigation incurred by the plaintiff. The foregoing provision shall not apply if the amount of the damages awarded, excluding court costs and other expenses of the litigation, does not exceed the sum which the carrier has offered in writing to the plaintiff within a period of six months from the date of the occurrence causing the damage, or before the commencement of the action, if that is later.

5. The sums mentioned in terms of the Special Drawing Right in this Article shall be deemed to refer to the Special Drawing Right as defined by the International Monetary Fund. Conversion of the sums into national currencies shall, in case of judicial proceedings, be made according to the value of currencies in terms of the Special Drawing Right at the date of the judgment. The value of a national currency, in terms of the Special Drawing Right, of a High Contracting Party which is a Member of the International Monetary Fund, shall be calculated in accordance with the method of valuation by the International Monetary Fund, in effect at the date of the judgment, for its operations and transactions. The value of a national currency, in terms of the Special Drawing Right, of a High Contracting Party is not a Member of the International Monetary Fund, shall be calculated in a manner determined by that High Contracting Party.

Nevertheless, those States which are not Members of the International Monetary Fund and whose law does not permit the application of the provisions of paragraphs 1, 2(a) and 3 of Article 22 may at the time of ratification or accession or at any time thereafter, declare that the limit of liability of the carrier in judicial proceedings in their territories is fixed at a sum of 250 000 monetary units per passenger with respect to paragraph 1 of Article 22; 250 monetary units per kilogramme with respect to paragraph 2(a) of Article 22; and 5 000 monetary units per passenger with respect to paragraph 3 of Article 22. This monetary unit corresponds to sixty-five and a half milligrammes of gold of millesimal fineness nine hundred. These sums may be converted into the national currency concerned in round figures. The of these sums into national currency shall be made according to the law of the State concerned."

Chapter II – Scope of application of the Convention as amended

Article III

The Warsaw Convention as amended at The Hague in 1955 and by this Protocol shall apply to international carriage as defined in Article 1 of the Convention, provided that the places of departure and destination referred to in that Article are situated either in the territories of two Parties to this Protocol or within the territory of a single Party to this Protocol with an agreed stopping place in the territory of another State.

Chapter III – Final Clauses

Article IV

As between the Parties to this Protocol, the Warsaw Convention as amended at The Hague in 1955 and this Protocol shall be read and interpreted together as one single instrument and shall be known as the *Warsaw Convention as amended at The Hague, 1955, and by Additional Protocol No. 2 of Montreal, 1975.*

Article V

Until the date on which this Protocol comes into force in accordance with the provisions of Article VII, it shall remain open for signature by any State.

Article VI

1. This Protocol shall be subject to ratification by the signatory States.
2. Ratification of this Protocol by any State which is not a Party to the Warsaw Convention or by any State which is not a Party to the Warsaw Convention

as amended at The Hague, 1955, shall have the effect of accession to the *Warsaw Convention as amended at The Hague, 1955, and by Additional Protocol No. 2 of Montreal, 1975.*

3. The instruments of ratification shall be deposited with the Government of the Polish People's Republic.

Article VII

1. As soon as thirty signatory States have deposited their instruments of ratification of this Protocol, it shall come into force between them on the ninetieth day after the deposit of the thirtieth instrument of ratification. It shall come into force for each State ratifying thereafter on the ninetieth day after the deposit of its instrument of ratification.
2. As soon as this Protocol comes into force it shall be registered with the United Nations by the Government of the Polish People's Republic.

Article VIII

1. This Protocol, after it has come into force, shall be open for accession by any non-signatory State.
2. Accession to this Protocol by any State which is not a Party to the Warsaw Convention or by any State which is not a Party to the Warsaw Convention as amended at The Hague, 1955, shall have the effect of accession to the *Warsaw Convention as amended at The Hague, 1955, and by Additional Protocol No. 2 of Montreal, 1975.*
3. Accession shall be effected by the deposit of an instrument of accession with the Government of the Polish People's Republic and shall take effect on the ninetieth day after the deposit.

Article IX

1. Any Party to this Protocol may denounce the Protocol by notification addressed to the Government of the Polish People's Republic.
2. Denunciation shall take effect six months after the date of receipt by the Government of the Polish People's Republic of the notification of denunciation.
3. As between the Parties to this Protocol, denunciation by any of them of the Warsaw Convention in accordance with Article 39 thereof or of the Hague Protocol in accordance with Article XXIV thereof shall not be construed in any way as a denunciation of the *Warsaw Convention as amended at The Hague, 1955, and by Additional Protocol No. 2 of Montreal, 1975.*

Article X

No reservation may be made to this Protocol except that a State may at any time declare by a notification addressed to the Government of the Polish People's Republic that the Convention as amended by this Protocol shall not apply to the carriage of persons, cargo and baggage for its military authorities on aircraft, registered in that State, the whole capacity of which has been reserved by or on behalf of such authorities.

Article XI

The Government of the Polish People's Republic shall promptly inform all States Parties to the Warsaw Convention or to that Convention as amended, all signatory or acceding States to the present Protocol, as well as the International Civil Aviation Organization, of the date of each signature, the date of deposit of each instrument of ratification or accession, the date of coming into force of this Protocol, and other relevant information.

Article XII

As between the Parties to this Protocol which are also Parties to the Convention, Supplementary to the Warsaw Convention, for the Unification of Certain Rules Relating to International Carriage by Air Performed by a Person Other than the Contracting Carrier, signed at Guadalajara on 18 September 1961 (hereinafter referred to as the "Guadalajara Convention") any reference to the "Warsaw Convention" contained in the Guadalajara Convention shall include reference to the *Warsaw Convention as amended at The Hague, 1955, and by Additional Protocol No. 2 of Montreal, 1975*, in cases where the carriage under the agreement referred to in Article 1, paragraph (b) of the Guadalajara Convention is governed by this Protocol.

Article XIII

This Protocol shall remain open for signature until 1 January 1976 at the Headquarters of the International Civil Aviation Organization and thereafter until it comes into force in accordance with Article VII at the Ministry for Foreign Affairs of the Polish People's Republic. The International Civil Aviation Organization shall promptly inform the Government of the Polish People's Republic of any signature and the date thereof during the time that the Protocol shall be open for signature at the Headquarters of the International Civil Aviation Organization.

IN WITNESS WHEREOF the undersigned Plenipotentiaries, having been duly authorized, have signed this Protocol.

DONE at Montreal on the twenty-fifth day of the month of September of the year One Thousand Nine Hundred and Seventy-five in four authentic texts in the English, French, Russian and Spanish languages. In the case of any inconsistency, the text in the French language, in which language the Warsaw Convention of 12 October 1929 was drawn up, shall prevail.

2.5 Montreal Additional Protocol No. 3, 1975

ADDITIONAL PROTOCOL NO. 3 TO AMEND CONVENTION FOR THE UNIFICATION OF CERTAIN RULES RELATING TO INTERNATIONAL CARRIAGE BY AIR SIGNED AT WARSAW ON 12 OCTOBER 1929, AS AMENDED BY THE PROTOCOL DONE AT THE HAGUE ON 28 SEPTEMBER 1955 AND AT GUATEMALA CITY ON 8 MARCH 1971, SIGNED AT MONTREAL, ON 25 SEPTEMBER 1975

THE GOVERNMENTS UNDERSIGNED

CONSIDERING that it is desirable to amend the Convention for the Unification of Certain Rules Relating to International Carriage by Air signed at Warsaw on 12 October 1929 as amended by the Protocols done at The Hague on 28 September 1955, and at Guatemala City on 8 March 1971,

HAVE AGREED as follows:

Chapter I – Amendments to the Convention

Article 1

The Convention which the provisions of the present Chapter modify is the Warsaw Convention as amended at The Hague in 1955, and at Guatemala City in 1971.

Article II

Article 22 of the Convention shall be deleted and replaced by the following:

"Article 22

1. (a) In the carriage of persons the liability of the carrier is limited to the sum of 100 000 Special Drawing Rights for the aggregate of the claims, however founded, in respect of damage suffered as a result of the death

or personal injury of each passenger. Where, in accordance with the law of the court seised of the case, damages may be awarded in the form of periodic payments, the equivalent capital value of the said payments shall not exceed 100 000 Special Drawing Rights.

(b) In the case of delay in the carriage of persons the liability of the carrier for each passenger is limited to 4 150 Special Drawing Rights.

(c) In the carriage of baggage the liability of the carrier in the case of destruction, loss, damage or delay is limited to 1 000 Special Drawing Rights for each passenger.

2. (a) In the carriage of cargo, the liability of the carrier is limited to a sum of 17 Special Drawing Rights per kilogramme, unless the consignor has made, at the time when the package was handed over to the carrier, a special declaration of interest in delivery at destination and has paid a supplementary sum if the case so requires. In that case the carrier will be liable to pay a sum not exceeding the declared sum, unless he proves that that sum is greater than the consignor's actual interest in delivery at destination.

(b) In the case of loss, damage or delay of part of the cargo, or of any object contained therein, the weight to be taken into consideration in determining the amount to which the carrier's liability is limited shall be the total weight of the package or packages concerned. Nevertheless, when the loss, damage or delay of a part of the cargo, or of an object contained therein, affects the value of other packages covered by the same air waybill, the total weight of such package or packages shall also be taken into consideration in determining the limit of liability.

3. (a) The courts of the High Contracting Parties which are not authorized under their law to award the costs of the action, including lawyers' fees, shall, in actions to which this Convention applies, have the power to award, in their discretion, to the claimant the whole or part of the costs of the action, including lawyers' fees which the court considers reasonable.

(b) The costs of the action including lawyers' fees shall be awarded in accordance with subparagraph (a) only if the claimant gives a written notice to the carrier of the amount claimed including the particulars of the calculation of that amount and the carrier does not make, within a period of six months after his receipt of such notice, a written offer of settlement in an amount at least equal to the compensation awarded within the applicable limit. This period will be extended until the time of commencement of the action if that is later.

(c) The costs of the action including lawyers' fees shall not be taken into account in applying the limits under this Article.

4. The sums mentioned in terms of Special Drawing Right in this Article and Article 42 shall be deemed to refer to the Special Drawing Right as defined by the International Monetary Fund. Conversion of the sums into national currencies shall, in case of judicial proceedings, be made according to the value of such currencies in terms of the Special Drawing Right at the date of the judgment. The value of a national currency, in terms of the Special Drawing Right, of a High Contracting Party which is a Member of the International Monetary Fund, shall be calculated in accordance with the method of valuation applied by the International Monetary Fund, in effect at the date of the judgment, for its operations and transactions. The value of a national currency, in terms of the Special Drawing Right, of a High Contracting Party which is not a Member of the International Monetary Fund, shall be calculated in a manner determined by that High Contracting Party.

Nevertheless, those States which are not Members of the International Monetary Fund and whose law does not permit the application of the provisions of paragraphs 1 and 2(a) of Article 22 may, at the time of ratification or accession or at any time thereafter, declare that the limit of liability of the carrier in judicial proceedings in their territories is fixed at a sum of 1 500 000 monetary units per passenger with respect to paragraph 1(a) of Article 22; 62 500 monetary units per passenger with respect to paragraph 1(b) of Article 22; 15 000 monetary units per passenger with respect to paragraph 1(c) of Article 22; and 250 monetary units per kilogramme with respect to paragraph 2(a) of Article 22. A State applying the provisions of this paragraph may also declare that the sum referred to in paragraphs 2 and 3 of Article 42 shall be the sum of 187 500 monetary units. This monetary unit corresponds to sixty-five and a half milligrammes of gold of millesimal fineness nine hundred. These sums may be converted into the national currency concerned in round figures. The conversion of these sums into national currency shall be made according to the law of the State concerned."

Article III

In Article 42 of the Convention paragraphs 2 and 3 shall be deleted and replaced by the following:

"2. At each of the Conferences mentioned in paragraph 1 of this Article the limit of liability in Article 22, paragraph 1 (a) in force at the respective dates of these Conferences shall not be increased by an amount exceeding 12 500 Special Drawing Rights.

3. Subject to paragraph 2 of this Article, unless before the thirty-first December of the fifth and tenth year after the date of entry into force of the Protocol referred to in paragraph 1 of this Article the aforesaid Conferences decide otherwise by a two-thirds majority vote of the Parties

present and voting, the limit of liability in Article 22, paragraph 1 (a) in force at the respective dates of these Conferences shall on those dates be increased by 12 500 Special Drawing Rights."

Chapter II – Scope of Application of the Convention as Amended

Article IV

The Warsaw Convention as amended at The Hague in 1955, and at Guatemala City in 1971 and by this Protocol shall apply to international carriage as defined in Article 1 of the Convention, provided that the places of departure and destination referred to in that Article are situated either in the territories of two Parties to this Protocol or within the territory of a single Party to this Protocol with an agreed stopping place in the territory of another State.

Chapter III – Final Clauses

Article V

As between the Parties to this Protocol, the Warsaw Convention as amended at The Hague in 1955 and at Guatemala City in 1971, and this Protocol shall be read and interpreted together as one single instrument and shall be known as the *Warsaw Convention as amended at The Hague, 1955, at Guatemala City, 1971, and by the Additional Protocol No. 3 of Montreal, 1975.*

Article VI

Until the date on which this Protocol comes into force in accordance with the provisions of Article VIII, it shall remain open for signature by any State.

Article VII

1. This Protocol shall be subject to ratification by the signatory States.
2. Ratification of this Protocol by any State which is not a Party to the Warsaw Convention or by any State which is not a Party to the Warsaw Convention as amended at The Hague, 1955, or by any State which is not a Party to the Warsaw Convention as amended at The Hague, 1955, and at Guatemala City, 1971, shall have the effect of accession to the *Warsaw Convention as amended at The Hague, 1955, at Guatemala City, 1971, and by the Additional Protocol No. 3 of Montreal, 1975.*
3. The instruments of ratification shall be deposited with the Government of the Polish People's Republic.

Article VIII

1. As soon as thirty signatory States have deposited their instruments of ratification of this Protocol, it shall come into force between them on the ninetieth day after the deposit of the thirtieth instrument of ratification. It shall come into force for each State ratifying thereafter on the ninetieth day after the deposit of its instrument of ratification.
2. As soon as this Protocol comes into force it shall be registered with the United Nations by the Government of the Polish People's Republic.

Article IX

1. This Protocol, after it has come into force, shall be open for accession by any non-signatory State.
2. Accession to this Protocol by any State which is not a Party to the Warsaw Convention or by any State which is not a Party to the Warsaw Convention as amended at The Hague, 1955, or by any State not a Party to the Warsaw Convention as amended at The Hague, 1955, and at Guatemala City, 1971, shall have the effect of accession to the *Warsaw Convention as amended at The Hague, 1955, at Guatemala City, 1971, and by the Additional Protocol No. 3 of Montreal, 1975.*
3. Accession shall be effected by the deposit of an instrument of accession with the Government of the Polish People's Republic and shall take effect on the ninetieth day after the deposit.

Article X

1. Any Party to this Protocol may denounce the Protocol by notification addressed to the Government of the Polish People's Republic.
2. Denunciation shall take effect six months after the date of receipt by the Government of the Polish People's Republic of the notification of denunciation.
3. As between the Parties to this Protocol, denunciation by any of them of the Warsaw Convention in accordance with Article 39 thereof or of The Hague Protocol in accordance with Article XXIV thereof or of the Guatemala City Protocol in accordance with Article XXII thereof shall not be construed in any way as a denunciation of the *Warsaw Convention as amended at The Hague, 1955, at Guatemala City, 1971, and by the Additional Protocol No. 3 of Montreal, 1975.*

Article XI

1. Only the following reservations may be made to this Protocol:

   (a) any State whose courts are not authorized under its law to award the costs of the action including lawyers' fees may at any time by a notification addressed to the Government of the Polish People's Republic declare that Article 22, paragraph 3(a) shall not apply to its courts;

(b) any State may at any time declare by a notification addressed to the Government of the Polish People's Republic that the *Warsaw Convention as amended at The Hague, 1955, at Guatemala City, 1971, and by the Additional Protocol No. 3 of Montreal, 1975*, shall not apply to the carriage of persons, baggage and cargo for its military authorities on aircraft, registered in that State, the whole capacity of which has been reserved by or on behalf of such authorities; and

(c) any State may declare at the time of ratification of or accession to the Montreal Protocol No. 4 of 1975, or at any time thereafter, that it is not bound by the provisions of the *Warsaw Convention as amended at The Hague, 1955, at Guatemala City, 1971, and by the Additional Protocol No. 3 of Montreal, 1975*, in so far as they relate to the carriage of cargo, mail and postal packages. Such declaration shall have effect ninety days after the date of receipt by the Government of the Polish People's Republic of the declaration.

2. Any State having made a reservation in accordance with the preceding paragraph may at any time withdraw such reservation by notification to the Government of the Polish People's Republic.

Article XII

The Government of the Polish People's Republic shall promptly inform all States Parties to the Warsaw Convention or to that Convention as amended, all signatory or acceding States to the present Protocol, as well as the International Civil Aviation Organization, of the date of each signature, the date of deposit of each instrument of ratification or accession, the date of coming into force of this Protocol, and other relevant information.

Article XIII

As between the Parties to this Protocol which are also Parties to the Convention, Supplementary to the Warsaw Convention, for the Unification of Certain Rules Relating to International Carriage by Air Performed by a Person Other than the Contracting Carrier, signed at Guadalajara on 18 September 1961 (hereinafter referred to as the "Guadalajara Convention") any reference to the "Warsaw Convention" contained in the Guadalajara Convention shall include reference to the Warsaw Convention as amended at The Hague, 1955, at Guatemala City, 1971, and by the Additional Protocol No. 3 of Montreal, 1975, in cases where the carriage under the agreement referred to in Article 1, paragraph (b) of the Guadalajara Convention is governed by this Protocol.

Article XIV

This Protocol shall remain open for signature until 1 January 1976 at the Headquarters of the International Civil Aviation Organization and thereafter until it comes into force in accordance with Article VIII at the Ministry for Foreign Affairs of the Polish People's Republic. The International Civil Aviation Organization shall promptly inform the Government of the Polish People's Republic of any signature and the date thereof during the time that the Protocol shall be open for signature at the Headquarters of the International Civil Aviation Organization.

IN WITNESS WHEREOF the undersigned Plenipotentiaries, having been duly authorized, have signed this Protocol.

DONE at Montreal on the twenty-fifth day of September of the year One Thousand Nine Hundred and Seventy-five in four authentic texts in the English, French, Russian and Spanish languages. In the case of any inconsistency, the text in the French language, in which language the Warsaw Convention of 12 October 1929 was drawn up, shall prevail.

2.6 Montreal Protocol No. 4, 1975

ADDITIONAL PROTOCOL NO. 4 TO AMEND
CONVENTION FOR THE UNIFICATION OF CERTAIN
RULES RELATING TO INTERNATIONAL CARRIAGE
BY AIR SIGNED AT WARSAW ON 12 OCTOBER 1929,
AS AMENDED BY THE PROTOCOL DONE AT THE
HAGUE ON 28 SEPTEMBER 1955, SIGNED AT
MONTREAL ON 25 SEPTEMBER 1975

THE GOVERNMENTS UNDERSIGNED

CONSIDERING that it is desirable to amend the Convention for the
Unification of Certain Rules Relating to International Carriage by Air signed
at Warsaw on 12 October 1929 as amended by the Protocol done at The Hague
on 28 September 1955,

HAVE AGREED as follows:

Chapter I – Amendments to the Convention

Article I

The Convention which the provisions of the present Chapter modify is the
Warsaw Convention as amended at The Hague in 1955.

Article II

In Article 2 of the Convention- paragraph 2 shall be deleted and replaced by
the following:

"2. In the carriage of postal items the carrier shall be liable only to the relevant
    postal administration in accordance with the rules applicable to the
    relationship between the carriers and the postal administrations.

3. Except as provided in paragraph 2 of this Article, the provisions of this Convention shall not apply to the carriage of postal items."

Article III

In Chapter II of the Convention- Section III (Articles 5 to 16) shall be deleted and replaced by the following:

"Section III – Documentation relating to cargo

Article 5

1. In respect of the carriage of cargo an air waybill shall be delivered.
2. Any other means which would preserve a record of the carriage to be performed may, with the consent of the consignor, be substituted for the delivery of an air waybill. If such other means are used, the carrier shall, if so requested by the consignor, deliver to the consignor a receipt for the cargo permitting identification of the consignment and access to the information contained in the record preserved by such other means.
3. The impossibility of using, at points of transit and destination, the other means which would preserve the record of the carriage referred to in paragraph 2 of this Article does not entitle the carrier to refuse to accept the cargo for carriage.

Article 6

1. The air waybill shall be made out by the consignor in three original parts.
2. The first part shall be marked "for the carrier"; it shall be signed by the consignor. The second part shall be marked "for the consignee"; it shall be signed by the consignor and by the carrier. The third part shall be signed by the carrier and handed by him to the consignor after the cargo has been accepted.
3. The signature of the carrier and that of the consignor may be printed or stamped.
4. If, at the request of the consignor, the carrier makes out the air waybill, he shall be deemed, subject to proof to the contrary, to have done so on behalf of the consignor.

Article 7

When there is more than one package:

(a) the carrier of cargo has the right to require the consignor to make out separate air waybills;
(b) the consignor has the right to require the carrier to deliver separate receipts when the other means referred to in paragraph 2 of Article 5 are used.

Article 8

The air waybill and the receipt for the cargo shall contain:

    (a) an indication of the places of departure and destination;

    (b) if the places of departure and destination are within the territory of a single High Contracting Party, one or more agreed stopping places being within the territory of another State, an indication of at least one such stopping place; and

    (c) an indication of the weight of the consignment.

Article 9

Non-compliance with the provisions of Articles 5 to 8 shall not affect the existence or the validity of the contract of carriage, which shall, none the less, be subject to the rules of this Convention including those relating to limitation of liability.

Article 10

1. The consignor is responsible for the correctness of the particulars and statements relating to the cargo inserted by him or on his behalf in the air waybill or furnished by him or on his behalf to the carrier for insertion in the receipt for the cargo or for insertion in the record preserved by the other means referred to in paragraph 2 of Article 5.

2. The consignor shall indemnify the carrier against all damage suffered by him, or by any other person to whom the carrier is liable, by reason of the irregularity, incorrectness or incompleteness of the particulars and statements furnished by the consignor or on his behalf.

3. Subject to the provisions of paragraphs 1 and 2 of this Article, the carrier shall indemnify the consignor against all damage suffered by him, or by any other person to whom the consignor is liable, by reason of the irregularity, incorrectness or incompleteness of the particulars and statements inserted by the carrier or on his behalf in the receipt for the cargo or in the record preserved by the other means referred to in paragraph 2 of Article 5.

Article 11

1. The air waybill or the receipt for the cargo is *prima facie* evidence of the conclusion of the contract, of the acceptance of the cargo and of the conditions of carriage mentioned therein.

2. Any statements in the air waybill or the receipt for the cargo relating to the weight, dimensions and packing of the cargo, as well as those relating to the number of packages, are *prima facie* evidence of the facts stated; those relating to the quantity, volume and condition of the cargo do not constitute evidence against the carrier except so far as they both have been,

and are stated in the air waybill to have been, checked by him in the presence of the consignor, or relate to the apparent condition of the cargo.

Article 12

1. Subject to his liability to carry out all his obligations under the contract of carriage, the consignor has the right to dispose of the cargo by withdrawing it at the airport of departure or destination, or by stopping it in the course of the journey on any landing, or by calling for it to be delivered at the place of destination or in the course of the journey to a person other than the consignee originally designated, or by requiring it to be returned to the airport of departure. He must not exercise this right of disposition in such a way as to prejudice the carrier or other consignors and he must repay any expenses occasioned by the exercise of this right.
2. If it is impossible to carry out the orders of the consignor the carrier must so inform him forthwith.
3. If the carrier obeys the orders of the consignor for the disposition of the cargo without requiring the production of the part of the air waybill or the receipt for the cargo delivered to the latter, he will be liable, without prejudice to his right of recovery from the consignor, for any damage which may be caused thereby to any person who is lawfully in possession of that part of the air waybill or the receipt for the cargo.
4. The right conferred on the consignor ceases at the moment when that of the consignee begins in accordance with Article 13. Nevertheless, if the consignee declines to accept the cargo, or if he cannot be communicated with, the consignor resumes his right of disposition.

Article 13

1. Except when the consignor has exercised his right under Article 12, the consignee is entitled, on arrival of the cargo at the place of destination, to require the carrier to deliver the cargo to him, on payment of the charges due and on complying with the conditions of carriage.
2. Unless it is otherwise agreed, it is the duty of the carrier to give notice to the consignee as soon as the cargo arrives.
3. If the carrier admits the loss of the cargo, or if the cargo has not arrived at the expiration of seven days after the date on which it ought to have arrived, the consignee is entitled to enforce against the carrier the rights which flow from the contract of carriage.

Article 14

The consignor and the consignee can respectively enforce all the rights given them by Articles 12 and 13, each in his own name, whether he is acting in his own interest or in the interest of another, provided that he carries out the obligations imposed by the contract of carriage.

Article 15

1. Articles 12, 13 and 14 do not affect either the relations of the consignor and the consignee with each other or the mutual relations of third parties whose rights are derived either from the consignor or from the consignee.
2. The provisions of Articles 12, 13 and 14 can only be varied by express provision in the air waybill or the receipt for the cargo.

Article 16

1. The consignor must furnish such information and such documents as are necessary to meet the formalities of customs, octroi or police before the cargo can be delivered to the consignee. The consignor is liable to the carrier for any damage occasioned by the absence, insufficiency or irregularity of any such information or documents, unless the damage is due to the fault of the carrier, his servants or agents.
2. The carrier is under no obligation to enquire into the correctness or sufficiency of such information or documents."

Article IV

Article 18 of the Convention shall be deleted and replaced by the following:

"Article 18

1. The carrier is liable for damage sustained in the event of the destruction or loss of, or damage to, any registered baggage, if the occurrence which caused the damage so sustained took place during the carriage by air.
2. The carrier is liable for damage sustained in the event of the destruction or loss of, or damage to, cargo upon condition only that the occurrence which caused the damage so sustained took place during the carriage by air.
3. However, the carrier is not liable if he proves that the destruction, loss of, or damage to, the cargo resulted solely from one or more of the following:

   (a) inherent defect, quality or vice of that cargo;
   (b) defective packing of that cargo performed by a person other than the carrier or his servants or agents;
   (c) an act of war or an armed conflict;
   (d) an act of public authority carried out in connexion with the entry, exit or transit of the cargo.

4. The carriage by air within the meaning of the preceding paragraphs of this Article comprises the period during which the baggage or cargo is in the charge of the carrier, whether in an airport or on board an aircraft, or, in the case of a landing outside an airport, in any place whatsoever.
5. The period of the carriage by air does not extend to any carriage by land, by sea or by river performed outside an airport. If, however, such carriage

takes place in the performance of a contract for carriage by air, for the purpose of loading, delivery or transhipment, any damage is presumed, subject to proof to the contrary, to have been the result of an event which took place during the carriage by air."

Article V

Article 20 of the Convention shall be deleted and replaced by the following:

"**Article 20**

In the carriage of passengers and baggage, and in the case of damage occasioned by delay in the carriage of cargo, the carrier shall not be liable if he proves that he and his servants and agents have taken all necessary measures to avoid the damage or that it was impossible for them to take such measures."

Article VI

Article 21 of the Convention shall be deleted and replaced by the following:

"**Article 21**

1. In the carriage of passengers and baggage, if the carrier proves that the damage was caused by or contributed to by the negligence of the person suffering the damage the Court may, in accordance with the provisions of its own law, exonerate the carrier wholly or partly from his liability.
2. In the carriage of cargo, if the carrier proves that the damage was caused by or contributed to by the negligence or other wrongful act or omission of the person claiming compensation, or the person from whom he derives his rights, the carrier shall be wholly or partly exonerated from his liability to the claimant to the extent that such negligence or wrongful act or omission caused or contributed to the damage."

Article VII

In Article 22 of the Convention –

(a) in paragraph 2 (a) the words "and of cargo" shall be deleted.
(b) after paragraph 2 (a) the following paragraph shall be inserted:

"(b) In the carriage of cargo, the liability of the carrier is limited to a sum of 17 Special Drawing Rights per kilogramme, unless the consignor has made, at the time when the package was handed over to the carrier, a special declaration of interest in delivery at destination and has paid a supplementary sum if the case so requires. In that case the carrier will be liable to pay a sum not exceeding the declared sum, unless he proves that the sum is greater than the consignor's actual interest in delivery at destination."

(c) paragraph 2 (b) shall be designated as paragraph 2 (c).

(d) after paragraph 5 the following paragraph shall be inserted:

"6. The sums mentioned in terms of the Special Drawing Right in this Article shall be deemed to refer to the Special Drawing Right as defined by the International Monetary Fund. Conversion of the sums into national currencies shall, in case of judicial proceedings, be made according to the value of such currencies in terms of the Special Drawing Right at the date of the judgment. The value of a national currency, in terms of the Special Drawing Right, of a High Contracting Party which is a Member of the International Monetary Fund, shall be calculated in accordance with the method of valuation applied by the International Monetary Fund, in effect at the date of the judgment, for its operations and transactions. The value of a national currency, in terms of the Special Drawing Right, of a High Contracting Party which is not a Member of the International Monetary Fund, shall be calculated in a manner determined by that High Contracting Party.

Nevertheless, those States which are not Members of the International Monetary Fund and whose law does not permit the application of the provisions of paragraph 2 (b) of Article 22 may, at the time of ratification or accession or at any time thereafter, declare that the limit of liability of the carrier in judicial proceedings in their territories is fixed at a sum of two hundred and fifty monetary units per kilogramme. This monetary unit corresponds to sixty-five and a half milligrammes of gold of millesimal fineness nine hundred. This sum may be converted into the national currency concerned in round figures. The conversion of this sum into the national currency shall be made according to the law of the State concerned.

Article VIII

Article 24 of the Convention shall be deleted and replaced by the following:

"Article 24

1. In the carriage of passengers and baggage, any action for damages, however founded, can only be brought subject to the conditions and limits set out in this Convention, without prejudice to the question as to who are the persons who have the right to bring suit and what are their respective rights.

2. In the carriage of cargo, any action for damages, however founded, whether under this Convention or in contract or in tort or otherwise, can only be brought subject to the conditions and limits of liability set out in this Convention without prejudice to the question as to who are the persons who have the right to bring suit and what are their respective rights. Such

limits of liability constitute maximum limits and may not be exceeded whatever the circumstances which gave rise to the liability."

Article IX

Article 25 of the Convention shall be deleted and replaced by the following:

"**Article 25**

In the carriage of passengers and baggage, the limits of liability specified in Article 22 shall not apply if it is proved that the damage resulted from an act or omission of the carrier, his servants or agents, done with intent to cause damage or recklessly and with knowledge that damage would probably result; provided that, in the case of such act or omission of a servant or agent, it is also proved that he was acting within the scope of his employment."

Article X

In Article 25 A of the Convention paragraph 3 shall be deleted and replaced by the following:

"3. In the carriage of passengers and baggage, the provisions of paragraphs 1 and 2 of this Article shall not apply if it is proved that the damage resulted from an act or omission of the servant or agent done with intent to cause damage or recklessly and with knowledge that damage would probably result."

Article XI

After Article 30 of the Convention, the following Article shall be inserted:

"**Article 30A**

Nothing in this Convention shall prejudice the question whether a person liable for damage in accordance with its provisions has a right of recourse against any other person."

Article XII

Article 33 of the Convention shall be deleted and replaced by the following:

"**Article 33**

Except as provided in paragraph 3 of Article 5, nothing in this Convention shall prevent the carrier either from refusing to enter into any contract of carriage or from making regulations which do not conflict with the provisions of this Convention."

Article XIII

Article 34 of the Convention shall be deleted and replaced by the following:

"Article 34

The provisions of Articles 3 to 8 inclusive relating to documents of carriage shall not apply in the case of carriage performed in extraordinary circumstances outside the normal scope of an air carrier's business."

Chapter II – Scope of Application of the Convention as Amended

Article XIV

The Warsaw Convention as amended at The Hague in 1955 and by this Protocol shall apply to international carriage as defined in Article 1 of the Convention, provided that the places of departure and destination referred to in that Article are situated either in the territories of two Parties to this Protocol or within the territory of a single Party to this Protocol with an agreed stopping place in the territory of another State.

Chapter III – Final Clauses

Article XV

As between the Parties to this Protocol, the Warsaw Convention as amended at The Hague in 1955 and this Protocol shall be read and interpreted together as one single instrument and shall be known as the *Warsaw Convention as amended at The Hague, 1955, and by Protocol No. 4 of Montreal, 1975.*

Article XVI

Until the date on which this Protocol comes into force in accordance with the provisions of Article XVIII, it shall remain open for signature by any State.

Article XVII

1. This Protocol shall be subject to ratification by the signatory States.
2. Ratification of this Protocol by any State which is not a Party to the Warsaw Convention or by any State which is not a Party to the Warsaw Convention as amended at The Hague, 1955, shall have the effect of accession to the *Warsaw Convention as amended at The Hague, 1955, and by Protocol No. 4 of Montreal, 1975.*
3. The instruments of ratification shall be deposited with the Government of the Polish People's Republic.

Article XVIII

1. As soon as thirty signatory States have deposited their instruments of ratification of this Protocol, it shall come into force between them on the ninetieth day after the deposit of the thirtieth instrument of ratification. It shall come into force for each State ratifying thereafter on the ninetieth day after the deposit of its instrument of ratification.
2. As soon as this Protocol comes into force it shall be registered with the United Nations by the Government of the Polish People's Republic.

Article XIX

1. This Protocol, after it has come into force, shall be open for accession by any non-signatory State.
2. Accession to this Protocol by any State which is not a Party to the Warsaw Convention or by any State which is not a Party to the Warsaw Convention as amended at The Hague, 1955, shall have the effect of accession to the *Warsaw Convention as amended at The Hague, 1955, and by Protocol No. 4 of Montreal, 1975.*
3. Accession shall be effected by the deposit of an instrument of accession with the Government of the Polish People's Republic and shall take effect on the ninetieth day after the deposit.

Article XX

1. Any Party to this Protocol may denounce the Protocol by notification addressed to the Government of the Polish People's Republic.
2. Denunciation shall take effect six months after the date of receipt by the Government of the Polish People's Republic of the notification of denunciation.
3. As between the Parties to this Protocol, denunciation by any of them of the Warsaw Convention in accordance with Article 39 thereof or of The Hague Protocol in accordance with Article XXIV thereof shall not be construed in any way as a denunciation of the *Warsaw Convention as amended at The Hague, 1955, and by Protocol No. 4 of Montreal, 1975.*

Article XXI

1. Only the following reservations may be made to this Protocol:

    (a) a State may at any time declare by a notification addressed to the Government of the Polish People's Republic that the *Warsaw Convention as amended at The Hague, 1955, and by Protocol No. 4 of Montreal, 1975,* shall not apply to the carriage of persons, baggage and cargo for its military authorities on aircraft, registered in that State, the whole capacity of which has been reserved by or on behalf of such authorities; and

(b) any State may declare at the time of ratification of or accession to the Additional Protocol No. 3 of Montreal, 1975, or at any time thereafter, that it is not bound by the provisions of the *Warsaw Convention as amended at The Hague, 1955, and by Protocol No. 4 of Montreal, 1975,* in so far as they relate to the carriage of passengers and baggage. Such declaration shall have effect ninety days after the date of receipt of the declaration by the Government of the Polish People's Republic.

2.   Any State having made a reservation in accordance with the preceding paragraph may at any time withdraw such reservation by notification to the Government of the Polish People's Republic.

Article XXII

The Government of the Polish People's Republic shall promptly inform all States Parties to the Warsaw Convention or to that Convention as amended, all signatory or acceding States to the present Protocol, as well as the International Civil Aviation Organization, of the date of each signature, the date of deposit of each instrument of ratification or accession, the date of coming into force of this Protocol, and other relevant information.

Article XXIII

As between the Parties to this Protocol which are also Parties to the Convention, Supplementary to the Warsaw Convention, for the Unification of Certain Rules Relating to International Carriage by Air Performed by a Person Other than the Contracting Carrier, signed at Guadalajara on 18 September 1961 (hereinafter referred to as the "Guadalajara Convention") any reference to the "Warsaw Convention" contained in the Guadalajara Convention shall include reference to the *Warsaw Convention as amended at The Hague, 1955, and by Protocol No. 4 of Montreal, 1975,* in cases where the carriage under the agreement referred to in Article 1, paragraph (b) of the Guadalajara Convention is governed by this Protocol.

Article XXIV

If two or more States are Parties both to this Protocol and to the Guatemala City Protocol, 1971, or to the Additional Protocol No. 3 of Montreal, 1975, the following rules shall apply between them:

(a) the provisions resulting from the system established by this Protocol, concerning cargo and postal items, shall prevail over the provisions resulting from the system established by the Guatemala City Protocol, 1971, or by the Additional Protocol No. 3 of Montreal, 1975;

(b) the provisions resulting from the system established by the Guatemala City Protocol, 1971, or by the Additional Protocol No. 3 of Montreal, 1975, concerning passengers and baggage, shall prevail over the provisions resulting from the system established by this Protocol.

Article XXV

This Protocol shall remain open for signature until 1 January 1976 at the Headquarters of the International Civil Aviation Organization and thereafter until it comes into force in accordance with Article XVIII at the Ministry for Foreign Affairs of the Polish People's Republic. The International Civil Aviation Organization shall promptly inform the Government of the Polish People's Republic of any signature and the date thereof during the time that the Protocol shall be open for signature at the Headquarters of the International Civil Aviation Organization.

IN WITNESS WHEREOF the undersigned Plenipotentiaries, having been duly authorized, have signed this Protocol.

DONE at Montreal on the twenty-fifth day of September of the year One Thousand Nine Hundred and Seventy-five in four authentic texts in the English, French, Russian and Spanish languages. In the case of any inconsistency, the text in the French language, in which language the Warsaw Convention of 12 October 1929 was drawn up, shall prevail.

Notes

1 Agreement CAB18900, approved by Order E-23680, May 13, 1966 (docket 17325).
2 Either alternative may be used.

Section 3

Intercarrier and Carrier Agreements

3.1 Montreal Intercarrier Agreement 1966

MONTREAL INTERCARRIER AGREEMENT, 1966 (CAB 18900) AGREEMENT RELATING TO LIABILITY LIMITATIONS OF THE WARSAW CONVENTION AND THE HAGUE PROTOCOL1

The undersigned carriers (hereinafter referred to as "the Carriers") hereby agree as follows:

1. Each of the Carriers shall effective May 16, 1966, include the following in its conditions of carriage, including tariffs embodying conditions of carriage filed by it with any government:

    The Carrier shall avail itself of the limitation of liability provided in the Convention for the Unification of Certain Rules Relating to International Carriage by Air signed at Warsaw October 12th, 1929, or provided in the said Convention as amended by the Protocol signed at The Hague September 28th, 1955. However, in accordance with Article 22(1) of said Convention, or said Convention as amended by said Protocol, the Carrier agrees that, as to all international transportation by the Carrier as defined in the said Convention or said Convention as amended by said Protocol, which, according to the Contract of Carriage, includes a point in the United States of America as a point of origin, point of destination, or agreed stopping place:

    (1) The limit of liability for each passenger for death, wounding, or other bodily injury shall be the sum of US$75,000 inclusive of legal fees and costs, except that, in case of a claim brought in a State where provision is made for separate award of legal fees and costs, the limit shall be the sum of US$58,000 exclusive of legal fees and costs.

    (2) The Carrier shall not, with respect to any claim arising out of the death, wounding, or other bodily injury of a passenger, avail itself of any defense under Article 20(1) of said Convention or said Convention as amended by said Protocol.

Nothing herein shall be deemed to affect the rights and liabilities of the Carrier with regard to any claim brought by, on behalf of, or in respect of any person who had wilfully caused damage which resulted in death, wounding, or other bodily injury of a passenger.

2. Each Carrier shall at the time of delivery of the ticket, furnish to each passenger whose transportation is governed by the Convention, or the Convention as amended by The Hague Protocol, and by the special contract described in paragraph 1, the following notice, which shall be printed in type at least as large as 10 point modern type and in ink contrasting with the stock on (i) each ticket; (ii) a piece of paper either placed in the ticked envelope with the ticket or attached to the ticket; or (iii) on the ticket envelope:

ADVICE TO INTERNATIONAL PASSENGER ON LIMITATION OF LIABILITY

Passengers on a journey involving an ultimate destination or a stop in a country other than the country of origin are advised that the provisions of a treaty known as the Warsaw Convention may be applicable to the entire journey, including any portion entirely within the country of origin or destination. For such passengers on a journey to, from, or with an agreed stopping place in the United States of America, the Convention and special contracts of carriage embodied in applicable tariffs provide that the liability of certain (name of carrier) and certain other[2] carriers parties to such special contracts for death of or personal injury to passengers is limited in most cases to proven damages not to exceed US $75,000 per passenger, and that this liability up to such limit shall not depend on negligence on the part of the carrier. For such passengers travelling by a carrier not a party to such special contracts or on a journey not to, from, or having an agreed stopping place in the United States of America, liability of the carrier for death or personal injury to passengers is limited in most cases to approximately US $8,290 or US $16,580.

The names of Carriers parties to such special contracts are available at all ticket offices of such carriers and may be examined on request.

Additional protection can usually be obtained by purchasing insurance from a private company. Such insurance is not affected by any limitation of the carrier's liability under the Warsaw Convention or such special contracts of carriage. For further information please consult your airline or insurance company representative.

3. This Agreement shall be filed with the Civil Aeronautics Board of the United States for approval pursuant to Section 412 of the Federal Aviation Act of 1958, as amended, and filed with other governments as required. The Agreement shall become effective upon approval by said Board pursuant to said Section 412.

4. This Agreement may be signed in any number of counterparts, all of which shall constitute one Agreement. Any carrier may become a party to this Agreement by signing a counterpart hereof and depositing it with the Civil Aeronautics Board.
5. Any carrier party hereto may withdraw from this Agreement by giving twelve (12) months' written notice of withdrawal to said Civil Aeronautics Board and the other Carriers parties to the Agreement.

3.2 Japanese Carriers – Conditions of Carriage and Waiver of Liability Limits 1992

JAPANESE CARRIERS' CONDITIONS OF CARRIAGE AND ADVICE ON WAIVER OF LIABILITY LIMITS

Conditions of Carriage

(a) [Carrier] agrees in accordance with Article 22(1) of the Convention that as to all international carriage hereunder as defined in the Convention:

   (i) [Carrier] shall not apply the applicable limit of liability based on Article 22(1) of the Convention in defence of any claim arising out of the death, wounding or other bodily injury of a passenger within the meaning of Article 17 of the Convention. Except as provided in paragraph (ii) below, [Carrier] does not waive any defence to such claims as is available under Article 20(1) of the Convention or any other applicable law.

   (ii) [Carrier] shall not, with respect to any claim arising out of the death, wounding or other bodily injury of a passenger within the meaning of Article 17 of the Convention, avail itself of any defence under Article 20(i) of the Convention up to the sum of 100,000 SDRs exclusive of the costs of the action including lawyers' fees which the court finds reasonable.

(b) Nothing herein shall be deemed to affect the rights of [Carrier] with regard to any claim brought by, on behalf of, or in respect of any person who has wilfully caused damage which resulted in death, wounding or other bodily injury of a passenger.

(c) The sum mentioned in terms of SDR in this Article shall be deemed to refer to the Special Drawing Rights as defined by the International Monetary Fund. Conversion of the sum into national currencies shall, in case of judicial proceedings, be made according to the value of such currencies in terms of the Special Drawing Rights at the date of conclusion of an oral argument, or, in case of not judicial proceedings, according to the value of such currencies in terms of the Special Drawing Rights at the date when the damages to be paid is agreed.

Advice on Waiver of Liability Limit by [Carrier]

With respect to carriage performed by [Carrier] only, the applicable liability limit for death or bodily injury under the Warsaw Convention ("Convention") has been waived in accordance with the Conditions of Carriage of [Carrier]. However, [Carrier] reserves the right to assert a defence under Article 20(1) of the Convention for claims in excess of 100,000 SDR.

3.3 IATA Intercarrier Agreement on Passenger Liability 1995

INTERCARRIER AGREEMENT ON PASSENGER LIABILITY

WHEREAS the Warsaw Convention system is of great benefit to international air transportation; and

NOTING THAT the Convention's limits of liability, which have not been amended since 1955, are now grossly inadequate in most countries and that international airlines have previously acted together to increase them to the benefit of passengers;

THE UNDERSIGNED CARRIERS AGREE

1. To take action to waive the limitation of liability on recoverable compensatory damages in Article 22 paragraph 1 of the Warsaw Convention★ as to claims for death, wounding or other bodily injury of a passenger within the meaning of Article 17 of the Convention, so that recoverable compensatory damages may be determined and awarded by reference to the law of the domicile of the passenger.
2. To reserve all available defences pursuant to the provisions of the Convention; nevertheless, any carrier may waive any defence, including the waiver of any defence up to a specified monetary amount of recoverable compensatory damages, as circumstances may warrant.
3. To reserve their rights of recourse against any other person, including rights of contribution or indemnity, with respect to any sums paid by the carrier.
4. To encourage other airlines involved in the international carriage of passengers to apply the terms of this Agreement to such carriage.
5. To implement the provisions of this Agreement no later than 1 November 1996 or upon receipt of requisite government approvals, whichever is later.
6. That nothing in this Agreement shall affect the rights of the passenger or the claimant otherwise available under the Convention.
7. That this Agreement may be signed in any number of counterparts, all of which shall constitute one Agreement. Any carrier may become a party

to this Agreement by signing a counterpart hereof and depositing it with the Director General of the International Air Transport Association (IATA).

8. That any carrier party hereto may withdraw from this Agreement by giving twelve (12) months' written notice of withdrawal to the Director General of IATA and to the other carriers parties to the Agreement.

Signed this_____ day of _____ 199_____

★ "WARSAW CONVENTION" as used herein means the Convention for the Unification of Certain Rules Relating to International Carriage by Air signed at Warsaw, 12th October 1929, or that Convention as amended at The Hague, 28th September 1955, whichever may be applicable.

INTERCARRIER AGREEMENT ON PASSENGER LIABILITY

Explanatory Note

The Intercarrier Agreement is an "umbrella accord"; the precise legal rights and responsibilities of the signatory carriers with respect to passengers will be spelled out in the applicable Conditions of Carriage and tariff filings.

The carriers signatory to the Agreement undertake to take action to waive such limitations of liability for death and bodily injury as are set out in the Warsaw Convention (1929), The Hague Protocol (1955), the Montreal Agreement of 1966, and/or limits they may have previously agreed to implement.

Such waiver by a carrier may be made conditional on the law of the domicile of the passenger governing the calculation of the recoverable compensatory damages under the Intercarrier Agreement. But this is an option. Should a carrier wish to waive the limits of liability but not insist on the law of the domicile of the passenger governing the calculation of the recoverable compensatory damages it may rely on the law of the court to which the case is submitted.

The Warsaw Convention system defences will remain available, in whole or in part, to the carriers signatory to the Agreement, unless a carrier decides to waive them or is so required by a governmental authority.

Section 4

European Regulations

4.1 Council Regulation (EC) No 2027/97 of 9 October 1997 on Air Carrier Liability in the Event of Accidents

COUNCIL REGULATION (EC) NO 2027/97 OF 9 OCTOBER 1997 ON AIR CARRIER LIABILITY IN THE EVENT OF ACCIDENTS

THE COUNCIL OF THE EUROPEAN UNION,

Having regard to the Treaty establishing the European Community, and in particular Article 84 (2) thereof,

Having regard to the proposal from the Commission ([1]),

Having regard to the opinion of the Economic and Social Committee ([2]),

Acting in accordance with the procedure laid down in Article 189 (c) of the Treaty ([3]),

(1) Whereas, in the framework of the common transport policy, it is necessary to improve the level of protection of passengers involved in air accidents;

(2) Whereas the rules on liability in the event of accidents are governed by the Convention for the Unification of Certain Rules Relating to International Carriage by Air, signed at Warsaw on 12 October 1929, or that Convention as amended at The Hague on 28 September 1955 and the Convention done at Guadalajara on 18 September 1961, whichever may be applicable each being hereinafter referred to, as applicable, as the 'Warsaw Convention'; whereas the Warsaw Convention is applied worldwide for the benefit of both passengers and air carriers;

(3) Whereas the limit set on liability by the Warsaw Convention is too low by today's economic and social standards and often leads to lengthy legal actions which damage the image of air transport; whereas as a result Member States have variously increased the liability limit, thereby leading to different terms and conditions of carriage in the internal aviation market;

(4) Whereas in addition the Warsaw Convention applies only to international transport; whereas, in the internal aviation market, the distinction between national and international transport has been eliminated; whereas it is therefore appropriate to have the same level and nature of liability in both national and international transport;

(5) Whereas a full review and revision of the Warsaw Convention is long overdue and would represent, in the long term, a more uniform and applicable response, at an international level, to the issue of air carrier liability in the event of accidents; whereas efforts to increase the limits of liability imposed in the Warsaw Convention should continue through negotiation at multilateral level;

(6) Whereas, in compliance with the principle of subsidiarity, action at Community level is desirable in order to achieve harmonization in the field of air carrier liability and could serve as a guideline for improved passenger protection on a global scale;

(7) Whereas it is appropriate to remove all monetary limits of liability within the meaning of Article 22 (1) of the Warsaw Convention or any other legal or contractual limits, in accordance with present trends at international level;

(8) Whereas, in order to avoid situations where victims of accidents are not compensated, Community air carriers should not, with respect of any claim arising out of the death, wounding or other bodily injury of a passenger under Article 17 of the Warsaw Convention, avail themselves of any defence under Article 20 (1) of the Warsaw Convention up to a certain limit;

(9) Whereas Community air carriers may be exonerated from their liability in cases of contributory negligence of the passenger concerned;

(10) Whereas it is necessary to clarify the obligations of this Regulation in the light of Article 7 of Council Regulation (EEC) No 2407/92 of 23 July 1992 on licensing of air carriers (⁴); whereas, in this regard, Community air carriers should be insured up to a certain limit laid down in this Regulation;

(11) Whereas Community air carriers should always be entitled to claim against third parties;

(12) Whereas prompt advance payments can considerably assist the injured passengers or natural persons entitled to compensation in meeting the immediate costs following an air accident;

(13) Whereas the rules on the nature and limitation of liability in the event of death, wounding or any other bodily injury suffered by a passenger form part of the terms and conditions of carriage in the air transport contract between carrier and passenger; whereas, in order to reduce the risk of distorting competition, third-country carriers should adequately inform passengers of their conditions of carriage;

(14) Whereas it is appropriate and necessary that the monetary limits expressed in this Regulation be reviewed in order to take into account economic developments and developments in international fora;

(15) Whereas the International Civil Aviation Organization (ICAO) is at present engaged in a review of the Warsaw Convention; whereas, pending the outcome of such review, actions on an interim basis by the Community will enhance the protection of passengers; whereas the Council should review this Regulation as soon as possible after the review by ICAO,

HAS ADOPTED THIS REGULATION:

Article 1

This Regulation lays down the obligations of Community air carriers in relation to liability in the event of accidents to passengers for damage sustained in the event of death or wounding of a passenger or any other bodily injury suffered by a passenger, if the accident which caused the damage so sustained took place on board an aircraft or in the course of any of the operations of embarking or disembarking.

This Regulation also clarifies some insurance requirements for Community air carriers.

In addition, this Regulation sets down some requirements on information to be provided by air carriers established outside the Community which operate to, from or within the Community.

Article 2

1. For the purpose of this Regulation:

    (a) 'air carrier' shall mean an air transport undertaking with a valid operating licence;

    (b) 'Community air carrier' shall mean an air carrier with a valid operating licence granted by a Member State in accordance with the provisions of Regulation (EEC) No 2407/92;

    (c) 'person entitled to compensation' shall mean a passenger or any person entitled to claim in respect of that passenger, in accordance with applicable law;

    (d) 'ecu' shall mean the unit of account in drawing up the general budget of the European Communities in accordance with Articles 207 and 209 of the Treaty;

    (e) 'SDR' shall mean a Special Drawing Right as defined by the International Monetary Fund;

    (f) 'Warsaw Convention' shall mean the Convention for the Unification of Certain Rules Relating to International Carriage by Air, signed at Warsaw on 12 October 1929, or the Warsaw Convention as amended at The Hague on 28 September 1955 and the Convention supplementary to the Warsaw Convention done at Guadalajara on 18 September 1961 – whichever is applicable to the passenger contract of carriage, together with all international instruments which supplement, and are associated with, it and are in force.

2. Concepts contained in this Regulation which are not defined in paragraph 1 shall be equivalent to those used in the Warsaw Convention.

Article 3

1. (a) The liability of a Community air carrier for damages sustained in the event of death, wounding or any other bodily injury by a passenger in the event of an accident shall not be subject to any financial limit, be it defined by law, convention or contract.

   (b) The obligation of insurance set out in Article 7 of Regulation (EEC) No 2407/92 shall be understood as requiring that a Community air carrier shall be insured up to the limit of the liability required under paragraph 2 and thereafter up to a reasonable level.

2. For any damages up to the sum of the equivalent in ecus of 100,000 SDR, the Community air carrier shall not exclude or limit his liability by proving that he and his agents have taken all necessary measures to avoid the damage or that it was impossible for him or them to take such measures.

3. Notwithstanding the provisions of paragraph 2, if the Community air carrier proves that the damage was caused by, or contributed to by, the negligence of the injured or deceased passenger, the carrier may be exonerated wholly or partly from its liability in accordance with applicable law.

Article 4

In the event of death, wounding or any other bodily injury suffered by a passenger in the event of an accident, nothing in this Regulation shall

   (a) imply that a Community air carrier is the sole party liable to pay damages; or

   (b) restrict any rights of a Community air carrier to seek contribution or indemnity from any other party in accordance with applicable law.

Article 5

1. The Community air carrier shall without delay, and in any event not later than fifteen days after the identity of the natural person entitled to compensation has been established, make such advance payments as may be required to meet immediate economic needs on a basis proportional to the hardship suffered.

2. Without prejudice to paragraph 1, an advance payment shall not be less than the equivalent in ecus of 15,000 SDR per passenger in the event of death.

3. An advance payment shall not constitute recognition of liability and may be offset against any subsequent sums paid on the basis of Community air carrier liability, but is not returnable, except in the cases prescribed in Article 3 (3) or in circumstances where it is subsequently proved that the person who received the advance payment caused, or contributed to, the damage by negligence or was not the person entitled to compensation.

Article 6

1. The provisions contained in Articles 3 and 5 shall be included in the Community air carrier's conditions of carriage.
2. Adequate information on the provisions contained in Articles 3 and 5 shall, on request, be available to passengers at the Community air carrier's agencies, travel agencies and check-in counters and at points of sale. The ticket document or an equivalent shall contain a summary of the requirements in plain and intelligible language.
3. Air carriers established outside the Community operating to, from or within the Community and not applying the provisions referred to in Articles 3 and 5 shall expressly and clearly inform the passengers thereof, at the time of purchase of the ticket at the carrier's agencies, travel agencies or check-in counters located in the territory of a Member State. Air carriers shall provide the passengers with a form setting out their conditions. The fact that only a liability limit is indicated on the ticket document or an equivalent shall not constitute sufficient information.

Article 7

No later than two years after the entry into force of this Regulation, the Commission shall draw up a report on the application of the Regulation which, *inter alia*, takes into account economic developments and developments in international fora. Such report may be accompanied by proposals for a revision of this Regulation.

Article 8

This Regulation shall enter into force one year after the date of its publication in the *Official Journal of the European Communities*.

This Regulation shall be binding in its entirety and directly applicable in all Member States.

Done at Luxembourg, 9 October 1997.
For the Council
The President
M. DELVAUX-STEHRES

Notes

1. OJ C 104, 10.4.1996, p. 18 and OJ No C 29, 30.1.1997, p. 10.
2. OJ C 212, 22.7.1996, p. 38.
3. Opinion of the European Parliament of 17 September 1996 (OJ No C 320, 28.10.1996, p. 30), Council Common Position of 24 February 1997 (OJ No C 123, 21.4.1997, p. 89) and Decision of the European Parliament of 29 May 1997 (OJ C 182, 16.6.1997).
4. (4) OJ L 240, 24.8.1992, p. 1.

4.2 Regulation (EC) No 889/2002 of the European Parliament and of the Council

REGULATION (EC) NO 889/2002 OF THE EUROPEAN PARLIAMENT AND OF THE COUNCIL OF 13 MAY 2002 AMENDING COUNCIL REGULATION (EC) NO 2027/97 ON AIR CARRIER LIABILITY IN THE EVENT OF ACCIDENTS

THE EUROPEAN PARLIAMENT AND THE COUNCIL OF THE EUROPEAN UNION,

Having regard to the Treaty establishing the European Community, and in particular Article 80(2) thereof,

Having regard to the proposal from the Commission ([1]),

Having regard to the opinion of the Economic and Social Committee ([2]),

Following consultation of the Committee of the Regions,

Acting in accordance with the procedure laid down in Article 251 of the Treaty ([3]),

Whereas:

(1) In the framework of the common transport policy, it is important to ensure a proper level of compensation for passengers involved in air accidents.

(2) A new Convention for the Unification of Certain Rules Relating to International Carriage by Air was agreed at Montreal on 28 May 1999 setting new global rules on liability in the event of accidents for international air transport replacing those in the Warsaw Convention of 1929 and its subsequent amendments ([4]).

(3) The Warsaw Convention will continue to exist alongside the Montreal Convention for an indefinite period.

(4) The Montreal Convention provides for a regime of unlimited liability in the case of death or injury of air passengers.

(5) The Community has signed the Montreal Convention indicating its intention to become a party to the agreement by ratifying it.

(6) It is necessary to amend Council Regulation (EC) No 2027/97 of 9 October 1997 on air carrier liability in the event of accidents(⁵) in order to align it with the provisions of the Montreal Convention, thereby creating a uniform system of liability for international air transport.

(7) This Regulation and the Montreal Convention reinforce the protection of passengers and their dependants and cannot be interpreted so as to weaken their protection in relation to the present legislation on the date of adoption of this Regulation.

(8) In the internal aviation market, the distinction between national and international transport has been eliminated and it is therefore appropriate to have the same level and nature of liability in both international and national transport within the Community.

(9) In compliance with the principle of subsidiarity, action at Community level is desirable in order to create a single set of rules for all Community air carriers.

(10) A system of unlimited liability in case of death or injury to passengers is appropriate in the context of a safe and modern air transport system.

(11) The Community air carrier should not be able to avail itself of Article 21(2) of the Montreal Convention unless it proves that the damage was not due to the negligence or other wrongful act or omission of the carrier or its servants or agents.

(12) Uniform liability limits for loss of, damage to, or destruction of, baggage and for damage occasioned by delay, which apply to all travel on Community carriers, will ensure simple and clear rules for both passengers and airlines and enable passengers to recognise when additional insurance is necessary.

(13) It would be impractical for Community air carriers and confusing for their passengers if they were to apply different liability regimes on different routes across their networks.

(14) It is desirable to relieve accident victims and their dependants of short-term financial concerns in the period immediately after an accident.

(15) Article 50 of the Montreal Convention requires parties to ensure that air carriers are adequately insured and it is necessary to take account of Article 7 of Council Regulation (EEC) No 2407/92 of 23 July 1992 on licensing of air carriers(⁶) in complying with this provision.

(16) It is desirable to provide basic information on the liability rules applicable to every passenger so that they can make additional insurance arrangements in advance of travel if necessary.

(17) It will be necessary to review the monetary amounts set down in this Regulation in order to take account of inflation and any review of the liability limits in the Montreal Convention.

(18)   To the extent that further rules are required in order to implement the Montreal Convention on points that are not covered by Regulation (EC) No 2027/97, it is the responsibility of the Member States to make such provisions,

HAVE ADOPTED THIS REGULATION:

Article 1

Regulation (EC) No 2027/97 is hereby amended as follows:

1.   The title shall be replaced by the following:

"Regulation (EC) No 2027/97 on air carrier liability in respect of the carriage of passengers and their baggage by air.";

2.   Article 1 shall be replaced by the following:

"Article 1

This Regulation implements the relevant provisions of the Montreal Convention in respect of the carriage of passengers and their baggage by air and lays down certain supplementary provisions. It also extends the application of these provisions to carriage by air within a single Member State.";

3.   Article 2 shall be replaced by the following:

"Article 2

1.   For the purpose of this Regulation:

   (a)   'air carrier' shall mean an air transport undertaking with a valid operating licence;
   (b)   'Community air carrier' shall mean an air carrier with a valid operating licence granted by a Member State in accordance with the provisions of Regulation (EEC) No 2407/92;
   (c)   'person entitled to compensation' shall mean a passenger or any person entitled to claim in respect of that passenger, in accordance with applicable law;
   (d)   'baggage', unless otherwise specified, shall mean both checked and unchecked baggage with the meaning of Article 17(4) of the Montreal Convention;
   (e)   'SDR' shall mean a special drawing right as defined by the International Monetary Fund;
   (f)   'Warsaw Convention' shall mean the Convention for the Unification of Certain Rules Relating to International Carriage

by Air, signed at Warsaw on 12 October 1929, or the Warsaw Convention as amended at The Hague on 28 September 1955 and the Convention supplementary to the Warsaw Convention done at Guadalajara on 18 September 1961;

(g) 'Montreal Convention' shall mean the 'Convention for the Unification of Certain Rules Relating to International Carriage by Air', signed at Montreal on 28 May 1999.

2. Concepts contained in this Regulation which are not defined in paragraph 1 shall be equivalent to those used in the Montreal Convention.";

4. Article 3 shall be replaced by the following:

"Article 3

1. The liability of a Community air carrier in respect of passengers and their baggage shall be governed by all provisions of the Montreal Convention relevant to such liability.
2. The obligation of insurance set out in Article 7 of Regulation (EEC) No 2407/92 as far as it relates to liability for passengers shall be understood as requiring that a Community air carrier shall be insured up to a level that is adequate to ensure that all persons entitled to compensation receive the full amount to which they are entitled in accordance with this Regulation.";

5. the following Article shall be inserted:

"Article 3a

The supplementary sum which, in accordance with Article 22(2) of the Montreal Convention, may be demanded by a Community air carrier when a passenger makes a special declaration of interest in delivery of their baggage at destination, shall be based on a tariff which is related to the additional costs involved in transporting and insuring the baggage concerned over and above those for baggage valued at or below the liability limit. The tariff shall be made available to passengers on request.";

6. Article 4 shall be deleted;

7. Article 5 shall be replaced by the following:

"Article 5

1. The Community air carrier shall without delay, and in any event not later than fifteen days after the identity of the natural person entitled to compensation has been established, make such advance payments as may be required to meet immediate economic needs on a basis proportional to the hardship suffered.

2.   Without prejudice to paragraph 1, an advance payment shall not be less than the equivalent in euro of 16,000 SDRs per passenger in the event of death.

3.   An advance payment shall not constitute recognition of liability and may be offset against any subsequent sums paid on the basis of Community air carrier liability, but is not returnable, except in the cases prescribed in Article 20 of the Montreal Convention or where the person who received the advance payment was not the person entitled to compensation.";

8.   Article 6 shall be replaced by the following:

"Article 6

1.   All air carriers shall, when selling carriage by air in the Community, ensure that a summary of the main provisions governing liability for passengers and their baggage, including deadlines for filing an action for compensation and the possibility of making a special declaration for baggage, is made available to passengers at all points of sale, including sale by telephone and via the Internet. In order to comply with this information requirement, Community air carriers shall use the notice contained in the Annex. Such summary or notice cannot be used as a basis for a claim for compensation, nor to interpret the provisions of this Regulation or the Montreal Convention.

2.   In addition to the information requirements set out in paragraph 1, all air carriers shall in respect of carriage by air provided or purchased in the Community, provide each passenger with a written indication of:

–   the applicable limit for that flight on the carrier's liability in respect of death or injury, if such a limit exists,
–   the applicable limit for that flight on the carrier's liability in respect of destruction, loss of or damage to baggage and a warning that baggage greater in value than this figure should be brought to the airline's attention at check-in or fully insured by the passenger prior to travel;
–   the applicable limit for that flight on the carrier's liability for damage occasioned by delay.

3.   In the case of all carriage performed by Community air carriers, the limits indicated in accordance with the information requirements of paragraphs 1 and 2 shall be those established by this Regulation unless the Community air carrier applies higher limits by way of voluntary undertaking. In the case of all carriage performed by non-Community air carriers, paragraphs 1 and 2 shall apply only in relation to carriage to, from or within the Community.";

9. Article 7 shall be replaced by the following:

"Article 7

No later than three years after the date on which Regulation (EC) No 889/2002(⁷) begins to apply, the Commission shall draw up a report on the application of this Regulation. In particular, the Commission shall examine the need to revise the amounts mentioned in the relevant Articles of the Montreal Convention in the light of economic developments and the notifications of the ICAO Depositary.";

10. the following Annex shall be added:

"ANNEX

Air carrier liability for passengers and their baggage

This information notice summarises the liability rules applied by Community air carriers as required by Community legislation and the Montreal Convention.

Compensation in the case of death or injury

There are no financial limits to the liability for passenger injury or death. For damages up to 100,000 SDRs (approximate amount in local currency) the air carrier cannot contest claims for compensation. Above that amount, the air carrier can defend itself against a claim by proving that it was not negligent or otherwise at fault.

Advance payments

If a passenger is killed or injured, the air carrier must make an advance payment, to cover immediate economic needs, within 15 days from the identification of the person entitled to compensation. In the event of death, this advance payment shall not be less than 16,000 SDRs (approximate amount in local currency).

Passenger delays

In case of passenger delay, the air carrier is liable for damage unless it took all reasonable measures to avoid the damage or it was impossible to take such measures. The liability for passenger delay is limited to 4,150 SDRs (approximate amount in local currency).

Baggage delays

In case of baggage delay, the air carrier is liable for damage unless it took all reasonable measures to avoid the damage or it was impossible to take such measures. The liability for baggage delay is limited to 1,000 SDRs (approximate amount in local currency).

Destruction, loss or damage to baggage

The air carrier is liable for destruction, loss or damage to baggage up to 1,000 SDRs (approximate amount in local currency). In the case of checked baggage, it is liable even if not at fault, unless the baggage was defective. In the case of unchecked baggage, the carrier is liable only if at fault.

Higher limits for baggage

A passenger can benefit from a higher liability limit by making a special declaration at the latest at check-in and by paying a supplementary fee.

Complaints on baggage

If the baggage is damaged, delayed, lost or destroyed, the passenger must write and complain to the air carrier as soon as possible. In the case of damage to checked baggage, the passenger must write and complain within seven days, and in the case of delay within 21 days, in both cases from the date on which the baggage was placed at the passenger's disposal.

Liability of contracting and actual carriers

If the air carrier actually performing the flight is not the same as the contracting air carrier, the passenger has the right to address a complaint or to make a claim for damages against either. If the name or code of an air carrier is indicated on the ticket, that air carrier is the contracting air carrier.

Time limit for action

Any action in court to claim damages must be brought within two years from the date of arrival of the aircraft, or from the date on which the aircraft ought to have arrived.

Basis for the information

The basis for the rules described above is the Montreal Convention of 28 May 1999, which is implemented in the Community by Regulation (EC) No 2027/97 (as amended by Regulation (EC) No 889/2002) and national legislation of the Member States."

Article 2

This Regulation shall enter into force on the day of its publication in the Official Journal of the European Communities.

It shall apply from the date of its entry into force or from the date of the entry into force of the Montreal Convention for the Community, whichever is the later.

This Regulation shall be binding in its entirety and directly applicable in all Member States.

Done at Brussels, 13 May 2002.

For the European Parliament
The President
P. Cox

For the Council
The President
J. Piqué I Camps

Notes

1   OJ C 337 E, 28.11.2000, p. 68 and OJ C 213 E, 31.7.2001, p. 298.
2   OJ C 123, 25.4.2001, p. 47.
3   Opinion of the European Parliament of 5 April 2001 (OJ C 21, 24.1.2002, p. 256), Council Common Position of 19 December 2001 (OJ C 58 E, 5.3.2002, p. 8) and Decision of the European Parliament of 12 March 2002.
4   OJ L 194, 18.7.2001, p. 38.
5   OJ L 285, 17.10.1997, p. 1.
6   OJ L 240, 24.8.1992, p. 1.
7   OJ L 140, 30.5.2002, p. 2.

4.3 Council Decision 2001/539/EC on the conclusion by the European Community of the Convention for the Unification of Certain Rules for International Carriage by Air

COUNCIL DECISION OF 5 APRIL 2001 ON THE
CONCLUSION BY THE EUROPEAN COMMUNITY OF
THE CONVENTION FOR THE UNIFICATION OF
CERTAIN RULES FOR INTERNATIONAL CARRIAGE
BY AIR (THE MONTREAL CONVENTION)
(2001/539/EC)

THE COUNCIL OF THE EUROPEAN UNION,

Having regard to the Treaty establishing the European Community, and in particular Article 80(2) in conjunction with the first sentence of the first subparagraph of Article 300(2) and the first subparagraph of Article 300(3) thereof,

Having regard to the proposal from the Commission (^{1}),

Having regard to the opinion of the European Parliament (^{2}),

Whereas:

1. It is beneficial for European Community air carriers to operate under uniform and clear rules regarding their liability for damage and that such rules should be the same as those applicable to carriers from third countries.
2. The Community took part in the International Diplomatic Conference on air law convened in Montreal from 10 to 28 May 1999, which resulted in the adoption of the Convention for the unification of certain rules for international carriage by air (the Montreal Convention), and it signed the said Convention on 9 December 1999.
3. Regional Economic Integration Organisations which have competence in respect of certain matters governed by the Montreal Convention may be parties to it.

4. The Community and its Member States share competence in the matters covered by the Montreal Convention and it is therefore necessary for them simultaneously to ratify it in order to guarantee uniform and complete application of its provisions within the European Union,

HAS DECIDED AS FOLLOWS:

Article 1

The Convention for the Unification of Certain Rules for International Carriage by Air ('the Montreal Convention') is hereby approved on behalf of the European Community.

The text of the Convention is attached to this Decision.

Article 2

The President of the Council shall deposit, on behalf of the European Community, the instrument provided for in Article 53(3) of the Montreal Convention with the International Civil Aviation Organisation, together with the Declaration of Competence.

The instrument shall be deposited simultaneously with the instruments of ratification of all the Member States.

Done at Luxembourg, 5 April 2001.

For the Council
The President
B. ROSENGREN

Notes

1   OJ C 337 E, 28.11.2000, p. 225.
2   Opinion of 16 January 2001 (not yet published in the Official Journal).

4.4 Regulation (EC) No. 261/2004 of the European parliament and of the Council of 11 February 2004 establishing common rules on compensation and assistance to passengers in the event of denied boarding and of cancellation or long delay of flights

REGULATION (EC) NO 261/2004 OF THE EUROPEAN PARLIAMENT AND OF THE COUNCIL OF 11 FEBRUARY 2004 ESTABLISHING COMMON RULES ON COMPENSATION AND ASSISTANCE TO PASSENGERS IN THE EVENT OF DENIED BOARDING AND OF CANCELLATION OR LONG DELAY OF FLIGHTS, AND REPEALING REGULATION (EEC) NO 295/91

THE EUROPEAN PARLIAMENT AND THE COUNCIL OF THE EUROPEAN UNION,

Having regard to the Treaty establishing the European Community, and in particular Article 80(2) thereof,

Having regard to the proposal from the Commission [1],

Having regard to the opinion of the European Economic and Social Committee [2],

After consulting the Committee of the Regions,

Acting in accordance with the procedure laid down in Article 251 of the Treaty [3], in the light of the joint text approved by the Conciliation Committee on 1 December 2003,

Whereas:

1. Action by the Community in the field of air transport should aim, among other things, at ensuring a high level of protection for passengers. Moreover, full account should be taken of the requirements of consumer protection in general.
2. Denied boarding and cancellation or long delay of flights cause serious trouble and inconvenience to passengers.
3. While Council Regulation (EEC) No 295/91 of 4 February 1991 establishing common rules for a denied boarding compensation system in scheduled air transport (⁴) created basic protection for passengers, the number of passengers denied boarding against their will remains too high, as does that affected by cancellations without prior warning and that affected by long delays.
4. The Community should therefore raise the standards of protection set by that Regulation both to strengthen the rights of passengers and to ensure that air carriers operate under harmonised conditions in a liberalised market.
5. Since the distinction between scheduled and non-scheduled air services is weakening, such protection should apply to passengers not only on scheduled but also on non-scheduled flights, including those forming part of package tours.
6. The protection accorded to passengers departing from an airport located in a Member State should be extended to those leaving an airport located in a third country for one situated in a Member State, when a Community carrier operates the flight.
7. In order to ensure the effective application of this Regulation, the obligations that it creates should rest with the operating air carrier who performs or intends to perform a flight, whether with owned aircraft, under dry or wet lease, or on any other basis.
8. This Regulation should not restrict the rights of the operating air carrier to seek compensation from any person, including third parties, in accordance with the law applicable.
9. The number of passengers denied boarding against their will should be reduced by requiring air carriers to call for volunteers to surrender their reservations, in exchange for benefits, instead of denying passengers boarding, and by fully compensating those finally denied boarding.
10. Passengers denied boarding against their will should be able either to cancel their flights, with reimbursement of their tickets, or to continue them under satisfactory conditions, and should be adequately cared for while awaiting a later flight.
11. Volunteers should also be able to cancel their flights, with reimbursement of their tickets, or continue them under satisfactory conditions, since they face difficulties of travel similar to those experienced by passengers denied boarding against their will.

12. The trouble and inconvenience to passengers caused by cancellation of flights should also be reduced. This should be achieved by inducing carriers to inform passengers of cancellations before the scheduled time of departure and in addition to offer them reasonable re-routing, so that the passengers can make other arrangements. Air carriers should compensate passengers if they fail to do this, except when the cancellation occurs in extraordinary circumstances which could not have been avoided even if all reasonable measures had been taken.

13. Passengers whose flights are cancelled should be able either to obtain reimbursement of their tickets or to obtain re-routing under satisfactory conditions, and should be adequately cared for while awaiting a later flight.

14. As under the Montreal Convention, obligations on operating air carriers should be limited or excluded in cases where an event has been caused by extraordinary circumstances which could not have been avoided even if all reasonable measures had been taken. Such circumstances may, in particular, occur in cases of political instability, meteorological conditions incompatible with the operation of the flight concerned, security risks, unexpected flight safety shortcomings and strikes that affect the operation of an operating air carrier.

15. Extraordinary circumstances should be deemed to exist where the impact of an air traffic management decision in relation to a particular aircraft on a particular day gives rise to a long delay, an overnight delay, or the cancellation of one or more flights by that aircraft, even though all reasonable measures had been taken by the air carrier concerned to avoid the delays or cancellations.

16. In cases where a package tour is cancelled for reasons other than the flight being cancelled, this Regulation should not apply.

17. Passengers whose flights are delayed for a specified time should be adequately cared for and should be able to cancel their flights with reimbursement of their tickets or to continue them under satisfactory conditions.

18. Care for passengers awaiting an alternative or a delayed flight may be limited or declined if the provision of the care would itself cause further delay.

19. Operating air carriers should meet the special needs of persons with reduced mobility and any persons accompanying them.

20. Passengers should be fully informed of their rights in the event of denied boarding and of cancellation or long delay of flights, so that they can effectively exercise their rights.

21. Member States should lay down rules on sanctions applicable to infringements of the provisions of this Regulation and ensure that these sanctions are applied. The sanctions should be effective, proportionate and dissuasive.

22. Member States should ensure and supervise general compliance by their air carriers with this Regulation and designate an appropriate body to

carry out such enforcement tasks. The supervision should not affect the rights of passengers and air carriers to seek legal redress from courts under procedures of national law.

23. The Commission should analyse the application of this Regulation and should assess in particular the opportunity of extending its scope to all passengers having a contract with a tour operator or with a Community carrier, when departing from a third country airport to an airport in a Member State.

24. Arrangements for greater cooperation over the use of Gibraltar airport were agreed in London on 2 December 1987 by the Kingdom of Spain and the United Kingdom in a joint declaration by the Ministers of Foreign Affairs of the two countries. Such arrangements have yet to enter into operation.

25. Regulation (EEC) No 295/91 should accordingly be repealed,

HAVE ADOPTED THIS REGULATION:

Article 1

Subject

1. This Regulation establishes, under the conditions specified herein, minimum rights for passengers when:

   (a) they are denied boarding against their will;
   (b) their flight is cancelled;
   (c) their flight is delayed.

2. Application of this Regulation to Gibraltar airport is understood to be without prejudice to the respective legal positions of the Kingdom of Spain and the United Kingdom with regard to the dispute over sovereignty over the territory in which the airport is situated.

3. Application of this Regulation to Gibraltar airport shall be suspended until the arrangements in the Joint Declaration made by the Foreign Ministers of the Kingdom of Spain and the United Kingdom on 2 December 1987 enter into operation. The Governments of Spain and the United Kingdom will inform the Council of such date of entry into operation.

Article 2

Definitions

For the purposes of this Regulation:

   (a) 'air carrier' means an air transport undertaking with a valid operating licence;

(b) 'operating air carrier' means an air carrier that performs or intends to perform a flight under a contract with a passenger or on behalf of another person, legal or natural, having a contract with that passenger;

(c) 'Community carrier' means an air carrier with a valid operating licence granted by a Member State in accordance with the provisions of Council Regulation (EEC) No 2407/92 of 23 July 1992 on licensing of air carriers ([5]);

(d) 'tour operator' means, with the exception of an air carrier, an organiser within the meaning of Article 2, point 2, of Council Directive 90/314/EEC of 13 June 1990 on package travel, package holidays and package tours ([6]);

(e) 'package' means those services defined in Article 2, point 1, of Directive 90/314/EEC;

(f) 'ticket' means a valid document giving entitlement to transport, or something equivalent in paperless form, including electronic form, issued or authorised by the air carrier or its authorised agent;

(g) 'reservation' means the fact that the passenger has a ticket, or other proof, which indicates that the reservation has been accepted and registered by the air carrier or tour operator;

(h) 'final destination' means the destination on the ticket presented at the check-in counter or, in the case of directly connecting flights, the destination of the last flight; alternative connecting flights available shall not be taken into account if the original planned arrival time is respected;

(i) 'person with reduced mobility' means any person whose mobility is reduced when using transport because of any physical disability (sensory or locomotory, permanent or temporary), intellectual impairment, age or any other cause of disability, and whose situation needs special attention and adaptation to the person's needs of the services made available to all passengers;

(j) 'denied boarding' means a refusal to carry passengers on a flight, although they have presented themselves for boarding under the conditions laid down in Article 3(2), except where there are reasonable grounds to deny them boarding, such as reasons of health, safety or security, or inadequate travel documentation;

(k) 'volunteer' means a person who has presented himself for boarding under the conditions laid down in Article 3(2) and responds positively to the air carrier's call for passengers prepared to surrender their reservation in exchange for benefits.

(l) 'cancellation' means the non-operation of a flight which was previously planned and on which at least one place was reserved.

Article 3

Scope

1. This Regulation shall apply:

    (a) to passengers departing from an airport located in the territory of a Member State to which the Treaty applies;

    (b) to passengers departing from an airport located in a third country to an airport situated in the territory of a Member State to which the Treaty applies, unless they received benefits or compensation and were given assistance in that third country, if the operating air carrier of the flight concerned is a Community carrier.

2. Paragraph 1 shall apply on the condition that passengers:

    (a) have a confirmed reservation on the flight concerned and, except in the case of cancellation referred to in Article 5, present themselves for check-in,

    –   as stipulated and at the time indicated in advance and in writing (including by electronic means) by the air carrier, the tour operator or an authorised travel agent, or, if no time is indicated,

    –   not later than 45 minutes before the published departure time; or

    (b) have been transferred by an air carrier or tour operator from the flight for which they held a reservation to another flight, irrespective of the reason.

3. This Regulation shall not apply to passengers travelling free of charge or at a reduced fare not available directly or indirectly to the public. However, it shall apply to passengers having tickets issued under a frequent flyer programme or other commercial programme by an air carrier or tour operator.

4. This Regulation shall only apply to passengers transported by motorised fixed wing aircraft.

5. This Regulation shall apply to any operating air carrier providing transport to passengers covered by paragraphs 1 and 2. Where an operating air carrier which has no contract with the passenger performs obligations under this Regulation, it shall be regarded as doing so on behalf of the person having a contract with that passenger.

6. This Regulation shall not affect the rights of passengers under Directive 90/314/EEC. This Regulation shall not apply in cases where a package tour is cancelled for reasons other than cancellation of the flight.

Article 4

Denied boarding

1. When an operating air carrier reasonably expects to deny boarding on a flight, it shall first call for volunteers to surrender their reservations in exchange for benefits under conditions to be agreed between the passenger concerned and the operating air carrier. Volunteers shall be assisted in accordance with Article 8, such assistance being additional to the benefits mentioned in this paragraph.
2. If an insufficient number of volunteers comes forward to allow the remaining passengers with reservations to board the flight, the operating air carrier may then deny boarding to passengers against their will.
3. If boarding is denied to passengers against their will, the operating air carrier shall immediately compensate them in accordance with Article 7 and assist them in accordance with Articles 8 and 9.

Article 5

Cancellation

1. In case of cancellation of a flight, the passengers concerned shall:

   (a) be offered assistance by the operating air carrier in accordance with Article 8; and
   (b) be offered assistance by the operating air carrier in accordance with Article 9(1)(a) and 9(2), as well as, in event of re-routing when the reasonably expected time of departure of the new flight is at least the day after the departure as it was planned for the cancelled flight, the assistance specified in Article 9(1)(b) and 9(1)(c); and
   (c) have the right to compensation by the operating air carrier in accordance with Article 7, unless:

      (i) they are informed of the cancellation at least two weeks before the scheduled time of departure; or
      (ii) they are informed of the cancellation between two weeks and seven days before the scheduled time of departure and are offered re-routing, allowing them to depart no more than two hours before the scheduled time of departure and to reach their final destination less than four hours after the scheduled time of arrival; or
      (iii) they are informed of the cancellation less than seven days before the scheduled time of departure and are offered re-routing, allowing them to depart no more than one hour before the scheduled time of departure and to reach their final destination less than two hours after the scheduled time of arrival.

2. When passengers are informed of the cancellation, an explanation shall be given concerning possible alternative transport.
3. An operating air carrier shall not be obliged to pay compensation in accordance with Article 7, if it can prove that the cancellation is caused by extraordinary circumstances which could not have been avoided even if all reasonable measures had been taken.
4. The burden of proof concerning the questions as to whether and when the passenger has been informed of the cancellation of the flight shall rest with the operating air carrier.

Article 6

Delay

1. When an operating air carrier reasonably expects a flight to be delayed beyond its scheduled time of departure:

   (a) for two hours or more in the case of flights of 1 500 kilometres or less; or
   (b) for three hours or more in the case of all intra-Community flights of more than 1 500 kilometres and of all other flights between 1 500 and 3 500 kilometres; or
   (c) for four hours or more in the case of all flights not falling under (a) or (b), passengers shall be offered by the operating air carrier:

      (i) the assistance specified in Article 9(1)(a) and 9(2); and
      (ii) when the reasonably expected time of departure is at least the day after the time of departure previously announced, the assistance specified in Article 9(1)(b) and 9(1)(c); and
      (iii) when the delay is at least five hours, the assistance specified in Article 8(1)(a).

2. In any event, the assistance shall be offered within the time limits set out above with respect to each distance bracket.

Article 7

Right to compensation

1. Where reference is made to this Article, passengers shall receive compensation amounting to:

   (a) EUR 250 for all flights of 1 500 kilometres or less;
   (b) EUR 400 for all intra-Community flights of more than 1 500 kilometres, and for all other flights between 1 500 and 3 500 kilometres;
   (c) EUR 600 for all flights not falling under (a) or (b).

In determining the distance, the basis shall be the last destination at which the denial of boarding or cancellation will delay the passenger's arrival after the scheduled time.

2. When passengers are offered re-routing to their final destination on an alternative flight pursuant to Article 8, the arrival time of which does not exceed the scheduled arrival time of the flight originally booked

   (a) by two hours, in respect of all flights of 1 500 kilometres or less; or
   (b) by three hours, in respect of all intra-Community flights of more than 1 500 kilometres and for all other flights between 1 500 and 3 500 kilometres; or
   (c) by four hours, in respect of all flights not falling under (a) or (b),

   the operating air carrier may reduce the compensation provided for in paragraph 1 by 50%.

3. The compensation referred to in paragraph 1 shall be paid in cash, by electronic bank transfer, bank orders or bank cheques or, with the signed agreement of the passenger, in travel vouchers and/or other services.

4. The distances given in paragraphs 1 and 2 shall be measured by the great circle route method.

Article 8

Right to reimbursement or re-routing

1. Where reference is made to this Article, passengers shall be offered the choice between:

   (a) – reimbursement within seven days, by the means provided for in Article 7(3), of the full cost of the ticket at the price at which it was bought, for the part or parts of the journey not made, and for the part or parts already made if the flight is no longer serving any purpose in relation to the passenger's original travel plan, together with, when relevant,
       – a return flight to the first point of departure, at the earliest opportunity;
   (b) re-routing, under comparable transport conditions, to their final destination at the earliest opportunity; or
   (c) re-routing, under comparable transport conditions, to their final destination at a later date at the passenger's convenience, subject to availability of seats.

2. Paragraph 1(a) shall also apply to passengers whose flights form part of a package, except for the right to reimbursement where such right arises under Directive 90/314/EEC.

3. When, in the case where a town, city or region is served by several airports, an operating air carrier offers a passenger a flight to an airport alternative

to that for which the booking was made, the operating air carrier shall bear the cost of transferring the passenger from that alternative airport either to that for which the booking was made, or to another close-by destination agreed with the passenger.

Article 9

Right to care

1. Where reference is made to this Article, passengers shall be offered free of charge:

   (a) meals and refreshments in a reasonable relation to the waiting time;
   (b) hotel accommodation in cases
       - where a stay of one or more nights becomes necessary, or
       - where a stay additional to that intended by the passenger becomes necessary;
   (c) transport between the airport and place of accommodation (hotel or other).

2. In addition, passengers shall be offered free of charge two telephone calls, telex or fax messages, or e-mails.
3. In applying this Article, the operating air carrier shall pay particular attention to the needs of persons with reduced mobility and any persons accompanying them, as well as to the needs of unaccompanied children.

Article 10

Upgrading and downgrading

1. If an operating air carrier places a passenger in a class higher than that for which the ticket was purchased, it may not request any supplementary payment.
2. If an operating air carrier places a passenger in a class lower than that for which the ticket was purchased, it shall within seven days, by the means provided for in Article 7(3), reimburse

   (a) 30% of the price of the ticket for all flights of 1 500 kilometres or less, or
   (b) 50% of the price of the ticket for all intra-Community flights of more than 1 500 kilometres, except flights between the European territory of the Member States and the French overseas departments, and for all other flights between 1 500 and 3 500 kilometres, or
   (c) 75% of the price of the ticket for all flights not falling under (a) or (b), including flights between the European territory of the Member States and the French overseas departments.

Article 11

Persons with reduced mobility or special needs

1. Operating air carriers shall give priority to carrying persons with reduced mobility and any persons or certified service dogs accompanying them, as well as unaccompanied children.
2. In cases of denied boarding, cancellation and delays of any length, persons with reduced mobility and any persons accompanying them, as well as unaccompanied children, shall have the right to care in accordance with Article 9 as soon as possible.

Article 12

Further compensation

1. This Regulation shall apply without prejudice to a passenger's rights to further compensation. The compensation granted under this Regulation may be deducted from such compensation.
2. Without prejudice to relevant principles and rules of national law, including case-law, paragraph 1 shall not apply to passengers who have voluntarily surrendered a reservation under Article 4(1).

Article 13

Right of redress

In cases where an operating air carrier pays compensation or meets the other obligations incumbent on it under this Regulation, no provision of this Regulation may be interpreted as restricting its right to seek compensation from any person, including third parties, in accordance with the law applicable. In particular, this Regulation shall in no way restrict the operating air carrier's right to seek reimbursement from a tour operator or another person with whom the operating air carrier has a contract. Similarly, no provision of this Regulation may be interpreted as restricting the right of a tour operator or a third party, other than a passenger, with whom an operating air carrier has a contract, to seek reimbursement or compensation from the operating air carrier in accordance with applicable relevant laws.

Article 14

Obligation to inform passengers of their rights

1. The operating air carrier shall ensure that at check-in a clearly legible notice containing the following text is displayed in a manner clearly visible to passengers: 'If you are denied boarding or if your flight is cancelled or

delayed for at least two hours, ask at the check-in counter or boarding gate for the text stating your rights, particularly with regard to compensation and assistance'.

2. An operating air carrier denying boarding or cancelling a flight shall provide each passenger affected with a written notice setting out the rules for compensation and assistance in line with this Regulation. It shall also provide each passenger affected by a delay of at least two hours with an equivalent notice. The contact details of the national designated body referred to in Article 16 shall also be given to the passenger in written form.

3. In respect of blind and visually impaired persons, the provisions of this Article shall be applied using appropriate alternative means.

Article 15

Exclusion of waiver

1. Obligations vis-à-vis passengers pursuant to this Regulation may not be limited or waived, notably by a derogation or restrictive clause in the contract of carriage.

2. If, nevertheless, such a derogation or restrictive clause is applied in respect of a passenger, or if the passenger is not correctly informed of his rights and for that reason has accepted compensation which is inferior to that provided for in this Regulation, the passenger shall still be entitled to take the necessary proceedings before the competent courts or bodies in order to obtain additional compensation.

Article 16

Infringements

1. Each Member State shall designate a body responsible for the enforcement of this Regulation as regards flights from airports situated on its territory and flights from a third country to such airports. Where appropriate, this body shall take the measures necessary to ensure that the rights of passengers are respected. The Member States shall inform the Commission of the body that has been designated in accordance with this paragraph.

2. Without prejudice to Article 12, each passenger may complain to any body designated under paragraph 1, or to any other competent body designated by a Member State, about an alleged infringement of this Regulation at any airport situated on the territory of a Member State or concerning any flight from a third country to an airport situated on that territory.

3. The sanctions laid down by Member States for infringements of this Regulation shall be effective, proportionate and dissuasive.

Article 17

Report

The Commission shall report to the European Parliament and the Council by 1 January 2007 on the operation and the results of this Regulation, in particular regarding:

- the incidence of denied boarding and of cancellation of flights,
- the possible extension of the scope of this Regulation to passengers having a contract with a Community carrier or holding a flight reservation which forms part of a 'package tour' to which Directive 90/314/EEC applies and who depart from a third-country airport to an airport in a Member State, on flights not operated by Community air carriers,
- the possible revision of the amounts of compensation referred to in Article 7(1).

The report shall be accompanied where necessary by legislative proposals.

Article 18

Repeal

Regulation (EEC) No 295/91 shall be repealed.

Article 19

Entry into force
This Regulation shall enter into force on 17 February 2005.

This Regulation shall be binding in its entirety and directly applicable in all Member States.

Done at Strasbourg, 11 February 2004.

For the European Parliament
The President

P. COX
For the Council
The President
M. McDOWELL

Notes

1 OJ C 103 E, 30.4.2002, p. 225 and OJ C 71 E, 25.3.2003, p. 188.
2 OJ C 241, 7.10.2002, p. 29.
3 Opinion of the European Parliament of 24 October 2002 (OJ C 300 E, 11.12.2003, p. 443), Council Common Position of 18 March 2003 (OJ C 125 E, 27.5.2003, p. 63) and Position of the European Parliament of 3 July 2003. Legislative Resolution of the European Parliament of 18 December 2003 and Council Decision of 26 January 2004.
4 OJ L 36, 8.2.1991, p. 5.
5 OJ L 240, 24.8.1992, p. 1.
6 OJ L 158, 23.6.1990, p. 59.

PART II

SAFETY AND SECURITY

Commentary

Since the beginning of the jet age, ensuring the safety and security of persons on board aircraft, as well as those on the ground, has been a paramount concern for international civil aviation. Over time, states have developed – largely through treaty-making – various legal frameworks for the protection of the travelling public. Increasing security concerns such as hijacking and acts of terror and offences committed on board aircraft, together with major air disasters, have led states to revise and strengthen measures to further safeguard both passengers and those on the ground against trouble in the skies.

In Part II we provide analysis of international air safety and security instruments and their evolution. These instruments address matters which involve passengers in the air and persons on the ground.

The terrorist attacks of September 2001 raised important issues in relation to the modernisation of international air safety laws and security regimes. These issues are also discussed in this section. We also look at the most appropriate mechanisms to further address aviation in general (such mechanisms not yet in force).

SAFETY AND SECURITY ON BOARD AIRCRAFT

The problem of jurisdiction over offences committed on board aircraft had been the subject of debate, although debate of no real urgency. A number of hijackings in the late 1950s and early 1960s, however, led to the Tokyo Convention of 1963, which represents the first comprehensive attempt to deal with the issue of crimes committed on board an aircraft. With ongoing concern regarding unlawful interference with and hijacking of aircraft in the late 1960s and early 1970s, a number of additional aviation security conventions were concluded to address such interference and hijacking, together with the threat of explosives on board aircraft.

Addressing safety and security issues on board aircraft had been on the agenda of ICAO for a number of years prior to the conclusion of the Tokyo Convention.

Tokyo Convention 1963

The Convention on Offences and Certain Other Acts Committed on Board Aircraft, known as the Tokyo Convention, was signed on 14 September 1963 in Tokyo, Japan. The Convention came into force on 4 December 1969. The aim of the Convention, as set out in Article 1, is to make an offence such acts which may (a) jeopardise the safety of the aircraft (or persons or property on the aircraft); or (b) which may jeopardise good order and discipline on board an aircraft.

> ... According to the Convention, the aircraft commander has the power to take measures and restrain a person even if his act did not amount to jeopardizing the safety of the aircraft or the person or the property therein. This provision directly leads to an analogous situation of an offensive act perpetrated by an unruly person. If for example the conduct of two or more persons, while on board the aircraft, appears to be leading to the commission of some illegal act (the conduct of a drunken sporting team on board would be a good example), the commander can restrain them on the suspicion that they are conspiring to commit an act which may jeopardize good order and discipline on board ...
>
> The aircraft commander, in discharging his duties according to the Convention, can require or authorize the assistance of the crew and request the assistance of persons for that purpose. Even persons and crew members are authorized under Article 6(2) to take reasonable preventive measures without any authorization from the aircraft commander whenever they have reasonable grounds to believe that such action is immediately necessary for safety reasons.
>
> [...]
>
> The powers entrusted to the commander in order to suppress any unlawful act that threatens the safety of the aircraft go as far as requiring the disembarking of any person in the territory of any State in which he lands and delivering him to its competent authorities. The State is under an obligation to allow the disembarkation and to take delivery of the person so apprehended by the aircraft commander, but such custody may only be continued for such time as is reasonably necessary to enable the criminal extradition proceedings (if any) to be instituted. In the meantime the State of landing should make a preliminary enquiry into the facts and notify the State of registration of the aircraft.
>
> In any event, the commander as well as the crew members and persons are given immunity from suits by the alleged offender against whom they acted. Article 10 expressly provides:
>
> > Neither the aircraft commander, any member of the crew, any person, the owner or operator of the aircraft, nor the person on whose behalf the flight is performed shall be held responsible in any proceedings on account of the treatment undergone by the person against whom the actions were taken.[1]

Aviation Security After the Tokyo Convention

The Hague Convention 1970 was the result of concerted action on the part of states to combat an increase in hijacking in the late 1960s. The Hague Convention, as against the Tokyo Convention 1963, deals more specifically with the offence of hijacking: it must be unlawful, must entail some use or threat of force, and the act of hijacking must consist of seizure or an attempted seizure and exercise or an attempted exercise of unlawful control over the aircraft. The primary purpose of The Hague Convention is to eliminate to the extent possible refuge for hijackers.

The Hague Convention was followed by the 1971 Montreal Convention. This 1971 Convention was intended to complement the Tokyo and Hague Conventions by providing for certain matters not dealt with in those conventions – that is, acts of sabotage and unlawful acts against the safety of civil aviation, and not confined to offences on board aircraft. It extends the range of offences against the safety of civil aviation to cover acts likely to endanger the safety of an aircraft in service, in addition to an aircraft in flight.

State action in the 1960s to address aviation security concerns has been set out by ICAO:

> As the number of hijackings rose through 1969 and 1970 (118 incidents of unlawful seizure of civil aircraft and 14 incidents of sabotage and armed attacks against civil aviation occurred), an Extraordinary Assembly (17th) was held in Montreal from 16 to 30 June 1970, specifically on the subject of aviation security; it produced a series of resolutions dealing with a wide range of security measures, eventually leading to the adoption of a completely new Annex 17 – Security. The primary objective of each Contracting State is safeguarding its passengers, ground personnel, crew as well as the general public against any acts of unlawful interference.
>
> During its 24th Session in December 1969, the United Nations General Assembly adopted Resolution 2551 (XXIV) in which the General Assembly stated its deep concern over acts of unlawful interference with international civil aviation. On 9 September 1970, the UN Security Council adopted Resolution 286 calling upon States to take all possible legal steps to prevent further hijackings or any other interference with international civil air travel. On 25 November 1970, the UN General Assembly adopted Resolution 2645 (XXV) which condemned without exception whatsoever all aerial hijacking or other interference with civil air travel caused through threat or use of force. The international community thus condemned terrorism against air transport by giving official recognition to such condemnation and called upon all States to contribute to the eradication of the offence by taking effective, preventive and deterrent measures. In the years after, the UN General Assembly adopted other resolutions calling for inter-national cooperation dealing with acts of international terrorism.
>
> In the atmosphere of crisis and on [the] legal side, two new Conventions were prepared. From 1 to 16 December 1970, 77 States and 12 international

organizations met in The Hague for a Diplomatic Conference ending with the signing of The Hague Convention for the Suppression of Unlawful Seizure of Aircraft (sometimes named the Anti-hijacking Convention), which came into force on 14 October 1971. This Convention provided for effective legal measures being taken to deter acts of unlawful seizure of aircraft through the cooperation of nations throughout the world. Action taken by ICAO and its Members States resulted in a considerable reduction of hijackings during 1971.

Prior to the Montréal Conference, the 18th Session of the ICAO Assembly, in Resolution A18–9 (held in Vienna, from 15 June to 7 July 1971), called for speedy adoption and ratification of what was to become the Montréal Convention. From 8 to 23 September 1971, a full Diplomatic Conference (attended by Delegates from 60 Member States and the United Nations, as well as by observers from one State and six international organizations) was held in Montréal and the Montréal Convention for the Suppression of Unlawful Acts against the Safety of Civil Aviation was opened for signature; it came into force on 26 January 1973. The Protocol for the Suppression of Unlawful Acts of Violence at Airports Serving International Civil Aviation, Supplementary to the Convention for the Suppression of Unlawful Acts against the Safety of Civil Aviation was signed at Montreal on 23 September 1971 (adopted on 24 February 1988).[2]

Montreal Convention 1991

The bombing of Pan Am Flight 103 over Lockerbie, Scotland in 1988 (which resulted in the deaths of 270 people) led directly to the conclusion of the Convention on the Marking of Plastic Explosives for the Purpose of Detection, commonly known as the Montreal Convention 1991. This Convention also arose out of a concern that plastic explosives were being used by terrorists in executing attacks on public targets including aircraft.

Under the Convention, state parties to it are required to prohibit and prevent the manufacture of unmarked explosives, and the import and export of such explosives, in their territory. Additionally, plastic explosives must be marked by manufacturers with an agreed detection agent. In general terms, the Convention sets out provisions relating to regulating, monitoring, manufacturing, possessing, and importing and exporting of plastic explosives.

The rationale for the Convention was made very clear by the United Nations in the months after the adoption of the Convention:

International controls to regulate plastic explosives adopted in Montreal

A human tragedy was the catalyst for the Convention-the destruction of Pan Am flight 103 over Lockerbie, Scotland, on 21 December 1988. A plastic explosive device was reportedly secreted inside a cassette player.

"The response of the international community to that act of terrorism was swift and unanimous", UN Secretary-General Javier Pérez de Cuéllar recalled as he opened the Conference. The United Kingdom and Czechoslovakia jointly proposed a convention that would make it harder for terrorists to obtain lethal explosives. The Security Council and the General Assembly unanimously supported that initiative.

"Nothing perhaps activates co-operation like a universally shared sense of danger. The threat of terrorism that spares few countries or individuals is indeed practically a universal one", Mr. Pérez de Cuéllar said.

Assad Kotaite, President of the ICAO Council, emphasized the alarming trend in recent years towards the destruction of aircraft in flight. ICAO would accomplish its security mission not only through the development of international law but "by marshalling the necessary resources to assist all States in introducing technical preventive measures to safeguard the security of international civil aviation", he said.[3]

The key provisions of the Convention have been concisely set out by an Australian Parliamentary committee:

Convention on the Marking of Plastic Explosives for the Purpose of Detection

Obligations under the Convention

As signator[ies] to the Convention, [parties are] . . . required to:

- use one of the four ICAO recommended chemical detection agents in its minimum concentration to mark plastic explosives
- prohibit and prevent the manufacture in its territory, and the movement into and out of its territory of unmarked plastic explosives
- take necessary measures to destroy, as soon as possible, unmarked plastic explosives manufactured upon the Convention's entry into force.

Control of existing stocks of plastic explosives

The Convention obliges States to exercise strict and effective control of the possession and transfer of existing stocks of unmarked plastic explosives.

Existing stocks of unmarked plastic explosives must be either consumed, destroyed, marked or rendered permanently ineffective, consistent with obligations under the Convention within [certain periods of time].[4]

COMPENSATION CONVENTIONS FOR DAMAGE TO THIRD PARTIES

Earlier sections of Part II considered safety and security measures pertaining to those in a contractual relationship with the carrier, and acts of terror on board aircraft. This section considers damage caused by aircraft to third parties on the ground – that is, parties not in a relationship with the carrier.

Perhaps the most devastating example of such damage to third parties on the ground is the deliberate crashing of four commercial passenger aircraft in the United States. Two of these aircraft were flown into the World Trade Center buildings in New York City. These terrorist attacks resulted in the deaths of almost 3,000 people and the injury of more than 6,000 others.

Damage Caused by Foreign Aircraft to Third Parties on the Surface

While the September 11 attacks may be the most obvious example of the catastrophic damage that can be caused by aircraft to third parties on the ground, they did not involve foreign (non-US) aircraft and the relevant flights were not the subject of international jurisdiction.

In terms of such jurisdiction, international conventions have been developed to deal with damage to third parties on the ground caused by foreign aircraft.

Rome Convention 1933

At a 1933 conference in Rome certain states agreed a Convention on Surface Damage, the purpose of which was to bring together rules in relation to damage caused by foreign aircraft to third parties on the ground. This 1933 convention, the Convention for the Unification of Certain Rules Relating to Damage Caused by Foreign Aircraft to Third Parties on the Surface, was adopted on 29 May 1933 and was only ratified by five countries, Belgium, Brazil, Guatemala, Romania and Spain.

> The 1933 Rome Convention did not achieve wide acceptance and is now obsolete. Nevertheless, it remains interesting since it determined some fundamental principles on which further considerations and decisions could build. Among them were:
>
> - liability attaches to the operator (not owner) of the aircraft;
> - strict liability is imposed on the operator of the aircraft from which he could be exonerated only if he proves intervention of a third party;
> - liability is limited to sums depending on the weight of the aircraft; it is expressed in gold clause (French gold franc), one third of the compensation to be reserved for material damage, two-thirds to persons with a limit of 200,000 francs per person killed or injured;

- a financial guarantee must be obtained by each aircraft operator in international air operations.

. . . CITEJA prepared a further document complementing the 1933 Rome Convention on matters of insurance guarantees and the Fourth International Private Air Law Conference adopted it [in] Brussels on the eve of World War II on 29 September 1938 as the "Protocol Supplementary to the Convention for the Unification of Certain Rules Relating to Damage Caused by Foreign Aircraft to Third Parties on the Surface, Signed in Rome on 29 May 1933, Done at Brussels on 29 September 1938."

The Brussels Protocol of 1938 was ratified only by two countries (Brazil and Guatemala) and the war interrupted further development of the international unification of private air law.[5]

Rome Convention 1952

In 1948, the Legal Committee of ICAO decided to draft a new convention to improve and supersede the 1933 Rome Convention. The draft was considered at an international conference in Rome in 1952, and a new Rome Convention was signed on 7 October, 1952.

Like its predecessor, the 1952 Convention sought to establish a system of liability for damage to persons and property on the surface caused by foreign aircraft. The Convention imposed liability on the operator of the aircraft, such liability limited in accordance with a formula based on the weight of the aircraft. As against its predecessor, and amongst other things, it more clearly defined a number of important terms such as when the plane was 'in-flight', and 'operator'. It provided improved details of rules of procedure, set out more detailed formulae for ascertaining the limits of liability based on weight, and provided that an aircraft above the high seas was regarded as part of the territory of the state in which it was registered.

The Convention was not ratified by the United States because of its opposition to the liability limits of aircraft operators under the Convention. Indeed, unlike the Warsaw Convention, the Convention has never achieved widespread international recognition.

. . . By the end of 2007 there were 49 parties to the Convention; some earlier parties (Australia, Canada, and Nigeria) have denounced it. The Convention represents a modernization and drafting improvement of the 1933 text and encompasses also the subjects covered in the 1938 Brussels Protocol. The positive aspects of this unification of law are:

- strict liability that attaches to the operator of the aircraft; the victim on the surface is entitled to compensation upon proof only that the damage was caused by an aircraft in flight or by any person or thing falling therefrom;

- the liability is guaranteed by detailed provisions on security or operator's liability;
- single forum jurisdiction; all claims must be brought to courts in the state where the damage occurred and all claims are to be consolidated for disposal in a single proceeding before the same court;
- the judgment is to be recognized and enforced in other contracting States.

The negative element of the Convention is the severed limitation of liability. That was in fact the very purpose of the Convention which in the Preamble declares

> desire to ensure adequate compensation for persons who suffer damage caused on the surface by foreign aircraft, while limiting in a reasonable manner the extent of the liability incurred for such damage in order not to hinder the development of international air transport . . .

Limitation of liability is thus clearly aimed at the protection of the infant industry and it is the innocent victims on the ground who are expected to 'subsidize' the development of international air transport.

Like in the 1933 Convention, the Rome 1952 limits are tied to the weight of the aircraft – a very unconvincing benchmark because even a very light aircraft may cause extensive damage if it crashes against a sensitive target (gas works, oil refinery, nuclear plant).

The typical aircraft in today's international transport are heavier than 50 tons, the highest category under Article 1, paragraph 1(d) of the Convention; there the limit is determined as 10,500,000 francs plus 100 francs for each additional kilogram. According to the parties applicable in 1952 that was US$773,850 plus $7.37 for each additional kilogram. The limit of liability for a crashed B-747 would be less than US$3 million – an unrealistically low amount if we consider the scenario of a crash in populous downtown area of an industrial plant.

The specific limit for death or personal injury is 500,000 francs – only twice the limit for passengers under the Warsaw/Hague system that is now obsolete. Moreover, this sum may be reduced 'proportionately' if the sum of all claims exceeds the overall limit.

With the exception of Italy, Russia and the United Arab Emirates no major aviation country is party to the Convention and the Convention does not reflect the current needs of the international community.[6]

Post–September 11, 2001

Liability to third parties on the ground garnered particular attention following the hijackings and terrorist attacks against targets in the United States on 11 September 2001.

> The nature of the 11 September 2001 disaster was purely domestic. The aircraft involved were registered in the United States, were operated by

airlines with principal place of business in the US and were on domestic flights; the damage occurred on US territory. Any event of this nature and the claims for compensation resulting from it would not attract the application of foreign law or need for an international instrument for the unification of private law.

However, the impact of '911' was felt throughout the world and has thrown the airlines of the world into crisis, threatening the future viability of aviation and insurance industries. The airlines lost billions of dollars in the years that followed '911' and many governments had to bail out their national airlines from the brink of bankruptcy by massive cash and loan subsidies.

The situation was aggravated by the steep increases in the price of fuel that accounted for 13% of the airlines' operating costs prior to '911' and by the end of 2007 reach over 30%. Intrusive and time-consuming preventative measures, insensitive searches and screening of passengers, coupled often with intimidating attitudes of the security officers, turned away for a long time many passengers from air transport or from some airports.

Risk management became a major problem for the airlines around the world. As of 23 September 2001 the aviation insurers invoked the often overlooked 'seven-day-clause' in the policies and cancelled all war and terrorism clauses from the aviation insurance policies; later they reintroduced such coverage but for limited amounts. The insurance market – underfunded and overexposed over many years – could have completely collapsed. The lack of available insurance for third-party risk would have grounded many airlines but some States stepped in with governmental guarantees.

ICAO attempted to facilitate the availability of third-party insurance with the unsuccessful effort to find an alternative to commercial insurance for airlines. The planned proposal of an "ICAO Global Scheme on Aviation War Risk Insurance" – generally referred to as "Globaltime" – would have set up a non-profit Insurance Entity collecting premiums payable by passengers and any pay-out for damage caused to third parties on the surface in cases of aviation terrorism would be guaranteed by the participating governments. The scheme was supposed to become operational when agreement on participation is reached from States responsible for 51% of the contributions to the ICAO budget; that target was not achieved since, *inter alia*, the largest potential contributors (USA and Japan) did not join.

The actions within ICAO included the establishment of the Special Group on Aviation Was Risk Insurance (SGWI), Council Study Group on Aviation War Risk Insurance (CGWI) and a Review Group (SGWI-RG), Council Special Group on the Modernization of the Rome Convention of 1952) SGMR) – all *ad hoc* bodies not foreseen in the applicable rues or established practices.

A Rapporteur of the Legal Committee was appointed in early 2002 and the issue was considered at the 32nd session of the Legal Committee held in Montreal from 15 to 21 March 2004; its only conclusion was that the problem required more work. Little enthusiasm was indicated for any 'modernization' of the 1952 Rome Convention, although the special problem of incidents caused by terrorist acts proved to be somewhat more attractive.

The result of these studies were two draft conventions – one dealing with liability and compensation in cases of damage caused by unlawful interference and the other dealing with liability and compensation where there is no unlawful interference.[7]

The General Risks Convention

One of the two treaties adopted at the International Conference on Air Law held in Montreal under the auspices of ICAO in April and May 2009 was the Convention on Compensation for Damage Caused by Aircraft to Third Parties, generally referred to as the General Risks Convention. State parties to the Convention recognised the need for adequate third-party compensation for damage suffered as a result of events involving aircraft in flight. States also recognised the need to modernise the Rome Convention 1952 and its 1978 amending protocol.

> . . . ICAO's initiative to convene the Conference has its genesis in the effort of the Organization to modernize the Rome Convention of 1952, which addressed damage caused to third parties on the surface by foreign aircraft. It must, however, be noted that even before ICAO was established in 1944 by the Chicago Convention there were established principles pertaining to damage caused by an aircraft in flight to persons or property on the surface, which gave rise to a right to compensation on proof only that damage exists and that it is attributable to the aircraft concerned. These principles were established by the Rome Convention of 1933 . . .
>
> In adopting the *General Risks Convention* there were several considerations that were taken into account by the ICAO Member States other than the need to modernize the Rome Convention. The States Parties also recognized the importance of ensuring protection of the interests of third-party victims and the need for equitable compensation, as well as the need to enable the continued stability of the aviation industry. They saw a compelling need for the orderly development of international air transport operations and the smooth flow of passengers, baggage, and cargo in accordance with the principles and objectives of the *Convention on International Civil Aviation*, done at Chicago on 7 December 1944. Furthermore, they were convinced that collective State action for further harmonization and codification of certain rules governing the compensation of third parties who suffer damage resulting from events involving aircraft

in flight through a new Convention is the most desirable and effective means of achieving an equitable balance of interests.

Some general features of the convention

The *General Risks Convention*, which imposes liability on the operator of aircraft, extends that liability to property and environmental damage, and allows for damages to be paid for death, bodily injury, and mental injury. It goes on to say that damages due to mental injury shall be compensable only if caused by a 'recognizable psychiatric illness' resulting either from bodily injury or from direct exposure to the likelihood of imminent death or bodily injury. The term 'recognizable psychiatric illness' has not been defined in the Convention, which has seemingly left the matter to judicial interpretation if litigation were to arise where this provision is invoked. Although there is a distinct *cursus curiae* admitting of compensation for mental injury which is caused as a direct result of bodily injury, this is the first instance of legislative provision in private air law that allows for compensation for mental injury caused from direct exposure to the likelihood of imminent death or bodily injury.[8]

The Unlawful Interference Compensation Convention

The second of the two treaties adopted at the 2009 International Conference of Air Law was the Convention on Compensation for Damage to Third Parties Resulting from Acts of Unlawful Interference Involving Aircraft (the Unlawful Interference Compensation Convention). This Convention provides for strict liability of an aircraft operator to pay compensation for damage (if that damage was caused by an aircraft in flight) to third parties. State responsibility, under the Convention, does not extend to private acts of unlawful interference with civil aviation.

The Convention, in its *Preamble*, gives its rationale as having emerged through an initial recognition of the States Parties that acts of unlawful interference with aircraft that cause damage to third parties and to property have serious consequences and that there are currently no harmonized rules relating to such consequences. The States Parties also recognized the importance of ensuring protection of the interests of third-party victims and the need for equitable compensation, as well as the need to protect the aviation industry from the consequences of damage caused by unlawful interference with aircraft. Accordingly, it was concluded there was a compelling need for a coordinated and concerted approach toward providing compensation to third-party victims, based on cooperation between all affected parties. It was therefore reaffirmed that there should be an orderly development of international air transport operations and smooth flow of passengers, baggage, and cargo in accordance with the principles and objectives of the Chicago Convention. The approach taken in the

Convention was therefore to ensure collective State action for harmonization and codification of certain rules governing compensation for the consequences of an event of unlawful interference with aircraft in flight, through
a new Convention which would achieve an equitable balance of interests.

Some general features of the convention

The *Unlawful Interference Compensation Convention*, which also imposes
liability for property and environmental damage, introduces an interesting
dimension of operator liability in that it extends the operator's liability
to its 'senior management'. The term 'senior management' is defined in
the Convention as members of an operator's supervisory board, members
of its board of directors, or other senior officers of the operator who have
the authority to make and have significant roles in making binding decisions
about how the whole of or a substantial part of the operator's activities
are to be managed or organized. This is an implicit reflection of a trend
at common law which admits of corporate negligence and negligent
entrustment.

  [. . .]

Another innovation of the *Unlawful Interference Compensation Convention* is
that, similar to the *General Risks Convention*, it allows for damages to be
paid for death, bodily injury, and mental injury and goes on to say that
damages due to mental injury shall be compensable only if caused by a
'recognizable psychiatric illness' resulting either from bodily injury or from
direct exposure to the likelihood of imminent death or bodily injury. As
stated earlier with regard to the General Risks Convention, the term
'recognizable psychiatric illness' has not been defined in the Convention,
which has seemingly left the matter to judicial interpretation if litigation
were to arise where this provision is invoked.[9]

THE FUTURE OF INTERNATIONAL AIR SAFETY AND SECURITY

Discussion of the 11 September, 2011 terrorist attacks raises issues regarding
modernisation of the international regime which provides for safety and security
in the commercial aviation industry. These issues include new and evolving
aviation threats, dangers confronting the international state system including
domestic and regional instability, the changing nature of terrorism and the need
for increased security, and the most appropriate mechanisms to further safeguard
aviation in general.

Beijing Convention and Protocol 2010 (not in force)

Two international agreements concluded in China in 2010 form an integral
part of the modernisation of air safety and security. These Conventions (together

with an amending protocol) amend the 1971 Hague Convention and replace the Montreal Convention 1973 and its 1988 Protocol.

Both agreements address the conduct of the 9/11 terrorist attacks and activity that may threaten international civil aviation and public security. They include international counterterrorism provisions which take account of modern standards concerning both jurisdictional issues and the activities of armed and military forces.

These agreements will enter into force following the deposit with ICAO of twenty-two instruments of state ratification, such agreements summarised as follows:

September 11 Inspired Aviation Counter-Terrorism Convention and Protocol Adopted

Overview of the Amendments to the Montreal and Hague Conventions

<u>New Principal Offenses</u>

The Beijing Convention includes several new principal offenses. The first criminalizes the use of a civil aircraft to cause death, serious bodily injury, or serious damage to property or the environment. In other words, using aircraft as a weapon is now a specific offense. This would cover such conduct as flying an aircraft into a building as occurred in the September 11 attacks.

The second new offense criminalizes the releasing or discharging from a civil aircraft any biological, chemical, or nuclear ("BCN") weapon or explosive, radioactive or similar substances in a manner that is likely to cause death, serious bodily injury, or serious damage to property or the environment.

The third new offense is similar to the second, but specifically criminalizes the use of the same dangerous items against or on board a civil aircraft. In this scenario, the target is the actual aircraft and the persons on board, rather than anything outside the aircraft. This is a situation that has occurred with some frequency over the recent years.

A major development is the inclusion of a provision criminalizing the transport of dangerous materials such as explosive or radioactive material, a BCN weapon, or source or special fissionable material if proof is shown of specific mental elements in relation to the transport of each type of dangerous material. For instance, the provision makes an individual liable under this offense if the person transported the explosive or radioactive materials knowing they will be used for a terrorist purpose, or if the person transported source or special fissionable material knowing that they will be used in a nuclear explosive activity. These requirements restrict the scope of the offenses to cover only transport connected with illicit proliferation or terrorism. The changes also preserve the rights of states parties to the NPT, ensuring that state officials are not prosecuted for transporting nuclear materials as permitted by the NPT.

For those not party to the NPT, the offense will apply, except that transport of source or special fissionable material is permitted if done pursuant to a safeguards agreement concluded with the International Atomic Energy Agency. This includes comprehensive, as well as voluntary or facility-specific, safeguards agreements.

The rationale for the transport offense is to deter and punish movement of materials of proliferation around the world by air into the hands of state or non-state actors in circumstances that would pose a threat to international peace and security. The offense parallels a similar transport offense contained in the 2005 Protocol to the Convention for the Suppression of Unlawful Acts.

Accordingly, transportation of these materials by sea or air is now an international criminal offense subject to the extradition or prosecution requirements of the Convention.

New Ancillary and Inchoate Offenses

The Beijing Convention and Protocol include several new ancillary and inchoate offenses. They provide that it is an offense to directly or indirectly threaten to commit one or more of the principal offenses, or to organize or direct the commission of an offense.

These provisions are meant to harmonize recent UN counter-terrorism conventions.

In addition, the instruments include a fugitives offense which criminalizes any assistance to persons evading investigation, prosecution, or punishment, knowing that he or she has committed one of the offenses or is wanted for prosecution or to serve a sentence. This crime is akin to an accessory after the fact offense known to many common law jurisdictions and will help restrict the movement of those seeking to flee states where they may face prosecution. The instruments also incorporate a conspiracy or association de malfaiteurs offense which criminalizes the planning of an offense in conjunction with others reflecting both the common law and civil law traditions. This is the first time a UN counter-terrorism convention has included such a provision. It is designed to allow enforcement officers to apprehend and prosecute offenders before terrorist attacks can be carried out.

Expanded Jurisdiction

Both the Beijing Convention and Protocol include nationality of the offender as a mandatory ground for jurisdiction for states parties. This will help to expand the extra-territorial scope of the instruments and ensure that a greater number of states parties will have jurisdiction to prosecute or extradite known offenders. The instruments also include optional jurisdiction on the basis of nationality of the victims of offenses.

Activities of Armed Forces

The Beijing Convention and Protocol exclude from their scope the activities of armed forces during an armed conflict.

This provision was the most controversial aspect of the negotiations. Essentially, it means that members of armed forces cannot be prosecuted if they undertake an act that would amount to an offense under the instruments. For example, the use of a bomb against a civil airliner by military forces during an armed conflict could not be prosecuted under the Beijing Convention. However, if this conduct amounted to a violation of IHL (because it was not a legitimate military objective), then it could be prosecuted under that body of law.

Extradition Safeguards

The instruments include new provisions aimed at supporting extradition and mutual legal assistance obligations. In particular, none of the offenses can be considered a political offense in order to avoid these obligations. However, no state may be compelled to extradite a person or provide mutual legal assistance if there are substantial grounds to believe that it would lead to prosecution on discriminatory grounds.

Entry into Force

The Beijing Convention and Protocol will enter into force two months after the twenty-second ratification.

Implications

The adoption of the Beijing Convention and Protocol is a significant development in international counter-terrorism and aviation law. The new principal offenses combined with the ancillary offenses, expanded jurisdiction, and strengthened extradition and mutual assistance regimes will help to ensure that a range of individuals can be brought to justice for their role in terrorist or proliferation activities, including those who participate before, during, and after such acts. If the instruments are widely accepted, they can help prevent a repetition of the September 11 attacks.[10]

Montreal Protocol 2014 (not in force)

The Tokyo Convention 1963 was amended in 2014 by the Montreal Protocol which, as yet, has not entered into force. When it does, it will broaden the jurisdictional grounds (in accordance with specified criteria) for offences and action on board aircraft of the state of the operating carrier and the state in which the aircraft lands. The exercise of jurisdiction is mandatory when the specified criteria is met.

State ability to limit the growing frequency and escalation of unruly behaviour in flight will be strengthened by the Protocol. IATA has noted that

> [u]nruly passengers are a very small minority. But unacceptable behavior on board an aircraft can have serious consequences for the safety of all on board. They inconvenience other passengers and lead to significant operational disruption and cost for airlines. But due to loopholes in existing laws, there are many cases where those who commit serious offenses are not punished.

The Protocol affords in-flight security personnel certain protections and addresses issues including inter-state coordination and other like procedural matters. Recovery can also be sought in accordance with domestic laws.

Joint Position Calling for States to Ratify the Montreal Protocol 2014 to Deter Unruly Passenger Incidents and Promote a Safer Air Travel Experience for All

The International Air Transport Association (IATA) has conducted a detailed analysis of unruly passenger incidents and their root causes, based on non-mandatory reports received from 170 airlines. These statistics . . . show a clear upward trend in unruly passenger incidents since 2007. Long-term analysis indicates that for the period 2007 to 2013, over 28,400 incidents were reported. This equates to an average of one incident per 1,600 flights. Of these incidents, almost 20% were serious enough to require the intervention of police or security services.

A key issue is that a significant number of unruly passengers that are involved in these events rarely face prosecution or other legal or economic sanction. This is because of jurisdictional and other gaps in the Tokyo Convention 1963 ("the Convention"), the international aviation law instrument that covers offenses and certain other acts committed on board aircraft. These gaps (explained overleaf) undermine the deterrent effect of the Convention.

In 2009, the increase in unruly passenger incidents led IATA to make a formal request to the International Civil Aviation Organization (ICAO) to review and enhance the Convention to allow law enforcement authorities adequate means to pursue offenders. A detailed and lengthy review process culminated in a Diplomatic Conference held between 26 March and 4 April 2014. Attended by 88 delegations from Member States, the Conference adopted the 'Protocol to amend the Convention on Offences and Certain other Acts Committed on board Aircraft' ("the Protocol").

Taken together with the operational measures already being implemented by airlines to prevent and manage unruly incidents, the Protocol will provide a more effective deterrent by making the consequences of such behavior clear and enforceable. This will lead to a safer and a more pleasant air travel experience for all.

[. . .]

Key benefits of the Montreal Protocol 2014

a. Extension of Jurisdiction

In a representative survey of over 50 airlines in 2013, over 60% indicated that lack of jurisdiction was the key reason for failure to prosecute unruly passengers at foreign destinations. In other cases countries lack specific language within their penal codes to allow for the arrest and prosecution of unruly passengers even when jurisdiction is not an issue.

The Tokyo Convention grants jurisdiction over offenses and other acts committed on board aircraft to the State of registration of the aircraft in question. This causes issues when the Captain of the aircraft delivers or disembarks an unruly passenger to the competent authorities who often determine that they do not have jurisdiction (as the State of landing) when the aircraft is registered in another State. Likewise, the police and authorities in the State of registration may have little connection with an incident taking place in another country. The result is that the unruly passenger may be released to continue their journey without facing punishment for their misconduct.

The new Protocol will give States the tools they require to deal with unruly passengers, whilst preserving prosecutional discretion. Specifically:

a. The Protocol gives mandatory jurisdiction to the intended State of landing (the scheduled destination). However, two safeguards were included to reflect the concerns of some states on legal certainty and proportionality. Firstly, the offense must be sufficiently serious i.e. where the safety of the aircraft or of persons or property therein, or good order and discipline on board is jeopardized. Secondly, the State of landing must consider if the offence is an offence in the State of operator.
b. If the aircraft diverts to a third State, the Protocol gives that State the competence to exercise jurisdiction at its discretion.
c. The Protocol establishes mandatory jurisdiction for the State of operator. This takes account of the increasing trend toward dry leasing aircraft where the State of aircraft registration is not necessarily the State of operator.

b. Definition of Offenses

The Protocol clarifies certain behaviours which should be considered, at a minimum, as an offense and encourages States to take appropriate criminal or other legal proceedings. These include physical assault or a threat to commit such assault against a crew member and refusal to follow a lawful instruction given by or on behalf of the aircraft Commander (for safety purposes). The elaboration of the types of conduct prohibited will improve certainty for passengers, law enforcement authorities and airlines.

c. Right of Recourse

Airlines usually have to bear the costs incurred as a result of unruly passenger incidents. Where this involves diversions to disembark an unruly passenger, the cost can be substantial, in some instances over US$200,000. The Protocol recognizes that airlines may have a right to seek compensation for costs incurred as a result of unruly passenger behavior. The presence of this clause should have strong deterrent value.[11]

Notes

1 Abeyratne, Ruwantissa I.R. "A Protocol to Amend the Tokyo Convention of 1963: Some Unanswered Questions", *Air and Space Law* 39(1) (2014): 48–49.
2 International Civil Aviation Organization. "The Postal History of ICAO: Legal Instruments related to Aviation Security". www.icao.int/secretariat/postalhistory/legal_instruments_related_to_aviation_security.htm. Accessed 7 June 2016.
3 UN Chronicle. "International Controls to Regulate Plastic Explosives Adopted in Montreal", *UN Chronicle* 28(2) (June 1991): 32.
4 The Parliament of the Commonwealth of Australia Joint Standing Committee on Treaties. "Convention on the Marking of Plastic Explosives for the Purpose of Detection". In *Review of Treaties tabled on 11 October 2005 (2), 28 February and 29 March 2006 (2)*. Canberra: Commonwealth of Australia, 2006, 6–7.
5 Milde, Michael. *International Air Law and ICAO*. The Hague: Eleven International Publishing, 2012, 286.
6 Milde. *International Air Law and ICAO*, 287–288.
7 Milde. *International Air Law and ICAO*, 289–290.
8 Abeyratne, Ruwantissa I.R. "The ICAO Conventions on Liability for Third Party Damage Caused by Aircraft", *Air and Space Law* 34 (6) (2009): 403–406.
9 Abeyratne, Ruwantissa I.R. "The ICAO Conventions", 407–410.
10 Van der Toorn, Damien. "September 11 Inspired Aviation Counter-Terrorism Convention and Protocol Adopted", *American Society of International Law Insights* 15(3) (2011). www.asil.org/insights/volume/15/issue/3/september-11-inspired-aviation-counter-terrorism-convention-and-protocol. Accessed 11 August 2016.
11 International Air Transport Association. "Joint Position Calling for States to Ratify the Montreal Protocol 2014 to Deter Unruly Passenger Incidents and Promote a Safer Air Travel Experience for All". www.iata.org/policy/Documents/tokyo-revision-position-paper.pdf. Accessed 7 June 2016.

Section 5

Safety and Security Conventions

5.1 Tokyo Convention 1963

CONVENTION ON OFFENCES AND CERTAIN OTHER ACTS COMMITTED ON BOARD AIRCRAFT

Signed at Tokyo on 14 September 1963

THE STATES PARTIES to this Convention

HAVE AGREED as follows:

Chapter I – Scope of the Convention

Article 1

1. This Convention shall apply in respect of:

    (a) offences against penal law;
    (b) acts which, whether or not they are offences, may or do jeopardize the safety of the aircraft or of persons or property therein or which jeopardize good order and discipline on board.

2. Except as provided in Chapter III, this Convention shall apply in respect of offences committed or acts done by a person on board any aircraft registered in a Contracting State, while that aircraft is in flight or on the surface of the high seas or of any other area outside the territory of any State.
3. For the purposes of this Convention, an aircraft is considered to be in flight from the moment when power is applied for the purpose of take-off until the moment when the landing run ends.
4. This Convention shall not apply to aircraft used in military, customs or police services.

Article 2

Without prejudice to the provisions of Article 4 and except when the safety of the aircraft or of persons or property on board so requires, no provision of this Convention shall be interpreted as authorizing or requiring any action in respect of offences against penal laws of a political nature or those based on racial or religious discrimination.

Chapter II – Jurisdiction

Article 3

1. The State of registration of the aircraft is competent to exercise jurisdiction over offences and acts committed on board.
2. Each Contracting State shall take such measures as may be necessary to establish its jurisdiction as the State of registration over offences committed on board aircraft registered in such State.
3. This Convention does not exclude any criminal jurisdiction exercised in accordance with national law.

Article 4

A Contracting State which is not the State of Registration may not interfere with an aircraft in flight in order to exercise its criminal jurisdiction over an offence committed on board except in the following cases:

   (a) the offence has effect on the territory of such State;
   (b) the offence has been committed by or against a national or permanent resident of such State;
   (c) the offence is against the security of such State;
   (d) the offence consists of a breach of any rules or regulations relating to the flight or manoeuvre of aircraft in force in such State;
   (e) the exercise of jurisdiction is necessary to ensure the observance of any obligation of such State under a multilateral international agreement.

Chapter III – Powers of the Aircraft Commander

Article 5

1. The provisions of this Chapter shall not apply to offences and acts committed or about to be committed by a person on board an aircraft in flight in the airspace of the State of registration or over the high seas or any other area outside the territory of any State unless the last point of take-off or the next point of intended landing is situated in a State other than that of registration, or the aircraft subsequently flies in the airspace of a State other than that of registration with such person still on board.

2. Notwithstanding the provisions of Article 1, paragraph 3, an aircraft shall for the purposes of this chapter, be considered to be in flight at any time from the moment when all its external doors are closed following embarkation until the moment when any such door is opened for disembarkation. In the case of a forced landing, the provisions of this chapter shall continue to apply with respect to offences and acts committed on board until competent authorities of a State take over the responsibility for the aircraft and for the persons and property on board.

Article 6

1. The aircraft commander may, when he has reasonable grounds to believe that a person has committed, or is about to commit, on board the aircraft, an offence or act contemplated in Article 1 paragraph 1, impose upon such person reasonable measures including restraint which are necessary;

   (a) to protect the safety of the aircraft, or of persons or property therein; or
   (b) to maintain good order and discipline on board; or
   (c) to enable him to deliver such person to competent authorities or to disembark him in accordance with the provisions of this Chapter.

2. The aircraft commander may require or authorise the assistance of other crew members and may request or authorise, but not require, the assistance of passengers to restrain any person whom he is entitled to restrain. Any crew member or passenger may also take reasonable preventive measures without such authorization when he has reasonable grounds to believe that such action is immediately necessary to protect the safety of the aircraft, or of persons or property therein.

Article 7

1. Measures of restraint imposed upon a person in accordance with Article 6 shall not be continued beyond any point at which the aircraft lands unless:

   (a) such point is in the territory of a non-Contracting State and its authorities refuse to permit disembarkation of that person or those measures have been imposed in accordance with Article 6, paragraph 1(c) in order to enable his delivery to competent authorities;
   (b) the aircraft makes a forced landing and the aircraft commander is unable to deliver that person to competent authorities; or
   (c) that person agrees to onward carriage under restraint.

2. The aircraft commander shall as soon as practicable, and if possible before landing in the territory of a State with a person on board who has been placed under restraint in accordance with the provisions of Article 6, notify the authorities of such State of the fact that a person on board is under restraint and of the reasons for such restraint.

Article 8

1. The aircraft commander may, in so far as it is necessary for the purpose of subparagraph (a) or (b) of paragraph 1 of Article 6, disembark in the territory of any state in which the aircraft lands any person who he has reasonable grounds to believe has committed, or is about to commit, on board the aircraft an act contemplated in Article 1, paragraph 1(b).
2. The aircraft commander shall report to the authorities of the State in which he disembarks any person pursuant to this Article, the fact of, and the reasons for, such disembarkation.

Article 9

1. The aircraft commander may deliver to the competent authorities of any Contracting State in the territory of which the aircraft lands any person who he has reasonable grounds to believe has committed on board the aircraft an act which, in his opinion, is a serious offence according to the penal law of the State of registration of the aircraft.
2. The aircraft commander shall as soon as practicable and if possible before landing in the territory of a Contracting State with a person on board whom the aircraft commander intends to deliver in accordance with the preceding paragraph, notify the authorities of such State of his intention to deliver such person and the reasons therefor.
3. The aircraft commander shall furnish the authorities to whom any suspected offender is delivered in accordance with the provisions of this Article with evidence and information which, under the law of the State of registration of the aircraft, are lawfully in his possession.

Article 10

For actions taken in accordance with this Convention, neither the aircraft commander, any other member of the crew, any passenger, the owner or operator of the aircraft, nor the person on whose behalf the flight was performed shall be held responsible in any proceeding on account of the treatment undergone by the person against whom the actions were taken.

Chapter IV – Unlawful Seizure of Aircraft

Article 11

1. When a person on board has unlawfully committed by force or threat thereof an act of interference, seizure, or other wrongful exercise of control of an aircraft in flight or when such an act is about to be committed, Contracting States shall take all appropriate measures to restore control of the aircraft to its lawful commander or to preserve his control of the aircraft.

2. In the cases contemplated in the preceding paragraph, the Contracting State in which the aircraft lands shall permit its passengers and crew to continue their journey as soon as practicable, and shall return the aircraft and its cargo to the persons lawfully entitled to possession.

Chapter V – Powers and Duties of States

Article 12

Any Contracting State shall allow the commander of an aircraft registered in another Contracting State to disembark any person pursuant to Article 8, paragraph 1.

Article 13

1. Any Contracting State shall take delivery of any person whom the aircraft commander delivers pursuant to Article 9, paragraph 1.
2. Upon being satisfied that the circumstances so warrant, any Contracting State shall take custody or other measures to ensure the presence of any person suspected of an act contemplated in Article 11, paragraph 1 and of any person of whom it has taken delivery. The custody and other measures shall be as provided in the law of the State but may only be continued for such time as is reasonably necessary to enable any criminal or extradition proceedings to be instituted.
3. Any person in custody pursuant to the previous paragraph shall be assisted in communicating immediately with the nearest appropriate representative of the State of which he is a national.
4. Any Contracting State, to which a person is delivered pursuant to Article 9, paragraph 1, or in whose territory an aircraft lands following the commission of an act contemplated in Article 11, paragraph 1, shall immediately make a preliminary enquiry into the facts.
5. When a State, pursuant to this Article, has taken a person into custody, it shall immediately notify the State of registration of the aircraft and the State of nationality of the detained person and, if it considers it advisable, any other interested State of the fact that such person is in custody and of the circumstances which warrant his detention. The State which makes the preliminary enquiry contemplated in paragraph 4 of this Article shall promptly report its findings to the said States and shall indicate whether it intends to exercise jurisdiction.

Article 14

1. When any person has been disembarked in accordance with Article 8, paragraph 1, or delivered in accordance with Article 9, paragraph 1, or

has disembarked after committing an act contemplated in Article 11, paragraph 1, and when such person cannot or does not desire to continue his journey and the State of landing refuses to admit him, that State may, if the person in question is not a national or permanent resident of that State, return him to the territory of the State of which he is a national or permanent resident or to the territory of the State in which he began his journey by air.

2. Neither disembarkation, nor delivery, nor the taking of custody or other measures contemplated in Article 13, paragraph 2, nor return of the person concerned, shall be considered as admission to the territory of the Contracting State concerned for the purpose of its law relating to entry or admission of persons and nothing in this Convention shall affect the law of a Contracting State relating to the expulsion of persons from its territory.

Article 15

1. Without prejudice to Article 14, any person who has been disembarked in accordance with Article 8, paragraph 1, or delivered in accordance with Article 9, paragraph 1, or has disembarked after committing an act contemplated in Article 11, paragraph 1, and who desires to continue his journey shall be at liberty as soon as practicable to proceed to any destination of his choice unless his presence is required by the law of the State of landing for the purpose of extradition or criminal proceedings.

2. Without prejudice to its law as to entry and admission to, and extradition and expulsion from its territory, a Contracting State in whose territory a person has been disembarked in accordance with Article 8, paragraph 1, or delivered in accordance with Article 9, paragraph 1 or has disembarked and is suspected of having committed an act contemplated in Article 11, paragraph 1, shall accord to such person treatment which is no less favourable for his protection and security than that accorded to nationals of such Contracting State in like circumstances.

Chapter VI – Other Provisions

Article 16

1. Offences committed on aircraft registered in a Contracting State shall be treated, for the purpose of extradition, as if they had been committed not only in the place in which they have occurred but also in the territory of the State of registration of the aircraft.

2. Without prejudice to the provisions of the preceding paragraph, nothing in this Convention shall be deemed to create an obligation to grant extradition.

Article 17

In taking any measures for investigation or arrest or otherwise exercising jurisdiction in connection with any offence committed on board an aircraft the Contracting States shall pay due regard to the safety and other interests of air navigation and shall so act as to avoid unnecessary delay of the aircraft, passengers, crew or cargo.

Article 18

If Contracting States establish joint air transport operating organizations or international operating agencies which operate aircraft not registered in any one State those States shall, according to the circumstances of the case, designate the State among them which, for the purposes of this Convention, shall be considered as the State of registration and shall give notice thereof to the International Civil Aviation Organisation which shall communicate the notice to all States Parties to this Convention.

Chapter VII – Final Clauses

Article 19

Until the date on which this Convention comes into force in accordance with the provisions of Article 21, it shall remain open for signature on behalf of any State which at that date is a Member of the United Nations or of any of the Specialized Agencies.

Article 20

1. This Convention shall be subject to ratification by the signatory States in accordance with their constitutional procedures.
2. The instruments of ratification shall be deposited with the International Civil Aviation Organisation.

Article 21

1. As soon as twelve of the signatory States have deposited their instruments of ratification of this Convention, it shall come into force between them on the ninetieth day after the date of the deposit of the twelfth instrument of ratification. It shall come into force for each State ratifying thereafter on the ninetieth day after the deposit of its instrument of ratification.
2. As soon as this Convention comes into force, it shall be registered with the Secretary-General of the United Nations by the International Civil Aviation Organisation.

Article 22

1. This Convention shall, after it has come into force, be open for accession by any State Member of the United Nations or of any of the Specialized Agencies.
2. The accession of a State shall be effected by the deposit of an instrument of accession with the International Civil Aviation Organisation and shall take effect on the ninetieth day after the date of such deposit.

Article 23

1. Any Contracting State may denounce this Convention by notification addressed to the International Civil Aviation Organisation.
2. Denunciation shall take effect six months after the date of receipt by the International Civil Aviation Organisation of the notification of denunciation.

Article 24

1. Any dispute between two or more Contracting States concerning the interpretation or application of this Convention which cannot be settled through negotiation, shall, at the request of one of them, be submitted to arbitration. If within six months from the date of the request for arbitration the Parties are unable to agree on the organization of the arbitration, any one of those Parties may refer the dispute to the International Court of Justice by request in conformity with the Statute of the Court.
2. Each State may at the time of signature or ratification of this Convention or accession thereto, declare that it does not consider itself bound by the preceding paragraph. The other Contracting States shall not be bound by the preceding paragraph with respect to any Contracting State having made such a reservation.
3. Any Contracting State having made a reservation in accordance with the preceding paragraph may at any time withdraw this reservation by notification to the International Civil Aviation Organisation.

Article 25

Except as provided in Article 24 no reservation may be made to this Convention.

Article 26

The International Civil Aviation Organisation shall give notice to all States Members of the United Nations or of any of the Specialized Agencies:

(a) of any signature of this Convention and the date thereof;

(b) of the deposit of any instrument of ratification or accession and the date thereof;

(c) of the date on which this Convention comes into force in accordance with Article 21, paragraph 1;

(d) of the receipt of any notification of denunciation and the date thereof; and

(e) of the receipt of any declaration or notification made under Article 24 and the date thereof.

IN WITNESS WHEREOF the undersigned Plenipotentiaries, having been duly authorized, have signed this Convention.

DONE at Tokyo on the fourteenth day of September, One Thousand Nine Hundred and Sixty-three in three authentic texts drawn up in the English, French and Spanish languages.

This Convention shall be deposited with the International Civil Aviation Organisation with which, in accordance with Article 19, it shall remain open for signature and the said Organisation shall send certified copies thereof to all States Members of the United Nations or of any Specialised Agency.

5.2 Hague Convention 1970

**CONVENTION FOR THE SUPPRESSION OF
UNLAWFUL SEIZURE OF AIRCRAFT**

Signed at The Hague on 16 December 1970

THE STATES PARTIES TO THIS CONVENTION

CONSIDERING that unlawful acts of seizure or exercise of control of aircraft in flight jeopardise the safety of persons and property, seriously affect the operation of air services, and undermine the confidence of the peoples of the world in the safety of civil aviation;

CONSIDERING that the occurrence of such acts is a matter of grave concern;

CONSIDERING that, for the purpose of deterring such acts, there is an urgent need to provide appropriate measures for punishment of offenders;

HAVE AGREED AS FOLLOWS:

Article 1

Any person who on board an aircraft in flight:

    (a) unlawfully, by force or threat thereof, or by any other form of intimidation, seizes, or exercises control of, that aircraft, or attempts to perform any such act, or

    (b) is an accomplice of a person who performs or attempts to perform any such act commits an offence (hereinafter referred to as "the offence").

Article 2

Each Contracting State undertakes to make the offence punishable by severe penalties.

Article 3

1. For the purposes of this Convention, an aircraft is considered to be in flight at any time from the moment when all its external doors are closed following embarkation until the moment when any such door is opened for disembarkation. In the case of a forced landing, the flight shall be deemed to continue until the competent authorities take over the responsibility for the aircraft and for persons and property on board.
2. This Convention shall not apply to aircraft used in military, customs or police services.
3. This Convention shall apply only if the place of take-off or the place of actual landing of the aircraft on board which the offence is committed is situated outside the territory of the State of registration of that aircraft; it shall be immaterial whether the aircraft is engaged in an international or domestic flight.
4. In the cases mentioned in Article 5, this Convention shall not apply if the place of take-off and the place of actual landing of the aircraft on board which the offence is committed are situated within the territory of the same State where that State is one of those referred to in that Article.
5. Notwithstanding paragraphs 3 and 4 of this Article, Articles 6, 7, 8 and 10 shall apply whatever the place of take-off or the place of actual landing of the aircraft, if the offender or the alleged offender is found in the territory of a State other than the State of registration of that aircraft.

Article 4

1. Each Contracting State shall take such measures as may be necessary to establish its jurisdiction over the offence and any other act of violence against passengers or crew committed by the alleged offender in connection with the offence, in the following cases:

   (a) when the offence is committed on board an aircraft registered in that State;
   (b) when the aircraft on board which the offence is committed lands in its territory with the alleged offender still on board;
   (c) when the offence is committed on board an aircraft leased without crew to a lessee who has his principal place of business or, if the lessee has no such place of business, his permanent residence, in that State.

2. Each Contracting State shall likewise take such measures as may be necessary to establish its jurisdiction over the offence in the case where the alleged offender is present in its territory and it does not extradite him pursuant to Article 8 to any of the States mentioned in paragraph 1 of this Article.
3. This Convention does not exclude any criminal jurisdiction exercised in accordance with national law.

Article 5

The Contracting States which establish joint air transport operating organisations or international operating agencies, which operate aircraft which are subject to joint or international registration shall, by appropriate means, designate for each aircraft the State among them which shall exercise the jurisdiction and have the attributes of the State of registration for the purpose of this Convention and shall give notice thereof to the International Civil Aviation Organisation which shall communicate the notice to all States Parties to this Convention.

Article 6

1. Upon being satisfied that the circumstances so warrant, any Contracting State in the territory of which the offender or the alleged offender is present, shall take him into custody or take other measures to ensure his presence. The custody and other measures shall be as provided in the law of that State but may only be continued for such time as is necessary to enable any criminal or extradition proceedings to be instituted.
2. Such State shall immediately make a preliminary enquiry into the facts.
3. Any person in custody pursuant to paragraph 1 of this Article shall be assisted in communicating immediately with the nearest appropriate representative of the State of which he is a national.
4. When a State, pursuant to this Article, has taken a person into custody, it shall immediately notify the State of registration of the aircraft, the State mentioned in Article 4, paragraph 1(c), the State of nationality of the detained person and, if it considers it advisable, any other interested States of the fact that such person is in custody and of the circumstances which warrant his detention. The State which makes the preliminary enquiry contemplated in paragraph 2 of this Article shall promptly report its findings to the said States and shall indicate whether it intends to exercise jurisdiction.

Article 7

The Contracting State in the territory of which the alleged offender is found shall, if it does not extradite him, be obliged, without exception whatsoever and whether or not the offence was committed in its territory, to submit the case to its competent authorities for the purpose of prosecution. Those authorities shall take their decision in the same manner as in the case of any ordinary offence of a serious nature under the law of that State.

Article 8

1. The offence shall be deemed to be included as an extraditable offence in any extradition treaty existing between Contracting States. Contracting

States undertake to include the offence as an extraditable offence in every extradition treaty to be concluded between them.

2. If a Contracting State which makes extradition conditional on the existence of a treaty receives a request for extradition from another Contracting State with which it has no extradition treaty, it may at its option consider this Convention as the legal basis for extradition in respect of the offence. Extradition shall be subject to the other conditions provided by the law of the requested State.

3. Contracting States which do not make extradition conditional on the existence of a treaty shall recognize the offence as an extraditable offence between themselves subject to the conditions provided by the law of the requested State.

4. The offence shall be treated, for the purpose of extradition between Contracting States, as if it had been committed not only in the place in which it occurred but also in the territories of the States required to establish their jurisdiction in accordance with Article 4, paragraph 1.

Article 9

1. When any of the acts mentioned in Article 1(a) has occurred or is about to occur, Contracting States shall take all appropriate measures to restore control of the aircraft to its lawful commander or to preserve his control of the aircraft.

2. In the cases contemplated by the preceding paragraph, any Contracting State in which the aircraft or its passengers or crew are present shall facilitate the continuation of the journey of the passengers and crew as soon as practicable, and shall without delay return the aircraft and its cargo to the persons lawfully entitled to possession.

Article 10

1. Contracting States shall afford one another the greatest measure of assistance in connection with criminal proceedings brought in respect of the offence and other acts mentioned in Article 4. The law of the State requested shall apply in all cases.

2. The provisions of paragraph 1 of this Article shall not affect obligations under any other treaty, bilateral or multilateral, which governs or will govern, in whole or in part, mutual assistance in criminal matters.

Article 11

Each Contracting State shall in accordance with its national law report to the Council of the International Civil Aviation Organisation as promptly as possible any relevant information in its possession concerning:

    (a) the circumstances of the offence;

    (b) the action taken pursuant to Article 9;

    (c) the measures taken in relation to the offender or the alleged offender, and, in particular, the results of any extradition proceedings or other legal proceedings.

Article 12

1. Any dispute between two or more Contracting States concerning the interpretation or application of this Convention which cannot be settled through negotiations, shall, at the request of one of them, be submitted to arbitration. If within six months from the date of the request for arbitration the Parties are unable to agree on the organisation of the arbitration, any one of those Parties may refer the dispute to the International Court of Justice by request in conformity with the Statute of the Court.

2. Each State may at the time of signature or ratification of this Convention or accession thereto, declare that it does not consider itself bound by the preceding paragraph. The other Contracting States shall not be bound by the preceding paragraph with respect to any Contracting State having made such a reservation.

3. Any Contracting State having made a reservation in accordance with the preceding paragraph may at any time withdraw this reservation by notification to the Depositary Governments.

Article 13

1. This Convention shall be open for signature at The Hague on 16 December 1970, by States participating in the International Conference on Air Law held at The Hague from 1 to 16 December 1970 (hereinafter referred to as The Hague Conference). After 31 December 1970, the Convention shall be open to all States for signature in Moscow, London and Washington. Any State which does not sign this Convention before its entry into force in accordance with paragraph 3 of this Article may accede to it at any time.

2. This Convention shall be subject to ratification by the signatory States. Instruments of ratification and instruments of accession shall be deposited with the Governments of the Union of Soviet Socialist Republics, the United Kingdom of Great Britain and Northern Ireland, and the United States of America, which are hereby designated the Depositary Governments.

3. This Convention shall enter into force thirty days following the date of the deposit of instruments of ratification by ten States signatory to this Convention which participated in The Hague Conference.

4. For other States, this Convention shall enter into force on the date of entry into force of this Convention in accordance with paragraph 3 of this Article,

or thirty days following the date of deposit of their instruments of ratification or accession, whichever is later.

5. The Depositary Governments shall promptly inform all signatory and acceding States of the date of each signature, the date of deposit of each instrument of ratification or accession, the date of entry into force of this Convention, and other notices.

6. As soon as this Convention comes into force, it shall be registered by the Depositary Governments pursuant to Article 102 of the Charter of the United Nations and pursuant to Article 83 of the Convention on International Civil Aviation (Chicago, 1944).

Article 14

1. Any Contracting State may denounce this Convention by written notification to the Depositary Governments.

2. Denunciation shall take effect six months following the date on which notification is received by the Depositary Governments.

IN WITNESS WHEREOF the undersigned Plenipotentiaries, being duly authorised thereto by their Governments, have signed this Convention.

DONE at The Hague, this sixteenth day of December, one thousand nine hundred and seventy, in three originals, each being drawn up in four authentic texts in the English, French, Russian and Spanish languages.

5.3 Montreal Convention 1971

CONVENTION FOR THE SUPPRESSION OF UNLAWFUL ACTS AGAINST THE SAFETY OF CIVIL AVIATION

Concluded at Montreal on 23 September 1971

THE STATES PARTIES TO THIS CONVENTION

CONSIDERING that unlawful acts against the safety of civil aviation jeopardize the safety of persons and property, seriously affect the operation of air services, and undermine the confidence of the peoples of the world in the safety of civil aviation;

CONSIDERING that the occurrence of such acts is a matter of grave concern;

CONSIDERING that, for the purpose of deterring such acts, there is an urgent need to provide appropriate measures for punishment of offenders;

HAVE AGREED AS FOLLOWS

Article 1

1. Any person commits an offence if he unlawfully and intentionally:

    (a) performs an act of violence against a person on board an aircraft in flight if that act is likely to endanger the safety of that aircraft; or
    (b) destroys an aircraft in service or causes damage to such an aircraft which renders it incapable of flight or which is likely to endanger its safety in flight; or
    (c) places or causes to be placed on an aircraft in service, by any means whatsoever, a device or substance which is likely to destroy that aircraft, or to cause damage to it which renders it incapable of flight, or to cause damage to it which is likely to endanger its safety in flight; or
    (d) destroys or damages air navigation facilities or interferes with their operation, if any such act is likely to endanger the safety of aircraft in flight; or

(e) communicates information which he knows to be false, thereby endangering the safety of an aircraft in flight.

2. Any person also commits an offence if he:

(a) attempts to commit any of the offences mentioned in paragraph 1 of this Article; or

(b) is an accomplice of a person who commits or attempts to commit any such offence.

Article 2

For the purposes of this Convention:

(a) an aircraft is considered to be in flight at any time from the moment when all its external doors are closed following embarkation until the moment when any such door is opened for disembarkation; in the case of a forced landing, the flight shall be deemed to continue until the competent authorities take over the responsibility for the aircraft and for persons and property on board;

(b) an aircraft is considered to be in service from the beginning of the preflight preparation of the aircraft by ground personnel or by the crew for a specific flight until twenty-four hours after any landing; the period of service shall, in any event, extend for the entire period during which the aircraft is in flight as defined in paragraph (a) of this Article.

Article 3

Each Contracting State undertakes to make the offences mentioned in Article 1 punishable by severe penalties.

Article 4

1. This Convention shall not apply to aircraft used in military, customs or police services.

2. In the cases contemplated in subparagraphs (a), (b), (c) and (e) of paragraph 1 of Article 1, this Convention shall apply, irrespective of whether the aircraft is engaged in an international or domestic flight, only if:

(a) the place of take-off or landing, actual or intended, of the aircraft is situated outside the territory of the State of registration of that aircraft; or

(b) the offence is committed in the territory of a State other than the State of registration of the aircraft.

3. Notwithstanding paragraph 2 of this Article, in the cases contemplated in subparagraphs (a), (b), (c) and (e) of paragraph 1 of Article 1, this

Convention shall also apply if the offender or the alleged offender is found in the territory of a State other than the State of registration of the aircraft.

4. With respect to the States mentioned in Article 9 and in the cases mentioned in subparagraphs (a), (b), (c) and (e) of paragraph 1 of Article 1, this Convention shall not apply if the places referred to in subparagraph (a) of paragraph 2 of this Article are situated within the territory of the same State where that State is one of those referred to in Article 9, unless the offence is committed or the offender or alleged offender is found in the territory of a State other than that State.

5. In the cases contemplated in subparagraph (d) of paragraph 1 of Article 1, this Convention shall apply only if the air navigation facilities are used in international air navigation.

6. The provisions of paragraphs 2, 3, 4 and 5 of this Article shall also apply in the cases contemplated in paragraph 2 of Article 1.

Article 5

1. Each Contracting State shall take such measures as may be necessary to establish its jurisdiction over the offences in the following cases:

   (a) when the offence is committed in the territory of that State;
   (b) when the offence is committed against or on board an aircraft registered in that State;
   (c) when the aircraft on board which the offence is committed lands in its territory with the alleged offender still on board;
   (d) when the offence is committed against or on board an aircraft leased without crew to a lessee who has his principal place of business or, if the lessee has no such place of business, his permanent residence, in that State.

2. Each Contracting State shall likewise take such measures as may be necessary to establish its jurisdiction over the offences mentioned in Article 1, paragraph 1(a), (b) and (c), and in Article 1, paragraph 2, in so far as that paragraph relates to those offences, in the case where the alleged offender is present in its territory and it does not extradite him pursuant to Article 8 to any of the States mentioned in paragraph 1 of this Article.

3. This Convention does not exclude any criminal jurisdiction exercised in accordance with national law.

Article 6

1. Upon being satisfied that the circumstances so warrant, any Contracting State in the territory of which the offender or the alleged offender is present, shall take him into custody or take other measures to ensure his presence. The custody and other measures shall be as provided in the law of that

State but may only be continued for such time as is necessary to enable any criminal or extradition proceedings to be instituted.

2. Such State shall immediately make a preliminary enquiry into the facts.

3. Any person in custody pursuant to paragraph 1 of this Article shall be assisted in communicating immediately with the nearest appropriate representative of the State of which he is a national.

4. When a State, pursuant to this Article, has taken a person into custody, it shall immediately notify the States mentioned in Article 5, paragraph 1, the State of nationality of the detained person and, if it considers it advisable, any other interested States of the fact that such person is in custody and of the circumstances which warrant his detention. The State which makes the preliminary enquiry contemplated in paragraph 2 of this Article shall promptly report its findings to the said States and shall indicate whether it intends to exercise jurisdiction.

Article 7

The Contracting State in the territory of which the alleged offender is found shall, if it does not extradite him, be obliged, without exception whatsoever and whether or not the offence was committed in its territory, to submit the case to its competent authorities for the purpose of prosecution. Those authorities shall take their decision in the same manner as in the case of any ordinary offence of a serious nature under the law of that State.

Article 8

1. The offences shall be deemed to be included as extraditable offences in any extradition treaty existing between Contracting States. Contracting States undertake to include the offences as extraditable offences in every extradition treaty to be concluded between them.

2. If a Contracting State which makes extradition conditional on the existence of a treaty receives a request for extradition from another Contracting State with which it has no extradition treaty, it may at its option consider this Convention as the legal basis for extradition in respect of the offences. Extradition shall be subject to the other conditions provided by the law of the requested State.

3. Contracting States which do not make extradition conditional on the existence of a treaty shall recognize the offences as extraditable offences between themselves subject to the conditions provided by the law of the requested State.

4. Each of the offences shall be treated, for the purpose of extradition between Contracting States, as if it had been committed not only in the place in which it occurred but also in the territories of the States required to establish their jurisdiction in accordance with Article 5, paragraph 1(b), (c) and (d).

Article 9

The Contracting States which establish joint air transport operating organisations or international operating agencies, which operate aircraft which are subject to joint or international registration shall, by appropriate means, designate for each aircraft the State among them which shall exercise the jurisdiction and have the attributes of the State of registration for the purpose of this Convention and shall give notice thereof to the International Civil Aviation Organisation which shall communicate the notice to all States Parties to this Convention.

Article 10

1. Contracting States shall, in accordance with international and national law, endeavour to take all practicable measures for the purpose of preventing the offences mentioned in Article 1.
2. When, due to the commission of one of the offences mentioned in Article 1, a flight has been delayed or interrupted, any Contracting State in whose territory the aircraft or passengers or crew are present shall facilitate the continuation of the journey of the passengers and crew as soon as practicable, and shall without delay return the aircraft and its cargo to the persons lawfully entitled to possession.

Article 11

1. Contracting States shall afford one another the greatest measure of assistance in connection with criminal proceedings brought in respect of the offences. The law of the State requested shall apply in all cases.
2. The provisions of paragraph 1 of this Article shall not affect obligations under any other treaty, bilateral or multilateral, which governs or will govern, in whole or in part, mutual assistance in criminal matters.

Article 12

Any Contracting State having reason to believe that one of the offences mentioned in Article 1 will be committed shall, in accordance with its national law, furnish any relevant information in its possession to those States which it believes would be the States mentioned in Article 5, paragraph 1.

Article 13

Each Contracting State shall in accordance with its national law report to the Council of the International Civil Aviation Organization as promptly as possible any relevant information in its possession concerning:

  (a) the circumstances of the offence;
  (b) the action taken pursuant to Article 10, paragraph 2;

(c) the measures taken in relation to the offender or the alleged offender and, in particular, the results of any extradition proceedings or other legal proceedings.

Article 14

1. Any dispute between two or more Contracting States concerning the interpretation or application of this Convention which cannot be settled through negotiation, shall, at the request of one of them, be submitted to arbitration. If within six months from the date of the request for arbitration the Parties are unable to agree on the organization of the arbitration, any one of those Parties may refer the dispute to the International Court of Justice by request in conformity with the Statute of the Court.
2. Each State may at the time of signature or ratification of this Convention or accession thereto, declare that it does not consider itself bound by the preceding paragraph. The other Contracting States shall not be bound by the preceding paragraph with respect to any Contracting State having made such a reservation.
3. Any Contracting State having made a reservation in accordance with the preceding paragraph may at any time withdraw this reservation by notification to the Depositary Governments.

Article 15

1. This Convention shall be open for signature at Montreal on 23 September 1971, by States participating in the International Conference on Air Law held at Montreal from 8 to 23 September 1971 (hereinafter referred to as the Montreal Conference). After 10 October 1971, the Convention shall be open to all States for signature in Moscow, London and Washington. Any State which does not sign this Convention before its entry into force in accordance with paragraph 3 of this Article may accede to it at any time.
2. This Convention shall be subject to ratification by the signatory States. Instruments of ratification and instruments of accession shall be deposited with the Governments of the Union of Soviet Socialist Republics, the United Kingdom of Great Britain and Northern Ireland, and the United States of America, which are hereby designated the Depositary Governments.
3. This Convention shall enter into force thirty days following the date of the deposit of instruments of ratification by ten States signatory to this Convention which participated in the Montreal Conference.
4. For other States, this Convention shall enter into force on the date of entry into force of this Convention in accordance with paragraph 3 of this Article, or thirty days following the date of deposit of their instruments of ratification or accession, whichever is later.

5. The Depositary Governments shall promptly inform all signatory and acceding States of the date of each signature, the date of deposit of each instrument of ratification or accession, the date of entry into force of this Convention, and other notices.
6. As soon as this Convention comes into force, it shall be registered by the Depositary Governments pursuant to Article 102 of the Charter of the United Nations and pursuant to Article 83 of the Convention on International Civil Aviation (Chicago, 1944).

Article 16

1. Any Contracting State may denounce this Convention by written notification to the Depositary Governments.
2. Denunciation shall take effect six months following the date on which notification is received by the Depositary Governments.

IN WITNESS WHEREOF the undersigned Plenipotentiaries, being duly authorized thereto by their Governments, have signed this Convention.

DONE at Montreal, this twenty-third day of September, one thousand nine hundred and seventy-one, in three originals, each being drawn up in four authentic texts in the English, French, Russian and Spanish languages.

5.4 Montreal Convention 1991

CONVENTION ON THE MARKING OF PLASTIC EXPLOSIVES FOR THE PURPOSE OF DETECTION

Done at Montreal on 1 March 1991

THE STATES PARTIES TO THIS CONVENTION

CONSCIOUS of the implications of acts of terrorism for international security;

EXPRESSING deep concern regarding terrorist acts aimed at destruction of aircraft, other means of transportation and other targets;

CONCERNED that plastic explosives have been used for such terrorist acts;

CONSIDERING that the marking of such explosives for the purpose of detection would contribute significantly to the prevention of such unlawful acts;

RECOGNIZING that for the purpose of deterring such unlawful acts there is an urgent need for an international instrument obliging States to adopt appropriate measures to ensure that plastic explosives are duly marked;

CONSIDERING United Nations Security Council Resolution 635 of 14 June 1989, and United Nations General Assembly Resolution 44/29 of 4 December 1989 urging the International Civil Aviation Organization to intensify its work on devising an international regime for the marking of plastic or sheet explosives for the purpose of detection;

BEARING IN MIND Resolution A27–8 adopted unanimously by the 27th Session of the Assembly of the International Civil Aviation Organization which endorsed with the highest and overriding priority the preparation of a new international instrument regarding the marking of plastic or sheet explosives for detection;

NOTING with satisfaction the role played by the Council of the International Civil Aviation Organization in the preparation of the Convention as well as its willingness to assume functions related to its implementation;

HAVE AGREED AS FOLLOWS:

Article I

For the purposes of this Convention:

1. "Explosives" mean explosive products, commonly known as "plastic explosives", including explosives in flexible or elastic sheet form, as described in the Technical Annex to this Convention.
2. "Detection agent" means a substance as described in the Technical Annex to this Convention which is introduced into an explosive to render it detectable.
3. "Marking" means introducing into an explosive a detection agent in accordance with the Technical Annex to this Convention.
4. "Manufacture" means any process, including reprocessing, that produces explosives.
5. "Duly authorized military devices" include, but are not restricted to, shells, bombs, projectiles, mines, missiles, rockets, shaped charges, grenades and perforators manufactured exclusively for military or police purposes according to the laws and regulations of the State Party concerned.
6. "Producer State" means any State in whose territory explosives are manufactured.

Article II

Each State Party shall take the necessary and effective measures to prohibit and prevent the manufacture in its territory of unmarked explosives.

Article III

1. Each State Party shall take the necessary and effective measures to prohibit and prevent the movement into or out of its territory of unmarked explosives.
2. The preceding paragraph shall not apply in respect of movements for purposes not inconsistent with the objectives of this Convention, by authorities of a State Party performing military or police functions, of unmarked explosives under the control of that State Party in accordance with paragraph 1 of Article IV.

Article IV

1. Each State Party shall take the necessary measures to exercise strict and effective control over the possession and transfer of possession of unmarked explosives which have been manufactured in or brought into its territory prior to the entry into force of this Convention in respect of that State, so as to prevent their diversion or use for purposes inconsistent with the objectives of this Convention.

2. Each State Party shall take the necessary measures to ensure that all stocks of those explosives referred to in paragraph 1 of this Article not held by its authorities performing military or police functions are destroyed or consumed for purposes not inconsistent with the objectives of this Convention, marked or rendered permanently ineffective, within a period of three years from the entry into force of this Convention in respect of that State.

3. Each State Party shall take the necessary measures to ensure that all stocks of those explosives referred to in paragraph 1 of this Article held by its authorities performing military or police functions and that are not incorporated as an integral part of duly authorized military devices are destroyed or consumed for purposes not inconsistent with the objectives of this Convention, marked or rendered permanently ineffective, within a period of fifteen years from the entry into force of this Convention in respect of that State.

4. Each State Party shall take the necessary measures to ensure the destruction, as soon as possible, in its territory of unmarked explosives which may be discovered therein and which are not referred to in the preceding paragraphs of this Article, other than stocks of unmarked explosives held by its authorities performing military or police functions and incorporated as an integral part of duly authorized military devices at the date of the entry into force of this Convention in respect of that State.

5. Each State Party shall take the necessary measures to exercise strict and effective control over the possession and transfer of possession of the explosives referred to in paragraph II of Part 1 of the Technical Annex to this Convention so as to prevent their diversion or use for purposes inconsistent with the objectives of this Convention.

6. Each State Party shall take the necessary measures to ensure the destruction, as soon as possible, in its territory of unmarked explosives manufactured since the coming into force of this Convention in respect of that State that are not incorporated as specified in paragraph II (d) of Part 1 of the Technical Annex to this Convention and of unmarked explosives which no longer fall within the scope of any other sub-paragraphs of the said paragraph II.

Article V

1. There is established by this Convention an International Explosives Technical Commission (hereinafter referred to as "the Commission") consisting of not less than fifteen nor more than nineteen members appointed by the Council of the International Civil Aviation Organization (hereinafter referred to as "the Council") from among persons nominated by States Parties to this Convention.

2. The members of the Commission shall be experts having direct and substantial experience in matters relating to the manufacture or detection of, or research in, explosives.

3. Members of the Commission shall serve for a period of three years and shall be eligible for re-appointment.

4. Sessions of the Commission shall be convened, at least once a year at the Headquarters of the International Civil Aviation Organization, or at such places and times as may be directed or approved by the Council.

5. The Commission shall adopt its rules of procedure, subject to the approval of the Council.

Article VI

1. The Commission shall evaluate technical developments relating to the manufacture, marking and detection of explosives.

2. The Commission, through the Council, shall report its findings to the States Parties and international organizations concerned.

3. Whenever necessary, the Commission shall make recommendations to the Council for amendments to the Technical Annex to this Convention. The Commission shall endeavour to take its decisions on such recommendations by consensus. In the absence of consensus the Commission shall take such decisions by a two-thirds majority vote of its members.

4. The Council may, on the recommendation of the Commission, propose to States Parties amendments to the Technical Annex to this Convention.

Article VII

1. Any State Party may, within ninety days from the date of notification of a proposed amendment to the Technical Annex to this Convention, transmit to the Council its comments. The Council shall communicate these comments to the Commission as soon as possible for its consideration. The Council shall invite any State Party which comments on or objects to the proposed amendment to consult the Commission.

2. The Commission shall consider the views of States Parties made pursuant to the preceding paragraph and report to the Council. The Council, after consideration of the Commission's report, and taking into account the nature of the amendment and the comments of States Parties, including producer States, may propose the amendment to all States Parties for adoption.

3. If a proposed amendment has not been objected to by five or more States Parties by means of written notification to the Council within ninety days from the date of notification of the amendment by the Council, it shall be deemed to have been adopted, and shall enter into force one hundred and eighty days thereafter or after such other period as specified in the proposed amendment for States Parties not having expressly objected thereto.

4. States Parties having expressly objected to the proposed amendment may, subsequently, by means of the deposit of an instrument of acceptance or approval, express their consent to be bound by the provisions of the amendment.

5. If five or more States Parties have objected to the proposed amendment, the Council shall refer it to the Commission for further consideration.

6. If the proposed amendment has not been adopted in accordance with paragraph 3 of this Article, the Council may also convene a conference of all States Parties.

Article VIII

1. States Parties shall, if possible, transmit to the Council information that would assist the Commission in the discharge of its functions under paragraph 1 of Article VI.

2. States Parties shall keep the Council informed of measures they have taken to implement the provisions of this Convention. The Council shall communicate such information to all States Parties and international organizations concerned.

Article IX

The Council shall, in co-operation with States Parties and international organizations concerned, take appropriate measures to facilitate the implementation of this Convention, including the provision of technical assistance and measures for the exchange of information relating to technical developments in the marking and detection of explosives.

Article X

The Technical Annex to this Convention shall form an integral part of this Convention.

Article XI

1. Any dispute between two or more States Parties concerning the interpretation or application of this Convention which cannot be settled through negotiation shall, at the request of one of them, be submitted to

254 Safety and Security

arbitration. If within six months from the date of the request for arbitration the Parties are unable to agree on the organization of the arbitration, any one of those Parties may refer the dispute to the International Court of Justice by request in conformity with the Statute of the Court.

2. Each State Party may, at the time of signature, ratification, acceptance or approval of this Convention or accession thereto, declare that it does not consider itself bound by the preceding paragraph. The other States Parties shall not be bound by the preceding paragraph with respect to any State Party having made such a reservation.

3. Any State Party having made a reservation in accordance with the preceding paragraph may at any time withdraw this reservation by notification to the Depositary.

Article XII

Except as provided in Article XI no reservation may be made to this Convention.

Article XIII

1. This Convention shall be open for signature in Montreal on 1 March 1991 by States participating in the International Conference on Air Law held at Montreal from 12 February to 1 March 1991. After 1 March 1991 the Convention shall be open to all States for signature at the Headquarters of the International Civil Aviation Organization in Montreal until it enters into force in accordance with paragraph 3 of this Article. Any State which does not sign this Convention may accede to it at any time.

2. This Convention shall be subject to ratification, acceptance, approval or accession by States. Instruments of ratification, acceptance, approval or accession shall be deposited with the International Civil Aviation Organization, which is hereby designated the Depositary. When depositing its instrument of ratification, acceptance, approval or accession, each State shall declare whether or not it is a producer State.

3. This Convention shall enter into force on the sixtieth day following the date of deposit of the thirty-fifth instrument of ratification, acceptance, approval or accession with the Depositary, provided that no fewer than five such States have declared pursuant to paragraph 2 of this Article that they are producer States. Should thirty-five such instruments be deposited prior to the deposit of their instruments by five producer States, this Convention shall enter into force on the sixtieth day following the date of deposit of the instrument of ratification, acceptance, approval or accession of the fifth producer State.

4. For other States, this Convention shall enter into force sixty days following the date of deposit of their instruments of ratification, acceptance, approval or accession.

5. As soon as this Convention comes into force, it shall be registered by the Depositary pursuant to Article 102 of the Charter of the United Nations and pursuant to Article 83 of the Convention on International Civil Aviation (Chicago, 1944).

Article XIV

The Depositary shall promptly notify all signatories and States Parties of:

1. each signature of this Convention and date thereof;
2. each deposit of an instrument of ratification, acceptance, approval or accession and date thereof, giving special reference to whether the State has identified itself as a producer State;
3. the date of entry into force of this Convention;
4. the date of entry into force of any amendment to this Convention or its Technical Annex;
5. any denunciation made under Article XV; and
6. any declaration made under paragraph 2 of Article XI.

Article XV

1. Any State Party may denounce this Convention by written notification to the Depositary.
2. Denunciation shall take effect one hundred and eighty days following the date on which notification is received by the Depositary.

IN WITNESS WHEREOF the undersigned Plenipotentiaries, being duly authorized thereto by their Governments, have signed this Convention.

DONE at Montreal, this first day of March, one thousand nine hundred and ninety-one, in one original, drawn up in five authentic texts in the English, French, Russian, Spanish and Arabic languages.

Compensation Conventions for Damage to Third Parties

6.1 Rome Convention 1933

INTERNATIONAL CONVENTION FOR THE UNIFICATION OF CERTAIN RULES RELATING TO DAMAGE CAUSED BY AIRCRAFT TO THIRD PARTIES ON THE SURFACE

Done at Rome on 29 May 1933

Article 1 – Undertaking to Give Effect

The High Contracting Parties agree to take the necessary measures to give effect to the rules established by this Convention.

Article 2 – Proof of Liability

1. Damage caused by an aircraft in flight to persons or property on the surface gives a right to compensation on proof only that the damage exists and that it is attributable to the aircraft.
2. The above provision includes-
   (a) damage caused by an object of any kind falling from the aircraft, even in the event of the proper discharge of ballast or of jettison made in case of necessity;
   (b) damage caused by any person on board the aircraft, save in the case of an act unconnected with the management of the aircraft committed intentionally by a person not being a member of the crew, and without the operator or his servants or agents having been able to prevent it.
3. The aircraft is deemed to be in flight from the beginning of the operations of departure until the end of the operations of arrival.

Article 3 – Contributory Negligence

The liability imposed by the preceding article can be diminished or set aside only if the damage has been caused or contributed to by the negligence of the injured party.

Article 4 – Incidence of Liability

1. The liability imposed by Article 2 falls on the operator of the aircraft.
2. By the term operator of the aircraft is meant any person who has the aircraft at his disposal and who makes use thereof for his own account.
3. If the name of the operator is not inscribed in the aeronautical register or on some other official document, the owner is deemed to be the operator until proof to the contrary.

Article 5

Any person who, without having the aircraft at his disposal, has made use thereof without the consent of the operator is liable for any damage caused, and where the operator has not taken all proper steps to prevent the unlawful use of his aircraft he and the said person are jointly and severally liable, the liability of each being subject to the conditions and limitations of this Convention.

Article 6

In case of damage caused on the surface by two or more aircraft which have been in collision, the operators of such aircraft are jointly and severally liable to third parties suffering damage, the liability of each operator being subject to the conditions and limitations of this Convention.

Article 7

The preceding provisions are without prejudice to the question whether or not the operator of the aircraft may have a right of recourse against the author of the damage.

Article 8 – Amount of Liability

1. The operator is liable for each occurrence up to an amount determined at the rate of 250 francs for each kilogramme of the weight of the aircraft. By the weight of the aircraft is meant its weight with total maximum load as indicated in the certificate of airworthiness or any other official document.
2. Nevertheless the limit of the operator's liability shall not be less than 600,000 francs, nor greater than 2,000,000 francs.
3. One-third of the amount of the maximum liability so determined shall be appropriated to compensation for damage caused to property, and the other two-third to compensation for damage caused to persons, provided that in the latter case the compensation payable shall not exceed 200,000 francs in respect of each person injured.

Article 9 – Apportionment of Compensation

If several persons have suffered damage in the same occurrence and if the total sum payable by way of compensation exceeds the limits fixed in Article 8, the compensation due to each of such persons shall be reduced proportionately so that the total does not exceed the above-mentioned limits.

Article 10 – Time Limit for Claims

1. Persons who have suffered damage in the same occurrence must enforce their rights or notify their claims to the operator within a period of six months at most from the date of the occurrence.
2. At the expiry of this period the settlement of the amounts payable by way of compensation may properly be proceeded with; any interested parties who have allowed the period in question to expire without enforcing their rights or notifying their claims shall only be able to exercise their rights against the amount which has not been distributed.

Article 11 – Multiple Proceedings

If several injured parties take proceedings under the provisions of the preceding articles and of Article 16 before tribunals situated in different countries, the defendant may, before each of such tribunals, give evidence of the total amount of the claims and liabilities, in order that the limits of his liability may not be exceeded.

Article 12 – Insurance Requirements

1. Every aircraft registered in the territory of a High Contracting Party shall, for the purpose of flying above the territory of another High Contracting Party, be insured, within the limits fixed by Article 8, in respect of the damages to which this Convention relates with a State insurance institution or with an insurer authorised in the territory in which the aircraft is registered to undertake such risk.
2. The Municipal law of each High Contracting Party may in whole or in part substitute for insurance another guarantee against the risks to which this Convention relates: –

   (a) in the form of a deposit of money made with a State institution or with a bank authorised for that purpose in the territory in which the aircraft is registered;
   (b) in the form of a guarantee given by a bank authorised for that purpose in the territory in which the aircraft is registered.

   Any such deposit of money or bank guarantee must be made up to the full amount as soon as the sums which it represents are liable to be diminished by a payment of compensation.

262 Safety and Security

3. The indemnity by way of insurance, the deposit of money and the bank guarantee must be appropriated specifically and preferentially to the payment of compensation due in respect of the damages to which this Convention relates.

Article 13

1. The nature, scope and duration of the securities mentioned in Article 12 shall be vouched either by an official certificate or by an official entry in one of the documents carried on board the aircraft. This certificate of document must be produced on the demand of a public authority or of any interested person.
2. The above-mentioned certificate or document shall be evidence of the position of the aircraft in relation to the obligations of this Convention.

Article 14 – Effect of Gross Negligence, Wilful Misconduct, or Failure to Insure

The operator may not avail himself of the provisions of this Convention limiting his liability –

    (a) if it is proved that the damage results from the gross negligence ("faute lourde") or wilful misconduct ("dol") of the operator, or his servants or agents, except where the operator proves that the damage results from negligence in the pilotage, handling or navigation of the aircraft, or, where his servants or agents are concerned, that he has taken all proper steps to prevent the damage;

    (b) if he has not furnished one of the securities prescribed by this Convention, or if the securities furnished are not valid or do not cover the liability of the operator for the damage caused under the conditions and within the limitations of this Convention.

Article 15 – Amount of Deposit, or Guarantee in Lieu of Insurance

Where the operator of several aircraft furnishes the security prescribed by this Convention in the form of a deposit of money or of a bank guarantee, the security shall be considered as covering the full limit of his liability in respect of all the aircraft operated, if the deposit or guarantee amounts to a sum determined by reducing the total amount of the security which he would otherwise have to furnish in respect of all his aircraft by one-third, if he operates two aircraft, and by one-half if he operates three or more aircraft. The security shall, moreover, be deemed to cover the full liability of the operator for all his aircraft if it amounts to the sum of 2,500,000 francs for two aircraft, or 3,000,000 francs for three or more aircraft.

Article 16 – Choice of Jurisdiction for Claims

In the territory of each of the High Contracting Parties the judicial authorities of the defendant's ordinary place of residence, and those of the place where the damage was caused, are at the plaintiff's choice (and without prejudice to any direct action on the part of the injured third party against the insurer in all cases where such direct action lies) competent to entertain actions for damages.

Article 17 – Time Limit for Proceedings

1. The above-mentioned actions are subject to a period of limitation of one year from the date of the damage. If the injured party shows that he could not have had knowledge of the damage, or of the identity of the person liable, the period of limitation runs as from the date on which he might have had such knowledge.
2. In all cases the action is subject to a period of limitation of three years from the date on which the damage was caused.
3. The method of calculating the period of limitation as well as the grounds for the suspension or interruption of that period are determined by the law of the tribunal seised.

Article 18 – Survival of Action after Death

In the event of the death of the person liable, an action in respect of the liability within the limits prescribed by this Convention lies against those legally representing his estate.

Article 19 – Conversion Rate of Sums in Francs

The sums given in francs in this Convention refer to the French franc, consisting of 65 ½ milligrammes of gold of millesimal fineness 900. These sums may be converted into the national currency in round figures.

Article 20 – Territorial Application of Convention

1. This Convention is applicable in all cases where damage is caused on the surface in the territory of one High Contracting Party by an aircraft registered in the territory of another High Contracting Party.
2. The expression "territory of a High Contracting Party", for the purposes of this Convention, includes every territory under the sovereignty, suzerainty, protectorate, mandate or authority of that High Contracting Party in respect of which the latter is a party to the Convention.

Article 21 – Excepted Aircraft

This Convention does not apply to military, customs or police aircraft.

Article 22 – Exception of Contractual Liability

This Convention does not apply to damage caused on the surface, compensation for which is governed by a contract of carriage, or a contract of employment concluded between the injured person and the person upon whom liability falls under the terms of this Convention.

Article 23 – Text in French

This Convention is drawn up in French in a single copy which shall remain deposited in the archives of the Ministry for Foreign Affairs of the Kingdom of Italy, and of which a certified true copy shall be transmitted by the Government of the Kingdom of Italy to each of the interested Governments.

Article 24 – Ratification

1. This Convention shall be ratified. The instruments of ratification shall be deposited in the archives of the Ministry for Foreign Affairs of the Kingdom of Italy, which shall notify their deposit to each of the interested Governments.
2. When five ratifications have been deposited, the Convention shall come into force between the High Contracting Parties who have ratified it ninety days after the deposit of the fifth ratification. Each ratification subsequently deposited shall take effect ninety days after deposit.
3. The Government of the Kingdom of Italy shall notify each of the interested Governments of the date of the entry into force of the Convention.

Article 25 – Accession

1. This Convention, after its entry into force, shall be open to accession.
2. Accession shall be effected by means of a notification addressed to the Government of the Kingdom of Italy, which will communicate it to each of the interested Governments.
3. The accession shall take effect ninety days after notification to the Government of the Kingdom of Italy.

Article 26 – Denunciation

1. Each of the High Contracting Parties may denounce this Convention by means of a notification to be made to the Government of the Kingdom of Italy, which will at once inform each of the interested Governments thereof.

2. Each denunciation shall take effect 6 months after notification and only in regard to the party making it.

Article 27 – Application to Colonies, Protectorates, etc

1. The High Contracting Parties may at the time of signature, ratification or accession declare that their acceptance of this Convention does not apply to all or any part of their colonies, protectorates, overseas territories, territories under mandate, or any other territories under their sovereignty, authority or suzerainty.
2. The High Contracting Parties may subsequently notify the Government of the Kingdom of Italy that they desire to render this Convention applicable to all or any part of their colonies, protectorates, overseas territories, territories under mandate, or any other territories under their sovereignty, authority or suzerainty thus excluded by their original declaration.
3. The High Contracting Parties may at any moment notify the Government of the Kingdom of Italy that they desire to terminate the application of this Convention to all or any part of their colonies, protectorates, overseas territories under mandate, or any other territories under their sovereignty, authority or suzerainty.
4. The Government of the Kingdom of Italy shall inform each of the interested Governments of any notifications made in pursuance of the two preceding paragraphs.

Article 28 – Summoning of New Conference

Each of the High Contracting Parties, shall have the right, but not before two years from the entry into force of this Convention, to call for the assembling of a new international conference with the object of investigating the improvements which might be made in this Convention. For this purpose such High Contracting Party shall communicate with the Government of the French Republic, which will take the necessary steps to prepare for the conference.

The present Convention, done at Rome, 29th May 1933, will remain open for signature until 1st January 1934.

6.2 Rome Convention 1952

CONVENTION ON DAMAGE CAUSED BY FOREIGN
AIRCRAFT TO THIRD PARTIES ON THE SURFACE

Done at Rome on 7 October 1952

THE STATES SIGNATORY TO THIS CONVENTION

MOVED by a desire to ensure adequate compensation for persons who suffer damage caused on the surface by foreign aircraft, while limiting in a reasonable manner the extent of the liabilities incurred for such damage in order not to hinder the development of international civil air transport, and also

CONVINCED of the need for unifying to the greatest extent possible, through an international convention, the rules applying in the various countries of the world to the liabilities incurred for such damage,

HAVE APPOINTED to such effect the undersigned Plenipotentiaries who, duly authorised, HAVE AGREED AS FOLLOWS:

Chapter I – Principles of Liability

Article 1

1. Any person who suffers damage on the surface shall, upon proof only that the damage was caused by an aircraft in flight or by any person or thing falling there from, be entitled to compensation as provided by this Convention. Nevertheless there shall be no right to compensation if the damage is not a direct consequence of the incident giving rise thereto, or if the damage results from the mere fact of passage of the aircraft through the airspace in conformity with existing air traffic regulations.
2. For the purpose of this Convention, an aircraft is considered to be in flight from the moment when power is applied for the purpose of actual take-

off until the moment when the landing run ends. In the case of an aircraft lighter than air, the expression "in flight" relates to the period from the moment when it becomes detached from the surface until it becomes again attached thereto.

Article 2

1. The liability for compensation contemplated by Article 1 of this Convention shall attach to the operator of the aircraft.

2. (a) For the purposes of this Convention the term "operator" shall mean the person who was making use of the aircraft at the time the damage was caused, provided that if control of the navigation of the aircraft was retained by the person from whom the right to make use of the aircraft was derived, whether directly or indirectly, that person shall be considered the operator.
   (b) A person shall be considered to be making use of an aircraft when he is using it personally or when his servants or agents are using the aircraft in the course of their employment, whether or not within the scope of their authority.

3. The registered owner of the aircraft shall be presumed to be the operator and shall be liable as such unless, in the proceedings for the determination of his liability, he proves that some other person was the operator and, in so far as legal procedures permit, takes appropriate measures to make that other person a party in the proceedings.

Article 3

If the person who was the operator at the time the damage was caused had not the exclusive right to use the aircraft for a period of more than fourteen days, dating from the moment when the right to use commenced, the person from whom such right was derived shall be liable jointly and severally with the operator, each of them being bound under the provisions and within the limits of liability of this Convention.

Article 4

If a person makes use of an aircraft without the consent of the person entitled to its navigational control, the latter, unless he proves that he has exercised due care to prevent such use, shall be jointly and severally liable with the unlawful user for damage giving a right to compensation under Article 1, each of them being bound under the provisions and within the limits of liability of this Convention.

Article 5

Any person who would otherwise be liable under the provisions of this Convention shall not be liable if the damage is the direct consequence of armed conflict or civil disturbance, or if such person has been deprived of the use of the aircraft by act of public authority.

Article 6

1. Any person who would otherwise be liable under the provisions of this Convention shall not be liable for damage if he proves that the damage was caused solely through the negligence or other wrongful act or omission of the person who suffers the damage or of the latter's servants or agents. If the person liable proves that the damage was contributed to by the negligence or other wrongful act or omission of the person who suffers the damage, or of his servants or agents, the compensation shall be reduced to the extent to which such negligence or wrongful act or omission contributed to the damage. Nevertheless there shall be no such exoneration or reduction if, in the case of the negligence or other wrongful act or omission of a servant or agent, the person who suffers the damage proves that his servant or agent was acting outside the scope of his authority.

2. When an action is brought by one person to recover damages arising from the death or injury of another person, the negligence or other wrongful act or omission of such other person, or of his servants or agents, shall also have the effect provided in the preceding paragraph.

Article 7

When two or more aircraft have collided or interfered with each other in flight and damage for which a right to compensation as contemplated in Article 1 results, or when two or more aircraft have jointly caused such damage, each of the aircraft concerned shall be considered to have caused the damage and the operator of each aircraft shall be liable, each of them being bound under the provisions and within the limits of liability of this Convention.

Article 8

The persons referred to in paragraph 3 of Article 2 and in Articles 3 and 4 shall be entitled to all defences which are available to an operator under the provisions of this Convention.

Article 9

Neither the operator, the owner, any person liable under Article 3 or Article 4, nor their respective servants or agents, shall be liable for damage on the surface caused by an aircraft in flight or any person or thing falling therefrom otherwise than as expressly provided in this Convention. This rule shall not apply to any such person who is guilty of a deliberate act or omission done with intent to cause damage.

Article 10

Nothing in this Convention shall prejudice the question whether a person liable for damage in accordance with its provisions has a right of recourse against any other person.

Chapter II – Extent of Liability

Article 11

1. Subject to the provisions of Article 12, the liability for damage giving a right to compensation under Article 1, for each aircraft and incident, in respect of all persons liable under this Convention, shall not exceed:

   (a) 500,000 francs for aircraft weighing 1,000 kilogrammes or less;
   (b) 500,000 francs plus 400 francs per kilogramme over 1,000 kilogrammes for aircraft weighing more than 1,000 but not exceeding 6,000 kilogrammes;
   (c) 2,500,000 francs plus 250 francs per kilogramme over 6,000 kilogrammes for aircraft weighing more than 6,000 but not exceeding 20,000 kilogrammes;
   (d) 6,000,000 francs plus 150 francs per kilogramme over 20,000 kilogrammes for aircraft weighing more than 20,000 but not exceeding 50,000 kilogrammes;
   (e) 10,500,000 francs plus 100 francs per kilogramme over 50,000 kilogrammes for aircraft weighing more than 50,000 kilogrammes.

2. The liability in respect of loss of life or personal injury shall not exceed 500,000 francs per person killed or injured.
3. "Weight" means the maximum weight of the aircraft authorised by the certificate of airworthiness for take-off, excluding the effect of lifting gas when used.
4. The sums mentioned in francs in this Article refer to a currency unit consisting of 65 ½ milligrammes of gold of millesimal fineness 900. These sums may be converted into national currencies in round figures. Conversion of the sums into national currencies other than gold shall, in case of judicial proceedings, be made according to the gold value of such currencies at the date of the judgment, or, in cases covered by Article 14, at the date of the allocation.

Article 12

1. If the person who suffers damage proves that it was caused by a deliberate act or omission of the operator, his servants or agents, done with intent to cause damage, the liability of the operator shall be unlimited; provided that in the case of such act or omission of such servant or agent, it is also proved that he was acting in the course of his employment and within the scope of his authority.
2. If a person wrongfully takes and makes use of an aircraft without the consent of the person entitled to use it, his liability shall be unlimited.

Article 13

1. Whenever, under the provisions of Article 3 or Article 4, two or more persons are liable for damage, or a registered owner who was not the operator is made liable as such as provided in paragraph 3 of Article 2, the persons who suffer damage shall not be entitled to total compensation greater than the highest indemnity which may be awarded under the provisions of this Convention against any one of the persons liable.
2. When the provisions of Article 7 are applicable, the person who suffers the damage shall be entitled to be compensated up to the aggregate of the limits applicable with respect to each of the aircraft involved, but no operator shall be liable for a sum in excess of the limit applicable to his aircraft unless his liability is unlimited under the terms of Article 12.

Article 14

If the total amount of the claims established exceeds the limit of liability applicable under the provisions of this Convention, the following rules shall apply, taking into account the provisions of paragraph 2 of Article 11:

(a) If the claims are exclusively in respect of loss of life or personal injury or exclusively in respect of damage to property, such claims shall be reduced in proportion to their respective amounts.

(b) If the claims are both in respect of loss of life or personal injury and in respect of damage to property, one half of the total sum distributable shall be appropriated preferentially to meet claims in respect of loss of life and personal injury and, if insufficient, shall be distributed proportionately between the claims concerned. The remainder of the total sum distributable shall be distributed proportionately among the claims in respect of damage to property and the portion not already covered of the claims in respect of loss of life and personal injury.

Chapter III – Security for Operator's Liability

Article 15

1. Any Contracting State may require that the operator of an aircraft registered in another Contracting State shall be insured in respect of his liability for damage sustained in its territory for which a right to compensation exists under Article 1 by means of insurance up to the limits applicable according to the provisions of Article 11.

2. (a) The insurance shall be accepted as satisfactory if it conforms to the provisions of this Convention and has been effected by an insurer authorised to effect such insurance under the laws of the State where the aircraft is registered or of the State where the insurer has his residence or principal place of business, and whose financial responsibility has been verified by either of those States.

   (b) If insurance has been required by any State under paragraph 1 of this Article, and a final judgment in that State is not satisfied by payment in the currency of that State, any Contracting State may refuse to accept the insurer as financially responsible until such payment, if demanded, has been made.

3. Notwithstanding the last preceding paragraph the State overflown may refuse to accept as satisfactory insurance effected by an insurer who is not authorised for that purpose in a Contracting State.

4. Instead of insurance, any of the following securities shall be deemed satisfactory if the security conforms to Article 17:

   (a) a cash deposit in a depository maintained by the Contracting State where the aircraft is registered or with a bank authorised to act as a depository by that State;

   (b) a guarantee given by a bank authorised to do so by the Contracting State where the aircraft is registered, and whose financial responsibility has been verified by that State;

   (c) a guarantee given by the Contracting State where the aircraft is registered, if that State undertakes that it will not claim immunity from suit in respect of that guarantee.

5. Subject to paragraph 6 of this Article, the State overflown may also require that the aircraft shall carry a certificate issued by the insurer certifying that insurance has been effected in accordance with the provisions of this Convention, and specifying the person or persons whose liability is secured thereby, together with a certificate or endorsement issued by the appropriate authority in the State where the aircraft is registered or in the State where the insurer has his residence or principal place of business certifying the financial responsibility of the insurer. If other security is furnished in accordance with the provisions of paragraph 4 of this Article, a certificate to that effect shall be issued by the appropriate authority in the State where the aircraft is registered.

6. The certificate referred to in paragraph 5 of this Article need not be carried in the aircraft if a certified copy has been filed with the appropriate authority designated by the State overflown or, if the International Civil Aviation Organisation agrees, with that Organisation, which shall furnish a copy of the certificate to each contracting State.

7. (a) Where the State overflown has reasonable grounds for doubting the financial responsibility of the insurer, or of the bank which issues a guarantee under paragraph 4 of this Article, that State may request additional evidence of financial responsibility, and if any question arises as to the adequacy of that evidence the dispute affecting the States concerned shall, at the request of one of those States, be submitted to an arbitral tribunal which shall be either the Council of the International Civil Aviation Organization or a person or body mutually agreed by the parties.

    (b) Until this tribunal has given its decision the insurance or guarantee shall be considered provisionally valid by the State overflown.

8. Any requirements imposed in accordance with this Article shall be notified to the Secretary General of the International Civil Aviation Organization who shall inform each Contracting State thereof.

9. For the purpose of this Article, the term "insurer" includes a group of insurers, and for the purpose of paragraph 5 of this Article, the phrase "appropriate authority in a State" includes the appropriate authority in the highest political subdivision thereof which regulates the conduct of business by the insurer.

Article 16

1. The insurer or other person providing security required under Article 15 for the liability of the operator may, in addition to the defences available to the operator, and the defence of forgery, set up only the following defences against claims based on the application of this Convention:

    (a) that the damage occurred after the security ceased to be effective. However, if the security expires during a flight, it shall be continued in force until the next landing specified in the flight plan, but no longer than twenty-four hours; and if the security ceases to be effective for any reason other than the expiration of its term, or a change of operator, it shall be continued until fifteen days after notification to the appropriate authority of the State which certifies the financial responsibility of the insurer or the guarantor that the security has ceased to be effective, or until effective withdrawal of the certificate of the insurer or the certificate of guarantee if such a certificate has been required under paragraph 5 of Article 15, whichever is the earlier;

(b) that the damage occurred outside the territorial limits provided for by the security, unless flight outside of such limits was caused by force majeure, assistance justified by the circumstances, or an error in piloting, operation or navigation.

2. The State which has issued or endorsed a certificate pursuant to paragraph 5 of Article 15 shall notify the termination or cessation, otherwise than by the expiration of its term, of the insurance or other security to the interested contracting States as soon as possible.

3. Where a certificate of insurance or other security is required under paragraph 5 of Article 15 and, the operator is changed during the period of the validity of the security, the security shall apply to the liability under this Convention of the new operator, unless he is already covered by other insurance or security or is an unlawful user, but not beyond fifteen days from the time when the insurer or guarantor notifies the appropriate authority of the State where the certificate was issued that the security has become ineffective or until the effective withdrawal of the certificate of the insurer if such a certificate has been required underparagraph 5 of Article 15, whichever is the shorter period.

4. The continuation in force of the security under the provisions of paragraph 1 of this Article shall apply only for the benefit of the person suffering damage.

5. Without prejudice to any right of direct action which he may have under the law governing the contract of insurance or guarantee, the person suffering damage may bring a direct action against the insurer or guarantor only in the following cases:

(a) where the security is continued in force under the provisions of paragraph 1 (a) and (b) of this Article;
(b) the bankruptcy of the operator.

6. Excepting the defences specified in paragraph 1 of this Article, the insurer or other person providing security may not, with respect to direct actions brought by the person suffering damage based upon application of this Convention, avail himself of any grounds of nullity or any right of retroactive cancellation.

7. The provisions of this Article shall not prejudice the question whether the insurer or guarantor has a right of recourse against any other person.

Article 17

1. If security is furnished in accordance with paragraph 4 of Article 15, it shall be specifically and preferentially assigned to payment of claims under the provisions of this Convention.

2. The security shall be deemed sufficient if, in the case of an operator of one aircraft, it is for an amount equal to the limit applicable according to

the provisions of Article 11, and in the case of an operator of several aircraft, if it is for an amount not less than the aggregate of the limits of liability applicable to the two aircraft subject to the highest limits.

3. As soon as notice of a claim has been given to the operator, the amount of the security shall be increased up to a total sum equivalent to the aggregate of:

    (a) the amount of the security then required by paragraph 2 of this Article,
    (b) the amount of the claim not exceeding the applicable limit of liability.

    This increased security shall be maintained until every claim has been disposed of.

Article 18

Any sums due to an operator from an insurer shall be exempt from seizure and execution by creditors of the operator until claims of third parties under this Convention have been satisfied.

Chapter IV – Rules of Procedure and Limitation of Actions

Article 19

If a claimant has not brought an action to enforce his claim or if notification of such claim has not been given to the operator within a period of six months from the date of the incident which gave rise to the damage, the claimant shall only be entitled to compensation out of the amount for which the operator remains liable after all claims made within that period have been met in full.

Article 20

1. Actions under the provisions of this Convention may be brought only before the courts of the Contracting State where the damage occurred. Nevertheless, by agreement between any one or more claimants and any one or more defendants, such claimants may take action before the courts of any other Contracting State, but no such proceedings shall have the effect of prejudicing in any way the rights of persons who bring actions in the State where the damage occurred. The parties may also agree to submit disputes to arbitration in any Contracting State.
2. Each Contracting State shall take all necessary measures to ensure that the defendant and all other parties interested are notified of any proceedings concerning them and have a fair and adequate opportunity to defend their interests.
3. Each Contracting State shall so far as possible ensure that all actions arising from a single incident and brought in accordance with paragraph 1 of this Article are consolidated for disposal in a single proceeding before the same court.

4. Where any final judgment, including a judgment by default, is pronounced by a court competent in conformity with this Convention, on which execution can be issued according to the procedural law of that court, the judgment shall be enforceable upon compliance with the formalities prescribed by the laws of the Contracting State, or of any territory, State or province thereof, where execution is applied for :

   (a) in the Contracting State where the judgment debtor has his residence or principal place of business or,

   (b) if the assets available in that State and in the State where the judgment was pronounced are insufficient to satisfy the judgment, in any other Contracting State where the judgment debtor has assets.

5. Notwithstanding the provisions of paragraph 4 of this Article, the court to which application is made for execution may refuse to issue execution if it is proved that any of the following circumstances exist:

   (a) the judgment was given by default and the defendant did not acquire knowledge of the proceedings in sufficient time to act upon it;

   (b) the defendant was not given a fair and adequate opportunity to defend his interests;

   (c) the judgment is in respect of a cause of action which had already, as between the same parties, formed the subject of a judgment or an arbitral award which, under the law of the State where execution is sought, is recognized as final and conclusive;

   (d) the judgment has been obtained by fraud of any of the parties;

   (e) the right to enforce the judgment is not vested in the person by whom the application for execution is made.

6. The merits of the case may not be reopened in proceedings for execution under paragraph 4 of this Article.

7. The court to which application for execution is made may also refuse to issue execution if the judgment concerned is contrary to the public policy of the State in which execution is requested.

8. If, in proceedings brought according to paragraph 4 of this Article, execution of any judgment is refused on any of the grounds referred to in subparagraphs (a), (b) or (d) of paragraph 5 or paragraph 7 of this Article, the claimant shall be entitled to bring a new action before the courts of the State where execution has been refused. The judgment rendered in such new action may not result in the total compensation awarded exceeding the limits applicable under the provisions of this Convention. In such new action the previous judgment shall be a defence only to the extent to which it has been satisfied. The previous judgment shall cease to be enforceable as soon as the new action has been started.

    The right to bring a new action under this paragraph shall, notwithstanding the provisions of Article 21, be subject to a period of limitation of one year from the date on which the claimant has received notification of the refusal to execute the judgment.

9. Notwithstanding the provisions of paragraph 4 of this Article, the court to which application for execution is made shall refuse execution of any judgment rendered by a court of a State other than that in which the damage occurred until all the judgments rendered in that State have been satisfied.

    The court applied to shall also refuse to issue execution until final judgment has been given on all actions filed in the State where the damage occurred by those persons who have complied with the time limit referred to in Article 19, if the judgment debtor proves that the total amount of compensation which might be awarded by such judgments might exceed the applicable limit of liability under the provisions of this Convention.

    Similarly such court shall not grant execution when, in the case of actions brought in the State where the damage occurred, by those persons who have complied with the time limit referred to in Article 19, the aggregate of the judgments exceeds the applicable limit of liability, until such judgments have been reduced in accordance with Article 14.

10. Where a judgment is rendered enforceable under this Article, payment of costs recoverable under the judgment shall also be enforceable. Nevertheless the court applied to for execution may, on the application of the judgment debtor, limit the amount of such costs to a sum equal to ten per centum of the amount for which the judgment is rendered enforceable. The limits of liability prescribed by this Convention shall be exclusive of costs.
11. Interest not exceeding four per centum per annum may be allowed on the judgment debt from the date of the judgment in respect of which execution is granted.
12. An application for execution of a judgment to which paragraph 4 of this Article applies must be made within five years from the date when such judgment became final.

Article 21

1. Actions under this Convention shall be subject to a period of limitation of two years from the date of the incident which caused the damage.
2. The grounds for suspension or interruption of the period referred to in paragraph 1 of this Article shall be determined by the law of the court trying the action; but in any case the right to institute an action shall be extinguished on the expiration of three years from the date of the incident which caused the damage.

Article 22

In the event of the death of the person liable, an action in respect of liability under the provisions of this Convention shall lie against those legally responsible for his obligations.

Chapter V – Application of the Convention and General Provisions

Article 23

1. This Convention applies to damage contemplated in Article 1 caused in the territory of a Contracting State by an aircraft registered in the territory of another Contracting State.
2. For the purpose of this Convention a ship or aircraft on the high seas shall be regarded as part of the territory of the State in which it is registered.

Article 24

This Convention shall not apply to damage caused to an aircraft in flight, or to persons or goods on board such aircraft.

Article 25

This Convention shall not apply to damage on the surface if liability for such damage is regulated either by a contract between the person who suffers such damage and the operator or the person entitled to use the aircraft at the time the damage occurred, or by the law relating to workmen's compensation applicable to a contract of employment between such persons.

Article 26

This Convention shall not apply to damage caused by military, customs or police aircraft.

Article 27

Contracting States will, as far as possible, facilitate payment of compensation under the provisions of this Convention in the currency of the State where the damage occurred.

Article 28

If legislative measures are necessary in any Contracting State to give effect to this Convention, the Secretary General of the International Civil Aviation Organisation shall be informed forthwith of the measures so taken.

Article 29

As between Contracting States which have also ratified the International Convention for the Unification of Certain Rules relating to Damage caused by Aircraft to Third Parties on the Surface opened for signature at Rome on the 29 May 1933,[1] the present Convention upon its entry into force shall supersede the said Convention of Rome.

Article 30

For the purposes of this Convention:

- "Person" means any natural or legal person, including a State.
- "Contracting State" means any State which has ratified or adhered to this Convention and whose denunciation thereof has not become effective.
- "Territory of a State" means the metropolitan territory of a State and all territories for the foreign relations of which that State is responsible, subject to the provisions of Article 36.

Chapter VI – Final Provisions

Article 31

This Convention shall remain open for signature on behalf of any State until it comes into force in accordance with the provisions of Article 33.

Article 32

1. This Convention shall be subject to ratification by the signatory States.
2. The instruments of ratification shall be deposited with the International Civil Aviation Organisation.

Article 33

1. As soon as five of the signatory States have deposited their instruments of ratification of this Convention, it shall come into force between them on the ninetieth day after the date of the deposit of the fifth instrument of ratification. It shall come into force, for each State which deposits its instrument of ratification after that date, on the ninetieth day after the deposit of its instrument of ratification.
2. As soon as this Convention comes into force, it shall be registered with the United Nations by the Secretary General of the International Civil Aviation Organisation.

Article 34

1. This Convention shall, after it has come into force, be open for adherence by any non-signatory State.
2. The adherence of a State shall be effected by the deposit of an instrument of adherence with the International Civil Aviation Organisation and shall take effect as from the ninetieth day after the date of the deposit.

Article 35

1. Any Contracting State may denounce this Convention by notification of denunciation to the International Civil Aviation Organisation.
2. Denunciation shall take effect six months after the date of receipt by the International Civil Aviation Organisation of the notification of denunciation; nevertheless, in respect of damage contemplated in Article 1 arising from an incident which occurred before the expiration of the six months period, the Convention shall continue to apply as if the denunciation had not been made.

Article 36

1. This Convention shall apply to all territories for the foreign relations of which a Contracting State is responsible, with the exception of territories in respect of which a declaration has been made in accordance with paragraph 2 of this Article or paragraph 3 of Article 37.
2. Any State may at the time of deposit of its instrument of ratification or adherence, declare that its acceptance of this Convention does not apply to any one or more of the territories for the foreign relations of which such State is responsible.
3. Any Contracting State may subsequently, by notification to the International Civil Aviation Organisation, extend the application of this Convention to any or all of the territories regarding which it has made a declaration in accordance with paragraph 2 of this Article or paragraph 3 of Article 37. The notification shall take effect as from the ninetieth day after its receipt by the Organisation.
4. Any Contracting State may denounce this Convention, in accordance with the provisions of Article 35, separately for any or all of the territories for the foreign relations of which such State is responsible.

Article 37

1. When the whole or part of the territory of a Contracting State is transferred to a non-contracting State, this Convention shall cease to apply to the territory so transferred, as from the date of the transfer.
2. When part of the territory of a Contracting State becomes an independent State responsible for its own foreign relations, this Convention shall cease to apply to the territory which becomes an independent State, as from the date on which it becomes independent.
3. When the whole or part of the territory of another State is transferred to a Contracting State, the Convention shall apply to the territory so transferred as from the date of the transfer; provided that, if the territory transferred does not become part of the metropolitan territory of the Contracting State concerned, that Contracting State may, before or at the

time of the transfer, declare by notification to the International Civil Aviation Organisation that the Convention shall not apply to the territory transferred unless a notification is made under paragraph 3 of Article 36.

Article 38

The Secretary General of the International Civil Aviation Organisation shall give notice to all signatory and adhering States and to all States members of the Organisation or of the United Nations:

(a) of the deposit of any instrument of ratification or adherence and the date thereof, within thirty days from the date of the deposit, and

(b) of the receipt of any denunciation or of any declaration or notification made under Article 36 or 37 and the date thereof, within thirty days from the date of the receipt.

The Secretary General of the Organisation shall also notify these States of the date on which the Convention comes into force in accordance with paragraph 1 of Article 33.

Article 39

No reservations may be made to this Convention.

IN WITNESS WHEREOF the undersigned Plenipotentiaries, having been duly authorised, have signed this Convention.

DONE at Rome on the seventh day of the month of October of the year One Thousand Nine Hundred and Fifty Two in the English, French and Spanish languages, each text being of equal authenticity.

This Convention shall be deposited with the International Civil Aviation Organisation where, in accordance with Article 31, it shall remain open for signature, and the Secretary General of the Organisation shall send certified copies thereof to all signatory and adhering States and to all States members of the Organisation or the United Nations.

6.3 Convention on Compensation for Damage Caused by Aircraft to Third Parties 2009

CONVENTION ON COMPENSATION FOR DAMAGE CAUSED BY AIRCRAFT TO THIRD PARTIES

Done at Montreal on 2 May 2009

THE STATES PARTIES TO THIS CONVENTION,

RECOGNIZING the need to ensure adequate compensation for third parties who suffer damage resulting from events involving an aircraft in flight;

RECOGNIZING the need to modernize the *Convention on Damage Caused by Foreign Aircraft to Third Parties on the Surface*, Signed at Rome on 7 October 1952, and the *Protocol to Amend the Convention on Damage Caused by Foreign Aircraft to Third Parties on the Surface*, Signed at Rome on 7 October 1952, Signed at Montreal on 23 September 1978;

RECOGNIZING the importance of ensuring protection of the interests of third-party victims and the need for equitable compensation, as well as the need to enable the continued stability of the aviation industry;

REAFFIRMING the desirability of the orderly development of international air transport operations and the smooth flow of passengers, baggage and cargo in accordance with the principles and objectives of the *Convention on International Civil Aviation*, done at Chicago on 7 December 1944; and

CONVINCED that collective State action for further harmonization and codification of certain rules governing the compensation of third parties who suffer damage resulting from events involving aircraft in flight through a new Convention is the most desirable and effective means of achieving an equitable balance of interests;

HAVE AGREED AS FOLLOWS:

Chapter I – Principles

Article 1 – Definitions

For the purposes of this Convention:

(a) an "act of unlawful interference" means an act which is defined as an offence in the *Convention for the Suppression of Unlawful Seizure of Aircraft*, Signed at The Hague on 16 December 1970, or the *Convention for the Suppression of Unlawful Acts Against the Safety of Civil Aviation*, Signed at Montreal on 23 September 1971, and any amendment in force at the time of the event;

(b) an "event" occurs when damage is caused by an aircraft in flight other than as a result of an act of unlawful interference;

(c) an aircraft is considered to be "in flight" at any time from the moment when all its external doors are closed following embarkation or loading until the moment when any such door is opened for disembarkation or unloading;

(d) "international flight" means any flight whose place of departure and whose intended destination are situated within the territories of two States, whether or not there is a break in the flight, or within the territory of one State if there is an intended stopping place in the territory of another State;

(e) "maximum mass" means the maximum certificated take-off mass of the aircraft, excluding the effect of lifting gas when used;

(f) "operator" means the person who makes use of the aircraft, provided that if control of the navigation of the aircraft is retained by the person from whom the right to make use of the aircraft is derived, whether directly or indirectly, that person shall be considered the operator. A person shall be considered to be making use of an aircraft when he or she is using it personally or when his or her servants or agents are using the aircraft in the course of their employment, whether or not within the scope of their authority;

(g) "person" means any natural or legal person, including a State;

(h) "State Party" means a State for which this Convention is in force; and

(i) "third party" means a person other than the operator, passenger or consignor or consignee of cargo.

Article 2 – Scope

1. This Convention applies to damage to third parties which occurs in the territory of a State Party caused by an aircraft in flight on an international flight, other than as a result of an act of unlawful interference.

2. If a State Party so declares to the Depositary, this Convention shall also apply where an aircraft in flight other than on an international flight causes damage in the territory of that State, other than as a result of an act of unlawful interference.

3. For the purposes of this Convention:

    (a) damage to a ship in or an aircraft above the High Seas or the Exclusive
         Economic Zone shall be regarded as damage occurring in the territory
         of the State in which it is registered; however, if the operator of the
         aircraft has its principal place of business in the territory of a State
         other than the State of Registry, the damage to the aircraft shall be
         regarded as having occurred in the territory of the State in which it
         has its principal place of business; and

    (b) damage to a drilling platform or other installation permanently fixed
         to the soil in the Exclusive Economic Zone or the Continental
         Shelf shall be regarded as having occurred in the territory of the State
         which has jurisdiction over such platform or installation in accordance
         with international law including the *United Nations Convention on the
         Law of the Sea*, done at Montego Bay on 10 December 1982.

4. This Convention shall not apply to damage caused by State aircraft. Aircraft
    used in military, customs and police services shall be deemed to be State
    aircraft.

Chapter II – Liability of the operator and related issues

Article 3 – Liability of the operator

1. The operator shall be liable for damage sustained by third parties upon
    condition only that the damage was caused by an aircraft in flight.
2. There shall be no right to compensation under this Convention if the
    damage is not a direct consequence of the event giving rise thereto, or if
    the damage results from the mere fact of passage of the aircraft through
    the airspace in conformity with existing air traffic regulations.
3. Damages due to death, bodily injury and mental injury shall be
    compensable. Damages due to mental injury shall be compensable only if
    caused by a recognizable psychiatric illness resulting either from bodily
    injury or from direct exposure to the likelihood of imminent death or
    bodily injury.
4. Damage to property shall be compensable.
5. Environmental damage shall be compensable, in so far as such compensation
    is provided for under the law of the State Party in the territory of which
    the damage occurred.
6. No liability shall arise under this Convention for damage caused by a nuclear
    incident as defined in the *Paris Convention on Third Party Liability in the
    Field of Nuclear Energy* (29 July 1960) or for nuclear damage as defined in
    the *Vienna Convention on Civil Liability for Nuclear Damage* (21 May 1963),
    and any amendment or supplements to these Conventions in force at the
    time of the event.

7. Punitive, exemplary or any other non-compensatory damages shall not be recoverable.
8. An operator who would otherwise be liable under the provisions of this Convention shall not be liable if the damage is the direct consequence of armed conflict or civil disturbance.

Article 4 – Limit of the operator's liability

1. The liability of the operator arising under Article 3 shall not exceed for an event the following limit based on the mass of the aircraft involved:

    (a) 750 000 Special Drawing Rights for aircraft having a maximum mass of 500 kilogrammes or less;
    (b) 1 500 000 Special Drawing Rights for aircraft having a maximum mass of more than 500 kilogrammes but not exceeding 1 000 kilogrammes;
    (c) 3 000 000 Special Drawing Rights for aircraft having a maximum mass of more than 1 000 kilogrammes but not exceeding 2 700 kilogrammes;
    (d) 7 000 000 Special Drawing Rights for aircraft having a maximum mass of more than 2 700 kilogrammes but not exceeding 6 000 kilogrammes;
    (e) 18 000 000 Special Drawing Rights for aircraft having a maximum mass of more than 6 000 kilogrammes but not exceeding 12 000 kilogrammes;
    (f) 80 000 000 Special Drawing Rights for aircraft having a maximum mass of more than 12 000 kilogrammes but not exceeding 25 000 kilogrammes;
    (g) 150 000 000 Special Drawing Rights for aircraft having a maximum mass of more than 25 000 kilogrammes but not exceeding 50 000 kilogrammes;
    (h) 300 000 000 Special Drawing Rights for aircraft having a maximum mass of more than 50 000 kilogrammes but not exceeding 200 000 kilogrammes;
    (i) 500 000 000 Special Drawing Rights for aircraft having a maximum mass of more than 200 000 kilogrammes but not exceeding 500 000 kilogrammes;
    (j) 700 000 000 Special Drawing Rights for aircraft having a maximum mass of more than 500 000 kilogrammes.

2. If an event involves two or more aircraft operated by the same operator, the limit of liability in respect of the aircraft with the highest maximum mass shall apply.
3. The limits in this Article shall only apply if the operator proves that the damage:

    (a) was not due to its negligence or other wrongful act or omission or that of its servants or agents; or
    (b) was solely due to the negligence or other wrongful act or omission of another person.

Article 5 – Priority of compensation

If the total amount of the damages to be paid exceeds the amounts available according to Article 4, paragraph 1, the total amount shall be awarded preferentially to meet proportionately the claims in respect of death, bodily injury and mental injury, in the first instance. The remainder, if any, of the total amount payable shall be awarded proportionately among the claims in respect of other damage.

Article 6 – Events involving two or more operators

1. Where two or more aircraft have been involved in an event causing damage to which this Convention applies, the operators of those aircraft are jointly and severally liable for any damage suffered by a third party.
2. If two or more operators are so liable, the recourse between them shall depend on their respective limits of liability and their contribution to the damage.
3. No operator shall be liable for a sum in excess of the limit, if any, applicable to its liability.

Article 7 – Court costs and other expenses

1. The court may award, in accordance with its own law, the whole or part of the court costs and of the other expenses of the litigation incurred by the claimant, including interest.
2. Paragraph 1 shall not apply if the amount of the damages awarded, excluding court costs and other expenses of the litigation, does not exceed the sum which the operator has offered in writing to the claimant within a period of six months from the date of the event causing the damage, or before the commencement of the action, whichever is the later.

Article 8 – Advance payments

If required by the law of the State where the damage occurred, the operator shall make advance payments without delay to natural persons who may be entitled to claim compensation under this Convention, in order to meet their immediate economic needs. Such advance payments shall not constitute a recognition of liability and may be offset against any amount subsequently payable as damages by the operator.

Article 9 – Insurance

1. Having regard to Article 4, States Parties shall require their operators to maintain adequate insurance or guarantee covering their liability under this Convention.

2.   An operator may be required by the State Party in or into which it operates to furnish evidence that it maintains adequate insurance or guarantee. In doing so, the State Party shall apply the same criteria to operators of other States Parties as it applies to its own operators.

Chapter III – Exoneration and recourse

Article 10 – Exoneration

If the operator proves that the damage was caused, or contributed to, by the negligence or other wrongful act or omission of a claimant, or the person from whom he or she derives his or her rights, the operator shall be wholly or partly exonerated from its liability to that claimant to the extent that such negligence or wrongful act or omission caused or contributed to the damage.

Article 11 – Right of recourse

Subject to Article 13, nothing in this Convention shall prejudice the question whether a person liable for damage in accordance with its provisions has a right of recourse against any person.

Chapter IV – Exercise of remedies and related provisions

Article 12 – Exclusive remedy

1.   Any action for compensation for damage to third parties caused by an aircraft in flight brought against the operator, or its servants or agents, however founded, whether under this Convention or in tort or otherwise, can only be brought subject to the conditions set out in this Convention without prejudice to the question as to who are the persons who have the right to bring suit and what are their respective rights.
2.   Article 3, paragraphs 6, 7 and 8, shall apply to any other person from whom the damages specified in those paragraphs would otherwise be recoverable or compensable, whether under this Convention or in tort or otherwise.

Article 13 – Exclusion of liability

Neither the owner, lessor or financier retaining title or holding security of an aircraft, not being an operator, nor their servants or agents, shall be liable for damages under this Convention or the law of any State Party relating to third-party damage.

Article 14 – Conversion of Special Drawing Rights

The sums mentioned in terms of Special Drawing Right in this Convention shall be deemed to refer to the Special Drawing Right as defined by the International Monetary Fund. Conversion of the sums into national currencies shall, in case of judicial proceedings, be made according to the value of such currencies in terms of the Special Drawing Right at the date of the judgement. The value in a national currency shall be calculated in accordance with the method of valuation applied by the International Monetary Fund for its operations and transactions. The value in a national currency, of a State Party which is not a Member of the International Monetary Fund, shall be calculated in a manner determined by that State to express in the national currency of the State Party as far as possible the same real value as the amounts in Article 4, paragraph 1.

Article 15 – Review of limits

1. Subject to paragraph 2 of this Article, the sums prescribed in Article 4, paragraph 1, shall be reviewed by the Depositary by reference to an inflation factor which corresponds to the accumulated rate of inflation since the previous revision or in the first instance since the date of entry into force of this Convention. The measure of the rate of inflation to be used in determining the inflation factor shall be the weighted average of the annual rates of increase or decrease in the Consumer Price Indices of the States whose currencies comprise the Special Drawing Right mentioned in Article 14.
2. If the review referred to in the preceding paragraph concludes that the inflation factor has exceeded 10 per cent, the Depositary shall notify the States Parties of a revision of the limits of liability. Any such revision shall become effective six months after the notification to the States Parties, unless a majority of the States Parties register their disapproval. The Depositary shall immediately notify all States Parties of the coming into force of any revision.

Article 16 – Forum

1. Subject to paragraph 2 of this Article, actions for compensation under the provisions of this Convention may be brought only before the courts of the State Party in whose territory the damage occurred.
2. Where damage occurs in more than one State Party, actions under the provisions of this Convention may be brought only before the courts of the State Party the territory of which the aircraft was in or about to leave when the event occurred.
3. Without prejudice to paragraphs 1 and 2 of this Article, application may be made in any State Party for such provisional measures, including protective measures, as may be available under the law of that State.

Article 17 – Recognition and enforcement of judgements

1. Subject to the provisions of this Article, judgements entered by a competent court under Article 16 after trial, or by default, shall when they are enforceable in the State Party of that court be enforceable in any other State Party as soon as the formalities required by that State Party have been complied with.
2. The merits of the case shall not be reopened in any application for recognition or enforcement under this Article.
3. Recognition and enforcement of a judgement may be refused if:

    (a) its recognition or enforcement would be manifestly contrary to public policy in the State Party where recognition or enforcement is sought;
    (b) the defendant was not served with notice of the proceedings in such time and manner as to allow him or her to prepare and submit a defence;
    (c) it is in respect of a cause of action which had already, as between the same parties, formed the subject of a judgement or an arbitral award which is recognized as final and conclusive under the law of the State Party where recognition or enforcement is sought;
    (d) the judgement has been obtained by fraud of any of the parties; or
    (e) the right to enforce the judgement is not vested in the person by whom the application is made.

4. Recognition and enforcement of a judgement may also be refused to the extent that the judgement awards damages, including exemplary or punitive damages, that do not compensate a third party for actual harm suffered.
5. Where a judgement is enforceable, payment of any court costs and other expenses incurred by the plaintiff, including interest recoverable under the judgement, shall also be enforceable.

Article 18 – Regional and multilateral agreements on the recognition and enforcement of judgements

1. States Parties may enter into regional and multilateral agreements regarding the recognition and enforcement of judgements consistent with the objectives of this Convention, provided that such agreements do not result in a lower level of protection for any third party or defendant than that provided for in this Convention.
2. States Parties shall inform each other, through the Depositary, of any such regional or multilateral agreements that they have entered into before or after the date of entry into force of this Convention.
3. The provisions of this Chapter shall not affect the recognition or enforcement of any judgement pursuant to such agreements.

Article 19 – Period of limitation

1. The right to compensation under Article 3 shall be extinguished if an action is not brought within two years from the date of the event which caused the damage.
2. The method of calculating such two-year period shall be determined in accordance with the law of the court seised of the case.

Article 20 – Death of person liable

In the event of the death of the person liable, an action for damages lies against those legally representing his or her estate and is subject to the provisions of this Convention.

Chapter V – Final clauses

Article 21 – Signature, ratification, acceptance, approval or accession

1. This Convention shall be open for signature in Montréal on 2 May 2009 by States participating in the International Conference on Air Law held at Montréal from 20 April to 2 May 2009. After 2 May 2009, the Convention shall be open to all States for signature at the Headquarters of the International Civil Aviation Organization in Montréal until it enters into force in accordance with Article 23.
2. This Convention shall be subject to ratification by States which have signed it.
3. Any State which does not sign this Convention may accept, approve or accede to it at any time.
4. Instruments of ratification, acceptance, approval or accession shall be deposited with the International Civil Aviation Organization, which is hereby designated the Depositary.

Article 22 – Regional Economic Integration Organizations

1. A Regional Economic Integration Organization which is constituted by sovereign States and has competence over certain matters governed by this Convention may similarly sign, ratify, accept, approve or accede to this Convention. The Regional Economic Integration Organization shall in that case have the rights and obligations of a State Party to the extent that that Organization has competence over matters governed by this Convention.
2. The Regional Economic Integration Organization shall, at the time of signature, ratification, acceptance, approval or accession, make a declaration to the Depositary specifying the matters governed by this Convention in respect of which competence has been transferred to that Organization

by its Member States. The Regional Economic Integration Organization shall promptly notify the Depositary of any changes to the distribution of competence, including new transfers of competence, specified in the declaration under this paragraph.

3. Any reference to a "State Party" or "States Parties" in this Convention applies equally to a Regional Economic Integration Organization where the context so requires.

Article 23 – Entry into Force

1. This Convention shall enter into force on the sixtieth day following the date of deposit of the thirty-fifth instrument of ratification, acceptance, approval or accession with the Depositary between the States which have deposited such instruments. An instrument deposited by a Regional Economic Integration Organization shall not be counted for the purpose of this paragraph.

2. For other States and for other Regional Economic Integration Organizations, this Convention shall take effect sixty days following the date of deposit of the instrument of ratification, acceptance, approval or accession.

Article 24 – Denunciation

1. Any State Party may denounce this Convention by written notification to the Depositary.

2. Denunciation shall take effect one hundred and eighty days following the date on which notification is received by the Depositary; in respect of damage contemplated in Article 3 arising from an event which occurred before the expiration of the one hundred and eighty day period, the Convention shall continue to apply as if the denunciation had not been made.

Article 25 – Relationship to other treaties

The rules of this Convention shall prevail over any rules in the following instruments which would otherwise be applicable to damage covered by this Convention:

(a) the *Convention on Damage Caused by Foreign Aircraft to Third Parties on the Surface*, Signed at Rome on 7 October 1952; or

(b) the *Protocol to Amend the Convention on Damage Caused by Foreign Aircraft to Third Parties on the Surface*, Signed at Rome on 7 October 1952, Signed at Montréal on 23 September 1978.

Article 26 – States with more than one system of law

1. If a State has two or more territorial units in which different systems of
    law are applicable in relation to matters dealt with in this Convention, it
    may at the time of signature, ratification, acceptance, approval or accession
    declare that this Convention shall extend to all its territorial units or only
    to one or more of them and may modify this declaration by submitting
    another declaration at any time.
2. Any such declaration shall be notified to the Depositary and shall state
    expressly the territorial units to which this Convention applies.
3. For a declaration made under Article 2, paragraph 2, by a State Party having
    two or more territorial units in which different systems of law are applicable,
    it may declare that this Convention shall apply to damage to third parties
    that occurs in all its territorial units or in one or more of them and may
    modify this declaration by submitting another declaration at any time.
4. In relation to a State Party which has made a declaration under this Article:

    (a) the reference in Article 8 to "the law of the State" shall be construed
        as referring to the law of the relevant territorial unit of that State; and
    (b) references in Article 14 to "national currency" shall be construed as
        referring to the currency of the relevant territorial unit of that State.

Article 27 – Reservations and declarations

1. No reservation may be made to this Convention but declarations authorized
    by Article 2, paragraph 2, Article 22, paragraph 2, and Article 26 may be
    made in accordance with these provisions.
2. Any declaration or any withdrawal of a declaration made under this
    Convention shall be notified in writing to the Depositary.

Article 28 – Functions of the Depositary

The Depositary shall promptly notify all signatories and States Parties of:

(a) each new signature of this Convention and the date thereof;
(b) each deposit of an instrument of ratification, acceptance, approval or
    accession and the date thereof;
(c) each declaration and the date thereof;
(d) the modification or withdrawal of any declaration and the date thereof;
(e) the date of entry into force of this Convention;
(f) the date of the coming into force of any revision of the limits of liability
    established under this Convention; and
(g) any denunciation with the date thereof and the date on which it takes
    effect.

IN WITNESS WHEREOF the undersigned Plenipotentiaries, having been duly authorized, have signed this Convention.

DONE at Montréal on the 2nd day of May of the year two thousand and nine in the English, Arabic, Chinese, French, Russian and Spanish languages, all texts being equally authentic, such authenticity to take effect upon verification by the Secretariat of the Conference under the authority of the President of the Conference within ninety days hereof as to the conformity of the texts with one another. This Convention shall remain deposited in the archives of the International Civil Aviation Organization, and certified copies thereof shall be transmitted by the Depositary to all Contracting States to this Convention, as well as to all States Parties to the Conventions and Protocol referred to in Article 25.

6.4 Convention on Compensation for Damage to Third Parties Resulting from Acts of Unlawful Interference Involving Aircraft 2009

CONVENTION ON COMPENSATION FOR DAMAGE TO THIRD PARTIES, RESULTING FROM ACTS OF UNLAWFUL INTERFERENCE INVOLVING AIRCRAFT

Done at Montreal on 2 May 2009

THE STATES PARTIES TO THIS CONVENTION,

RECOGNIZING the serious consequences of acts of unlawful interference with aircraft which cause damage to third parties and to property;

RECOGNIZING that there are currently no harmonized rules relating to such consequences;

RECOGNIZING the importance of ensuring protection of the interests of third-party victims and the need for equitable compensation, as well as the need to protect the aviation industry from the consequences of damage caused by unlawful interference with aircraft;

CONSIDERING the need for a coordinated and concerted approach to providing compensation to third-party victims, based on cooperation between all affected parties;

REAFFIRMING the desirability of the orderly development of international air transport operations and the smooth flow of passengers, baggage and cargo in accordance with the principles and objectives of the *Convention on International Civil Aviation*, done at Chicago on 7 December 1944; and

CONVINCED that collective State action for harmonization and codification of certain rules governing compensation for the consequences of an event of unlawful interference with aircraft in flight through a new Convention is the most desirable and effective means of achieving an equitable balance of interests;

HAVE AGREED AS FOLLOWS:

Chapter I – Principles

Article 1 – Definitions

For the purposes of this Convention:

(a) an "act of unlawful interference" means an act which is defined as an offence in the Convention for the Suppression of Unlawful Seizure of Aircraft, Signed at The Hague on 16 December 1970, or the Convention for the Suppression of Unlawful Acts Against the Safety of Civil Aviation, Signed at Montréal on 23 September 1971, and any amendment in force at the time of the event;

(b) an "event" occurs when damage results from an act of unlawful interference involving an aircraft in flight;

(c) an aircraft is considered to be "in flight" at any time from the moment when all its external doors are closed following embarkation or loading until the moment when any such door is opened for disembarkation or unloading;

(d) "international flight" means any flight whose place of departure and whose intended destination are situated within the territories of two States, whether or not there is a break in the flight, or within the territory of one State if there is an intended stopping place in the territory of another State;

(e) "maximum mass" means the maximum certificated take-off mass of the aircraft, excluding the effect of lifting gas when used;

(f) "operator" means the person who makes use of the aircraft, provided that if control of the navigation of the aircraft is retained by the person from whom the right to make use of the aircraft is derived, whether directly or indirectly, that person shall be considered the operator. A person shall be considered to be making use of an aircraft when he or she is using it personally or when his or her servants or agents are using the aircraft in the course of their employment, whether or not within the scope of their authority. The operator shall not lose its status as operator by virtue of the fact that another person commits an act of unlawful interference;

(g) "person" means any natural or legal person, including a State;

(h) "senior management" means members of an operator's supervisory board, members of its board of directors, or other senior officers of the operator who have the authority to make and have significant roles in making binding decisions about how the whole of or a substantial part of the operator's activities are to be managed or organized;

(i) "State Party" means a State for which this Convention is in force; and

(j) "third party" means a person other than the operator, passenger or consignor or consignee of cargo.

Article 2 – Scope

1. This Convention applies to damage to third parties which occurs in the territory of a State Party caused by an aircraft in flight on an international flight, as a result of an act of unlawful interference. This Convention shall also apply to such damage that occurs in a State non-Party as provided for in Article 28.
2. If a State Party so declares to the Depositary, this Convention shall also apply to damage to third parties that occurs in the territory of that State Party which is caused by an aircraft in flight other than on an international flight, as a result of an act of unlawful interference.
3. For the purposes of this Convention:

   (a) damage to a ship in or an aircraft above the High Seas or the Exclusive Economic Zone shall be regarded as damage occurring in the territory of the State in which it is registered; however, if the operator of the aircraft has its principal place of business in the territory of a State other than the State of Registry, the damage to the aircraft shall be regarded as having occurred in the territory of the State in which it has its principal place of business; and

   (b) damage to a drilling platform or other installation permanently fixed to the soil in the Exclusive Economic Zone or the Continental Shelf shall be regarded as having occurred in the territory of the State Party which has jurisdiction over such platform or installation in accordance with international law, including the *United Nations Convention on the Law of the Sea*, done at Montego Bay on 10 December 1982.

4. This Convention shall not apply to damage caused by State aircraft. Aircraft used in military, customs and police services shall be deemed to be State aircraft.

Chapter II – Liability of the operator and related issues

Article 3 – Liability of the operator

1. The operator shall be liable to compensate for damage within the scope of this Convention upon condition only that the damage was caused by an aircraft in flight.
2. There shall be no right to compensation under this Convention if the damage is not a direct consequence of the event giving rise thereto.
3. Damages due to death, bodily injury and mental injury shall be compensable. Damages due to mental injury shall be compensable only if caused by a recognizable psychiatric illness resulting either from bodily injury or from direct exposure to the likelihood of imminent death or bodily injury.
4. Damage to property shall be compensable.

5. Environmental damage shall be compensable, in so far as such compensation is provided for under the law of the State in the territory of which the damage occurred.
6. No liability shall arise under this Convention for damage caused by a nuclear incident as defined in the Paris Convention on Third Party Liability in the Field of Nuclear Energy (29 July 1960) or for nuclear damage as defined in the Vienna Convention on Civil Liability for Nuclear Damage (21 May 1963), and any amendment or supplements to these Conventions in force at the time of the event.
7. Punitive, exemplary or any other non-compensatory damages shall not be recoverable.

Article 4 – Limit of the operator's liability

1. The liability of the operator arising under Article 3 shall not exceed for an event the following limit based on the mass of the aircraft involved:

    (a) 750 000 Special Drawing Rights for aircraft having a maximum mass of 500 kilogrammes or less;
    (b) 1 500 000 Special Drawing Rights for aircraft having a maximum mass of more than 500 kilogrammes but not exceeding 1 000 kilogrammes;
    (c) 3 000 000 Special Drawing Rights for aircraft having a maximum mass of more than 1 000 kilogrammes but not exceeding 2 700 kilogrammes;
    (d) 7 000 000 Special Drawing Rights for aircraft having a maximum mass of more than 2 700 kilogrammes but not exceeding 6 000 kilogrammes;
    (e) 18 000 000 Special Drawing Rights for aircraft having a maximum mass of more than 6 000 kilogrammes but not exceeding 12 000 kilogrammes;
    (f) 80 000 000 Special Drawing Rights for aircraft having a maximum mass of more than 12 000 kilogrammes but not exceeding 25 000 kilogrammes;
    (g) 150 000 000 Special Drawing Rights for aircraft having a maximum mass of more than 25 000 kilogrammes but not exceeding 50 000 kilogrammes;
    (h) 300 000 000 Special Drawing Rights for aircraft having a maximum mass of more than 50 000 kilogrammes but not exceeding 200 000 kilogrammes;
    (i) 500 000 000 Special Drawing Rights for aircraft having a maximum mass of more than 200 000 kilogrammes but not exceeding 500 000 kilogrammes;
    (j) 700 000 000 Special Drawing Rights for aircraft having a maximum mass of more than 500 000 kilogrammes.

2. If an event involves two or more aircraft operated by the same operator, the limit of liability in respect of the aircraft with the highest maximum mass shall apply.

Article 5 – Events involving two or more operators

1. Where two or more aircraft have been involved in an event causing damage to which this Convention applies, the operators of those aircraft are jointly and severally liable for any damage suffered by a third party.
2. If two or more operators are so liable, the recourse between them shall depend on their respective limits of liability and their contribution to the damage.
3. No operator shall be liable for a sum in excess of the limit, if any, applicable to its liability.

Article 6 – Advance payments

If required by the law of the State where the damage occurred, the operator shall make advance payments without delay to natural persons who may be entitled to claim compensation under this Convention, in order to meet their immediate economic needs. Such advance payments shall not constitute a recognition of liability and may be offset against any amount subsequently payable as damages by the operator.

Article 7 – Insurance

1. Having regard to Article 4, States Parties shall require their operators to maintain adequate insurance or guarantee covering their liability under this Convention. If such insurance or guarantee is not available to an operator on a per event basis, the operator may satisfy this obligation by insuring on an aggregate basis. States Parties shall not require their operators to maintain such insurance or guarantee to the extent that they are covered by a decision made pursuant to Article 11, paragraph 1(e) or Article 18, paragraph 3.
2. An operator may be required by the State Party in or into which it operates to furnish evidence that it maintains adequate insurance or guarantee. In doing so, the State Party shall apply the same criteria to operators of other States Parties as it applies to its own operators. Proof that an operator is covered by a decision made pursuant to Article 11, paragraph 1(e) or Article 18, paragraph 3, shall be sufficient evidence for the purpose of this paragraph.

Chapter III – The International Civil Aviation Compensation Fund

Article 8 – The constitution and objectives of the International Civil Aviation Compensation Fund

1. An organization named the International Civil Aviation Compensation Fund, hereinafter referred to as "the International Fund", is established by this Convention. The International Fund shall be made up of a Conference of Parties, consisting of the States Parties, and a Secretariat headed by a Director.

2. The International Fund shall have the following purposes:

    (a) to provide compensation for damage according to Article 18, paragraph 1, pay damages according to Article 18, paragraph 3, and provide financial support under Article 28;

    (b) to decide whether to provide supplementary compensation to passengers on board an aircraft involved in an event, according to Article 9, paragraph (j);

    (c) to make advance payments under Article 19, paragraph 1, and to take reasonable measures after an event to minimize or mitigate damage caused by an event, according to Article 19, paragraph 2; and

    (d) to perform other functions compatible with these purposes.

3. The International Fund shall have its seat at the same place as the International Civil Aviation Organization.

4. The International Fund shall have international legal personality.

5. In each State Party, the International Fund shall be recognized as a legal person capable under the laws of that State of assuming rights and obligations, entering into contracts, acquiring and disposing of movable and immovable property and of being a party in legal proceedings before the courts of that State. Each State Party shall recognize the Director of the International Fund as the legal representative of the International Fund.

6. The International Fund shall enjoy tax exemption and such other privileges as are agreed with the host State. Contributions to the International Fund and its funds, and any proceeds from them, shall be exempted from tax in all States Parties.

7. The International Fund shall be immune from legal process, except in respect of actions relating to credits obtained in accordance with Article 17 or to compensation payable in accordance with Article 18. The Director of the International Fund shall be immune from legal process in relation to acts performed by him or her in his or her official capacity. The immunity of the Director may be waived by the Conference of Parties. The other personnel of the International Fund shall be immune from legal process in relation to acts performed by them in their official capacity. The immunity of the other personnel may be waived by the Director.

8. Neither a State Party nor the International Civil Aviation Organization shall be liable for acts, omissions or obligations of the International Fund.

Article 9 – The Conference of Parties

The Conference of Parties shall:

(a) determine its own rules of procedure and, at each meeting, elect its officers;

(b) establish the Regulations of the International Fund and the Guidelines for Compensation;

(c) appoint the Director and determine the terms of his or her employment and, to the extent this is not delegated to the Director, the terms of employment of the other employees of the International Fund;

(d) delegate to the Director, in addition to powers given in Article 11, such powers and authority as may be necessary or desirable for the discharge of the duties of the International Fund and revoke or modify such delegations of powers and authority at any time;

(e) decide the period for, and the amount of, initial contributions and fix the contributions to be made to the International Fund for each year until the next meeting of the Conference of Parties;

(f) in the case where the aggregate limit on contributions under Article 14, paragraph 3, has been applied, determine the global amount to be disbursed to the victims of all events occurring during the time period with regard to which Article 14, paragraph 3, was applied;

(g) appoint the auditors;

(h) vote budgets and determine the financial arrangements of the International Fund including the Guidelines on Investment, review expenditures, approve the accounts of the International Fund, and consider the reports of the auditors and the comments of the Director thereon;

(i) examine and take appropriate action on the reports of the Director, including reports on claims for compensation, and decide on any matter referred to it by the Director;

(j) decide whether and in what circumstances supplementary compensation may be payable by the International Fund to passengers on board an aircraft involved in an event in circumstances where the damages recovered by passengers according to applicable law did not result in the recovery of compensation commensurate with that available to third parties under this Convention. In exercising this discretion, the Conference of Parties shall seek to ensure that passengers and third parties are treated equally;

(k) establish the Guidelines for the application of Article 28, decide whether to apply Article 28 and set the maximum amount of such assistance;

(l)   determine which States non-Party and which intergovernmental and international non-governmental organizations shall be admitted to take part, without voting rights, in meetings of the Conference of Parties and subsidiary bodies;

(m) establish any body necessary to assist it in its functions, including, if appropriate, an Executive Committee consisting of representatives of States Parties, and define the powers of such body;

(n)   decide whether to obtain credits and grant security for credits obtained pursuant to Article 17, paragraph 4;

(o)   make such determinations as it sees fit under Article 18, paragraph 3;

(p)   enter into arrangements on behalf of the International Fund with the International Civil Aviation Organization;

(q)   request the International Civil Aviation Organization to assume an assistance, guidance and supervisory role with respect to the International Fund as far as the principles and objectives of the Convention on International Civil Aviation, done at Chicago on 7 December 1944, are concerned. ICAO may assume these tasks in accordance with pertinent decisions of its Council;

(r)   as appropriate, enter into arrangements on behalf of the International Fund with other international bodies; and

(s)   consider any matter relating to this Convention that a State Party or the International Civil Aviation Organization has referred to it.

Article 10 – The meetings of the Conference of Parties

1.   The Conference of Parties shall meet once a year, unless a Conference of Parties decides to hold its next meeting at another interval. The Director shall convene the meeting at a suitable time and place.

2.   An extraordinary meeting of the Conference of Parties shall be convened by the Director:

(a)   at the request of no less than one-fifth of the total number of States Parties;

(b)   if an aircraft has caused damage falling within the scope of this Convention, and the damages are likely to exceed the applicable limit of liability according to Article 4 by more than 50 per cent of the available funds of the International Fund;

(c)   if the aggregate limit on contributions according to Article 14, paragraph 3, has been reached; or

(d)   if the Director has exercised the authority according to Article 11, paragraph 1 (d) or (e).

3.   All States Parties shall have an equal right to be represented at the meetings of the Conference of Parties and each State Party shall be entitled to one vote. The International Civil Aviation Organization shall have the right to be represented, without voting rights, at the meetings of the Conference of Parties.

4. A majority of the States Parties is required to constitute a quorum for the meetings of the Conference of Parties. Decisions of the Conference of Parties shall be taken by a majority vote of the States Parties present and voting. Decisions under Article 9, subparagraphs (a), (b), (c), (d), (e), (k), (m), (n) and (o) shall be taken by a two-thirds majority of the States Parties present and voting.
5. Any State Party may, within ninety days after the deposit of an instrument of denunciation the result of which it considers will significantly impair the ability of the International Fund to perform its functions, request the Director to convene an extraordinary meeting of the Conference of Parties. The Director may convene the Conference of Parties to meet not later than sixty days after receipt of the request.
6. The Director may convene, on his or her own initiative, an extraordinary meeting of the Conference of Parties to meet within sixty days after the deposit of any instrument of denunciation, if he or she considers that such denunciation will significantly impair the ability of the International Fund to perform its functions.
7. If the Conference of Parties at an extraordinary meeting convened in accordance with paragraph 5 or 6 decides by a two-thirds majority of the States Parties present and voting that the denunciation will significantly impair the ability of the International Fund to perform its functions, any State Party may, not later than one hundred and twenty days before the date on which the denunciation takes effect, denounce this Convention with effect from that same date.

Article 11 – The Secretariat and the Director

1. The International Fund shall have a Secretariat led by a Director. The Director shall hire personnel, supervise the Secretariat and direct the day-to-day activities of the International Fund. In addition, the Director:

    (a) shall report to the Conference of Parties on the functioning of the International Fund and present its accounts and a budget;
    (b) shall collect all contributions payable under this Convention, administer and invest the funds of the International Fund in accordance with the Guidelines on Investment, maintain accounts for the funds, and assist in the auditing of the accounts and the funds in accordance with Article 17;
    (c) shall handle claims for compensation in accordance with the Guidelines for Compensation, and prepare a report for the Conference of Parties on how each has been handled;
    (d) may decide to temporarily take action under Article 19 until the next meeting of the Conference of Parties;
    (e) shall decide to temporarily take action under Article 18, paragraph 3, until the next meeting of the Conference of Parties called in accordance with Article 10, paragraph 2 (d);

(f)   shall review the sums prescribed under Articles 4 and 18 and inform the Conference of Parties of any revision to the limits of liability in accordance with Article 31; and

(g)   shall discharge any other duties assigned to him or her by or under this Convention and decide any other matter delegated by the Conference of Parties.

2.   The Director and the other personnel of the Secretariat shall not seek or receive instructions in regard to the discharge of their responsibilities from any authority external to the International Fund. Each State Party undertakes to fully respect the international character of the responsibilities of the personnel and not seek to influence any of its nationals in the discharge of their responsibilities.

Article 12 – Contributions to the International Fund

1.   The contributions to the International Fund shall be:

(a)   the mandatory amounts collected in respect of each passenger and each tonne of cargo departing on an international commercial flight from an airport in a State Party. Where a State Party has made a declaration under Article 2, paragraph 2, such amounts shall also be collected in respect of each passenger and each tonne of cargo departing on a commercial flight between two airports in that State Party; and

(b)   such amounts as the Conference of Parties may specify in respect of general aviation or any sector thereof.

The operator shall collect these amounts and remit them to the International Fund.

2.   Contributions collected in respect of each passenger and each tonne of cargo shall not be collected more than once in respect of each journey, whether or not that journey includes one or more stops or transfers.

Article 13 – Basis for fixing the contributions

1.   Contributions shall be fixed having regard to the following principles:

(a)   the objectives of the International Fund should be efficiently achieved;

(b)   competition within the air transport sector should not be distorted;

(c)   the competitiveness of the air transport sector in relation to other modes of transportation should not be adversely affected; and

(d)   in relation to general aviation, the costs of collecting contributions shall not be excessive in relation to the amount of such contributions, taking into account the diversity that exists in this sector.

2.   The Conference of Parties shall fix contributions in a manner that does not discriminate between States, operators, passengers and consignors or consignees of cargo.

3. On the basis of the budget drawn up according to Article 11, paragraph 1 (a), the contributions shall be fixed having regard to:

    (a) the upper limit for compensation set out in Article 18, paragraph 2;
    (b) the need for reserves where Article 18, paragraph 3, is applied;
    (c) claims for compensation, measures to minimize or mitigate damages and financial assistance under this Convention;
    (d) the costs and expenses of administration, including the costs and expenses incurred by meetings of the Conference of Parties;
    (e) the income of the International Fund; and
    (f) the availability of additional funds for compensation pursuant to Article 17, paragraph 4.

Article 14 – Period and rate of contributions

1. At its first meeting, the Conference of Parties shall decide the period and the rate of contributions in respect of passengers and cargo departing from a State Party to be made from the time of entry into force of this Convention for that State Party. If a State Party makes a declaration under Article 2, paragraph 2, initial contributions shall be paid in respect of passengers and cargo departing on flights covered by such declaration from the time it takes effect. The period and the rate shall be equal for all States Parties.
2. Contributions shall be fixed in accordance with paragraph 1 so that the funds available amount to 100 per cent of the limit of compensation set out in Article 18, paragraph 2, within four years. If the funds available are deemed sufficient in relation to the likely compensation or financial assistance to be provided in the foreseeable future and amount to 100 per cent of that limit, the Conference of Parties may decide that no further contributions shall be made until the next meeting of the Conference of Parties, provided that both the period and rate of contributions shall be applied in respect of passengers and cargo departing from a State in respect of which this Convention subsequently enters into force.
3. The total amount of contributions collected by the International Fund within any period of two consecutive calendar years shall not exceed three times the maximum amount of compensation according to Article 18, paragraph 2.
4. Subject to Article 28, the contributions collected by an operator in respect of a State Party may not be used to provide compensation for an event which occurred in its territory prior to the entry into force of this Convention for that State Party.

Article 15 – Collection of the contributions

1. The Conference of Parties shall establish in the Regulations of the International Fund a transparent, accountable and cost-effective mechanism

supporting the collection, remittal and recovery of contributions. When establishing the mechanism, the Conference of Parties shall endeavour not to impose undue burdens on operators and contributors to the funds of the International Fund. Contributions which are in arrears shall bear interest as provided for in the Regulations.

2.   Where an operator does not collect or does not remit contributions it has collected to the International Fund, the International Fund shall take appropriate measures against such operator with a view to the recovery of the amount due. Each State Party shall ensure that an action to recover the amount due may be taken within its jurisdiction, notwithstanding in which State Party the debt actually accrued.

Article 16 – Duties of States Parties

1.   Each State Party shall take appropriate measures, including imposing such sanctions as it may deem necessary, to ensure that an operator fulfils its obligations to collect and remit contributions to the International Fund.

2.   Each State Party shall ensure that the following information is provided to the International Fund:

   (a)   the number of passengers and quantity of cargo departing on international commercial flights from that State Party;
   (b)   such information on general aviation flights as the Conference of Parties may decide; and
   (c)   the identity of the operators performing such flights.

3.   Where a State Party has made a declaration under Article 2, paragraph 2, it shall ensure that information detailing the number of passengers and quantity of cargo departing on commercial flights between two airports in that State Party, such information on general aviation flights as the Conference of Parties may decide, and the identity of the operators performing such flights, are also provided. In each case, such statistics shall be *prima facie* evidence of the facts stated therein.

4.   Where a State Party does not fulfil its obligations under paragraphs 2 and 3 of this Article and this results in a shortfall in contributions for the International Fund, the State Party shall be liable for such shortfall. The Conference of Parties shall, on recommendation by the Director, decide whether the State Party shall pay for such shortfall.

Article 17 – The funds of the International Fund

1.   The funds of the International Fund may only be used for the purposes set out in Article 8, paragraph 2.

2.   The International Fund shall exercise the highest degree of prudence in the management and preservation of its funds. The funds shall be preserved in accordance with the Guidelines on Investment determined by the

Conference of Parties under Article 9, subparagraph (h). Investments may only be made in States Parties.

3. Accounts shall be maintained for the funds of the International Fund. The auditors of the International Fund shall review the accounts and report on them to the Conference of Parties.

4. Where the International Fund is not able to meet valid compensation claims because insufficient contributions have been collected, it may obtain credits from financial institutions for the payment of compensation and may grant security for such credits.

Chapter IV – Compensation from the International Fund

Article 18 – Compensation

1. The International Fund shall, under the same conditions as are applicable to the liability of the operator, provide compensation to persons suffering damage in the territory of a State Party. Where the damage is caused by an aircraft in flight on a flight other than an international flight, compensation shall only be provided if that State Party has made a declaration according to Article 2, paragraph 2. Compensation shall only be paid to the extent that the total amount of damages exceeds the limits according to Article 4.

2. The maximum amount of compensation available from the International Fund shall be 3 000 000 000 Special Drawing Rights for each event. Payments made according to paragraph 3 of this Article and distribution of amounts recovered according to Article 25 shall be in addition to the maximum amount for compensation.

3. If and to the extent that the Conference of Parties determines and for the period that it so determines that insurance in respect of the damage covered by this Convention is wholly or partially unavailable with respect to amounts of coverage or the risks covered, or is only available at a cost incompatible with the continued operation of air transport generally, the International Fund may, at its discretion, in respect of future events causing damage compensable under this Convention, pay the damages for which the operators are liable under Articles 3 and 4 and such payment shall discharge such liability of the operators. The Conference of Parties shall decide on a fee, the payment of which by the operators, for the period covered, shall be a condition for the International Fund taking the action specified in this paragraph.

Article 19 – Advance payments and other measures

1. Subject to the decision of the Conference of Parties and in accordance with the Guidelines for Compensation, the International Fund may make advance payments without delay to natural persons who may be entitled

to claim compensation under this Convention, in order to meet their immediate economic needs. Such advance payments shall not constitute recognition of a right to compensation and may be offset against any amount subsequently payable by the International Fund.

2.   Subject to the decision of the Conference of Parties and in accordance with the Guidelines for Compensation, the International Fund may also take other measures to minimize or mitigate damage caused by an event.

Chapter V – Special provisions on compensation and recourse

Article 20 – Exoneration

If the operator or the International Fund proves that the damage was caused, or contributed to, by an act or omission of a claimant, or the person from whom he or she derives his or her rights, done with intent or recklessly and with knowledge that damage would probably result, the operator or the International Fund shall be wholly or partly exonerated from its liability to that claimant to the extent that such act or omission caused or contributed to the damage.

Article 21 – Court costs and other expenses

1.   The limits prescribed in Articles 4 and 18, paragraph 2, shall not prevent the court from awarding, in accordance with its own law, in addition, the whole or part of the court costs and of the other expenses of the litigation incurred by the claimant, including interest.

2.   Paragraph 1 shall not apply if the amount of the damages awarded, excluding court costs and other expenses of the litigation, does not exceed the sum which the operator has offered in writing to the claimant within a period of six months from the date of the event causing the damage, or before the commencement of the action, whichever is the later.

Article 22 – Priority of compensation

If the total amount of the damages to be paid exceeds the amounts available according to Articles 4 and 18, paragraph 2, the total amount shall be awarded preferentially to meet proportionately the claims in respect of death, bodily injury and mental injury, in the first instance. The remainder, if any, of the total amount payable shall be awarded proportionately among the claims in respect of other damage.

Article 23 – Additional compensation

1.   To the extent the total amount of damages exceeds the aggregate amount payable under Articles 4 and 18, paragraph 2, a person who has suffered damage may claim additional compensation from the operator.

2. The operator shall be liable for such additional compensation to the extent the person claiming compensation proves that the operator or its employees have contributed to the occurrence of the event by an act or omission done with intent to cause damage or recklessly and with knowledge that damage would probably result.

3. Where an employee has contributed to the damage, the operator shall not be liable for any additional compensation under this Article if it proves that an appropriate system for the selection and monitoring of its employees has been established and implemented.

4. An operator or, if it is a legal person, its senior management shall be presumed not to have been reckless if it proves that it has established and implemented a system to comply with the security requirements specified pursuant to Annex 17 to the *Convention on International Civil Aviation* (Chicago, 1944) in accordance with the law of the State Party in which the operator has its principal place of business, or if it has no such place of business, its permanent residence.

Article 24 – Right of recourse of the operator

The operator shall have a right of recourse against:
   (a) any person who has committed, organized or financed the act of unlawful interference; and
   (b) any other person.

Article 25 – Right of recourse of the International Fund

The International Fund shall have a right of recourse against:

   (a) any person who has committed, organized or financed the act of unlawful interference;
   (b) the operator subject to the conditions set out in Article 23; and
   (c) any other person.

Article 26 – Restrictions on rights of recourse

1. The rights of recourse under Article 24, subparagraph (b), and Article 25, subparagraph (c), shall only arise to the extent that the person against whom recourse is sought could have been covered by insurance available on a commercially reasonable basis.

2. Paragraph 1 shall not apply if the person against whom recourse is sought under Article 25, subparagraph (c) has contributed to the occurrence of the event by an act or omission done recklessly and with knowledge that damage would probably result.

3. The International Fund shall not pursue any claim under Article 25, subparagraph (c) if the Conference of Parties determines that to do so would give rise to the application of Article 18, paragraph 3.

Article 27 – Exoneration from recourse

No right of recourse shall lie against an owner, lessor, or financier retaining title of or holding security in an aircraft, not being an operator, or against a manufacturer if that manufacturer proves that it has complied with the mandatory requirements in respect of the design of the aircraft, its engines or components.

Chapter VI – Assistance in case of events in States non-Party

Article 28 – Assistance in case of events in States non-Party

Where an operator, which has its principal place of business, or if it has no such place of business, its permanent residence, in a State Party, is liable for damage occurring in a State non-Party, the Conference of Parties may decide, on a case by case basis, that the International Fund shall provide financial support to that operator. Such support may only be provided:

(a) in respect of damage that would have fallen under the Convention if the State non-Party had been a State Party;

(b) if the State non-Party agrees in a form acceptable to the Conference of Parties to be bound by the provisions of this Convention in respect of the event giving rise to such damage;

(c) up to the maximum amount for compensation set out in Article 18, paragraph 2; and

(d) if the solvency of the operator liable is threatened even if support is given, where the Conference of Parties determines that the operator has sufficient arrangements protecting its solvency.

Chapter VII – Exercise of remedies and related provisions

Article 29 – Exclusive remedy

1. Without prejudice to the question as to who are the persons who have the right to bring suit and what are their respective rights, any action for compensation for damage to a third party due to an act of unlawful interference, however founded, whether under this Convention or in tort or in contract or otherwise, can only be brought against the operator and, if need be, against the International Fund and shall be subject to the conditions and limits of liability set out in this Convention. No claims by a third party shall lie against any other person for compensation for such damage.

2. Paragraph 1 shall not apply to an action against a person who has committed, organized or financed an act of unlawful interference.

Article 30 – Conversion of Special Drawing Rights

The sums mentioned in terms of Special Drawing Right in this Convention shall be deemed to refer to the Special Drawing Right as defined by the International Monetary Fund. Conversion of the sums into national currencies shall, in case of judicial proceedings, be made according to the value of such currencies in terms of the Special Drawing Right at the date of the judgement. The value in a national currency shall be calculated in accordance with the method of valuation applied by the International Monetary Fund for its operations and transactions. The value in a national currency, of a State Party which is not a Member of the International Monetary Fund, shall be calculated in a manner determined by that State to express in the national currency of the State Party as far as possible the same real value as the amounts in Article 4.

Article 31 – Review of limits

1. Subject to paragraph 2 of this Article, the sums prescribed in Articles 4 and 18, paragraph 2, shall be reviewed by the Director of the International Fund, by reference to an inflation factor which corresponds to the accumulated rate of inflation since the previous revision or in the first instance since the date of entry into force of this Convention. The measure of the rate of inflation to be used in determining the inflation factor shall be the weighted average of the annual rates of increase or decrease in the Consumer Price Indices of the States whose currencies comprise the Special Drawing Right mentioned in Article 30.
2. If the review referred to in the preceding paragraph concludes that the inflation factor has exceeded 10 per cent, the Director shall inform the Conference of Parties of a revision of the limits of liability. Any such revision shall become effective six months after the meeting of the Conference of Parties, unless a majority of the States Parties register their disapproval. The Director shall immediately notify all States Parties of the coming into force of any revision.

Article 32 – Forum

1. Subject to paragraph 2 of this Article, actions for compensation under the provisions of this Convention may be brought only before the courts of the State Party in whose territory the damage occurred.
2. Where damage occurs in more than one State Party, actions under the provisions of this Convention may be brought only before the courts of the State Party the territory of which the aircraft was in or about to leave when the event occurred.
3. Without prejudice to paragraphs 1 and 2 of this Article, application may be made in any State Party for such provisional measures, including protective measures, as may be available under the law of that State.

Article 33 – Intervention by the International Fund

1. Each State Party shall ensure that the International Fund has the right to intervene in proceedings brought against the operator in its courts.
2. Except as provided in paragraph 3 of this Article, the International Fund shall not be bound by any judgement or decision in proceedings to which it has not been a party or in which it has not intervened.
3. If an action is brought against the operator in a State Party, each party to such proceedings shall be entitled to notify the International Fund of the proceedings. Where such notification has been made in accordance with the law of the court seised and in such time that the International Fund had time to intervene in the proceedings, the International Fund shall be bound by a judgement or decision in proceedings even if it has not intervened.

Article 34 – Recognition and enforcement of judgements

1. Subject to the provisions of this Article, judgements entered by a competent court under Article 32 after trial, or by default, shall when they are enforceable in the State Party of that court be enforceable in any other State Party as soon as the formalities required by that State Party have been complied with.
2. The merits of the case shall not be reopened in any application for recognition or enforcement under this Article.
3. Recognition and enforcement of a judgement may be refused if:

    (a) its recognition or enforcement would be manifestly contrary to public policy in the State Party where recognition or enforcement is sought;
    (b) the defendant was not served with notice of the proceedings in such time and manner as to allow him or her to prepare and submit a defence;
    (c) it is in respect of a cause of action which had already, as between the same parties, formed the subject of a judgement or an arbitral award which is recognized as final and conclusive under the law of the State Party where recognition or enforcement is sought;
    (d) the judgement has been obtained by fraud of any of the parties; or
    (e) the right to enforce the judgement is not vested in the person by whom the application is made.

4. Recognition and enforcement of a judgement may also be refused to the extent that the judgement awards damages, including exemplary or punitive damages, that do not compensate a third party for actual harm suffered.
5. Where a judgement is enforceable, payment of any court costs and other expenses incurred by the plaintiff, including interest recoverable under the judgement, shall also be enforceable.

Article 35 – Regional and multilateral agreements on the recognition and enforcement of judgements

1. States Parties may enter into regional and multilateral agreements regarding the recognition and enforcement of judgements consistent with the objectives of this Convention, provided that such agreements do not result in a lower level of protection for any third party or defendant than that provided for in this Convention.
2. States Parties shall inform each other, through the Depositary, of any such regional or multilateral agreements that they have entered into before or after the date of entry into force of this Convention.
3. The provisions of this Chapter shall not affect the recognition or enforcement of any judgement pursuant to such agreements.

Article 36 – Period of limitation

1. The right to compensation under Article 3 shall be extinguished if an action is not brought within two years from the date of the event which caused the damage.
2. The right to compensation under Article 18 shall be extinguished if an action is not brought, or a notification pursuant to Article 33, paragraph 3, is not made, within two years from the date of the event which caused the damage.
3. The method of calculating such two-year period shall be determined in accordance with the law of the court seized of the case.

Article 37 – Death of person liable

In the event of the death of the person liable, an action for damages lies against those legally representing his or her estate and is subject to the provisions of this Convention.

Chapter VIII – Final clauses

Article 38 – Signature, ratification, acceptance, approval or accession

1. This Convention shall be open for signature in Montréal on 2 May 2009 by States participating in the International Conference on Air Law held at Montréal from 20 April to 2 May 2009. After 2 May 2009, the Convention shall be open to all States for signature at the headquarters of the International Civil Aviation Organization in Montréal until it enters into force in accordance with Article 40.
2. This Convention shall be subject to ratification by States which have signed it.
3. Any State which does not sign this Convention may accept, approve or accede to it at any time.

4. Instruments of ratification, acceptance, approval or accession shall be deposited with the International Civil Aviation Organization, which is hereby designated the Depositary.

Article 39 – Regional Economic Integration Organizations

1. A Regional Economic Integration Organization which is constituted by sovereign States and has competence over certain matters governed by this Convention may similarly sign, ratify, accept, approve or accede to this Convention. The Regional Economic Integration Organization shall in that case have the rights and obligations of a State Party, to the extent that the Organization has competence over matters governed by this Convention. Where the number of States Parties is relevant in this Convention, including in respect of Article 10, the Regional Economic Integration Organization shall not count as a State Party in addition to its Member States which are States Parties.
2. The Regional Economic Integration Organization shall, at the time of signature, ratification, acceptance, approval or accession, make a declaration to the Depositary specifying the matters governed by this Convention in respect of which competence has been transferred to that Organization by its Member States. The Regional Economic Integration Organization shall promptly notify the Depositary of any changes to the distribution of competence, including new transfers of competence, specified in the declaration under this paragraph.
3. Any reference to a "State Party" or "States Parties" in this Convention applies equally to a Regional Economic Integration Organization where the context so requires.

Article 40 – Entry into force

1. This Convention shall enter into force on the one hundred and eightieth day after the deposit of the thirty-fifth instrument of ratification, acceptance, approval or accession on condition, however, that the total number of passengers departing in the previous year from airports in the States that have ratified, accepted, approved or acceded is at least 750 000 000 as appears from the declarations made by ratifying, accepting, approving or acceding States. If, at the time of deposit of the thirty-fifth instrument of ratification, acceptance, approval or accession this condition has not been fulfilled, the Convention shall not come into force until the one hundred and eightieth day after this condition shall have been satisfied. An instrument deposited by a Regional Economic Integration Organization shall not be counted for the purpose of this paragraph.
2. This Convention shall come into force for each State ratifying, accepting, approving or acceding after the deposit of the last instrument of ratification, acceptance, approval or accession necessary for entry into force of this

Convention on the ninetieth day after the deposit of its instrument of ratification, acceptance, approval or accession.

3. At the time of deposit of its instrument of ratification, acceptance, approval or accession a State shall declare the total number of passengers that departed on international commercial flights from airports in its territory in the previous year. The declaration at Article 2, paragraph 2, shall include the number of domestic passengers in the previous year and that number shall be counted for the purposes of determining the total number of passengers required under paragraph 1.

4. In making such declarations a State shall endeavour not to count a passenger that has already departed from an airport in a State Party on a journey including one or more stops or transfers. Such declarations may be amended from time to time to reflect passenger numbers in subsequent years. If a declaration is not amended, the number of passengers shall be presumed to be constant.

Article 41 – Denunciation

1. Any State Party may denounce this Convention by written notification to the Depositary.

2. Denunciation shall take effect one year following the date on which notification is received by the Depositary; in respect of damage contemplated in Article 3 arising from events which occurred before the expiration of the one-year period and the contributions required to cover such damage, the Convention shall continue to apply as if the denunciation had not been made.

Article 42 – Termination

1. This Convention shall cease to be in force on the date when the number of States Parties falls below eight or on such earlier date as the Conference of Parties shall decide by a two-thirds majority of States that have not denounced the Convention.

2. States which are bound by this Convention on the day before the date it ceases to be in force shall enable the International Fund to exercise its functions as described under Article 43 of this Convention and shall, for that purpose only, remain bound by this Convention.

Article 43 – Winding up of the International Fund

1. If this Convention ceases to be in force, the International Fund shall nevertheless:

    (a) meet its obligations in respect of any event occurring before the Convention ceased to be in force and of any credits obtained pursuant to paragraph 4 of Article 17 while the Convention was still in force; and

(b) be entitled to exercise its rights to contributions to the extent that these contributions are necessary to meet the obligations under subparagraph (a), including expenses for the administration of the International Fund necessary for this purpose.

2. The Conference of Parties shall take all appropriate measures to complete the winding up of the International Fund including the distribution in an equitable manner of any remaining assets for a purpose consonant with the aims of this Convention or for the benefit of those persons who have contributed to the International Fund.

3. For the purposes of this Article the International Fund shall remain a legal person.

Article 44 – Relationship to other treaties

1. The rules of this Convention shall prevail over any rules in the following instruments which would otherwise be applicable to damage covered by this Convention:

   (a) the Convention on Damage Caused by Foreign Aircraft to Third Parties on the Surface, Signed at Rome on 7 October 1952; or

   (b) the Protocol to Amend the Convention on Damage Caused by Foreign Aircraft to Third Parties on the Surface, Signed at Rome on 7 October 1952, Signed at Montréal on 23 September 1978.

Article 45 – States with more than one system of law

1. If a State has two or more territorial units in which different systems of law are applicable in relation to matters dealt with in this Convention, it may at the time of signature, ratification, acceptance, approval or accession declare that this Convention shall extend to all its territorial units or only to one or more of them and may modify this declaration by submitting another declaration at any time.

2. Any such declaration shall be notified to the Depositary and shall state expressly the territorial units to which the Convention applies.

3. For a declaration made under Article 2, paragraph 2, by a State Party having two or more territorial units in which different systems of law are applicable, it may declare that this Convention shall apply to damage to third parties that occurs in all its territorial units or in one or more of them and may modify this declaration by submitting another declaration at any time.

4. In relation to a State Party which has made a declaration under this Article:

   (a) the reference in Article 6 to "the law of the State" shall be construed as referring to the law of the relevant territorial unit of that State; and

   (b) references in Article 30 to "national currency" shall be construed as referring to the currency of the relevant territorial unit of that State.

Article 46 – Reservations and declarations

1. No reservation may be made to this Convention but declarations authorized by Article 2, paragraph 2, Article 39, paragraph 2, Article 40, paragraph 3, and Article 45 may be made in accordance with these provisions.
2. Any declaration or any withdrawal of a declaration made under this Convention shall be notified in writing to the Depositary.

Article 47 – Functions of the Depositary

The Depositary shall promptly notify all signatories and States Parties of:

(a) each new signature of this Convention and the date thereof;
(b) each deposit of an instrument of ratification, acceptance, approval or accession and the date thereof;
(c) the date of entry into force of this Convention;
(d) the date of the coming into force of any revision of the limits of liability established under this Convention;
(e) each declaration or modification thereto, together with the date thereof;
(f) the withdrawal of any declaration and the date thereof;
(g) any denunciation together with the date thereof and the date on which it takes effect; and
(h) the termination of the Convention.

IN WITNESS WHEREOF the undersigned Plenipotentiaries, having been duly authorized, have signed this Convention.

DONE at Montréal on the 2nd day of May of the year two thousand and nine in the English, Arabic, Chinese, French, Russian and Spanish languages, all texts being equally authentic, such authenticity to take effect upon verification by the Secretariat of the Conference under the authority of the President of the Conference within ninety days hereof as to the conformity of the texts with one another.

This Convention shall remain deposited in the archives of the International Civil Aviation Organization, and certified copies thereof shall be transmitted by the Depositary to all Contracting States to this Convention, as well as to all States Parties to the Convention and Protocol referred to in Article 44.

PART III

CIVIL AVIATION REGULATION

Commentary

As set out in Part I, international air carrier liability regimes were developed as early as 1929. In Part II, 'Safety and Security,' it became clear that regimes dealing with safety and security both on board aircraft and on the ground developed, in part, in response to specific incidents or series of incidents.

In this final section – Part III – we set out the evolution of civil aviation regulation. Although such regulation begins in the aftermath of World War I with the 1919 Paris Convention (as part of the Versailles Peace Conference), the most significant piece of regulation was and remains the Chicago Convention, signed towards the end of another world war in 1944.

The Chicago Convention begins with the dawn of the passenger jet age and proved – proves – remarkably prescient in dealing with aviation regulatory matters and issues. The Convention provides a foundation for the practical development of air law in terms of civil (but not state) aircraft and regulation. Matters addressed in this regard in this Part III include international scheduled and non-scheduled flight; access; certain 'freedoms of the air' – rights which facilitate the global development of international air services; increasing liberalisation of such air services; 'rules of the air'; and the UN body responsible for international aviation, ICAO.

HISTORY: PARIS CONVENTION AND AIRSPACE SOVEREIGNTY

The 1919 Paris Convention, convened by the French Government, was the first multilateral treaty to provide for the regulation of international flight. It set out a number of foundation principles, many of which subsequently found voice in the 1944 Chicago Convention. The key principle governing the drafting of the Paris Convention was the notion of absolute sovereignty over the airspace of a state.

Most of the controversy about state sovereignty of airspace began around the start of the twentieth century. It was at this time that serious consideration was being given to the use of balloons, dirigibles, and airplanes for both commercial and military purposes. The leaders of the two main schools of thought were Fauchille and Westlake. Fauchille introduced the celebrated theory of "freedom of the air" in 1902. Professor Westlake, at a 1906 meeting of the Institute of International Law, expressed the thought that the state's sovereignty had no limit upward. Apparently the main basis for his opinion was the idea that there was danger of greater damage from falling objects the higher the altitude from which they fell.

At that time, the states mainly concerned with the problem, because of their size and geographical location, were the European nations. In May, 1910, the French Government sponsored a Paris meeting of an International Conference on Air Navigation. The nineteen state conference which followed, though technically a diplomatic failure, was of great historical importance. When the conference met, there existed no acceptable plan for international flight regulation. When the conference adjourned, it had completed a draft convention of fifty-five articles and three annexes, including such subjects as aircraft nationality, registration, rules of the road and photographic and radio equipment in aircraft. The conference agreed on the following principles which were to re-appear in the Paris Convention of 1919 and which influenced the Chicago Convention of 1944: the subjacent State may set up prohibited zones above which no international flight was lawful; cabotage traffic may be reserved for national aircraft; the establishment of international airlines will depend upon the assent of interested States. In Professor Cooper's opinion, the conference first evidenced general international agreement that usable space above the lands and waters of a State is part of the territory of that State. Thus, the cause of failure of the conference was not, as generally supposed, the impossibility of reaching agreement as to the legal status of airspace. The real causes of breakdown were political.

The next important event was the Versailles Peace Conference of 1919 which established the Paris Convention. Article 1 of the Convention stated: "The High Contracting Parties recognize that every Power has complete and exclusive sovereignty over the airspace above its territory." Since this idea was used almost verbatim in later international agreements, one of the problems still existing today is what was meant by the term "air- space" as it was used there. It has been argued convincingly that this "air- space" refers to the atmosphere with sufficient air to support mechanics dependent on reaction with the air for their aerodynamic lift." . . .

The United States, although a strong advocate of freedom of the air, assisted in drafting the final convention and later signed but did not ratify it. It then formally asserted this country's sovereignty over its airspace by means of the Air Commerce Act of 1926 and the Civil Aeronautics Act of 1938, and by signing the Pan American Convention at Havana in 1928.

In 1929, the United States, along with thirty other nations, took part in an International Air Conference . . . [A]t the Air Conference of

1929, twenty-seven of the thirty-one states represented completely abandoned the principle of freedom of traffic. Only the Netherlands, Sweden, the United Kingdom, and the United States continued to consider the restriction of air sovereignty as necessary. As to the motives for the attitude of the great majority of states:

> Considerations of security were put forward, but it was fear of competition and uncertainty with regard to the state's own ability by which this un-imaginative attitude was prompted. Not the slightest attention was paid to the question what consequences the proclamation of the principle of total unrestrictedness (of sovereignty) would have on the development of world airlines.

With such feelings among the various nations, modified or possibly strengthened by World War II, the International Civil Aviation Conference convened at Chicago in 1944. The United States:

> insisted on the maintenance of sovereignty of the airspace but, subject to such sovereignty, desired that air international transport restrictions be kept at a minimum . . .. The United States desired that each government should have transit privileges for its aircraft engaged in scheduled international service and commercial rights approaching those long customary in the carriage of commerce at sea, but without the wide and wandering privileges of a typical tramp steamer.

However, the American delegation failed in its efforts, and Article I of the Chicago Convention was adopted in words almost identical to those used in the Paris Convention of 1919: "The contracting States recognize that every State has complete and exclusive sovereignty over the airspace above its territory."[1]

CHICAGO CONVENTION 1944

The Convention on International Civil Aviation was signed on 7 December 1944 by 52 state parties – for the time, a significant number of signatories which indicated the growing importance of the aviation industry both in terms of passengers and cargo. The 1944 treaty, commonly referred to as the Chicago Convention, is the bedrock of international civil aviation law, the foundations of which were established in the last two years of the Second World War. That war made clear the importance of aviation in terms of the military, the economy and political systems both domestically and internationally.

> [United States] President Franklin D. Roosevelt – responding to a British initiative – brought fifty-four Allied and neutral States to Chicago during the winter months of 1944 with the goal of developing an ordering mechanism for the world's airspace and the nascent international air

transport industry. The United States hoped that it could steer the negotiations towards affirming a (relatively) free market in aviation services, one which would give the U.S. airline industry – at the time the most developed and technologically sophisticated in the world – the opportunity to dominate the global marketplace. That ambition was not realized. Instead, the Convention's scope was curtailed to solve technical coordination problems relating to, among other things, aircraft registry, air traffic management, cross-border recognition of licensing certificates, and the kinds of taxes and charges that could be imposed on international air services.

States, Not Airlines, Define Chicago's Commercial Environment

. . . States, not their airlines, are vested with the right to define international aviation's commercial environment. That fact is not terribly surprising if one recalls the Chicago Convention's historical context. Memories of the 1929 worldwide economic collapse were still fresh, and economic advisors on both sides of the Atlantic were flirting with the supposed benefits of a Soviet-style command economy. Even the United States, eventually a bastion of neoliberalism and globalization, tempered the market freedoms of its industrial sectors in the late nineteenth century when Congress passed the Sherman Antitrust Act and established the Interstate Commerce Commission. That regulatory impulse spread to the privately owned U.S. air transport industry, which since 1938 had been placed under the economic supervision of a public agency, the now-defunct Civil Aeronautics Board . . .[2]

Civil and State Aircraft

Article 3 confines the scope of the Convention to civil aircraft only; the Convention, thus, does not apply to state aircraft. This provision is one of the Convention's most contentious, and has been the subject of much comment. While neither Article 3 nor any of the definitions in Article 96 (the definitions section) provide an exhaustive list of aircraft deemed to be 'state' aircraft, it is clear that aircraft used in military, customs and police services as described in Article 3 (b) could be – depending on the circumstances – included in such a definition.

. . . Article 3 (a) explicitly excludes from the application of the Convention State aircraft the legal framework of which was left behind in favour of national legislation. However, where should a line be drawn between civil and State aviation, i.e. the line that would state that a particular aircraft should be operated under either a uniform international regime or under non-uniform national legal frameworks? It is submitted that Article 3 (b) is due to take the place of the provision that will solve this question. Nevertheless, interpretation of the given paragraph of Article 3 varies and the paragraph is attributed with different roles. Therefore, one faces difficulty in determining whether the Chicago Convention clearly states what its scope is. The present state of confusion in the interpretation of paragraphs (a) and (b) is strengthened by the existence of paragraphs (c) and (d), which contain regulatory provisions for State aircraft, though it is excluded from the application of the Convention.

. . . If the aircraft is classed as a civil aircraft, then there is no doubt that the aircraft will be subject to the legal framework of the Chicago Convention. Not being a civil aircraft means that the aircraft will be considered as a State aircraft, and thus excluded from the scope of the Convention. As the consequence of this exclusion, a legal framework for navigation of State aircraft has to be developed at the national level.

The first problem I dealt with concerned the question how to distinguish civil and State aircraft. There are different views with regard to this question. My view, as implied from the analysis accomplished above, is in sum as follows:

1. The Chicago Convention makes a distinction between civil and State aircraft, however, it does not encompass conditions according to which such a distinction should be provided.
2. Article 3 (b) is not a definition of 'State aircraft', nor does it play a substantial role in defining this term.
3. Article 3 (b) is a presumption according to which civil aircraft that are normally subject to the Convention are, under certain conditions, 'deemed to be' State aircraft.
4. The presumption included in Article 3 (b) cannot be applied *vice versa*. This means that a State aircraft cannot ever be deemed to be a civil aircraft and it still remains a State aircraft regardless of the purposes for which the aircraft is being operated.
5. Article 3 (b) has to be interpreted in relation to Article 4 of the Convention.[3]

Non-Scheduled Flight, Scheduled Air Services and Cabotage

Articles 5 and 6 respectively provide for non-scheduled flight and scheduled air services. *Non-scheduled* air traffic (Article 5 traffic), including private flights and charter operations, comprises a comparatively small component of international flights and is subject to far less stringent restrictions than for scheduled air services. Restrictions on any 'right' to fly are not imposed under international air law; they are matters for domestic policy and state agreements (by virtue of the principle of state sovereignty over airspace).

Scheduled international air services, provided for in Article 6, make up the majority of international air traffic. Article 6 is perhaps the most commercially significant of the Chicago Convention provisions. For international air services flown either pursuant to a schedule or with sufficient regularity, and subject to rates and tariffs (that is, commercial passenger flight), special permissions or other state authorisations must be obtained. Again, airspace over states is sovereign; thus, agreement to traverse such airspace is generally required.

A Concessionary Principle of Market Access: Article 6

Article 6 of the Chicago Convention perfects the restrictive logic of the airspace sovereignty principle through a concessionary principle of market access. Thus, "[n]o scheduled international air service may be operated over or into the territory of a contracting State, except with special permission or authorization of that State, and in accordance with the terms of such permission and authorization." This is not only an application of *noli me tangere* ("touch me not") sovereignty by States to the airlines of the world, however. There is also a strong national security component to the Article. Given aviation's capacity to penetrate the territorial integrity of a State as no mode of transportation had heretofore allowed, governments understandably wanted to limit access to the airspace over their territories to prevent activities such as unauthorized photographing of military installations. In the intervening decades, that concern has lost much of its salience. Satellites and high-resolution photography make aerial photography less important; anyone with an Internet connection has free access to global satellite imagery on websites such as Google Earth. Additionally, improvements in air traffic management technology have proven sophisticated enough to monitor and keep aircraft away from sensitive areas.[4]

Scheduled international air services are not defined in the Chicago Convention. An enduring definition for these international services was adopted by the ICAO Council in 1952 in Doc 7278-C/841:

A scheduled international air service is a series of flights that possesses all the following characteristics:

(a) it passes through the airspace over the territory of more than one State;
(b) it is performed by aircraft for the transport of passengers, mail or cargo for remuneration, in such a manner that each flight is open to use by members of the public;
(c) it is operated so as to serve traffic between the same two or more points, either 1: according to a published timetable, or 2: with flights so regular or frequent that they constitute a recognizable systematic series.

State parties at the 1944 Chicago Conference were together unable to reach a multilateral agreement to provide for the exchange of air traffic rights for scheduled international air services. This failure resulted in the post-World War II system of basic 'freedoms of the air' being exchanged in bilateral agreements between states pursuant to Article 6. This bilateral system has endured for many decades.

> The first interim Assembly of ICAO (Resolution IV in June 1946) affirmed the opinion that a multilateral agreement on commercial rights constituted "the only solution compatible with the character of the International Civil Aviation Organization created at Chicago". However, in November 1947, consequent upon exhaustive deliberations and discussion, the Commission on Multilateral Agreement on Commercial Rights in International Civil Air Transport which was convened prior to the adoption of Resolution A1–38 decided that the divergence of views on certain important issues rendered impossible any agreement that would find wide acceptance. This notwithstanding, the Commission produced Annex III to its report which contained provisions that would form part of a future multilateral agreement.
>
> The member States of ICAO at ICAO's 7th Assembly (Brighton 16 June – 6 July 1953) adopted Resolution A7–15 (Prospects and Methods of Future International Agreement on Commercial Rights in International Air Transport – Scheduled International Air Services) whereby the Assembly gave its opinion that there was no prospect at that time of achieving a universal multilateral agreement, although multilateralism in commercial rights to the greatest possible extent continues to be the objective of the Organization. Through Resolution A7–15, the Assembly requested favourable consideration of the ICAO Council towards convening regional conference in Europe (upon a request of the Council of Europe at that time).
>
> Article 6 is arguably the most contentious in the Chicago Convention. In brief, it contends the following:
>
> • All scheduled international commercial air transport services are prohibited except to the extent they are permitted;
> • All bilateral and open skies agreements are reciprocal and subject to the nuances of aeropolitics and protectionism and arbitrary demarcations of market share;
> • Therefore airlines do not have freedom to access of markets;
> • There are rigid and archaic ownership and control regulations governing so called "national carriers";
> • In many instances, this effectively precludes direct foreign investment in airlines;
> • All of the above unduly prevent connectivity, which is the meaning and purpose of meeting the needs of the people of the world for regular, efficient and economical air transport.
>
> . . . With all this ambivalent rhetoric, Article 6 makes us ask: What do we stand for as a global aviation community? How do we strike the balance between growth and development? Where does aviation and its governance

fit into a world transformed by the winds of globalization and change through technology? Have we a strategic direction and have be achieved our goals in aviation?[5]

The ideal aviation economic environment – and more specifically, the degree of market access to be afforded states for the operation of international scheduled air services – was not created by delegates at the Chicago conference of 1944. While delegates failed to agree on the exchange of freedoms multilaterally, two side agreements annexed to the Convention allow the *possibility* of such freedoms being exchanged.

Five freedoms or 'privileges' are set out in two agreements. The first agreement, the International Air Services Transit Agreement, includes two freedoms: the freedoms to overfly and make a technical landing in a foreign state. The second agreement, the International Air Transport Agreement, contains three additional commercial transport freedoms.

Very few states have ratified these two agreements. Absent a multilateral exchange of rights, these commercial freedoms are negotiated and then exchanged through state-based bilateral agreements.

Bilateral Agreements

Prior to any airline operating services to another state, the airline's home state must negotiate an agreement (an international treaty) with that destination state. Such agreements – bilateral air services agreements – now number than 3000. The net effect is a complex web of international agreements providing for the ability of airlines to fly from one state to another (and often beyond that destination state).

Bilateral agreements are not mandated in the Chicago Conventions. States did adopt a resolution – Resolution VIII – which provides for a standard form of bilateral agreement which states may choose to implement in either an unamended or amended form.

Bilateral air services agreements/arrangements contain provisions on;

- **Traffic rights**–the routes airlines can fly, including cities that can be served within, between and beyond the bilateral partners.
- **Capacity**–the number of flights that can be operated or passengers that can be carried between the bilateral partners.
- **Designation, Ownership and Control**–the number of airlines the bilateral partners can nominate to operate services and the ownership criteria airlines must meet to be designated under the bilateral agreement. This clause sometimes includes foreign ownership restrictions.
- **Tariffs**–i.e. prices. Some agreements require airlines to submit ticket prices to aeronautical authorities for approval (it is not current practice for Australian aeronautical authorities to require this), and
- Many other clauses addressing competition policy, safety and security.[6]

Freedoms of the Air

The exchange of certain freedoms of the air are central to international air services agreements, whether bilateral or multilateral. The right (or lack thereof) of a carrier to fly passengers, cargo or both between, over, within and beyond a state can have significant commercial advantages (or deleterious commercial impacts).

> The expression "freedoms of the air" has been used in the parlance of international air transport since the Chicago Conference on International Civil Aviation of 1944. It is mostly parlance, because nowhere can one find an international legal instrument stating that freedom x or y is 'defined as follows'. The multilateral International Air Services Transit Agreement (IASTA) and the International Air Transport Agreement of 1944 do, however, use the expression "freedoms of the air" in a general fashion and come closest to giving definitions of freedoms 1 through 5 of the air. Ever since the Chicago Conference, freedoms 1 through 4 have had very specific meaning in international air transport, whereas freedom 5 received very broad, general definition. Since 1944, authors and practitioners have often distinguished more than just 5 freedoms of the air, although authoritative legal definitions are lacking and although there is great fluidity in the definitions themselves of these further freedoms.
>
> The IASTA and the International Air Transport Agreement express the freedoms of the air as 'privileges' to fly, to land, etc; the Chicago Convention, in Article 5 and 7, and bilateral agreements speak of the 'right' to make flights, to operate air services.
>
> It is submitted that 'right' is the more proper term: multilateral and bilateral agreements between States exchange contractual rights to fly aircraft, to operate air services that derogate from the customary international law principle of Article 1 of the Chicago Convention to the effect that each State has complete and exclusive sovereignty in the airspace above its territory.[7]

In addition to the five freedoms contained in the two agreements annexed to the Chicago Convention, further freedoms have been developed and established in the post-World War II period. The most commonly recognised freedoms, then, are as follows:

> First Freedom of the Air – the right or privilege, in respect of scheduled international air services, granted by one State to another State or States to fly across its territory without landing (also known as a First Freedom Right).
>
> Second Freedom of the Air – the right or privilege, in respect of scheduled international air services, granted by one State to another State or States to land in its territory for non-traffic purposes (also known as a Second Freedom Right).

Third Freedom of [t]he Air – the right or privilege, in respect of scheduled international air services, granted by one State to another State to put down, in the territory of the first State, traffic coming from the home State of the carrier (also known as a Third Freedom Right).

Fourth Freedom of [t]he Air – the right or privilege, in respect of scheduled international air services, granted by one State to another State to take on, in the territory of the first State, traffic destined for the home State of the carrier (also known as a Fourth Freedom Right).

Fifth Freedom of [t]he Air – the right or privilege, in respect of scheduled international air services, granted by one State to another State to put down and to take on, in the territory of the first State, traffic coming from or destined to a third State (also known as a Fifth Freedom Right).

ICAO characterizes all "freedoms" beyond the Fifth as "so-called" because only the first five "freedoms" have been officially recognized as such by international treaty.

Sixth Freedom of [t]he Air – the right or privilege, in respect of scheduled international air services, of transporting, via the home State of the carrier, traffic moving between two other States (also known as a Sixth Freedom Right). The so-called Sixth Freedom of the Air, unlike the first five freedoms, is not incorporated as such into any widely recognized air service agreements such as the "Five Freedoms Agreement".

Seventh Freedom of [t]he Air – the right or privilege, in respect of scheduled international air services, granted by one State to another State, of transporting traffic between the territory of the granting State and any third State with no requirement to include on such operation any point in the territory of the recipient State, i.e the service need not connect to or be an extension of any service to/from the home State of the carrier.

Eighth Freedom of [t]he Air – the right or privilege, in respect of scheduled international air services, of transporting cabotage traffic between two points in the territory of the granting State on a service which originates or terminates in the home country of the foreign carrier or (in connection with the so-called Seventh Freedom of the Air) outside the territory of the granting State (also known as an Eighth Freedom Right or "consecutive cabotage").

Ninth Freedom of [t]he Air – the right or privilege of transporting cabotage traffic of the granting State on a service performed entirely within the territory of the granting State (also known as an Eighth Freedom Right or "stand alone" cabotage).[8]

Increasing Liberalisation

Over time and, in particular, in recent years, countries and groups of countries have negotiated multilateral air service agreements. Notwithstanding this development, the great majority of freedoms of the air are still exchanged bilaterally. Both multilateral and bilateral air services agreements are, however, increasingly becoming more liberal.

Multilateral Approaches to Market Access

. . . while there have been calls in some quarters for restraint on opening markets due to a number of factors, outright demands to roll back liberal agreements have been rare, and the industry has advocated more, not less, commercial freedom and liberalization. The question has again been raised whether future expansion of market access can be better achieved by continued reliance on bilateral exchanges of market access, or whether the time has come to renew attempts to establish a multilateral framework. For example, WP/13 proposes that ICAO assume a leadership role in developing a multilateral market access agreement.

. . . Notwithstanding the gradual erosion of bilateral restrictions and the accelerating liberalization of market access over the past three decades, the bilateral system has been widely criticized for perpetuating limitations and acting as a barrier to a wider exchange of rights due to its cumbersome nature.

A broad multilateral exchange of market opportunities has remained an ambitious vision, and several attempts have been made to overcome the limitations of the bilateral system: (1) inclusion of air services in the Global Agreement on Trade in Services (GATS), (2) liberalized regional and sub- regional agreements, and (3) broader plurilateral agreements such as the Multilateral Agreement on Liberalization of International Air Transportation (MALIAT). These efforts have generally yielded at best mixed results. Inclusion of traffic rights and services directly related to their exercise in GATS has been unacceptable because States remain reluctant to grant rights on [a most favoured nation] basis, without any assurance that they will receive comparable rights. With the notable exception of the EU, regional agreements have had mixed success to date due to insufficient liberalization and/or implementation difficulties. Accession to MALIAT has been disappointing. Since its 2001 signature by Brunei, Chile, New Zealand, Singapore and the U.S., the MALIAT has been joined by Peru (which later withdrew), Samoa, Tonga, Mongolia (cargo only) and Cook Islands.

Nevertheless, the MALIAT, if more widely accepted, would provide all the benefits of a new multilateral instrument. MALIAT, in addition to incorporating the full open-skies model of unrestricted route access including all-cargo 7th freedoms, capacity and pricing freedom, and pro-competitive doing-business and airline cooperative provisions, provides a straightforward framework that allows all parties to enjoy full open-skies treatment from all other parties, as well as an option for enhanced access to capital investment, and for the accession of new parties without the need for a series of time-consuming bilateral negotiations. It was later amended to permit accession on a cargo-only basis.

In order to advance liberalization and broaden economic benefits, a multilateral air services agreement would have to include the full set of open-skies elements. As noted in WP/13, such an undertaking would require substantial incremental work and allocation of resources, not only by ICAO but also by interested States. Development of such an instrument, including one along the lines set forth in WP/13, would essentially re-create the MALIAT. A fuller understanding of the reasons for the lack of broader adherence to MALIAT would provide indispensable insights into the prospects for widespread acceptance of a multilateral open-skies air services agreement . . .

Conclusions

Liberalization provides broad and deep economic benefits for States' consumers, airlines, airports, communities and economies. Increased access to the international market for air service providers is a key component for allowing the air transport sector to maximize its contribution to the global economy.

Air services agreements that couple increased market access (in addition to 3rd and 4th freedom) with the full set of other open-skies elements, including provisions that eliminate government interference in airlines' commercial decisions on capacity and pricing and establish pro-competitive elements on user charges, doing-business matters and cooperative arrangements, deliver broad economic benefits to States and aviation stakeholders.

The considerable progress that Member States have achieved in liberalization is evidence that the current system has been very effective in increasing liberalization, and that the momentum should be maintained through the use of open-skies agreements at the bilateral, regional, pluri-lateral and multilateral levels.

The Multilateral Agreement on Liberalization of International Air Transportation (MALIAT) offers the potential for a broader exchange of market access opportunities and significant progress in liberalization on a multilateral basis, but has attracted limited accession.

Recommendations

The following recommendations are proposed for adoption by the Conference:

(a) that States that have not yet entered into open-skies agreements should do so at the earliest practicable opportunity with as many partners as possible;

(b) that when negotiating liberalized market access agreements, States should actively consult with aviation stakeholders, including labor, airlines, airports and communities; and

(c) that ICAO should conduct a survey circulating the MALIAT and requesting States to respond by explaining the basis for their decisions to accede, or not to accede, and their willingness to accede to MALIAT or a similar instrument in the future.[9]

One of the keys to successful liberalisation of the skies is the grant of so called 'beyond' or sixth freedom rights – that is, the right to fly between two states with an intermediate stop being in the home state of the relevant carrier. For political, commercial and other domestic reasons, these rights are not easily granted or 'surrendered' by states.

Sixth Freedom Revisited in the Twenty-First Century

[. . .]
While the bilateral aviation system remains intact, sixth freedom rights will continue to play a role in making the carriage of passenger's economical viable and maximizing the usage of landing rights that have been granted under bilateral air service agreements. Which sixth freedom rights are used and where in the world they are used will depend strongly on both technology and economic needs, not very different than the years before. . . . The questions for the twenty-first century will be how many sixth freedom hubs can a region sustain given the rising competition at all levels and will it remain an economical viable model for all those banking on its success to enhance their economies. Furthermore, will it remain viable for smaller countries with limited origin and destination traffic to continue to take a large share of the pie of international transit passengers and will first mover advantages continue to pay dividend?[10]

Rules of the Air

State jurisdiction over national airspace and territorial waters (which have been extended to 12 nautical miles) is a cornerstone of the Chicago Convention. The airspace above national territory – and a state's territorial waters – is sovereign.

Article 12 of the Chicago Convention provides that aircraft must observe the rules of the air of the state over which or in which they operate. The rules of the air are further delineated in Annexes 2, 6, 11 and 12 of the Chicago Convention. In addition, Article 12 should be read together with Articles 11, 13 and 16 for a complete understanding of state jurisdictional matters.

State jurisdiction can be distinguished from the airspace above the High Seas (to which the provisions of the Chicago Convention apply by virtue of Article 12). Generally, the law to be applied on board the aircraft over the High Seas is the law of the state of registration of the aircraft.

. . . ICAO possesses formal legislative authority for civil aviation over the high seas, except for state (non-commercial aircraft). The Chicago

Convention authorizes the ICAO Council to adopt international standards and recommended practices concerning, *inter alia*, the rules of the air. The Council has adopted Rules of the Air in the form of international standards, without any recommended practices. These include Rules of the Air over the high seas, pursuant to Article 12 of the Chicago Convention. It provides in part: "Over the high seas, the rules in force shall be those established under this Convention."

It is arguable that all ICAO international standards are formally binding on member states, except to the extent that a member has opted out under a procedure set forth in the Convention. However that may be for most international standards, those in force over ocean areas recognized as the high seas or their equivalents for navigational purposes are formally binding by virtue of Article 12. Moreover, ICAO does not acknowledge any right to opt out of any standards that apply over free navigation ocean areas.[11]

Charges

Under Article 15, states may charge for the use of airport and air traffic management facilities but must not discriminate in terms of the imposition of such charges. It is generally accepted that Article 15 allows taxes or fees to be levied solely on a cost recovery basis. Any charge that does not go to the provision of such facilities and services – for example, a charge relating to environmental harm – would likely exceed the scope of the Article.

> There is no controversial issue that divides government tax collectors and the modern international airline industry more than the industry's apparently favourable tax treatment under Articles 15 and 24 of the Chicago Convention. Article 15, which covers "airports and similar charges," has moved to the foreground as States have adopted so-called eco-charges or green taxes to offset the purportedly harmful environmental effects of aircraft carbon emissions. Article 15 permits States to levy nondiscriminatory charges for the use of airport and air navigation (air traffic management) facilities, subject to a general exception which provides that "[n]o . . . charges [i.e., other than charges imposed for the use of airports and air navigation facilities] shall be imposed by any contracting State in respect solely of the right of transit over or entry into or exit from its territory of any aircraft of a contracting State or persons or property thereon." Although not a paragon of clear draftsmanship, the text of Article 15 has been interpreted by the Convention's State parties, acting through ICAO, to permit only the imposition of charges (which may also be called dues, fees or taxes) specifically to recover the costs to the charging State of providing facilities and services to international civil aviation. A general charge, such as a "Green tax", that is unrelated to the provision of services would arguably be a charge imposed in respect "solely" of the right of

transit over or entry into or exit from the State, and thus would be impermissible under the Convention.[12]

The parameters and the limitations of a charge levied under Article 15 were tested in the Dutch Supreme Court resulting in a decision that a domestic tax levied on passenger departure by The Netherlands did not contravene Article 15 on the basis that "charges" under Article 15 do not necessarily include taxes; the Article 15 heading includes reference to "airport *and similar charges*" [emphasis added]; and, if any restriction on the ability of states to levy domestic taxes had been intended, such restriction would have been made clear in the language of the provision.

Dutch Ticket Tax and Article 15 of the Chicago Convention

[. . .]

According to the [Dutch] Government, the aim of the Chicago Convention is not to award tax privileges to the aviation sector, but to enhance the safe and economic development of civil aviation. Article 15 of the Chicago Convention prohibits discriminatory charging by a State where it could levy a charge on foreign air carriers (or their passengers or cargo) that it does not extend to its national carriers. The Dutch Government argued, however, that Article 15 does not prohibit the imposition of a non-discriminatory national tax.

The Advocate-General continued by arguing that the drafters of the Chicago Convention could not have contemplated in 1944 the establishment of environmental measures or issues relating to the taxation thereof. He continued by stating that the drafters probably never heard of the contemporary concept of the '*natural* environment'. The Preamble to the Convention evidences that the purpose of the treaty is to ensure as many international flights as possible for those able to afford it. Thus, according to the Advocate-General, the notion that the Convention's drafters considered prohibiting the taxation of fuel for environmental purposes should be ruled out. Moreover, the Advocate-General opined that it is very unlikely that in 1944 the drafters opposed the visualization of the actual social cost triggered by aviation. At that time no transportation system comparable to today's international aviation industry was envisioned. Therefore, the Advocate-General concluded that it was unlikely that Article 15 flatly prohibits cost adjustment through taxation by way of excise duties or imposing consumer taxes on air fares (provided they are non-discriminatory).

[. . .]

Recalling case law of the Dutch Supreme Court applying the 1969 Vienna Convention on the Law of Treaties to agreements which preceded Vienna's ratification, the Advocate-General applied the Convention's canons of interpretation to Article 15. He reasoned that the final part of Article 15 only stipulates that the mere provision of air-space is not a service for which a fee, due, or other charge can be calculated. This final part prohibits a State from levying any charge merely because a civil aircraft finds itself in the airspace over its territory . . .. The Advocate-General did not find a prohibition on levying a regulated ticket tax. The Ticket Tax, in his view, focuses on the correction of the 'socially unacceptable' low consumer price of tickets but cannot be regarded as a charge '*uniquement pour le droit de transit, d'entrée ou de sortie de son territoire*'. The Advocate-General concluded that no 'unmistakable violation' of the Ticket Tax under Article 15 of the Chicago Convention existed.

[. . .]

The taxation of passengers departing from The Netherlands, in the Court's view, was not related to charging certain service performances, but rather projected the social cost of aviation to society in general. This was in order to create awareness that there are non-pecuniary costs associated with environmental polluting activities which are not sufficiently reflected in the ticket price. The price of air fares in relation to other modes of transportation, according to the Court, was too low due to the lack of any form of consumer tax (excise, duty, or value added tax . . .) for international aviation. With respect to the Ticket Tax, the Court viewed it as a levy for departing passengers, against which no counter-obligation in law exists.

The Supreme Court went on to state that the Court of Appeal rightfully concluded that the Ticket Tax is not 'unmistakably' in conflict with the Chicago Convention. According to the Court of Appeal's view, the final part of Article 15 of the Chicago Convention does not prevent taxation for which *no* counter-service is provided, such as the Ticket Tax . . .

The Dutch Supreme Court confirmed that the exercise of the sovereign right of taxation by a State is not restricted by the Chicago Convention.[13]

Aircraft Nationality and Registration

Chapter III of the Chicago Convention addresses issues associated with the nationality and registration of aircraft. Aircraft have the nationality of the state of registration and cannot be registered simultaneously in multiple states. Registration can, however, be transferred from one state to another, such registration and transfer governed by national law. Chapter III also provides for the display of aircraft nationality and registration marks and for the supply of information concerning ownership and control of aircraft from one state to another.

. . . States from the inception of aviation required, by domestic law, prescribed terms and conditions under which a person or corporation may own an aircraft and operate it.

One of the generally applied conditions was the registration of the aircraft . . . The national practice requiring registration of aircraft was soon adopted in the international regulation, The 1919 Paris Convention contained substantial restrictions – no aircraft to be entered on the register of one of the contracting States unless it belongs wholly to nationals of such state; moreover, no incorporated company can be registered as the owner of an aircraft unless it possesses the nationality of the State in which the aircraft is registered, unless the president of chairman of the company and at least two-thirds of the directors possess such nationality, and unless the company fulfils all other conditions which may be prescribed by the laws of the said State.

What could have been the cause for such substantial restriction? Perhaps the fierce opposition of States to 'flags of convenience' from the early beginning of aviation, perhaps also an effort to block the defeated Germany from advancing its aviation development in other States.

The current international regulation based on the Chicago Convention is far less restrictive: Article 19 [essentially provides that it is] a sovereign power of each State to decide by its legislation who and under what conditions can register an aircraft in its register – perhaps not only a citizen but also a permanent resident, corporate body either registered or having its principal place of business in that state, etc. Such laws would also determine whether a foreign owned aircraft . . . could be entered on the national register.

A limitation is imposed by international regulation in Article 18 of the Chicago Convention that prohibits dual registration . . .

The Chicago Convention also imposes an international duty to report to ICAO on the registration and ownership of any aircraft registered in that State. The relevant Article 21 of the Convention is for all practical purposes a 'dead letter' since there is no record that it ever was applied . . .

The registration marks of an aircraft should be letters, numbers, or a combination of letters and numbers, and are to be assigned by the State of Registry.

In international law more important than the registration of aircraft and the registration marks is the nationality of the aircraft and the nationality marks . . . Nationality of a person denotes a legal relation between that person and a particular state – a relation from which legal consequences follow in the form of rights and duties.

The 1919 Paris Convention introduced into international law a provision that aircraft possess the nationality of the State on the register of which they are entered. This principle is currently reflected in Article 17 of the Chicago Convention . . .

Annex 7 to the Chicago Convention prescribes the size, format and position of the nationality and registration marks on the hull of the aircraft and also the format of the Certificate of Registration that is to be carried in the aircraft at all times. Such certificate contains the name of the registering State, description of the nationality and registration mark, manufacturer's designation of the aircraft, aircraft serial number, name and address of the owner and the date of registration.[14]

The International Civil Aviation Organisation

The Chicago Convention established an independent aviation body, ICAO, based in Montreal. ICAO came into being on 4 April 1947 (30 days after the requirement of ratification of the Chicago Convention by 26 states was met). The Convention functions as the constitution for ICAO and includes rules on ICAO's objectives, structure and composition and main activities. According to ICAO's official list, the organisation now has 191 member states (out of a global total of 195 independent states).

Objectives

ICAO became a Specialized Agency of the United Nations Organisation on 13 May 1947, and is for that reason invested with special powers, pursuant to Article 64 of the Chicago Convention.

The objectives of ICAO are laid down in the Chicago Convention as to which see Article 44. ICAO has as its principal objectives the promotion of safety and the orderly development of civil aviation throughout the world. ICAO must also contribute to taking measures regarding aviation security and the protection of the environment. Since the so called 9/11 events in the US, and the debate around global warming, these latter tasks receive special attention from ICAO and its bodies . . .

ICAO is mandated to regulate and introduce measures for the benefit of *civil* aircraft and *civil* aviation. State aircraft are subject to other regimes, including national law and international regulations. Domestic civil aviation is generally – but not always – a matter of state responsibility, without intervention from ICAO.

The General Assembly

The principal and sovereign body of ICAO is the General Assembly. The General Assembly meets at least once every three years. Each contracting State has one voice. The Assembly is convened by the Council, in accordance with Article 48. All Member States have an equal right to representation whereby each State has one vote. The Assembly's functions are summarised in Article 49; they comprise, among other duties, examining the Council's reports and voting and controlling budgets.

Decisions are taken by majority vote. In special cases, such as admission of new members, an amendment of the Chicago Convention decisions must be taken by a qualified majority. Membership of ICAO, and, consequently, participation in the work of the General Assembly, is open for *States* who are members of the United Nations as formulated by the Chicago Convention (as to which see Articles 92(a), 93 and 93*bis*). There is no provision regarding membership of Regional Economic Integration Organisations such as the EU . . .

The General Assembly also adopts Resolutions on all aspects of international civil aviation, including but not limited to: constitutional and general policy matters; membership and relations with Contracting States; air navigation; airworthiness; accident and incident investigation licensing of personnel; air transport establishment of charges; taxation and facilitation; financing of the organisation; unlawful interference with international civil aviation; and organisation and personnel. The legal effect of General Assembly Resolutions must be determined in accordance with international law principles on the legal force of resolutions adopted by the supreme bodies of other organisations, including the UN.

The Council

The Council is a permanent body whose head office is located in Montreal, Canada. It may be regarded as the Organisation's executive committee . . .

A principal function of the ICAO Council concerns the adoption of *Standards and Recommended Practices* (SARPs) which are laid down in 18 technical Annexes to the Chicago Convention and Procedures for Air Navigation Services (PANS). Also, the Council has a judicial function as is it is tasked by the Chicago Convention to settle a dispute between two or more Contracting States by way of a decision (see above).

The Council also has – albeit restricted – enforcement powers as it is entitled to bar an airline of a Contracting State from flying into the airspace of another State in case when the Council has decided that the concerned airline is not complying with the provisions of the Chicago Convention . . .

Under Article 86 of the Chicago Convention, the Council may decide on the compatibility of the operation of international air services with the rules made by and under this Convention. The Council has a strong enforcement mechanism at its disposal as it may decide that Contracting States must prevent non-compliant airlines from flying through the airspace above their territories . . .

The Air Navigation Commission

. . . The Air Navigation Commission assists the Council with respect to the development of the above mentioned SARPs and PANS. The Air Navigation Commission makes proposals for SARPs before their adoption by the Council and advises the Council regarding all matters which may help to advance air navigation.

The Air Navigation Commission is comprised of nineteen members who are appointed by the Council on the basis of professional expertise while taking into account geographical representation . . .

The Secretariat

The third important body of ICAO is the *Secretariat* which is headed by the Secretary General. The Chicago Convention does not mention the Secretariat. The Secretariat must provide technical, legal and administrative support to the Council. It is sub-divided into five departments called *Bureaux* . . .

The Establishment of Standards and Recommended Practices

The eighteen Annexes provide technical rules, comprising Standards and Recommended Practices. They are designed to implement the articles of the Convention and regulate the following subjects.

(1) Personnel Licensing
(2) Rules of the Air
(3) Meteorological Service for International Air Navigation
(4) Aeronautical Charts
(5) Units of Measurement to be Used in Air and Ground Operations
(6) Operation of Aircraft
(7) Aircraft Nationality and Registration Marks
(8) Airworthiness of Aircraft
(9) Facilitation
(10) Aeronautical Telecommunications
(11) Air Traffic Services
(12) Search and Rescue
(13) Aircraft Accident Investigation
(14) Aerodromes
(15) Aeronautical Information Services
(16) Environmental Protection
(17) Security – Safeguarding International Civil Aviation against Acts of Unlawful Interference
(18) Safe Transport of Dangerous Goods by Air

. . . 'Standards' are any specifications 'the uniform application of which is recognized as necessary for the safety or regularity of international air navigation'. 'Recommended practices' are, of course, not of a mandatory nature but are considered as desirable.

Departures from Standards must be notified to the ICAO Council under Article 38 of the Convention. States do not always comply with this obligation: they may depart from, that is, not implement and enforce a Standard without notifying ICAO of such a move.

The legal status of Standards and Recommended Practices has raised questions in courts, in literature and in practice, Standards have been attributed binding force; this is especially so if national law treats them as part of the Chicago Convention and attaches them, for instance, to their national aviation codes as secondary regulations. In yet other cases they are regarded as guidance material or 'soft law', as States may choose not to comply with them. Indeed, Article 54(1) of the Chicago Convention dictates that the ICAO Council must, as a matter of 'convenience', adopt Standards and Recommended Practices and attach them to this Convention.

In 2001, the ICAO General Assembly adopted a resolution encouraging ICAO Contracting States to implement SARPs 'by all available means'. Safety oversight must help to strengthen the legal force of ICAO SARPs which are so vital for the 'safe and orderly' development of international civil aviation. Compliance with the Standards is also normally a prerequisite for the exercise of traffic rights by an air carrier under a bilateral or multilateral air services agreement and States reserve the right to check to ensure that the Standards are indeed being met. This principle is enshrined in the US International Aviation Safety Assessment . . . programme . . . as well as in the European Safety Assessment of Foreign Aircraft . . . programme.[15]

Notes

1 Moon, Jr., Albert I. "A Look at Airspace Sovereignty", *Journal of Air Law and Commerce* 29(4) (1963): 330–332.
2 Havel, Brian F. and Sanchez, Gabriel S. *The Principles and Practice of International Aviation Law.* New York: Cambridge University Press, 2014, 28–29.
3 Hornik, Jiri. "Article 3 of the Chicago Convention", *Air and Space Law* 27(3) (2002): 161, 193–194.
4 Havel and Sanchez, *Principles and Practice*, 41–42.
5 Abeyratne, Ruwantissa I.R. *Convention on International Civil Aviation: A Commentary.* Cham, Switzerland: Springer Science & Business Media, 2013, 101–102.
6 Department of Infrastructure and Regional Development. "The Bilateral System – How International Air Services Work". Australian Government. https://infrastructure.gov.au/aviation/international/bilateral_system.aspx. Accessed 7 June 2016.
7 Haanappel, Peter P.C. *The Law and Policy of Air Space and Outer Space: A Comparative Approach.* The Hague: Kluwer Law International, 2003, 104–105.
8 International Civil Aviation Organization. "Freedoms of the Air". www.icao.int/Pages/freedomsAir.aspx. Accessed 7 June 2016.
9 International Civil Aviation Organization, "Liberalization of Market Access". Paper presented at the Worldwide Air Transport Conference, Sixth Meeting, Montreal, 18–22 March 2013): 3–5.
10 Van Brandenburg-Kulkami, Prachee. "'Sixth Freedom' Revisited in the Twenty-First Century", *Air and Space Law* 40(1) (2015): 63.
11 Joyner, Christopher C. *The United Nations and International Law.* Cambridge: Cambridge University Press, 1999, 77.

12 Havel and Sanchez, *Principles and Practice*, 44–45.
13 Havel, Brian F. and van Antwerpen, Niels. "Dutch Ticket Tax and Article 15 of the Chicago Convention (Continued)", *Air and Space Law* 34(6) (2009): 449–451.
14 Milde, Michael. *International Air Law and ICAO*. The Hague: Eleven International Publishing, 2012, 75–77.
15 Diederiks-Verschoor, I.H. Ph. and Mendes de Leon, Pablo. *An Introduction to Air Law*. Alphen aan den Rijn: Kluwer Law International, 2012, 9th edition, 32–37.

Section 7

International Civil Aviation

7.1 Chicago Convention 1944

CONVENTION ON INTERNATIONAL CIVIL AVIATION

Signed in Chicago on 7 December 1944

WHEREAS the future development of international civil aviation can greatly help to create and preserve friendship and understanding among the nations and peoples of the world, yet its abuse can become a threat to the general security; and

WHEREAS it is desirable to avoid friction and to promote that cooperation between nations and peoples upon which the peace of the world depends;

THEREFORE, the undersigned governments having agreed on certain principles and arrangements in order that international civil aviation may be developed in a safe and orderly manner and that international air transport services may be established on the basis of equality of opportunity and operated soundly and economically;

Have accordingly concluded this Convention to that end.

PART I – AIR NAVIGATION

Chapter I – General Principles and Application of the Convention

Article 1 – Sovereignty

The contracting States recognize that every State has complete and exclusive sovereignty over the airspace above its territory.

Article 2 – Territory

For the purposes of this Convention the territory of a State shall be deemed to be the land areas and territorial waters adjacent thereto under the sovereignty, suzerainty, protection or mandate of such State.

Article 3 – Civil and State Aircraft

(a) This Convention shall be applicable only to civil aircraft, and shall not be applicable to state aircraft.
(b) Aircraft used in military, customs and police services shall be deemed to be state aircraft.
(c) No state aircraft of a contracting State shall fly over the territory of another State or land thereon without authorization by special agreement or otherwise, and in accordance with the terms thereof.
(d) The contracting States undertake, when issuing regulations for their state aircraft, that they will have due regard for the safety of navigation of civil aircraft.

Article 3 **bis**

(a) The contracting States recognize that every State must refrain from resorting to the use of weapons against civil aircraft in flight and that, in case of interception, the lives of persons on board and the safety of aircraft must not be endangered. This provision shall not be interpreted as modifying in any way the rights and obligations of States set forth in the Charter of the United Nations.
(b) The contracting States recognize that every State, in the exercise of its sovereignty, is entitled to require the landing at some designated airport of a civil aircraft flying above its territory without authority or if there are reasonable grounds to conclude that it is being used for any purpose inconsistent with the aims of this Convention; it may also give such aircraft any other instructions to put an end to such violations. For this purpose, the contracting States may resort to any appropriate means consistent with relevant rules of international law, including the relevant provisions of this Convention, specifically paragraph (a) of this Article. Each contracting State agrees to publish its regulations in force regarding the interception of civil aircraft.
(c) Every civil aircraft shall comply with an order given in conformity with paragraph (b) of this Article. To this end each contracting State shall establish all necessary provisions in its national laws or regulations to make such compliance mandatory for any civil aircraft registered in that State or operated by an operator who has his principal place of business or permanent residence in that State. Each contracting State shall make any violation of such applicable laws or regulations

punishable by severe penalties and shall submit the case to its competent
authorities in accordance with its laws or regulations.

(d) Each contracting State shall take appropriate measures to prohibit the
deliberate use of any civil aircraft registered in that State or operated
by an operator who has his principal place of business or permanent
residence in that State for any purpose inconsistent with the aims of this
Convention. This provision shall not affect paragraph (a) or derogate
from paragraphs (b) and (c) of this Article.

Article 4 – Misuse of Civil Aviation

Each contracting State agrees not to use civil aviation for any purpose inconsistent with the aims of this Convention.

Chapter II – Flight Over Territory of Contracting States

Article 5 – Right of Non-Scheduled Flight

Each contracting State agrees that all aircraft of the other contracting States, being aircraft not engaged in scheduled international air services shall have the right, subject to the observance of the terms of this Convention, to make flights into or in transit non-stop across its territory and to make stops for non-traffic purposes without the necessity of obtaining prior permission, and subject to the right of the State flown over to require landing. Each contracting State nevertheless reserves the right, for reasons of safety of flight, to require aircraft desiring to proceed over regions which are inaccessible or without adequate air navigation facilities to follow prescribed routes, or to obtain special permission for such flights.

Such aircraft, if engaged in the carriage of passengers, cargo, or mail for remuneration or hire on other than scheduled international air services, shall also, subject to the provisions of Article 7, have the privilege of taking on or discharging passengers, cargo, mail, subject to the right of any State where such embarkation or discharge takes place to impose such regulations, conditions or limitations at it may consider desirable.

Article 6 – Scheduled Air Services

No scheduled international air service may be operated over or into the territory of a contracting State, except with the special permission or other authorization of that State, and in accordance with the terms of such permission or authorization.

Article 7 – Cabotage

Each contracting State shall have the right to refuse permission to the aircraft of other contracting States to take on in its territory passengers, mail and cargo carried for remuneration or hire and destined for another point within its territory. Each contracting State undertakes not to enter into any arrangements which specifically grant any such privilege on an exclusive basis, to any other State or an airline of any other State, and not to obtain any such exclusive privilege from any other State.

Article 8 – Pilotless Aircraft

No aircraft capable of being flown without a pilot shall be flown without a pilot over the territory of a contracting State without special authorization by that State and in accordance with the terms of such authorization. Each contracting State undertakes to insure that the flight of such aircraft without a pilot in regions open to civil aircraft shall be so controlled as to obviate danger to civil aircraft.

Article 9 – Prohibited Areas

(a) Each contracting State may, for reasons of military necessity or public safety, restrict or prohibit uniformly the aircraft of other States from flying over certain areas of its territory, provided that no distinction in this respect is made between the aircraft of the State whose territory is involved, engaged in international scheduled airline services, and the aircraft of the other contracting States likewise engaged. Such prohibited areas shall be of reasonable extent and location so as not to interfere unnecessarily with air navigation. Descriptions of such prohibited areas in the territory of a contracting State, as well as any subsequent alterations therein, shall be communicated as soon as possible to the other contracting States and to the International Civil Aviation Organization.

(b) Each contracting State reserves also the right, in exceptional circumstances or during a period of emergency, or in the interest of public safety, and with immediate effect, temporarily to restrict or prohibit flying over the whole or any part of its territory, on condition that such restriction or prohibition shall be applicable without distinction of nationality to aircraft of all other States.

(c) Each contracting State, under such regulations as it may prescribe, may require any aircraft entering the areas contemplated in subparagraphs (a) or (b) above to effect a landing as soon as practicable thereafter at some designated airport within its territory.

Article 10 – Landing at Customs Airport

Except in a case where, under the terms of this Convention or a special authorization, aircraft are permitted to cross the territory of a contracting State without landing, every aircraft which enters the territory of a contracting

State shall, if the regulations of that State so require, land at an airport designated by that State for the purpose of customs and other examination. On departure from the territory of a contracting State, such aircraft shall depart from a similarly designated customs airport. Particulars of all designated customs airports shall be published by the State and transmitted to the International Civil Aviation Organization established under Part II of this Convention for communication to all other contracting States.

Article 11 – Applicability of Air Regulations

Subject to the provisions of this Convention, the laws and regulations of a contracting State relating to the admission to or departure from its territory of aircraft engaged in international air navigation, or to the operation and navigation of such aircraft while within its territory, shall be applied to the aircraft of all contracting States without distinction as to nationality, and shall be complied with by such aircraft upon entering or departing from or while within the territory of that State.

Article 12 – Rules of the Air

Each contracting State undertakes to adopt measures to insure that every aircraft flying over or maneuvering within its territory and that every aircraft carrying its nationality mark, wherever such aircraft may be, shall comply with the rules and regulations relating to the flight and maneuver of aircraft there in force. Each contracting State undertakes to keep its own regulations in these respects uniform, to the greatest possible extent, with those established from time to time under this Convention. Over the high seas, the rules in force shall be those established under this Convention. Each contracting State undertakes to insure the prosecution of all persons violating the regulations applicable.

Article 13 – Entry and Clearance Regulations

The laws and regulations of a contracting State as to the admission to or departure from its territory of passengers, crew or cargo of aircraft, such as regulations relating to entry, clearance, immigration, passports, customs, and quarantine shall be complied with by or on behalf of such passengers, crew or cargo upon entrance into or departure from, or while within the territory of that State.

Article 14 – Prevention of Spread of Disease

Each contracting State agrees to take effective measures to prevent the spread by means of air navigation of cholera, typhus (epidemic), smallpox, yellow fever, plague, and such other communicable diseases as the contracting States shall from time to time decide to designate, and to that end contracting States will keep in close consultation with the agencies concerned with international regulations relating to sanitary measures, applicable to aircraft. Such consultation shall be without prejudice to the application of any existing international convention on this subject to which the contracting States may be parties.

Article 15 – Airport and Similar Charges

Every airport in a contracting State which is open to public use by its national aircraft shall likewise, subject to the provisions of Article 68, be open under uniform conditions to the aircraft of all the other contracting States. The like uniform conditions shall apply to the use, by aircraft of every contracting State, of all air navigation facilities, including radio and meteorological services, which may be provided for public use for the safety and expedition of air navigation.

Any charges that may be imposed or permitted to be imported by a contracting State for the use of such airports and air navigation facilities by the aircraft of any other contracting State shall not be higher,

  (a) As to aircraft not engaged in scheduled international air services, than those that would be paid by its national aircraft of the same class engaged in similar operations, and
  (b) As to aircraft engaged in scheduled international air services, than those that would be paid by its national aircraft engaged in similar international air services.

All such charges shall be published and communicated to the International Civil Aviation Organization, provided that, upon representation by an interested contracting State, the charger, imposed for the use of airports and other facilities shall be subject to review by the Council, which shall report and make recommendations thereon for the consideration of the State or States concerned. No fees, dues or other charges shall be imposed by any contracting State in respect solely of the right of transit over or entry into or exit from its territory of any aircraft of a contracting State or persons or property thereon.

Article 16 – Search of Aircraft

The appropriate authorities of each of the contracting States shall have the right, without unreasonable delay, to search aircraft of the other contracting States on landing or departure, and to inspect the certificates and other documents prescribed by this Convention.

Chapter III – Nationality of Aircraft

Article 17 – Nationality of Aircraft

Aircraft have the nationality of the State in which they are registered.

Article 18 – Dual Registration

An aircraft cannot be validly registered in more than one State, but its registration may be changed from one State to another.

Article 19 – National Laws Governing Registration

The registration or transfer of registration of aircraft in any contracting State shall be made in accordance with its laws and regulations.

Article 20 – Display of Marks

Every aircraft engaged in international air navigation shall bear its appropriate nationality and registration marks.

Article 21 – Report of Registrations

Each contracting State undertakes to supply to any other contracting State or to the International Civil Aviation Organization, on demand, information concerning the registration and ownership of any particular aircraft registered in that State. In addition, each contracting State shall furnish reports to the International Civil Aviation Organization, under such regulations as the latter may prescribe, giving such pertinent data as can be made available concerning the ownership and control of aircraft registered in that State and habitually engaged in international air navigation. The data thus obtained by the International Civil Aviation Organization shall be made available by it on request to the other contracting States.

Chapter IV – Measures to Facilitate Air Navigation

Article 22 – Facilitation of Formalities

Each contracting State agrees to adopt all practicable measures, through the issuance of special regulations or otherwise, to facilitate and expedite navigation by aircraft between the territories of contracting States, and to prevent unnecessary delays to aircraft, crews, passengers and cargo, especially in the administration of the laws relating to immigration, quarantine, customs and clearance.

Article 23 – Customs and Immigration Procedures

Each contracting State undertakes, so far as it may find practicable, to establish customs and immigration procedures affecting international air navigation in accordance with the practices which may be established or recommended from time to time, pursuant to this Convention. Nothing in this Convention shall be construed as preventing the establishment of customs-free airports.

Article 24 – Customs Duty

(a) Aircraft on a flight to, from, or across the territory of another contracting State shall be admitted temporarily free of duty, subject to the customs regulations of the State. Fuel, lubricating oils, spare parts, regular equipment and aircraft stores on board an aircraft of a contracting State, on arrival in the territory of another contracting State and retained on board on leaving the territory of that State shall be exempt from customs duty, inspection fees or similar national or local duties and charges. This exemption shall not apply to any quantities or articles unloaded, except in accordance with the customs regulations of the State, which may require that they shall be kept under customs supervision.

(b) Spare parts and equipment imported into the territory of a contracting State for incorporation in or use on an aircraft of another contracting State engaged in international air navigation shall be admitted free of customs duty, subject to compliance with the regulations of the State concerned, which may provide that the articles shall be kept under customs supervision and control.

Article 25 – Aircraft in Distress

Each contracting State undertakes to provide such measures of assistance to aircraft in distress in its territory as it may find practicable, and to permit, subject to control by its own authorities, the owners of the aircraft or authorities of the State in which the aircraft is registered to provide such measures of assistance as may be necessitated by the circumstances. Each contracting State, when undertaking search for missing aircraft, will collaborate in coordinated measures which may be recommended from time to time pursuant to this Convention.

Article 26 – Investigation of Accidents

In the event of an accident to an aircraft of a contracting State occurring in the territory of another contracting State, and involving death or serious injury, or indicating serious technical defect in the aircraft or air navigation facilities, the State in which the accident occurs will institute an inquiry into the circumstances of the accident, in accordance, so far as its laws permit, with the procedure which may be recommended by the International Civil Aviation Organization. The State in which the aircraft is registered shall be given the opportunity to appoint observers to be present at the inquiry and the State holding the inquiry shall communicate the report and findings in the matter to that State.

Article 27 – Exemption from Seizure on Patent Claims

(a) While engaged in international air navigation, any authorized entry of aircraft of a contracting State into the territory of another contracting State or authorized transit across the territory of such State with or without landings shall not entail any seizure or detention of the aircraft or any claim against the owner or operator thereof or any other interference therewith by or on behalf of such State or any person therein, on the ground that the construction, mechanism, parts, accessories or operation of the aircraft is an infringement of any patent, design, or model duly granted or registered in the State whose territory is entered by the aircraft, it being agreed that no deposit of security in connection with the foregoing exemption from seizure or detention of the aircraft shall in any case be required in the State entered by such aircraft.

(b) The provisions of paragraph (a) of this Article shall also be applicable to the storage of spare parts and spare equipment for the aircraft and the right to use and install the same in the repair of an aircraft of a contracting State in the territory of any other contracting State, provided that any patented part or equipment so stored shall not be sold or distributed internally in or exported commercially from the contracting State entered by the aircraft.

(c) The benefits of this Article shall apply only to such States, parties to this Convention, as either (1) are parties to the International Convention for the Protection of Industrial Property and to any amendments thereof; or (2) have enacted patent laws which recognize and give adequate protection to inventions made by the nationals of the other States parties to this Convention.

Article 28 – Air Navigation Facilities and Standard Systems

Each contracting State undertakes, so far as it may find practicable, to:

(a) Provide, in its territory, airports, radio services, meteorological services and other air navigation facilities to facilitate international air navigation, in accordance with the standards and practices recommended or established from time to time, pursuant to this Convention;

(b) Adopt and put into operation the appropriate standard systems of communications procedure, codes, markings, signals, lighting and other operational practices and rules which may be recommended or established from time to time, pursuant to this Convention;

(c) Collaborate in international measures to secure the publication of aeronautical maps and charts in accordance with standards which may be recommended or established from time to time, pursuant to this Convention.

Chapter V – Conditions to Be Fulfilled with Respect to Aircraft

Article 29 – Documents Carried in Aircraft

Every aircraft of a contracting State, engaged in international navigation, shall carry the following documents in conformity with the conditions prescribed in this Convention:

(a) Its certificate of registration;
(b) Its certificate of airworthiness;
(c) The appropriate licenses for each member of the crew;
(d) Its journey log book;
(e) If it is equipped with radio apparatus, the aircraft radio station license;
(f) If it carries passengers, a list of their names and places of embarkation and destination;
(g) If it carries cargo, a manifest and detailed declarations of the cargo.

Article 30 – Aircraft Radio Equipment

(a) Aircraft of each contracting State may, in or over the territory of other contracting States, carry radio transmitting apparatus only if a license to install and operate such apparatus has been issued by the appropriate authorities of the State in which the aircraft is registered. The use of radio transmitting apparatus in the territory of the contracting State whose territory is flown over shall be in accordance with the regulations prescribed by that State.
(b) Radio transmitting apparatus may be used only by members of the flight crew who are provided with a special license for the purpose, issued by the appropriate authorities of the State in which the aircraft is registered.

Article 31 – Certificates of Airworthiness

Every aircraft engaged in international navigation shall be provided with a certificate of airworthiness issued or rendered valid by the State in which it is registered.

Article 32 Licenses of Personnel

(a) The pilot of every aircraft and the other members of the operating crew of every aircraft engaged in international navigation shall be provided with certificates of competency and licenses issued or rendered valid by the State in which the aircraft is registered.

(b) Each contracting State reserves the right to refuse to recognize, for the purpose of flight above its own territory, certificates of competency and licenses granted to any of its nationals by another contracting State.

Article 33 – Recognition of Certificates and Licenses

Certificates of airworthiness and certificates of competency and licenses issued or rendered valid by the contracting State in which the aircraft is registered, shall be recognized as valid by the other contracting States, provided that the requirements under which such certificates or licenses were issued or rendered valid are equal to or above the minimum standards which may be established from time to time pursuant to this Convention.

Article 34 – Journey Log Books

There shall be maintained in respect of every aircraft engaged in international navigation a journey log book in which shall be entered particulars of the aircraft, its crew and of each journey, in such form as may be prescribed from time to time pursuant to this Convention.

Article 35 – Cargo Restrictions

(a) No munitions of war or implements of war may be carried in or above the territory of a State in aircraft engaged in international naviga-tion, except by permission of such State. Each State shall determine by regulations what constitutes munitions of war or implement, of war for the purposes of this Article, giving due consideration, for the purposes of uniformity, to such recommendations as the International Civil Aviation Organization may from time to time make.

(b) Each contracting State reserves the right, for reasons of public order and safety, to regulate or prohibit the carriage in or above its territory of articles other than those enumerated in paragraph (a): provided that no distinction is made in this respect between its national aircraft engaged in international navigation and the aircraft of the other States so engaged; and provided further that no restriction shall be imposed which may interfere with the carriage and use on aircraft of apparatus necessary for the operation or navigation of the aircraft or the safety of the personnel or passengers.

Article 36 – Photographic Apparatus

Each contracting State may prohibit or regulate the use of photographic apparatus in aircraft over its territory.

Chapter VI – International Standards and Recommended Practices

Article 37 – Adoption of International Standards and Procedures

Each contracting State undertakes to collaborate in securing the highest practicable degree of uniformity in regulations, standards, procedures, and organization in relation to aircraft, personnel, airways and auxiliary services in all matters in which such uniformity will facilitate and improve air navigation.

To this end the International Civil Aviation Organization shall adopt and amend from time to time, as may be necessary, international standards and recommended practices and procedures dealing with:

(a) Communications systems and air navigation aids, including ground marking;
(b) Characteristics of airports and landing areas;
(c) Rules of the air and air traffic control practices;
(d) Licensing of operating and mechanical personnel;
(e) Airworthiness of aircraft;
(f) Registration and identification of aircraft;
(g) Collection and exchange of meteorological information;
(h) Log books;
(i) Aeronautical maps and charts;
(j) Customs and immigration procedures;
(k) Aircraft in distress and investigation of accidents;

and such other matters concerned with the safety, regularity, and efficiency of air navigation as may from time to time appear appropriate.

Article 38 – Departures from International Standards and Procedures

Any State which finds it impracticable to comply in all respects with any such international standards or procedure, or to bring its own regulations or practices into full accord with any international standard or procedure after amendment of the latter, or which deems it necessary to adopt regulations or practices differing in any particular respect from those established by an international standard, shall give immediate notification to the International Civil Aviation Organization of the differences between its own practice and that established by the international standard. In the case of amendments to international standards, any State which does not make the appropriate amendments to its own regulations or practices shall give notice to the Council within sixty days of the adoption of the amendment to the international standard, or indicate the action which it proposes to take. In any such case, the Council shall make immediate notification to all other States of the difference which exists between one or more features of an international standard and the corresponding national practice of that State.

Article 39 – Endorsement of Certificates and Licenses

(a) Any aircraft or part thereof with respect to which there exists an international standard of airworthiness or performance, and which failed in any respect to satisfy that standard at the time of its certification, shall have endorsed on or attached to its airworthiness certificate a complete enumeration of the details in respect of which it so failed.

(b) Any person holding a license who does not satisfy in full the conditions laid down in the international standard relating to the class of license or certificate which he holds shall have endorsed on or attached to his license a complete enumeration of the particulars in which he does not satisfy such conditions.

Article 40 – Validity of Endorsed Certificates and Licenses

No aircraft or personnel having certificates or licenses so endorsed shall participate in international navigation, except with the permission of the State or States whose territory is entered. The registration or use of any such aircraft, or of any certificated aircraft part, in any State other than that in which it was originally certificated shall be at the discretion of the State into which the aircraft or part is imported.

Article 41 – Recognition of Existing Standards of Airworthiness

The provisions of this Chapter shall not apply to aircraft and aircraft equipment of types of which the prototype is submitted to the appropriate national authorities for certification prior to a date three years after the date of adoption of an international standard of airworthiness for such equipment.

Article 42 – Recognition of Existing Standards of Competency of Personnel

The provisions of this Chapter shall not apply to personnel whose licenses are originally issued prior to a date one year after initial adoption of an international standard of qualification for such personnel; but they shall in any case apply to all personnel whose licenses remain valid five years after the date of adoption of such standard.

PART II – THE INTERNATIONAL CIVIL AVIATION ORGANIZATION

Chapter VII – The Organization

Article 43 – Name and Composition

An organization to be named the International Civil Aviation Organization is formed by the Convention. It is made up of an Assembly, a Council, and such other bodies as may be necessary.

Article 44 – Objectives

The aims and objectives of the Organization are to develop the principles and techniques of international air navigation and to foster the planning and development of international air transport so as to:

(a) Insure the safe and orderly growth of international civil aviation throughout the world;

(b) Encourage the arts of aircraft design and operation for peaceful purposes;

(c) Encourage the development of airways, airports, and air navigation facilities for international civil aviation;

(d) Meet the needs of the peoples of the world for safe, regular, efficient and economical air transport;

(e) Prevent economic waste caused by unreasonable competition;

(f) Insure that the rights of contracting States are fully respected and that every contracting State has a fair opportunity to operate international airlines;

(g) Avoid discrimination between contracting States;

(h) Promote safety of flight in international air navigation;

(i) Promote generally the development of all aspects of international civil aeronautics.

Article 45 – Permanent Seat

The permanent seat of the Organization shall be at such place as shall be determined at the final meeting of the Interim Assembly of the Provisional International Civil Aviation Organization set up by the Interim Agreement on International Civil Aviation signed at Chicago on December 7, 1944. The seat may be temporarily transferred elsewhere by decision of the Council, and otherwise than temporarily by decision of the Assembly, such decision to be taken by the number of votes specified by the Assembly. The number of votes so specified will not be less than three-fifths of the total number of contracting States.

Article 46 – First Meeting of Assembly

The first meeting of the Assembly shall be summoned by the Interim Council of the above-mentioned Provisional Organization as soon as the Convention has come into force, to meet at a time and place to be decided by the Interim Council.

Article 47 – Legal Capacity

The Organization shall enjoy in the territory of each contracting State such legal capacity as may be necessary for the performance of its functions. Full juridical personality shall be granted wherever compatible with the constitution and laws of the State concerned.

Chapter VIII – The Assembly

Article 48 – Meetings of Assembly and Voting

(a) The Assembly shall meet not less than once in three years and shall be convened by the Council at a suitable time and place. An extraordinary meeting of the Assembly may be held at any time upon the call of the Council or at the request of not less than one-fifth of the total number of contracting States addressed to the Secretary General.

(b) All contracting States shall have an equal right to be represented at the meetings of the Assembly and each contracting State shall be entitled to one vote. Delegates representing contracting States may be assisted by technical advisers who may participate in the meetings but shall have no vote.

(c) A majority of the contracting States is required to constitute a quorum for the meetings of the Assembly. Unless otherwise provided in this Convention, decisions of the Assembly shall be taken by a majority of the votes cast.

Article 49 – Powers and Duties of Assembly

The powers and duties of the Assembly shall be to:

(a) Elect at each meeting its President and other officers;
(b) Elect the contracting States to be represented on the Council, in accordance with the provisions of Chapter IX;
(c) Examine and take appropriate action on the reports of the Council and decide on any matter referred to it by the Council;
(d) Determine its own rules of procedure and establish such subsidiary commissions as it may consider to be necessary or desirable;

(e) Vote annual budgets and determine the financial arrangements of the Organization, in accordance with the provisions of Chapter XII;

(f) Review expenditures and approve the accounts of the Organization;

(g) Refer, at its discretion, to the Council, to subsidiary commissions or to any other body any matter within its sphere of action;

(h) Delegate to the Council the powers and authority necessary or desirable for the discharge of the duties of the Organization and revoke or modify the delegations of authority at any time;

(i) Carry out the appropriate provisions of Chapter XIII;

(j) Consider proposals for the modification or amendment of the provisions of this Convention and, if it approves of the proposals, recommend them to the contracting States in accordance with the provisions of Chapter XXI;

(k) Deal with any matter within the sphere of action of the Organization not specifically assigned to the Council.

Chapter IX – The Council

Article 50 – Composition and Election of Council

(a) The Council shall be a permanent body responsible to the Assembly. It shall be composed of thirty-six contracting States elected by the Assembly. An election shall be held at the first meeting of the Assembly and thereafter every three years, and the members of the Council so elected shall hold office until the next following election.

(b) In electing the members of the Council, the Assembly shall give adequate representation to (1) the States of chief importance in air transport; (2) the States not otherwise included which make the largest contribution to the provision of facilities for international civil air navigation; and (3) the States not otherwise included whose designation will insure that all major geographic areas of the world are represented on the Council. Any vacancy on the Council shall be filled by the Assembly as soon as possible; any contracting State so elected to the Council shall hold office for the unexpired portion of its predecessor's term of office.

(c) No representative of a contracting State on the Council shall be actively associated with the operation of an international air service or financially interested in such a service.

Article 51 – President of Council

The Council shall elect its President for a term of three years. He may be re-elected. He shall have no vote. The Council shall elect from among its members one or more Vice Presidents who shall retain their right to vote when serving as acting President. The President need not be selected from among the representatives of the members of the Council but, if a representative is elected, his seat shall be deemed vacant and it shall be filled by the State which he represented. The duties of the President shall be to:

(a) Convene meetings of the Council, the Air Transport Committee, and the Air Navigation Commission;
(b) Serve as representative of the Council; and
(c) Carry out on behalf of the Council the functions which the Council assigns to him.

Article 52 – Voting in Council

Decisions by the Council shall require approval by a majority of its members. The Council may delegate authority with respect to any particular matter to a committee of its members. Decisions of any committee of the Council may be appealed to the Council by any interested contracting State.

Article 53 – Participation Without a Vote

Any contracting State may participate, without a vote, in the consideration by the Council and by its committees and commissions on any question which especially affects its interests. No member of the Council shall vote in the consideration by the Council of a dispute to which it is a party.

Article 54 – Mandatory Functions of Council

The Council shall:

(a) Submit annual reports to the Assembly;
(b) Carry out the directions of the Assembly and discharge the duties and obligations which are laid on it by this Convention;
(c) Determine its organization and rules of procedure;
(d) Appoint and define the duties of an Air Transport Committee, which shall be chosen from among the representatives of the members of the Council, and which shall be responsible to it;
(e) Establish an Air Navigation Commission, in accordance with the provisions of Chapter X;
(f) Administer the finances of the Organization in accordance with the provisions of Chapters XII and XV;
(g) Determine the emoluments of the President of the Council;
(h) Appoint a chief executive officer who shall be called the Secretary General, and make provision for the appointment of such other personnel as may be necessary, in accordance with the provisions of Chapter XI;

(i)   Request, collect, examine and publish information relating to the advancement of air navigation and the operation of international air services, including information about the costs of operation and particulars of subsidies paid to airlines from public funds;

(j)   Report to contracting States any infraction of this Convention, as well as any failure to carry out recommendations or determinations of the Council;

(k)   Report to the Assembly any infraction of this Convention where a contracting State has failed to take appropriate action within a reasonable time after notice of the infraction;

(l)   Adopt, in accordance with the provisions of Chapter VI of this Convention, international standards and recommended practices; for convenience, designate them as Annexes to this Convention; and notify all contracting States of the action taken;

(m) Consider recommendations of the Air Navigation Commission for amendment of the Annexes and take action in accordance with the provisions of Chapter XX;

(n)   Consider any matter relating to the Convention which any contracting State refers to it.

Article 55 – Permissive Functions of Council

The Council may:

(a)   Where appropriate and as experience may show to be desirable, create subordinate air transport commissions on a regional or other basis and define groups of states or airlines with or through which it may deal to facilitate the carrying out of the aims of this Convention;

(b)   Delegate to the Air Navigation Commission duties additional to those set forth in the Convention and revoke or modify such delegations of authority at any time;

(c)   Conduct research into all aspects of air transport and air navigation which are of international importance, communicate the results of its research to the contracting States, and facilitate the exchange of information between contracting States on air transport and air navigation matters;

(d)   Study any matters affecting the organization and operation of international air transport, including the international ownership and operation of international air services on trunk routes, and submit to the Assembly plans in relation thereto;

(e)   Investigate, at the request of any contracting State, any situation which may appear to present avoidable obstacles to the development of international air navigation; and, after such investigation, issue such reports as may appear to it desirable.

Chapter X – The Air Navigation Commission

Article 56 – Nomination and Appointment of Commission

The Air Navigation Commission shall be composed of nineteen members appointed by the Council from among persons nominated by contracting States. These persons shall have suitable qualifications and experience in the science and practice of aeronautics. The Council shall request all contracting States to submit nominations. The President of the Air Navigation Commission shall be appointed by the Council.

Article 57 – Duties of Commission

The Air Navigation Commission shall:

(a) Consider, and recommend to the Council for adoption, modifications of the Annexes to this Convention;
(b) Establish technical subcommissions on which any contracting State may be represented, if it so desires;
(c) Advise the Council concerning the collection and communication to the contracting States of all information which it considers necessary and useful for the advancement of air navigation.

Chapter XI – Personnel

Article 58 – Appointment of Personnel

Subject to any rules laid down by the Assembly and to the provisions of this Convention, the Council shall determine the method of appointment and of termination of appointment, the training, and the salaries, allowances, and conditions of service of the Secretary General and other personnel of the Organization, and may employ or make use of the services of nationals of any contracting State.

Article 59 – International Character of Personnel

The President of the Council, the Secretary General, and other personnel shall not seek or receive instructions in regard to the discharge of their responsibilities from any authority external to the Organization. Each contracting State undertakes fully to respect the international character of the responsibilities of the personnel and not to seek to influence any of its nationals in the discharge of their responsibilities.

Article 60 – Immunities and Privileges of Personnel

Each contracting State undertakes, so far as possible under its constitutional procedure, to accord to the President of the Council, the Secretary General, and the other personnel of the Organization, the immunities and privileges which are accorded to corresponding personnel of other public international organizations. If a general international agreement on the immunities and privileges of international civil servants is arrived at, the immunities and privileges accorded to the President, the Secretary General, and the other personnel of the Organization shall be the immunities and privileges accorded under that general international agreement.

Chapter XII – Finance

Article 61 – Budget and Apportionment of Expenses

The Council shall submit to the Assembly annual budgets, annual statements of accounts and estimates of all receipts and expenditures. The Assembly shall vote the budgets with whatever modification it sees fit to prescribe, and, with the exception of assessments under Chapter XV to States consenting thereto, shall apportion the expenses of the Organization among the contracting States on the basis which it shall from time to time determine.

Article 62 – Suspension of Voting Power

The Assembly may suspend the voting power in the Assembly and in the Council of any contracting State that fails to discharge within a reasonable period its financial obligations to the Organization.

Article 63 – Expenses of Delegations and Other Representatives

Each contracting State shall bear the expenses of its own delegation to the Assembly and the remuneration, travel, and other expenses of any person whom it appoints to serve on the Council, and of its nominees or representatives on any subsidiary committees or commissions of the Organization.

Chapter XIII – Other International Arrangements

Article 64 – Security Arrangements

The Organization may, with respect to air matters within its competence directly affecting world security, by vote of the Assembly enter into appropriate arrangements with any general organization set up by the nations of the world to preserve peace.

Article 65 – Arrangements with Other International Bodies

The Council, on behalf of the Organization, may enter into agreements with other international bodies for the maintenance of common services and for common arrangements concerning personnel and, with the approval of the Assembly, may enter into such other arrangements as may facilitate the work of the Organization.

Article 66 – Functions Relating to Other Agreements

(a) The Organization shall also carry out the functions placed upon it by the International Air Services Transit Agreement and by the International Air Transport Agreement drawn up at Chicago on December 7, 1944 in accordance with the terms and conditions therein set forth.

(b) Members of the Assembly and the Council who have not accepted the International Air Services Transit Agreement or the International Air Transport Agreement drawn up at Chicago on December 7, 1944 shall not have the right to vote on any questions referred to the Assembly or Council under the provisions of the relevant Agreement.

PART III – INTERNATIONAL AIR TRANSPORT

Chapter XIV – Information and Reports

Article 67 – File Reports with Council

Each contracting State undertakes that its international airlines shall, in accordance with requirements laid down by the Council, file with the Council traffic reports, cost statistics and financial statements showing among other things all receipts and the sources thereof.

Chapter XV – Airports and Other Air Navigation Facilities

Article 68 – Designation of Routes and Airports

Each contracting State may, subject to the provisions of this Convention, designate the route to be followed within its territory by any international air service and the airports which any such service may use.

Article 69 – Improvement of Air Navigation Facilities

If the Council is of the opinion that the airports or other air navigation facilities, including radio and meteorological services, of a contracting State are not reasonably adequate for the safe, regular, efficient, and economical operation of international air services, present or contemplated, the Council shall consult with the State directly concerned, and other States affected, with a view to finding means by which the situation may be remedied, and may make recommendations for that purpose. No contracting State shall be guilty of an infraction of this Convention if it fails to carry out these recommendations.

Article 70 – Financing of Air Navigation Facilities

A contracting State, in the circumstances arising under the provisions of Article 69, may conclude an arrangement with the Council for giving effect to such recommendations. The State may elect to bear all of the costs involved in any such arrangement. If the States does not so elect, the Council may agree, at the request of the State, to provide for all or a portion of the cost.

Article 71 – Provision and Maintenance of Facilities by Council

If a contracting State so requests, the Council may agree to provide, man, maintain, and administer any or all of the airports and other air navigation facilities, including radio and meteorological services, required in its territory for the safe, regular, efficient and economical operation of the international air services of the other contracting States, and may specify just and reasonable charges for the use of the facilities provided.

Article 72 – Acquisition or Use of Land

Where land is needed for facilities financed in whole or in part by the Council at the request of a contracting State, that State shall either provide the land itself, retaining title if it wishes, or facilitate the use of the land by the Council on just and reasonable terms and in accordance with the laws of the State concerned.

Article 73 – Expenditure and Assessment of Funds

Within the limit of the funds which may be made available to it by the Assembly under Chapter XII, the Council may make current expenditures for the purposes of this Chapter from the general funds of the Organization. The Council shall assess the capital funds required for the purposes of this Chapter in previously agreed proportions over a reasonable period of time to the contracting States consenting thereto whose airlines use the facilities. The Council may also assess to States that consent any working funds that are required.

Article 74 – Technical Assistance and Utilization of Revenues

When the Council, at the request of a contracting State, advances funds or provides airports or other facilities in whole or in part, the arrangement may provide, with the consent of that State, for technical assistance in the supervision and operation of the airports and other facilities, and for the payment, from the revenues derived from the operation of the airports and other facilities, of the operating expenses of the airports and the other facilities, and of interest and amortization charges.

Article 75 – Taking Over of Facilities from Council

A contracting State may at any time discharge any obligation into which it has entered under Article 70, and take over airports and other facilities which the Council has provided in its territory pursuant to the provisions of Articles 71 and 72, by paying to the Council an amount which in the opinion of the Council is reasonable in the circumstances. If the State considers that the amount fixed by the Council is unreasonable it may appeal to the Assembly against the decision of the Council and the Assembly may confirm or amend the decision of the Council.

Article 76 – Return of Funds

Funds obtained by the Council through reimbursement under Article 75 and from receipts of interest and amortization payments under Article 74 shall, in the case of advances originally financed by States under Article 73, be returned to the States which were originally assessed in the proportion of their assessments, as determined by the Council.

Chapter XVI – Joint Operating Organizations and Pooled Services

Article 77 – Joint Operating Organizations Permitted

Nothing in this Convention shall prevent two or more contracting States from constituting joint air transport operating organizations or international operating agencies and from pooling their air services on any routes or in any regions, but such organizations or agencies and such pooled services shall be subject to all the provisions of this Convention, including those relating to the registration of agreements with the Council. The Council shall determine in what manner the provisions of this Convention relating to nationality of aircraft shall apply to aircraft operated by international operating agencies.

Article 78 – Function of Council

The Council may suggest to contracting States concerned that they form joint organizations to operate air services on any routes or in any regions.

Article 79 – Participation in Operating Organizations

A State may participate in joint operating organizations or in pooling arrangements, either through its government or through an airline company or companies designated by its government. The companies may, at the sole discretion of the State concerned, be state-owned or partly state-owned or privately owned.

PART IV – FINAL PROVISIONS

Chapter XVII – Other Aeronautical Agreements and Arrangements

Article 80 – Paris and Habana Conventions

Each contracting State undertakes, immediately upon the coming into force of this Convention, to give notice of denunciation of the Convention relating to the Regulation of Aerial Navigation signed at Paris on October 13, 1919 or the Convention on Commercial Aviation signed at Habana on February 20, 1928, if it is a party to either. As between contracting States, this Convention supersedes the Conventions of Paris and Habana previously referred to.

Article 81 – Registration of Existing Agreements

All aeronautical agreements which are in existence on the coming into force of this Convention, and which are between a contracting State and any other State or between an airline of a contracting State and any other State or the airline of any other State, shall be forthwith registered with the Council.

Article 82 – Abrogation of Inconsistent Arrangements

The contracting States accept this Convention as abrogating all obligations and understandings between them which are inconsistent with its terms, and undertake not to enter into any such obligations and understandings. A contracting State which, before becoming a member of the Organization has under taken any obligations toward a non-contracting State or a national of a contracting State or of a non-contracting State inconsistent with the terms of this Convention, shall take immediate steps to procure its release from the obligations. If an airline of any contracting State has entered into any such inconsistent obligations, the State of which it is a national shall use its best efforts to secure their termination forthwith and shall in any event cause them to be terminated as soon as such action can lawfully be taken after the coming into force of this Convention.

Article 83 – Registration of New Arrangements

Subject to the provisions of the preceding Article, any contracting State may make arrangements not inconsistent with the provisions of this Convention

Any such arrangement shall be forthwith registered with the Council, which shall make it public as soon as possible.

Article 83 bis – Transfer of Certain Functions and Duties

(a) Notwithstanding the provisions of Articles 12, 30, 31 and 32(a), when an aircraft registered in a contracting State is operated pursuant to an agreement for the lease, charter or interchange of the aircraft or any similar arrangement by an operator who has his principal place of business or, or if he has no such place of business, his permanent residence in another contracting State, the State of registry may, by agreement with such other State, transfer to it all or part of its functions and duties as State of registry in respect of that aircraft under Articles 12, 30, 31 and 32(a). The State of registry shall be relieved of responsibility in respect of the functions and duties transferred.

(b) The transfer shall not have effect in respect of other contracting States before either the agreement between States in which it is embodied has been registered with the Council and made public pursuant to Article 83 or the existence and scope of the agreement have been directly communicated to the authorities of the other contracting State or States concerned by a State party to the agreement.

(c) The provisions of paragraphs (a) and (b) above shall also be applicable to cases covered by Article 77.

Chapter XVIII – Disputes and Default

Article 84 – Settlement of Disputes

If any disagreement between two or more contracting States relating to the interpretation or application of this Convention and its Annexes cannot be settled by negotiation, it shall, on the application of any State concerned in the disagreement, be decided by the Council. No member of the Council shall vote in the consideration by the Council of any dispute to which it is a party. Any contracting State may, subject to Article 85, appeal from the decision of the Council to an ad hoc arbitral tribunal agreed upon with the other parties to the dispute or to the Permanent Court of International Justice. Any such appeal shall be notified to the Council within sixty days of receipt of notification of the decision of the Council.

Article 85 – Arbitration Procedure

If any contracting State party to a dispute in which the decision of the Council is under appeal has not accepted the Statute of the Permanent Court of International Justice and the contracting States parties to the dispute cannot agree on the choice of the arbitral tribunal, each of the contracting States parties to the dispute shall name a single arbitrator who shall name an umpire. If either contracting State party to the dispute fails to name an arbitrator within a period of three months from the date of the appeal, an arbitrator shall be named on behalf of that State by the President of the Council from a list of qualified and available persons maintained by the Council. If, within thirty days, the arbitrators cannot agree on an umpire, the President of the Council shall designate an umpire from the list previously referred to. The arbitrators and the umpire shall then jointly constitute an arbitral tribunal. Any arbitral tribunal established under this or the preceding Article shall settle its own procedure and give its decisions by majority vote, provided that the Council may determine procedural questions in the event of any delay which in the opinion of the Council is excessive.

Article 86 – Appeals

Unless the Council decides otherwise, any decision by the Council on whether an international airline is operating in conformity with the provisions of this Convention shall remain in effect unless reversed on appeal. On any other matter, decisions of the Council shall, if appealed from, be suspended until the appeal is decided. The decisions of the Permanent Court of International Justice and of an arbitral tribunal shall be final and binding.

Article 87 – Penalty for Non-Conformity of Airline

Each contracting State undertakes not to allow the operation of an airline of a contracting State through the airspace above its territory if the Council has decided that the airline concerned is not conforming to a final decision rendered in accordance with the previous Article.

Article 88 – Penalty for Non-Conformity by State

The Assembly shall suspend the voting power in the Assembly and in the Council of any contracting State that is found in default under the provisions of this Chapter.

Chapter XIX – War

Article 89 – War and Emergency Conditions

In case of war, the provisions of this Convention shall not affect the freedom of action of any of the contracting States affected, whether as belligerents or as neutrals. The same principle shall apply in the case of any contracting State which declares a state of national emergency and notifies the fact to the Council.

Chapter XX – Annexes

Article 90 – Adoption and Amendment of Annexes

(a) The adoption by the Council of the Annexes described in Article 54, subparagraph (l), shall require the vote of two-thirds of the Council at a meeting called for that purpose and shall then be submitted by the Council to each contracting State. Any such Annex or any amendment of an Annex shall become effective within three months after its submission to the contracting States or at the end of such longer period of time as the Council may prescribe, unless in the meantime a majority of the contracting States register their disapproval with the Council.

(b) The Council shall immediately notify all contracting States of the coming into force of any Annex or amendment thereto.

Chapter XXI – Ratifications, Adherences, Amendments, and Denunciations

Article 91 – Ratification of Convention

(a) This Convention shall be subject to ratification by the signatory States. The instruments of ratification shall be deposited in the archives of the Government of the United States of America, which shall give notice of the date of the deposit to each of the signatory and adhering States.

(b) As soon as this Convention has been ratified or adhered to by twenty six States it shall come into force between them on the thirtieth day after deposit of the twenty-sixth instrument. It shall come into force for each State ratifying thereafter on the thirtieth day after the deposit of its instrument of ratification.

(c) It shall be the duty of the Government of the United States of America to notify the government of each of the signatory and adhering States of the date on which this Convention comes into force.

Article 92 – Adherence to Convention

(a) This Convention shall be open for adherence by members of the United Nations and States associated with them, and States which remained neutral during the present world conflict.

(b) Adherence shall be effected by a notification addressed to the Government of the United States of America and shall take effect as from the thirtieth day from the receipt of the notification by the Government of the United States of America, which shall notify all the contracting States.

Article 93 – Admission of Other States

States other than those provided for in Articles 91 and 92 (a) may, subject to approval by any general international organization set up by the nations of the world to preserve peace, be admitted to participation in this Convention by means of a four-fifths vote of the Assembly and on such conditions as the Assembly may prescribe: provided that in each case the assent of any State invaded or attacked during the present war by the State seeking admission shall be necessary.

Article 93 **bis**

(a) Notwithstanding the provisions of Articles 91, 92 and 93 above:

  1. A State whose government the General Assembly of the United Nations has recommended be debarred from membership in international agencies established by or brought into relationship with the United Nations shall automatically cease to be a member of the International Civil Aviation Organisation;
  2. A State which has been expelled from membership in the United Nations shall automatically cease to be a member of the International Civil Aviation Organisation unless the General Assembly of the United Nations attaches to its act of expulsion a recommendation to the contrary.

(b) A State which ceases to be a member of the International Civil Aviation Organisation as a result of the provisions of paragraph (a) above may, after approval by the General Assembly of the United Nations, be readmitted to the International Civil Aviation Organisation upon application and upon approval by a majority of the Council.

(c) Members of the Organisation which are suspended from the exercise of the rights and privileges of membership in the United Nations shall, upon the request of the latter, be suspended from the rights and privileges of membership in this Organisation.

Article 94 – Amendment of Convention

(a) Any proposed amendment to this Convention must be approved by a two-thirds vote of the Assembly and shall then come into force in respect of States which have ratified such amendment when ratified by the number of contracting States specified by the Assembly. The number so specified shall not be less than two-thirds of the total number of contracting States.

(b) If in its opinion the amendment is of such a nature as to justify this course, the Assembly in its resolution recommending adoption may provide that any State which has not ratified within a specified period after the amendment has come into force shall thereupon cease to be a member of the Organization and a party to the Convention.

Article 95 – Denunciation of Convention

(a) Any contracting State may give notice of denunciation of this Convention three years after its coming into effect by notification addressed to the Government of the United States of America, which shall at once inform each of the contracting States.

(b) Denunciation shall take effect one year from the date of the receipt of the notification and shall operate only as regards the State effecting the denunciation.

Chapter XXII – Definitions

Article 96

For the purpose of this Convention the expression:

(a) "Air service" means any scheduled air service performed by air craft for the public transport of passengers, mail or cargo.

(b) "International air service" means an air service which pass through the air space over the territory of more than one State.

(c) "Airline" means any air transport enterprise offering or operating an international air service.

(d) "Stop for non-traffic purposes" means a landing for any purpose other than taking on or discharging passengers, cargo or mail.

SIGNATURE OF CONVENTION

IN WITNESS WHEREOF, the undersigned plenipotentiaries, having been duly authorized, sign this Convention on behalf of their respective governments on the dates appearing opposite their signatures.

DONE at Chicago the seventh day of December 1944 in the English language. The texts of this Convention drawn up in the English, French, Russian and Spanish languages are of equal authenticity. These texts shall be deposited in the archives of the Government of the United States of America, and certified copies shall be transmitted by that Government to the Governments of all the States which may sign or adhere to this Convention. This Convention shall be open for signature at Washington, D.C.

Bibliography

Abeyratne, Ruwantissa I.R. "Regulatory Management of the Warsaw System of Air Carrier Liability", *Journal of Air Transport Management* 3 (1997): 37–45.

Abeyratne, Ruwantissa I.R. "The Role of the International Civil Aviation Organization (ICAO) in the Twenty-First Century", *Annals of Air and Space Law* 34 (2009): 529–544.

Abeyratne, Ruwantissa I.R. "A Critical Look at ICAO Policies on Charges Levied for Airports and Air Navigation Services", *Air and Space Law* 34(3) (2009): 177–188.

Abeyratne, Ruwantissa I.R. "The ICAO Conventions on Liability for Third Party Damage Caused by Aircraft", *Air and Space Law* 34(6) (2009): 403–416.

Abeyratne, Ruwantissa I.R. "Ensuring Regional Safety in Air Transport", *Air and Space Law* 35(3) (2010): 249–262.

Abeyratne, Ruwantissa I.R. *Convention on International Civil Aviation: A Commentary.* Cham, Switzerland: Springer Science & Business Media, 2013.

Abeyratne, Ruwantissa I.R. "A Protocol to Amend the Tokyo Convention of 1963: Some Unanswered Questions", *Air and Space Law* 39(1) (2014): 47–58.

Abeyratne, Ruwantissa I.R. "Protocol to the Tokyo Convention of 1963: A Legal Triumph or Damp Squib?", *Air and Space Law* 39(4/5) (2014): 245–260.

Australian Government, Department of Infrastructure and Regional Development. "The Bilateral System – how international air services work". https://infrastructure.gov.au/aviation/international/bilateral_system.aspx. Accessed 7 June 2016.

Baden, Naneen K. "The Japanese Initiative on the Warsaw Convention", *Journal of Air Law and Commerce* 61 (1996): 437–466.

Balfour, John. "EC Aviation Scene (No 1: 2002)", *Air and Space Law* 27(4/5) (2002): 249–265.

Bokareva, Olena. "Air Passengers' Rights in the EU: International Uniformity versus Regional Harmonization", *Air and Space Law* 41(1) (2016): 3–24.

Boyle, Robert P. and Pulsifer, Roy. "The Tokyo Convention on Offenses and Certain Other Acts Committed On Board Aircraft", *Journal of Air Law and Commerce* 30 (1964): 305–354.

Brise, Sven. "Economic Implications of Changing Passenger Limits in the Warsaw Liability System", *Annals of Air and Space Law* 22 (1997): 121.

Caplan, H. "Liability for Third Party Damage on the Ground", *Air and Space Law* 33(3) (2008): 183–213.

Cheng, Bin. *The Law of International Air Transport.* London: Stevens & Sons Limited, 1962.

Cheng, Bin. "A Fifth Jurisdiction Without Montreal Additional Protocol No. 3, and Full Compensation Without the Supplemental Compensation Plan", *Air and Space Law* 20 (1995): 118–124.

Cheng, Bin. "A New-Look Warsaw Convention on the Eve of the Twenty-First Century", *Annals of Air and Space Law* 22 (1997): 45.

Cobbs, Louise. "The Shifting Meaning of 'Accident' under Article 17 of the Warsaw Convention: What did the Airline know and what did it do about it?", *Air and Space Law* 24(3) (1999): 121–127.

Cunningham, McKay. "The Montreal Convention: Can Passengers Finally Recover for Mental Injuries?", *Vanderbilt Journal of Transnational Law* 41 (2008): 1043–1082.

Dean, Warren L. Jr. "Aviation Liability Regimes in the New Millennium: Beyond the Wild Blue Yonder", *Transportation Law Journal* 28 (2001): 239.

Dempsey, Paul S. "Aerial Piracy and Terrorism: Unilateral and Multilateral Responses to Aircraft Hijackings", *Connecticut Journal of International Law* 2 (1987): 427–462.

Dempsey, Paul S. "Pennies from Heaven: Breaking Through the Liability Limitations of Warsaw", *Annals of Air and Space Law* 22 (1997): 267–278.

Dempsey, Paul S. "Aviation Security: The Role of Law in the War Against Terrorism", *Columbia Journal of Transnational Law* 41(3) (2003): 649–733.

Dempsey, Paul S. *Public International Air Law*. Montreal: McGill University, 2008.

Dempsey, Paul S. and Milde, Michael. *International Air Carrier Liability: The Montreal Convention of 1999*. Montreal: McGill University Centre for Research in Air & Space Law, 2005.

Diederiks-Verschoor, I.H. Ph. and Mendes de Leon, Pablo. *An Introduction to Air Law*. Alphen aan den Rijn, The Netherlands: Kluwer Law International, 2012. 9th edition.

Fitzgerald, G.F. "The Protocol to Amend the Convention on Damage Caused by Foreign Aircraft to Third Parties on the Surface (Rome, 1952) signed at Montreal, 23 September 1978", *Annals of Air and Space Law* 4 (1979): 29–73.

Franklin, M. "Is a Successful New Convention on Airline Liability for Surface damage Achievable?", *Air and Space Law* 31(2) (2006): 87–97.

Gates, Sean and LeLoudas, George. "From Rome to Montreal in 57 Years: Worth the Wait?", *Air and Space Lawyer* 22(1) (2009): 4–7.

Giemulla, Elmar and Schmid, Ronald. "Council Regulation (EC) No. 2027/97 on Air Carrier Liability in the Event of Accidents and its Implications for Air Carriers", *Air and Space Law* 23(3) (1998): 98–105.

Goldhirsch, Lawrence. "Definition of 'Accident': Revisiting *Air France v. Saks*", *Air and Space Law* 26(2) (2001): 86–89.

Haanappel, Peter P.C. *The Law and Policy of Air Space and Outer Space: A Comparative Approach*. The Hague: Kluwer Law International, 2003.

Havel, Brian F. *Beyond Open Skies: A New Regime for International Aviation*. Alphen aan den Rijn, The Netherlands: Kluwer Law International, 2009.

Havel, Brian F. and van Antwerpen, Niels. "Dutch Ticket Tax and Article 15 of the Chicago Convention", *Air and Space Law* 34(2) (2009): 141–146.

Havel, Brian F. and van Antwerpen, Niels. "Dutch Ticket Tax and Article 15 of the Chicago Convention (Continued)", *Air and Space Law* 34(6) (2009): 447–451.

Havel, Brian F. and Sanchez, Gabriel S. *The Principles and Practice of International Aviation Law*. New York: Cambridge University Press, 2014.

Hornik, Jiri. "Article 3 of the Chicago Convention", *Air and Space Law* 27(3) (2002): 161–195.

International Air Transport Association. "Joint Position Calling for States to Ratify the Montreal Protocol 2014 to Deter Unruly Passenger Incidents and Promote a Safer Air Travel Experience for All". www.iata.org/policy/Documents/tokyo-revision-position-paper.pdf. Accessed 7 June 2016.

International Civil Aviation Organization. "Freedoms of the Air". www.icao.int/Pages/freedomsAir.aspx. Accessed 7 June 2016.

International Civil Aviation Organization. "Liberalization of Market Access". Paper presented at the Worldwide Air Transport Conference, Sixth Meeting, Montreal, 18–22 March 2013.

International Civil Aviation Organization. "The Postal History of ICAO: Legal Instruments related to Aviation Security". www.icao.int/secretariat/postalhistory/legal_instruments_related_to_aviation_security.htm. Accessed 7 June 2016.

Joyner, Christopher C. *The United Nations and International Law*. Cambridge: Cambridge University Press, 1999.

Kjelin, H. "The new International regime for third party liability", *Air and Space Law* 33(2) (2008): 63–80.

Koning, I. "Liability in Air Carriage: Carriage of Cargo under the Warsaw and Montreal Conventions", *Air and Space Law* 33(4/5) (2008): 318–345.

Larsen, P.B., Sweeney, J.C. and Gillick, J.E. *Aviation Law: Cases Laws and Related Sources*. Ardsley, UK: Transnational Publishers, 2006.

Levine, Michael E. "Scope and Limits of Multilateral Approaches to International Air Transport", in Organization for Economic Cooperation and Development, *International Air Transport: The Challenges Ahead* (Paris: OECD, 1993), 75.

Lowenfeld, Andreas F. and Mendelson, Allan I. "The United States and the Warsaw Convention", *Harvard Law Review* 80 (1967): 497–602.

Lyall, Francis. "The Warsaw Convention – Cutting the Gordian Knot and the 1995 Intercarrier Agreement", *Syracuse Journal of International Law and Commerce* 22 (1996): 67–78.

Mankiewicz, Rene H. "The 1971 Protocol of Guatemala City to Further Amend the 1929 Warsaw Convention", *Journal of Air Law and Commerce* 38 (1972): 519–545.

Mendes de Leon, Pablo. *Cabotage in Air Transport Regulation*. Dordrecht, The Netherlands: Martinus Nijhoff Publishers, 1981.

Mendes de Leon, Pablo and Eyskens, Werner. "The Montreal Convention: Analysis of Some Aspects of the Attempted Modernization and Consolidation of the Warsaw System", *Journal of Air Law and Commerce* 66 (2001): 1155–1185.

Milde, Michael. *Essential Air and Space Law Series: International Air Law and ICAO*. The Hague: Eleven International Publishing, 2008.

Milde, Michael. "Liability for Damage Caused by Aircraft on the Surface: Past and Current Efforts to Unify the Law", *Zeitschrift für Luft- und Weltraumrecht* 57 (2008): 532–557.

Milde, Michael. *International Air Law and ICAO*. The Hague: Eleven International Publishing, 2012.

Milde, Michael. "The Warsaw System of Liability in International Carriage by Air: History, Merits and Flaws and the New 'Non-Warsaw' Convention of 28 May 1999", *Annals of Air and Space Law* 24 (1999): 155–186.

Moon, Albert I. Jr. "A Look at Airspace Sovereignty", *Journal of Air Law and Commerce* 29(4) (1963): 328–345.

Moore, Larry. "The New Montreal Liability Convention, Major Changes in International Air Law: An End to the Warsaw Convention", *Tulane Journal of International and Comparative Law* 9 (2001): 223–231.

Neenan, Peter. "The Damaged Quilt: Inadequate Coverage of the Montreal Convention", *Air and Space Law* 37(1) (2012): 51–64.

Parliament of the Commonwealth of Australia Joint Standing Committee on Treaties. "Convention on the Marking of Plastic Explosives for the Purpose of Detection".

In Commonwealth of Australia, *Review of Treaties tabled on 11 October 2005 (2), 28 February and 29 March 2006 (2)* 5–20. Canberra: Commonwealth of Australia, 2006.

Pickelman, Matthew R. "Draft Convention for the Unification of Certain Rules for International Carriage By Air: The Warsaw Convention Revisited for The Last Time?", *Journal of Air Law and Commerce* 64 (1998): 273–306.

Prassl, Jeremias. "Reforming Air Passenger Rights in the European Union", *Air and Space Law* 39(1) (2014): 59–82.

Shawcross, C.N. and Beaumont, K.C. *Shawcross and Beaumont: Air Law*. London: Lexis Nexis Butterworths, 1997, as updated (loose-leaf service).

Tompkins, George N. Jr. "The Montreal Convention of 1999: This Is the Answer", *The Aviation Quarterly* 3 (July 1999): 114–139.

Tompkins, George N. Jr. "The Montreal Convention and the Meaning of 'Destination' in Art. 33(1)", *Air and Space Law* 32 (2007): 228–229.

Tompkins, George N. Jr. "Some Thoughts to Ponder when Considering Whether to Adopt the New Aviation General Risks and Unlawful Interference Conventions Proposed by ICAO", *Air and Space Law* 33(2) (2008): 81–84.

Tompkins, George N. Jr. "The Montreal Convention 1999, the Fifth Jurisdiction in the United States and the *Doctrine of Forum Non Conveniens*", *Air and Space Law* 33(3) (2008): 233–243.

Tompkins, George N. Jr. "The 1999 Montreal Convention: Alive, Well and Growing", *Air and Space Law* 34(6) (2009): 421–426.

Tompkins, George N. Jr. *Liability Rules Applicable to International Air Transportation as Developed by the Courts in the United States*. Alphen aan den Rijn, The Netherlands: Kluwer Law International, 2010.

Tompkins, George N. Jr. "Are the Objectives of the 1999 Montreal Convention in Danger of Failure?", *Air and Space Law* 39(3) (2014) 203–214.

UN Chronicle. "International Controls to Regulate Plastic Explosives Adopted in Montreal", *UN Chronicle* 28(2) (June 1991): 32.

van Brandenburg-Kulkarni, Prachee. "'Sixth Freedom' Revisited in the Twenty-First Century", *Air and Space Law* 40(1) (2015): 55–64.

van der Toorn, Damien. "September 11 Inspired Aviation Counter-Terrorism Convention and Protocol Adopted", *American Society of International Law Insights* 15(3) (2011). www.asil.org/insights/volume/15/issue/3/september-11-inspired-aviation-counter-terrorism-convention-and-protocol. Accessed 11 August 2016.

Vietor, Richard H.K., Yergin, Daniel and Evans, Peter C. *Fettered Flight: Globalization and the Airline Industry*. Cambridge: Global Decisions Group, 2000.

Wassenbergh, Henry A. *Aspects of Air Law and Civil Air Policy in the Seventies*. Dordrecht, The Netherlands: Springer, 1970.

Wassenbergh, Henry A. *Public International Air Transportation Law in a New Era*. Deventer, The Netherlands: Kluwer, 1986.

Wassenbergh, Henry A. *Principles and Practices in Air Transport Regulations*. Paris: Institute of Air Transport, 1993.

Weber, Ludwig. "ICAO's Initiative to Reform the Legal Framework for Air Carrier Liability", *Annals of Air and Space Law* 22 (1997): 59.

Weber, Ludwig. "Recent Developments in International Air Law", *Air and Space Law* 29 (2004): 280–312.

Weber, Ludwig. *International Civil Aviation Organization: An Introduction*. Alphen aan den Rijn, The Netherlands: Kluwer Law International, 2007.

Weber, Ludwig. *International Civil Aviation Organization (ICAO)*. Alphen aan den Rijn, The Netherlands: Kluwer Law International, 2012.

Wegter, J. "The ECJ decision of 10 January 2006 on the Validity of Regulation 261/2004: Ignoring the Exclusivity of the Montreal Convention", *Air and Space Law* 31(2) (2006): 133–148.

Weigand, Tory. "Accident, Exclusivity, and Passenger Disturbances Under the Warsaw Convention", *American University International Law Review* 16 (2001): 891–968.

Whalen, Thomas. "The New Warsaw Convention: The Montreal Convention", *Air and Space Law* 25(1) (2000): 12–26.

Index

For Product Safety Concerns and Information please contact our EU
representative GPSR@taylorandfrancis.com
Taylor & Francis Verlag GmbH, Kaufingerstraße 24, 80331 München, Germany

www.ingramcontent.com/pod-product-compliance
Ingram Content Group UK Ltd.
Pitfield, Milton Keynes, MK11 3LW, UK
UKHW021022180425
457613UK00020B/1023